D0049248

Day by Day

WITH
CHARLES SWINDOLL

❧ *Day by Day* ❧

WITH
CHARLES SWINDOLL

WORD PUBLISHING
NASHVILLE
A Thomas Nelson Company

DAY BY DAY WITH CHARLES SWINDOLL

ISBN 0-8499-1557-0

Printed in the United States of America
00   01   02   03   04   05   06   BVG   9   8   7   6   5   4   3   2   1

INTRODUCTION

❧❧❧❧

*I*n our culture today anything, even news about God, can be sold if it is packaged freshly; but when it loses its novelty, it goes on the garbage heap. There is a great market for religious experience in our world; there is little enthusiasm for the patient acquisition of virtue, little inclination to sign up for a long apprenticeship in what earlier generations of Christians called holiness.

Our generation toys dangerously with an I'm-getting-tired-so-let's-just-quit mentality. And this is not limited to the spiritual realm. Dieting is a daily discipline, so we stay fat. Finishing school is an everyday thing, so we bail out. Cultivating a close relationship is painful, so we back off. Working through conflicts in a marriage is a tiring struggle day by day, so we walk away. Sticking with an occupation is tough on given days, so we change jobs.

The let's-just-quit mentality is upon us.

Ignace Jan Paderewski, the famous Polish pianist and statesman, was once scheduled to perform at a great concert hall in America. It was a black-tie affair—a high society extravaganza.

Present in the audience that evening was a woman who had brought her nine-year-old son, hoping that he would be encouraged to practice the piano if he could just hear the great Paderewski at the keyboard. Weary of waiting for the concert to begin, and being there against his wishes anyway, the lad squirmed restlessly in his seat. Then, as his mother turned to talk with friends, the boy slipped out of his seat and down the aisle, strangely drawn by the ebony concert grand sitting majestic and alone at the center of the huge stage. He sat down on the tufted leather stool, placed his small hands on the black-and-white keys, and began to play "Chop Sticks."

Suddenly the crowd hushed, and hundreds of frowning faces turned in his direction. Irritated and embarrassed, some began to shout, "Hey, get that boy away from there!" "Where's his mother?" "Somebody stop him!"

Backstage, Paderewski heard the uproar and the sound of the simple tune. When he saw what was happening, he hurried onto the stage. Without a word to the audience, he walked up behind the lad, reached his arms around either side of him, and began to improvise a countermelody. As the two made music together, the master pianist kept whispering in the boy's ear, "Keep going. Don't quit, son. Keep on playing . . . don't stop . . . don't quit."

So it is with us. We hammer away at life day by day, and sometimes it seems about as significant as "Chop Sticks." Then, about the time we are ready to give up, along comes the Master, who leans over and whispers, "Don't quit. Keep going," as He provides His divine countermelody of grace, love, and joy at just the right moment.

Are you one of those weary pilgrims? Is the road getting long? Is hope wearing a little thin?

Don't quit. Keep on . . . day by day. Finish the course.

Are you discouraged? Do you wonder if you'll ever get this parenting business right? Will your hopes and dreams ever be realized? Does it seem too long a wait?

Don't give up . . . at least not today.

Just keep listening to the good news of the Master day by day, and joy and holiness will be yours until the day Jesus comes to take you home.

Day by day,

in the temple courts

and from house to house,

they never stopped teaching

and proclaiming the good news that

Jesus is the Christ

Acts 5:42, NIV

NOW DON'T JUST SIT THERE!

❧ *Psalm 108* ❧

*A*n old year has completed its course. A new year is smiling at us with twelve months of the unknown. An entire ocean of possibilities, including both sun-drenched days and a few storms with howling winds and giant waves, stretch out across the uncharted waters. If we let ourselves, we could become so afraid of the potential dangers, so safety conscious, we would miss the adventure.

That's one option, of course—becoming a beach-dwelling couch potato, someone who looks toward the horizon, entertains a few thoughts that start with "Someday . . . " or "In a year or two I'm gonna . . ." but then leans back and just keeps looking. What if Christopher Columbus had been content to build sandcastles along the shores of Spain?

Now, admittedly, some go a little nuts when they decide a change is needed. Larry Walters did. The thirty-three-year-old truck driver had been sitting around doing zilch week in, week out, until boredom got the best of him. That was back in the summer of '82. He decided enough was enough; what he needed was an adventure. So, on July 2 of that year he rigged forty-two helium-filled weather balloons to a Sears lawn chair in San Pedro, California, and lifted off. Armed with a pellet gun to shoot out a few balloons should he fly too high, Walters was shocked to reach 16,000 feet rather rapidly. He wasn't the only one. Surprised pilots reported seeing "some guy in a lawn chair floating in the sky" to perplexed air-traffic controllers.

Finally, Walters had enough sense to start shooting a few balloons, which allowed him to land safely in Long Beach some forty-five minutes later. When asked why he did such a weird thing, Walters usually gave the same answer: "It was something I had to do . . . I couldn't just sit there."

Between doing nothing and trying something *that* ridiculous, there's a wide expanse worth probing. Think of the dozens of things God is going to teach us and the many ways we are going to see Him work in the coming year!

But I should warn you, you will have to change . . . and that won't come easily. Mark Twain was correct when he said, "The only one who likes change is a wet baby."

Breaking out of old, tired routines is one of the secrets
for staying young and energetic.

A DIET THAT WORKS

❧ *Psalm 119: 1–16* ❧

*W*e're off! Ready or not, 364 days stretch out in front of us, waiting to be invested with all our high hopes and new motivation. Tops on the list for a lot of folks is attacking the age-old battle of the bulge. Just check the magazine rack and your local newspaper. They are filled with ads, fads, before-and-after pictures, and high-powered promises.

As concerned as I may be about our physical fitness as we enter this new year, I'm even more concerned about our spiritual fitness. I know of no scripture that teaches we'll be weighed in before entering heaven. But I am forever bumping into verses that mention our appearing before the Lord for some type of spiritual accountability.

With a new year sprawled out in front of you, what's your spiritual game plan? A good guide is Psalm 119:1–16.

You'll notice that the first eight verses affirm three absolutes: the reality of God's blessing, the authority of God's Word, and the necessity of God's presence. With that, the psalmist asks the same question all of us ask on the edge of twelve new months: How can I keep my life pure (v. 9)? What's the secret? The answer is found in the next six verses.

Seek the Lord on a regular basis (v. 10). Pursue Him daily. Include Him in your decisions, your plans, your fun times, your struggles.

Treasure His truth in your heart (v. 11). Commit verses of Scripture to memory. A heart full of treasure leaves little room for trash.

Openly tell others of Him (v. 13). Something wonderful happens when we open our own lips and speak to others about how God has changed our lives.

Rejoice and delight in God's workings (vv. 14, 16). Smile more. Let your delight shine.

Spend more of your free moments meditating on His principles (v. 15). Weave them into your driving time, your workouts, while waiting for an appointment, before going to sleep.

Give God your full respect (vv. 15–16). Don't hold back. Make this the year you dare to live by faith.

Forget the superficial ads and fads. Follow the Psalm 119 diet. When you stand before Him at the end of the race, He won't frown and ask, "How much did you lose?" He will smile and say, "You have finished well!"

If you don't already keep a daily journal, begin doing so now. Get yourself a note-book—any size that's comfortable for you—and start by writing down that which has spoken to your heart today. Be painfully specific.

How to Waste Time

❧ *James 4:13—17* ❧

*H*ave you noticed how many day-planners are available these days? And then there are the time-management self-help books: how to increase your efficiency, how to make every moment count, how to invest your time wisely and productively.

While all those voices and handy products scream for your attention, I'd like to play devil's advocate and tell you how to waste your time. Five proven ideas come immediately to mind:

First, worry a lot. Start worrying early in the morning and intensify your anxiety as the day passes. Worry about your own failures and mistakes—about what you should or could have done but didn't. To add variety, worry about things you should not have done but did. Hanging around negative people is another secret you won't want to forget. Remember: Potential ulcers need fresh acid.

Second, make hard-and-fast predictions. Of course, you'll need to ignore that little throwaway line in the fourth chapter of James: "you do not know what your life will be like tomorrow." But forget that comment and set your expectations in motion. Be as specific as you can. For example, one month before his July 1975 disappearance, Jimmy Hoffa announced: "I don't need bodyguards."

Third, fix your attention on getting rich. You'll get a lot of innovative ideas from the secular bookshelves (I counted fourteen books on the subject last time I was in a bookstore), plus you'll fit right in with most of the hype that's pouring out of entrepreneurial seminars and high-pressure sales meetings.

Fourth, compare yourself with others. Not only will you ricochet between the extremes of arrogance and discouragement, you will also spend the time not knowing who you are.

Fifth, lengthen your list of enemies. If there's one thing above all others that will keep your wheels spinning, it's perfecting your skill at the Blame Game. With a full arsenal of suspicion, paranoia, and resentment, you can waste endless evenings stewing over those folks who have made your life miserable.

Put these five surefire suggestions in motion, and you can forget about all the hassles connected with being happy, efficient, productive, and contented. Within a couple of months, those things won't even be on your agenda.

All this sounds like foolish exaggeration, doesn't it? But just stop and think: How much time are you already wasting on some of these things?

UPHOLDING HUMAN DIGNITY

❧ *Psalm 139* ❧

A few winters ago in Stockholm, Sweden, an eighty-four-year-old woman sat for two months on her balcony before a neighbor discovered she was dead. The woman was found sitting in a chair, dressed in a coat and hat, her forehead leaning against the railing.

A neighbor realized something was wrong when she saw the woman sitting on her balcony around the clock, despite freezing temperatures. "I accused myself for not having seen her earlier," she said later. "I hope this dreadful story makes us better at keeping in touch with our old neighbors."

Isolationism is not a Scandinavian phenomenon; it is a human tragedy. For fear of poking our nose in someone else's business or getting involved in something that could backfire on us, we have trained ourselves not to stop, look, or listen.

But in a fast-paced world where only the fit survive, it sure is easy to feel dehumanized. Our technological age has made us more aware of our insignificance. Our suspicion that we are not loved for who we are is confirmed daily by the impersonal nature of twentieth-century living. We make a phone call and "voice mail" takes over. If folks are not home, we can talk to an answering machine. If we need money at 2:00 A.M., we can drop by the local ATM machine.

Machines write for us, answer phones for us, get money for us, shop for us, think for us, rent cars for us. They can even sign our letters. And the result is scary. A subtle erosion of individuality, followed by a no-touch, don't-bother-me-I'm-too-busy coldness, leading to a total absence of eyeball-to-eyeball interaction, resulting in the ultimate: more loss of human dignity. This is excused because it saves time and keeps us from getting hung up on knotty things like relationships. They say that's healthier?

What's so healthy about becoming completely untouchable?

Machines can't hug you when you're grieving. Machines don't care when you need a sounding board. Machines never affirm you when you are low or confront you when you are wrong. When you need reassurance and hope and strength to go on, you cannot replace the essential presence of another human being.

Christ came to save *people*. Human beings with names and personalities and fingerprints and faces. Upholding human dignity is worth the effort every time.

There's no substitute for the personal touch.

MEASURING SPIRITUAL GROWTH

🦋 *Hebrews 5:12–14* 🦋

*H*umans are strange creatures. We run faster when we lose our way. Instead of pausing to regroup, we ricochet from place to place. Three words describe our times: hurry, worry, and bury.

In this race called life, when the pressing demands of time are upon us, we need to stop and get oriented. We need to discover that the Lord is God. He will be exalted; He is with us; He is our stronghold.

Remember during your growing-up years how your mother had a specially designed wall with some pencil marks on it where, as you grew from year to year, she marked where your head reached? We had such a wall in our home. It was interesting to see how our children went through certain growth spurts at times.

On occasions, it was convicting when I came back from a trip and one of the smaller children asked, "Daddy, how much did you grow while you were away?" No, they didn't have spiritual growth in mind, but I often thought about their question in that light. They wanted to know, "Do you keep growing:? When does it stop?"

God uses an infinite number of vehicles in the process of helping us grow. I do not know of any means that leads to instant growth. I've never met anyone who became instantly mature. It's a painstaking process that God takes us through, and it includes such things as waiting, failing, losing, and being misunderstood—each one calling for extra doses of perseverance. In your own spiritual growth, where are the marks on the wall of your life? Where do you stand in light of last year? Or how about the last decade?

Christian growth comes through hard-core, gutsy perseverance of applying what you hear and obeying it.

New Year Stats and Lists

✣ *Exodus 20:3–17* ✣

*I*nvariably, a new year prompts us to make our own list of things deserving our diligent attention and pursuit. Let me suggest that we work off the lists of two men who have gone before us. The lists are attainable, 100% wholesome, and a constant encouragement.

Moses' List (Exodus 20:3–17)

> Don't ever place substitute gods before the Lord your God.
> Don't make an idol out of anyone or anything.
> Don't take the Lord's name in vain. It is holy.
> Remember to observe a Sabbath rest every week.
> Honor and respect your dad and mom.
> Don't murder anyone for any reason.
> Never, ever commit adultery.
> Don't take things that aren't yours.
> Never lie or give a false impression.
> Don't covet another person's mate, benefits, or belongings.

Peter's List (2 Peter 1:5–8)

> Be a diligent person.
> Don't waver in your faith.
> Be known for uncompromising moral excellence.
> Enlarge your reservoir of knowledge; keep learning.
> Stay balanced; guard against extremes.
> Persevere.
> Make sure your godliness is free of hypocrisy.
> Treat others tactfully, graciously.
> Let your Christian love flow, let it flow, let it flow.

If you take these lists seriously, two things are certain: 1) You won't be the same person you were last year, and 2) You certainly won't get bored.

Without God, life is a monotonous repetition of weeks, months, seasons, years, decades, and generations.

THINK IT OVER

❧❧❧

*W*ith prayer and thoughtfulness, spend some time thinking about the year ahead and where God may be leading you.

You may want to write down some of your conclusions below so that you can pray about them and refer back to them from time to time in the coming year.

My List:

MEMORIES ARE MADE OF THIS

🕮 *Mark 3* 🕮

*D*uring the Thanksgiving holiday a few years ago, I experienced a moving moment as I watched our younger daughter, Colleen, with her baby, Ashley Alissa, who at that time was a newborn. Colleen had nursed her back to sleep and was holding Ashley ever so tenderly, as only a mother can do. Colleen didn't see me as I stood in the shadows, thinking . . . reflecting . . . remembering.

In my flashback, it was I who held our darling Colleen nestled in my arms. She had been born only a month or so earlier, and her arrival had brought a fresh ray of hope and happiness to our lives. In her tiny eyes, which danced with delight, I found a reason to smile. Her chubby little hands gripped my fingers, as if saying, "I love you, Daddy . . . you're special to me."

As these reflections passed through my mind, I realized anew the profound importance of caring for the young and being sensitive to their needs. I also realized again that both require sacrifice and commitment.

There stood the young mother, who was once our little baby, in the glow of a night light . . . exhausted from too little sleep, yet committed to her baby's comfort, whispering, "I love you" and determined to do whatever was necessary through the silent hours before dawn.

For many, I realize, such pleasant, nostalgic scenes of home are foreign, even nonexistent. Home was a battleground where only the fittest survived. Some of you who read this may not recall even a handful of pleasant memories springing from your original family. Not until Christ found you, won you over, and entered your life, did you begin to discover what love is all about.

To you, the *church*—those folks who people the place, who reach out in compassion, who provide you a healthy and a safe environment in which to grow—has become "home" and "family" as well.

Which is a needed reminder to us that the people of faith are the only models many have to look to, to learn from, to count on.

What can we in the church do? We can help those who have no memories of parental commitment and sacrifice to build new memories.

This requires commitment and sacrifice from us, no doubt about it. But, oh, isn't it worth it all?

Think of some young person(s) in your church who has a need for a family touch.
Take the opportunity to build a memory that impressionable individual
will never forget.

GUT-LEVEL AUTHENTICITY

❧ *1 Kings 2:1–4* ❧

*I*n 1991 James Patterson and Peter Kim released *The Day America Told the Truth,* a study based on an extensive opinion survey which guaranteed the anonymity of its participants. And the truth was shocking! Let me give you a brief sampling of their findings: Only 13% of Americans see all Ten Commandments as binding and relevant; 91% lie regularly, both at work and in their homes; most American workers admit to goofing off for an average of seven hours—almost one whole day—per week; and half of our work force admits that they regularly call in sick when they feel perfectly well.

One particular question on the survey really grabbed me: "What are you willing to do for $10 million?" (Are you sitting down?) Twenty-five percent would abandon their families; 23% would become a prostitute for a week; 7% would murder a stranger!

Now, a word of caution here. Sometimes it's easy for Christians to feel a little smug-to look down our pious noses and sigh in pharisaical tones, "I'm a Christian. I would never do that." Not so fast, my friend. You don't want to hear this, but there's not all that much difference between "us" and "them."

Two other authors, both Christians, did their own sampling of the populace and built their own embarrassing case based on hard evidence. According to their book, *Keeping Your Ethical Edge Sharp,* Doug Sherman and William Hendricks concluded that "the general ethical conduct of Christians varies only slightly from non-Christians" (with some grand exceptions, of course). Believers, they said, are almost as likely as unbelievers to do such things as falsify their income tax returns, steal from the workplace, and selectively obey the laws.

No question about it, depravity is alive and well with non-Christians and Christians alike. Why? Because "inauthenticity" became the art form of the 1990s.

Want a challenge? Start modeling the truth . . . the whole truth and nothing but the truth, so help you God. Think truth. Confess truth. Face truth. Love truth. Pursue truth. Walk truth. Talk truth. Ah, that last one! That's a good place to begin. From this day forward, deliberately, consciously, and conscientiously speak the truth. Start practicing gut-level authenticity.

Do your own honest soul search. What would you do for $10 million?

THE IDEAL COMBINATION

❧ *John 17:1–8* ❧

*W*hat is your favorite feeling?" When my sister, Luci, asked me that question recently, my brain began to click through a dozen or more possibilities. Being a person to whom feelings are extremely important, I had a tough time selecting one. Finally, I landed on "accomplishment." There is nothing quite as satisfying as crossing off the last item on my to-do list at the end of a busy day.

I have often thought of Jesus' words when He was only hours removed from the cross. In His prayer to the Father, after doing a quick mental pass in review, He said, "I glorified Thee on the earth, *having accomplished* the work which Thou hast given Me to do" (John 17:4). A little over thirty-three years after His arrival in Bethlehem, there He stood in Jerusalem, saying, in effect, "It's a wrap." He had done everything the Father sent Him to do . . . and in the final analysis, that's what mattered.

Oh, the satisfaction that comes from the accomplishment . . . *the accomplishment.*

Since my conversation with Luci was a dialogue, I naturally was curious about her favorite feeling. Actually, her answer was somewhat akin to mine. "My favorite feeling is relief," she said.

The relief from pain by finding the right medication. The relief from financial pressure by an unexpected gift or raise or bonus. The relief from panic by finding the lost wallet. The relief from loneliness by seeing the face of a loved one. The relief from despair by hearing your once-rebellious son or daughter say, "I love you." The relief from guilt and shame by God's promise of forgiveness.

Who hasn't swallowed a big knot when entering through imagination's gate to witness the return of the prodigal son? What relief that father must have felt when he caught his first glimpse of his boy on the horizon. And what relief that son must have felt! When wayward lad and waiting dad embraced, time stood still. Eyes that once burned in anger were soothed in tears as relief on both sides erased all fear. Ah, the relief . . . *the relief.*

Which is better, accomplishment or relief? Perhaps, like teeth in matching gears, one follows the other. After years of thinking, praying, planning, and dreaming, working to accomplish that goal, we then bask in the magnificent relief such accomplishment brings. Both feelings are heightened.

Think of the years of God's faithfulness. He saw us through one nagging obstacle after another until the objective was accomplished . . . and the relief experienced.

We don't need more strength than the strength God gives us. We don't need more knowledge than we already have. All we need is the will to do what needs to be done.

LISTS

❧ *Micah 6:8* ❧

*L*ists are everywhere. The sports page is full of them. Elsewhere we find lists of Academy Award winners, Pulitzer Prize winners, and beauty contest winners. The publishing world has its best-seller list, the music world its gold and platinum album lists, the financial world its Fortune 500 list. Even the religious world has its list of super churches, largest Sunday schools, biggest worship centers, or those giving most to missions.

Usually after looking over such lists, I wonder, Who really cares? It is doubtful that God has ever been impressed with the size of anything. His Book invariably ranks quality above quantity. As a matter of fact, He seems to delight in reminding us that greater glory to Him takes place when victory occurs in spite of the odds. As in David vs. Goliath. Or the Hebrews vs. the Egyptians at the Red Sea. Or Gideon's few. Or Jesus' small band of disciples.

But about the time I'm ready to suggest that we ignore all lists, I come across a list in the Scriptures! Dozens of them, in fact!

For example, God not only lists the Ten Commandments that depict His holy character, He lists the things He hates to find among His creatures. Remember them? Haughty eyes, a lying tongue, hands that shed innocent blood, a heart that devises wicked plans, feet that run rapidly to evil, a false witness who utters lies, one who spreads strife among brothers (Prov. 6:16–19).

The apostle Paul helps us out by listing "the fruit of the Spirit" (Gal. 5:22–23). Elsewhere, Paul lists the gifts of the Spirit in several of his letters (Rom. 12:6–8; 1 Cor. 12:28; Eph. 4:11), Peter lists the qualities of a maturing Christian (2 Pet. 1:5–8), and John lists the first-century churches that represented examples worth noting (Rev. 2:1–3, 22). There are lists of qualifications for being an elder and also for being a deacon.

Lists, lists, and more lists! And since they are authored by the living Lord, we'd be wise to read and heed each one.

Even though it finds its origin in one whose life was not centered on Christ our Lord, Mahatma Gandhi's own list of "seven deadly sins" in the form of contrasts deserves our attention: wealth without work, pleasure without conscience, knowledge without character, commerce without morality, science without humanity, worship without sacrifice, politics without principle.

Now, there's a list to heed and not carry out!

The prophet Micah names the absolute basics "required" by the Lord. The next time you're feeling that living for God is getting too complicated, blow the dust off Micah's list: to do justice, to love kindness, to walk humbly with God.

WAITING IN SILENCE

❧ *James 1:2—4* ❧

*M*y soul waits in silence for God only," (Psalm 62:1). Some of the best times in prayer are wordless times. I stop speaking, close my eyes, and meditate upon what I have been reading or upon what I have been saying, and I listen inside of myself. I listen deeply. I listen for reproofs. I think of myself as a home with many doors. As I am meditating—and often it helps to close my eyes so I won't be distracted—I unlock doors and open them as I wait. It is here that the Holy Spirit invades. Then, I take circumstances before Him and I listen with doors open.

Please be assured that I have never heard an audible voice. It isn't that kind of answering. It's a listening down inside. It's sensing what God is saying about the situation. His promise is, after all, that He will inscribe His law—His will—upon our hearts and our minds.

It's like what you do when you're in love with a person. Isn't it true—the deeper the love, the less that has to be said? You can actually sit alone together by a fireplace for an hour or two and say very, very little, but it can be the deepest encounter and relationship you know anything about.

Those who wait upon the Lord will gain new strength according to Isaiah, but remember: the key is waiting.

There's a sense of stability in trusting the Lord. That's how we wait silently and with a sense of confidence. When we wait for God to direct our steps, He does! When we trust Him to meet our needs, He will!

God tempers us and seasons us, making us mellow and mature when we wait on Him.

CLOSING THE GAP

❧ *Nehemiah 1–6* ❧

I sat down and looked over Nehemiah's shoulder for a couple of hours last week, refreshing my mind on the things he recorded during a critical segment of his life. As I reread this account of rebuilding the wall around Jerusalem, it began to dawn on me that this book is a veritable storehouse of insights on leadership and should be required reading for all who are in leadership or wish to be. I have found no less than seven qualities Nehemiah demonstrated as a leader.

First, he had a passion for the project. Whatever the project may be, passion, vision, enthusiasm, drive, and determination are absolutely essential. Nehemiah could hardly sleep as he pictured the need and imagined himself involved in accomplishing the objective.

Second, he had the ability to motivate others. What good is leadership if it cannot move people to action? Leaders like Nehemiah inspire others to do their best.

Third, he had an unswerving confidence in God. Nehemiah's journal is filled with prayers, constantly reminding the people of the Lord's presence and protection.

Fourth, he was resilient and patient through opposition. Nehemiah endured it all—sarcasm, suspicion, gossip, mockery, threats, false accusations—but he refused to let that sidetrack him.

Fifth, he had a practical, balanced grip on reality. Nehemiah had the workers stay at the job with diligence, but he also stationed others to guard the wall from attack. Good leaders maintain that needed balance between being positive and being aware of the negative.

Sixth, he had a willingness to work hard and remain unselfish. Nehemiah is a pattern of servant-hearted leadership.

Seventh, he had the discipline to finish the job. When the task loses its luster, good leaders don't rush elsewhere. As Nehemiah recorded, "So the wall was completed . . . in fifty-two days" (6:15). Mission accomplished!

Good, solid Christian leaders are as much in demand today as in Nehemiah's time. Perhaps more so. The problem is not a decline in opportunities but a dearth of candidates.

Are you in a position of leadership or being called to such a position?
Think long and hard about God's requirements. If you are not in such a position,
you certainly know those who are. Pray for them.

THINK IT OVER

❧ *Nehemiah 8* ❧

*A*nd all the people gathered as one man at the square which was in front of the Water Gate, and they asked Ezra the scribe to bring the book of the law of Moses which the LORD had given to Israel. Then Ezra the priest brought the law before the assembly of men, women, and all who could listen with understanding, on the first day of the seventh month.

And he read from it before the square which was in front of the Water Gate from early morning until midday, in the presence of men and women, those who could understand; and all the people were attentive to the book of the law. . . . And Ezra opened the book in the sight of all the people for he was standing above all the people; and when he opened it, all the people stood up.

Then Ezra blessed the LORD the great God. And all the people answered, "Amen, Amen! while lifting up their hands; then they bowed low and worshiped the LORD with their faces to the ground. . . . Then Nehemiah, who was the governor, and Ezra the priest and scribe, and the Levites who taught the people said to all the people, "This day is holy to the LORD your God; do not mourn or weep." For all the people were weeping when they heard the words of the law.

"Do not be grieved, for the joy of the LORD is your strength." So the Levites calmed all the people, saying, "Be still, for the day is holy; do not be grieved." . . . And there was great rejoicing.

And he read from the book of the law of God daily.

A FULL EMPTY NEST

❧ *2 Corinthians 5:17–21* ❧

*A*s the bride and groom roared off on their shiny black-and-purple Harley-Davidson Heritage Classic, my heart skipped a beat. I waved, put my arm around Cynthia, and found myself drifting back thirty-seven years to our own wedding.

Now, here we stood, watching our last child ride off into the sunset. I looked Cynthia in the eyes, wrapped her in my arms, whispered the three greatest words in the English language in her ear, and added, "Well, Hon . . . we're back where we started."

And so we are.

We started without knowing what the future held. We still don't. We started in simple faith, excited about God's leading. We're there again. If our God does not lead, we're still not interested in going. We started with hearts in tune to each other. Though young, we had no disagreement over who would have the final word. Our Lord, who had called us to become one, would remain preeminent. We started with a mutual desire to have a family and love each one with equal affection. We were determined not to let anything decrease the priority of our home—not school, not church, not the teenage years, not our own careers. We made it, all praise to His name. And we're still friends . . . still close . . . still committed.

I looked down at Cynthia and smiled. Thirty-seven years rushed between us. Our primary job of parenting was done. Our roles of hands-on mom and dad were changing. Instead of telling our four what to do or how to do it, we would be available, keep our mouths shut, be willing to wait, happy to help, quick to affirm—but definitely would not get in their way. Or control. Or preach. Or manipulate. Their lives are theirs to live, free of our presence or counsel, unless requested. For Chuck and Cynthia, it's back to where we started.

According to the book *Passages of Marriage,* we have reached the fifth and final stage, "Transcendent Love"—"a profound and peaceful perspective toward your partner and toward life."

That sounds pretty good to me. Frankly, my wife still looks so great to me, has such depth of character, and fulfills my life so thoroughly, I get excited just thinking about cultivating this "transcendent perspective."

Cultivate your own transcendent perspective with the one you love. Find one way this week to rekindle the intimacy you had in the beginning.

CONFESSIONS

❧ *Galatians 5:13* ❧

*L*et me be the first to tell you: Cynthia and I have a new baby. Yep, nice 'n healthy, strong body, a loud cry. Lots of fun, this kid. We haven't chosen a name yet, but we're workin' on it. Oh, did I mention that it weighs in at 750 pounds?

In case you haven't guessed it, baby is a Harley Heritage Softail Classic, black and blue, with big, bold, white sidewall tires (Harley-Davidson calls them "gangster whitewalls"!) and enough chrome to sink a small boat.

Okay, okay . . . maybe all this "motorcycle nonsense" needs a little background—especially for those of you who think something like this is "beneath the dignity" of a man of the cloth (or better still, the wife of a man of the cloth).

As I watched my son and his new wife roar off after their wedding on their black-and-purple Harley, it occurred to me that this grandfather and his sweetheart of thirty-seven years could enjoy one of those too. When I first visited the showroom and sat on one of those big machines, Cynthia didn't know whether to laugh out loud or witness to me. She compromised and hopped on behind after I winked at her (she couldn't resist). And suddenly, it was 1952 and we were cruising the back streets of Houston. She was wearing my letterman sweater with a ballerina skirt and her red-and-white saddle oxfords . . . and I had a flattop with a ducktail and a black leather jacket with fringe and chrome studs.

She leaned up and whispered, "You know, I could get used to this, but do you think we ought to be here?"

"Of course, honey. I'm a marine. All I need is a pair of black jeans, leather chaps—and all you need is a tattoo, and we'll blend right in."

What's happening? you may be asking. What on earth would possess a man of my age to start messing around with a motorcycle? What is all this about?

It's about forgetting the ridiculous idea that every single moment in life must be grim and sober. It's about being with one of our kids in a world that is totally his turf (for a change), not mine. It's about breaking the bondage of tunnel vision. It's about stepping into an anxiety-free world where I feel the wind and smell the wildflowers and hug my wife and laugh until I'm hoarse.

It's about freedom. That's it, plain and simple. And, bottom line . . . it's about grace.

Have you laughed yourself hoarse recently? Have you appropriated God's grace and freedom? Smelled any wildflowers? Maybe you should give yourself permission instead of worrying about who might say what.

HOW ABOUT 99.9%?

🙚 *Romans 4:4–5; Psalm 103* 🙚

*W*hen the Ritz-Carlton Hotels won the Malcolm Baldrige National Quality Award, the owner of that outstanding organization, Mr. William Johnson, stated that now they would need to work even harder to earn the respect that came with the award. "Quality," he said, "is a race with no finish line."

He is correct. Competitive excellence requires 100% all of the time. Ever tracked the consequences of "almost but not quite"? According to some fine research by Natalie Gabal, if 99.9% were considered good enough, then this year alone . . . 2,000,000 documents would be lost by the IRS; 12 babies would be given to the wrong parents each day; 291 pacemaker operations would be performed incorrectly; 20,000 incorrect drug prescriptions would be written (to cite just a few examples).

Instead of applying this negatively to the practical side of life, I'd much rather compare it positively to the theological. Remember that forgotten word "justification"? Justification is the sovereign act of God whereby He declares righteous the believing sinner while that person is still in a sinning state. He doesn't suddenly make us righteous (we still sin). He *declares* us righteous. How righteous does God declare us? One hundred percent righteous. Stop and think: Upon believing in Jesus Christ's substitutionary death and bodily resurrection, the once-lost sinner is instantly, unconditionally, and permanently "declared 100% righteous." Anything less and we are not righteous . . . we're *almost* righteous.

If we were declared 99.9% righteous, some verses would have to be rewritten. Like Isaiah 1:18, which might then read: "'Come now, and let us reason together,' says the LORD, 'though your sins are as scarlet, they will be light pink.'"

Nonsense! The promise of sins forgiven is all or nothing.

Unlike the earthly race for excellence, the race against sin had a finish line. Otherwise, when Jesus breathed His last breath, He would've said, "It is *almost* finished." And we would have to keep working at it, adding to something Christ didn't finish at the cross.

Let's never, ever forget that God is into "white as snow," not light pink.

*If Christ had paid 99.9% of the debt of sin,
not one of us would have a chance at heaven.*

It's Time to Take Time

❧ *Psalm 31* ❧

*Y*ears ago my older son, then a teenager, and I dropped by the local Hallmark shop to find Cynthia a card for Mother's Day. Somewhat bored with the process, Curt wandered back to the posters and soon called me to come look at one he liked. It was a picture of a boat on a very still lake at dawn. A father was sitting at one end, his son at the other, fishing. Both were smiling, obviously enjoying those leisure hours together. Two words were neatly printed at the bottom of that exquisite scene of solitude: TAKE TIME.

It got me thinking about how seldom we really take time to be with our children. Some time later, I saw a column in *Newsweek* entitled "Dear Dads, Save Your Sons," by Christopher Bacorn, a psychologist living in Boerne, Texas. I still can't shake myself free from his words.

> I have come to believe that most adolescent boys can't make use of professional counseling. . . . What a boy can use, and all too often doesn't have, is the fellowship of men—at least one man who pays attention to him, who spends time with him, who admires him. A boy needs a man he can look up to. What he doesn't need is a shrink. . . . The great majority of youthful offenders are male, most without fathers involved in their lives in any useful way. Many have never even met their fathers.
>
> What's become of the fathers of these boys? Where are they? Well, I can tell you where they're not. They're not at PTA meetings or piano recitals. They're not teaching Sunday school. . . .
>
> Where are the fathers? They are on golf courses, tennis courts, in bowling alleys, fishing on lakes and rivers. They are working in their jobs, many from early morning to late at night. Some are home watching television, out mowing the lawn or tuning up the car. In short, they are everywhere except in the company of their children.

What do you do when you have a free day, a holiday, or even a few available hours? Are you tempted to fill this time with "necessary" work projects or a whole day on the links with a few of your buddies? Before saying yes to the above, stop and ask yourself, "Why not spend some quiet time with one of my kids?"

Before it's too late . . . take time.

When was the last time you really spent time—real time—with your child? Make time right now to do it. Take time to rebuild a relationship.

BE GRACIOUS

❧ *2 Peter 3:18* ❧

aul deals with the value of being gracious in your Christian walk in 1 Thessalonians 2:7–11: "But we proved to be gentle among you, as a nursing mother tenderly cares for her own children. Having thus a fond affection for you, we were well-pleased to impart to you not only the gospel of God but also our own lives, because you had become very dear to us. For you recall, brethren, our labor and hardship, how working night and day so as not to be a burden to any of you, we proclaimed to you the gospel of God. You are witnesses, and so is God, how devoutly and uprightly and blamelessly we behaved toward you believers; just as you know how we were exhorting and encouraging and imploring each one of you as a father would his own children."

What a gracious, tolerant spirit! The man was both approachable and tender. Did you notice the word pictures? He cared for others "as a nursing mother" and dealt with them in their needs "as a father." He had compassion. Of high priority to this capable, brilliant man of God was a gracious, compassionate attitude.

If there is one specific criticism we hear against our evangelical "camp" more than any other, it is this: We lack compassion. We are more abrasive and judgmental than thoughtful, tactful, compassionate, and tolerant. If we're not careful, we tend to use people rather than love them, don't we? We try to change them and later help them, rather than accept them as they are.

Our world of hungry, hurting humanity longs for and deserves the message of truth presented in attractive, gentle, gracious wrappings. Don't forget: "As a mother . . . as a father." There is positive affirmation implied rather than negative nitpicking.

People are far more important than rigid rules and demanding expectations.

MILES THAT MATTER

❧ *Psalm 24* ❧

*J*ohn Steinbeck's delightful little volume *Travels with Charley* fascinates me each time I read it. It tells how the author and his dog took to the highways, traveling hundreds of miles, encountering all sorts of interesting people and intriguing situations.

I find myself charmed by that sort of thing, and I got a quick taste of it a few years ago when I drove our youngest son across eight states to get him settled in an apartment near a school he would be attending. We swapped turns driving his pickup, spent several nights in motels, and by the time we rolled into the last driveway, we'd covered 2,569 miles.

We drove through towns we'd never heard of, over rivers we couldn't pronounce, ate at a few spots we wouldn't recommend. Small talk and silence. Deep discussions and laughter. Hamburgers and Cokes, jokes and snoozes. But the best part of all? Being with my twenty-year-old son. Sharing feelings we hadn't talked about for much too long. With a 5 x 8 U-Haul behind us and nothing but miles of highway in front of us, life was distilled to stuff that mattered.

Why did I love the trip? Because I love my son. I cannot tell you the number of times I found myself overcome with nostalgia as I thought about the inescapable reality of six simple words: He is now on his own.

As the two of us walked together toward the airline terminal where I was to catch a return flight home, we arrived at a small sign: "Only ticketed passengers beyond this point." Suddenly he wrapped his long arms around me and whispered the words every father longs to hear from his own: "I love you, Dad." I held him tightly and recalled two decades of hugs from this boy who is now a man. I replayed childhood scenes of that little towhead and forced myself not to cling.

As my plane lifted high above the blue highways, I asked the Lord for four things: the unselfishness to release him, the vision to encourage him, the faithfulness to pray for him, and the wisdom to be there for him whenever or wherever that may be. God knows I'm willing to do whatever.

I was even willing to crawl back into that pickup when school was over and take on those same 2,569 miles in the opposite direction.

Get off the freeway and travel some blue highways.
You'll love the scenery. And, more importantly, you need the break.

THINK IT OVER

❧ *Nehemiah 8* ❧

*A*lmost always, the answer was the same. "How did your game go?" I'd ask. "Good," he would reply. "How did you do?" . . . "Good." The response wasn't a curt put-off, nor was it a rote reaction. It was offered honestly, and almost always with enthusiasm. . . . It didn't matter if the final score was 1–0 or 100–0. It didn't matter if he had knocked home the winning run or if he had struck out every time at bat. It didn't matter if the subject was sports, or school, or family or something else.

"How were things?" . . . "Good."

He had so much perspective for a little boy. . . . Sports were like the rest of life. Taking part was what made it worthwhile. . . . Gus found happiness just in taking part.

It wasn't just sports. It was choir and student council at school. It was violin lessons. It was a birthday party at a friend's house. . . . Every day was a new day, a time for a new experience. Life was good.

But life ended for a positive and uncomplaining and involved little boy last Sunday in a fire in Silver Plume, Colorado.

There were so many things undone. We hadn't gone to get Junior Zephyrs cards for this next year yet. We hadn't made our trek north to watch the dirt-track races at Erie, Colorado. . . . What we had done, though, was communicate through ten short years. And we had ended every night we were together with the same words: "I love you."

Please let me say it one more time. "Gus, I love you."

—TODD PHIPERS, *The Denver Post*

Three little words. Because they are often hard to say, because we so easily forget, we need to stay in practice. Todd would give everything he owns to be able to say them to Gus tonight.

OUR ULTIMATE HOORAY

❧ *John 11* ❧

*W*hat gives a widow courage as she stands beside a fresh grave? What is the ultimate hope of the handicapped, the abused, the burn victim? What is the final answer to pain, mourning, senility, insanity, terminal diseases, sudden calamities, and fatal accidents?

The answer to each of these questions is the same: *the hope of bodily resurrection.*

We draw strength from this single truth almost every day of our lives—more than we realize. It becomes the mental glue that holds our otherwise shattered thoughts together. Impossible though it may be for us to understand the details of how God is going to pull it off, we hang our hopes on fragile, threadlike thoughts that say, "Someday, He will make it right," and "Thank God, all this will change," and "When we're with Him, we shall be like Him."

More than a few times a year I look into red, swollen eyes and remind the despairing and the grieving that "there's a land that is fairer than day" where, as John promised in the Revelation, "He shall wipe away every tear . . . there shall no longer be any death . . . any mourning or crying or pain . . . there shall no longer be any curse . . . any night . . . because the Lord God shall illumine them; and they shall reign forever and ever" (21:4; 22:3, 5). Hooray for such wondrous hope!

Just imagine . . . those who are physically disabled today will one day leap in ecstatic joy. Those who spend their lives absorbed in total darkness will see every color in the spectrum of light. In fact, the very first face they will see will be the One who gives them sight!

There's nothing like the hope of resurrection to lift the agonizing spirits of the heavy-hearted.

But how can we know for sure, some may ask. What gives us such assurance, such unshakable confidence? Those questions have the same answer: *the fact of Christ's resurrection.*

Because He has been raised, we too shall rise! No wonder we get so excited every Easter! No wonder we hold nothing back as we smile and sing and celebrate His miraculous resurrection from the grave!

Jesus Himself promised: "I am the resurrection and the life; he who believes in Me shall live even if he dies" (John 11:25).

Easter is a double-barreled celebration:
His triumphant hurrah over agony and our ultimate hooray of ecstasy.

A Fox in the Henhouse

🐛 *Galatians 6:7–8* 🐛

I have been a Magic Johnson basketball fan ever since he made All-American at Michigan State. Magic was a champion without arrogance, an MVP without a peer.

And then, in one day, that love affair turned sour for some of us. We sat stunned. Magic had HIV! And to make the unbelievable hurt even more, he openly admitted that he had been promiscuous with numerous women. As he told *Sports Illustrated:* "The problem is that I can't pinpoint the time, the place, or the woman. It's a matter of numbers. . . . I confess that after I arrived in L.A., in 1979, I did my best to accommodate as many women as I could— most of them through unprotected sex."

Will someone please point out to me how those words resulted in such an avalanche of praise and approval, admiration and sympathy? While all the world seems impressed, I am both saddened and angry. Another national hero had been caught with his pants down . . . and now suffers the consequences.

At the risk of sounding terribly severe and perhaps unsympathetic, I must remind you that God's warning came over nineteen hundred years ago and has been true ever since mankind has inhabited this old planet: "Do not be deceived, God is not mocked; for whatever a man sows, this he will also reap. For the one who sows to his own flesh shall from the flesh reap corruption" (Gal. 6:7–8).

Am I concerned over the AIDS epidemic? You bet your life I am. Do we need to warn the public and use every means possible to find ways to combat the disease? Absolutely.

But if we're looking for individuals who have the right to speak publicly, let's choose those who really have been victimized, like innocent folks who were given contaminated blood transfusions or the innocent children who were born with it or brokenhearted parents whose homes have been ripped apart as they helplessly watch their son or daughter die. These and others like them are the real victims of the AIDS virus. Their words will carry far more weight than some athletic fox who spent too much time in the henhouse.

"And oftentimes, to win us to our harm, / The instruments of darkness tell us truths, / Win us with honest trifles, to betray us / In deepest consequence"
(William Shakespeare).

KNOWING THE FUTURE

❧ *James 4* ❧

*Q*uick now, what woman in recent years not only won the prestigious "Woman of the World" award but was named the "Most Admired Woman" in the world for three consecutive years? Former First Lady Barbara Bush or perhaps Supreme Court justice Sandra Day O'Conner? Maybe Mrs. Thatcher of Great Britain? All wrong.

She was the world's leading astrologer and "voice of prophecy"—none other than Jeanne Dixon. Among other unsolicited mailing lists, I'm on the list of the Franklin Mint, and a mailing was timed perfectly—as the last century drew to a close. When all of us were thinking about—what else? The future.

The offer? Jeanne Dixon's "Crystal Ball"—"an heirloom work of art to enhance your home . . . and your future." In Ms. Dixon's own words, "Behold the revelation of your destiny." What was once practiced behind closed doors and considered part hoax and part superstitious hocus-pocus is now big-time business.

But if you really desire to "behold the revelation of your destiny," stay away from "exquisite" crystal balls and sophisticated "astrological" software. Getting involved with all that will not only empty your purse, it will mess up your head.

Remember, the enemy of our souls has a field day when we take the restraints off our curiosity and plunge full-bore into the so-called mystical world. Substitute the word "demonic" for "mystical," and you won't be nearly so tempted.

If our God had wanted us to gaze into our own crystal ball, He would never have prompted James to write: "Come now, you who say, 'Today or tomorrow, we shall go to such and such a city, and spend a year there and engage in business and make a profit.' Yet you do not know what your life will be like tomorrow. You are just a vapor that appears for a little while and then vanishes away. Instead you ought to say, 'If the Lord wills, we shall live and also do this or that'" (James 4:13–15).

I want to walk with God by faith now and leave the future completely in His capable hands.

Our problem is not needing to know the truth about tomorrow;
it's needing to live the truth we know today.

GOOD THINGS, BAD WORLD

❧ *Psalm 1* ❧

*P*aul certainly proved himself a prophet when he wrote: "But the Spirit explicitly says that in later times some will fall away from the faith, paying attention to deceitful spirits and doctrines of demons" (1 Tim. 4:1).

And when he predicted: "But realize this, that in the last days difficult times will come. For men will be lovers of self, lovers of money, boastful, arrogant, revilers, disobedient to parents, ungrateful, unholy, unloving, irreconcilable, malicious gossips, without self-control, brutal, haters of good, treacherous, reckless, conceited, lovers of pleasure rather than lovers of God; holding to a form of godliness, although they have denied its power; and avoid such men as these" (2 Tim. 3:1–5), he foresaw exactly what would transpire. Sounds like he was describing life in the twentieth century.

Cynthia and I have a long-time friend who is fighting colon cancer. Following major surgery she is now undergoing extensive chemotherapy. The other day she and another woman went shopping at a mall in Fort Lauderdale. As they got out of the car, our friend was mugged. The attacker slammed her against the car, then brutally flung her to the pavement and began kicking her mercilessly—all in broad daylight. A stranger stepped in to rescue her, and the attacker punched him repeatedly, breaking several of his teeth. The motive? Rape? No. Robbery? No. Carjacking? No. The police said it's a new fad . . . randomly assaulting strangers for the sadistic excitement of bringing blood and causing another human being pain.

Ours is a bad, bad world, but does that mean nothing's good? Does it mean we have run out of things for which to be grateful? No, no, a thousand times, no!

Bob Green, a newspaper columnist, invited his readers to look on the bright side for a change and send him some of the good things about life in America. More than 50,000 things came pouring across his desk. Things like a newborn baby's cry of life, Mr. Rogers, literacy volunteers, Special Olympics, sweet corn in August, town meetings, state fairs, and fresh blackberry cobbler. There are thousands more. Let's deliberately take time to smell the flowers as we call to mind all the good things in a bad, bad world.

Make your own list of "good things."

GETTING INVOLVED

❧ *1 Corinthians 12:20–27* ❧

*C*hristians have at least four areas of involvement to maintain with Christ through life:

- To maintain a close connection with our Lord, we think of Him as we make our plans, we pray, we explore the rich treasures of His Word.
- Our involvement with members of our family: Parents, children, relatives, mates . . . Christian or not—all of these people comprise our circle of close contact.
- Our involvement with other Christians: Usually, these people are selected from the church we attend. The number grows as we connect with others through areas of mutual interest. This becomes a major factor in our ability to cope with life on this planet, otherwise a lonely and discouraging pilgrimage.
- Our involvement with non-Christians: We work alongside them, do business with them, live near them, go to school next to them, and are usually entertained by them. Unfortunately, most Christians cut off all close ties with non-Christians within a few months after their salvation. Small wonder we find it difficult to share our faith with others.

Difficult thought it may be to believe, there are Christian people who are out of touch and uninvolved in the town or city where you live. And also in the church where you worship. They need you. What's more, you need them.

Never forget, isolation is a potent killer.

FROM A DAD TO A DAUGHTER

❧ *Psalm 45* ❧

*W*ell, Colleen, my now grown-up daughter, Saturday is the big day. *The Big Day.* It's the one we have talked about, planned on, and pictured in our minds since you were just a tot playing make-believe. Remember? I sure do. Those moments of imaginary ecstasy have spilled over into our conversation dozens (maybe even *hundreds*) of times during your twenty-three years under our roof. Wonderful dreamlike moments, which today seem terribly significant to this proud father of the bride. They are moments your mother and I will forever cherish. But come Saturday, you will trade the make-believe for the real thing. The Big Day will begin—for you and Mark, the best there is.

Forgive me, sweetheart, but memories of yesteryear flood my mind. Camping. Listening to the rain from inside our tent, sitting around the campfire roasting marshmallows, and shooting the rapids on inner tubes. Hasn't it been fun washing cars together? And picking out Mother's Day cards together? And getting yogurt together? And jogging together? And doing dishes together?

You are a spiritually sensitive young woman. By bringing that quality to your marriage, your presence can only enhance your husband's devotion to Christ. You are also an encourager. Mark's years in seminary will take on new dimensions, and those tough days of study won't seem nearly so hard, thanks to your affirmation and confidence. Your sense of humor will give light to otherwise dark and dismal tunnels through which the two of you must travel . . . so, whatever else you do, laugh often and prompt your man to do the same.

When the two of you slip away on Saturday evening, your mother and I will step aside, arm in arm, and smile through tears of joy as we happily let you go to enjoy the best years of your life.

It's okay if I miss you from time to time, isn't it?

With all my love,

Dad

Have you ever written a letter to your son or daughter or to a good friend upon a special occasion? How about doing it now.

THINK IT OVER

❧ *1 Corinthians 12:20–27* ❧

Like apples of gold in settings of silver
is a word spoken in right circumstances.
—PROVERBS 25:11

T he days, weeks, months, and years fly by so quickly. Before you know it, it's too late. Don't let those words go unspoken, unwritten, unsaid.

Like cold water to a weary soul
So is good news from a distant land.
—PROVERBS 25:25

How long has it been since you have written to your parents, to your best friend, to old friends long unseen but not forgotten?

Have you ever written to your favorite teachers (school or Sunday school) and told them how much their influence has meant in your life? Can you imagine what news like that might mean to them?

A MONTH FOR LOVE

🐝 *1 Corinthians 13* 🐝

*I*t is February. Overcast, chilly, bleak-and-barren February. If you're not into skiing the slopes, skating on ice, or singin' in the rain, there's not a lot outside to excite you. Sure was gracious of God to make it last only twenty-eight days . . . well, sometimes twenty-nine. No wonder bears hibernate at this time of year—there's not even Monday Night Football!

But wait. There is something extra special about February. Valentine's Day. Hearts 'n flowers. Sweetheart banquets. A fresh and needed reminder that there is still a heart-shaped vacuum in the human breast that only the three most wonderful words in the English language can fill.

To love and to be loved is the bedrock of our existence. But love must also flex and adapt. Rigid love is not true love. It is veiled manipulation, a conditional time bomb that explodes when frustrated. Genuine love willingly waits! It isn't pushy or demanding. While it has its limits, its boundaries are far-reaching. It neither clutches nor clings. Real love is not short-sighted, selfish, or insensitive. It detects needs and does what is best for the other person without being told.

As we read in that greatest treatise ever written on the subject: "Love is patient, love is kind, and is not jealous; love does not brag and is not arrogant, does not act unbecomingly; it does not seek its own, is not provoked, does not take into account a wrong suffered, does not rejoice in unrighteousness, but rejoices with the truth; bears . . . believes . . . hopes . . . endures all things" (1 Cor. 13:4–7).

"I LOVE YOU." Simple, single-syllable words, yet they cannot be improved upon. Nothing even comes close. And because we don't have any guarantee we'll have each other forever, it's a good idea to say them as often as possible.

Tell each one of your kids you love 'em. Don't just say, "Love ya."
Say, "I love you." There's a difference. If you don't have any kids, tell your mate.
If you're single, call up a close friend and say those three powerful words
with feeling.

FORGOTTEN SIDE OF SUCCESS

🕮 *Matthew 6:24–34* 🕮

*W*e are a success-saturated society. The telltale signs are everywhere. Each year dozens of books and magazines, scores of audiotapes and videotapes, and hundreds of seminars offer ideas, motivation, techniques, and promises of prosperity.

Curiously, however, few ever address what most folks want (but seldom find) in their pursuit of success: contentment, fulfillment, satisfaction, and relief. On the contrary, as the *Executives' Digest* once reported, "The trouble with success is that the formula is the same as the one for a nervous breakdown."

And what is that? Work longer hours, push ahead, let nothing hinder your quest—not your marriage or family, not your convictions or conscience, not your health or friends. Be aggressive, if necessary mean, as you press toward the top.

At the risk of sounding ultra-simplistic, I'd like to offer some counsel that stands 180 degrees in contrast to all the above: "You younger men, likewise, be subject to your elders; and all of you, clothe yourselves with humility toward one another, for God is opposed to the proud, but gives grace to the humble. Humble yourselves, therefore, under the mighty hand of God, that He may exalt you at the proper time, casting all your anxiety upon Him, because He cares for you" (1 Pet. 5:5–7).

These verses address three crucial realms related to true success: authority, attitude, and anxiety. And the best part is this: Following God's directives will bring the one benefit not found in the world's empty promises—a deep sense of lasting satisfaction. It's what we could call the forgotten side of success.

First, submit yourself to those who are wise. Listen to their counsel, be accountable and open to their reproofs, accept their suggestions, respect their seasoned years, follow their model.

Second, humble yourself under God's mighty hand, allowing Him to grant you His kind of success in His own time and way.

Third, throw yourself on the mercy and care of God. This does not mean there is no place for planning or goal-setting or diligence; it just means we refuse to make success our private shrine. When God is in it, we're surprised at it rather than smug about it.

Instead of spending all those hours pushing and promoting, we'll wind up with more time for friends and family—and ourselves. Seems almost too good to be true, doesn't it? It isn't.

Submission + Humility - Worry = God-Honoring Success with Satisfaction.

HANDWRITING

ॐ

Read through the greetings and closings of the apostle Paul's letters to the churches in the New Testament, noting his tone of warmth and concern.

ॐ

*T*here is nothing quite like the charm and personal touch conveyed by a handwritten note. Since our penmanship, like our fingerprint, is altogether unique, each curve of the letter or stroke of the pen bears its own originality. There is personality and warmth and, yes, special effort too; for, after all, it's much more efficient to click on the PC, bang out a few lines on the keyboard, and print it. But, occasionally, it's nice to think some still care enough to throw efficiency to the winds and look you right in the eye with the harmonious movement of their thoughts and fingers.

To this day I remember receiving such notes and letters from my father. His handwriting came in strong rhythmic swirls, a heavy pen that at times drove the point through the paper, exaggerated commas and slashes above each "i," a determined manner in which he slammed a period at the end of each sentence. His letters revealed much more than words; there was passion mixed with beauty, not to mention color and true concern. His choice of terms yielded clear reasoning, a dash of humor, and always logical thought, but the handwriting (with a broad, bold stylus on his fountain pen) added a depth and elegance mere type on paper would have lacked.

I never fail to pause over those rare occasions in Scripture when the writer mentions some facet of the actual writing of the book or letter. My imagination explodes with ideas as I picture Paul, for example, pen in hand, sitting beneath the flicker of a candle as a chilly draft blows through the room, the flow of ink, and such moving words as these being formed by his fingers: "I, Paul, write this greeting with my own hand" (Col. 4:18). "See with what large letters I am writing to you with my own hand" (Gal. 6:11). Have you forgotten that God etched into stone the original Ten Commandments with His finger (Exod. 31:18)?

To have such words typeset in a carefully preserved text is indeed a treasure. But to gaze at the actual manuscript scripted by Paul would be far better. Why? Because his handwriting would communicate a host of valuable things that can't be duplicated or detected in type.

Let's not allow the speed and efficiency of our high-tech society to crowd out the personal touch. The meaning and expression your fingers add to your words is worth all the effort, regardless of how poor your penmanship may be.

Take the time to write out in longhand your words to a friend.

BRING BACK THE JOY

❧ *Proverbs 15:13; 15; 17:22* ❧

*R*ules, regulations, and statutes aren't meant to be amusing, but at times they are. Maybe it's because they are supposed to be so all-fired serious that I find some of them downright hilarious. Some examples?

A San Francisco ordinance forbids the reuse of confetti. In Danville, Pennsylvania, "fire hydrants must be checked one hour before all fires." In Seattle, it is illegal to carry a concealed weapon of more than six feet in length. An Oklahoma law states that a driver of "any vehicle involved in an accident resulting in death shall immediately stop . . . and give his name and address to the person struck." A piece of noise-abatement legislation was passed in the village of Lakefield, Ontario, which permits birds to sing for thirty minutes during the day and fifteen minutes at night.

Furthermore, we preachers are an incredibly funny lot. And when I study the faces and read about the lives and lifestyles of the pulpiteers of yesteryear, I confess I often chuckle. Many of them—deep down—were wild 'n crazy characters.

Such humor is not making jokes out of life; it's recognizing the ones that are there.

Now, I'm not suggesting that everybody start reading the comics or watch all those mindless sitcoms (frankly, most of them aren't even amusing) or tell a lot of silly jokes to each other. That's external, superficial, and shallow. I'm suggesting a project far more significant: developing a lighter heart that comes from a confidence in the living God, the loving Creator, the sovereign Lord who gave us humor and who smiles every time we enjoy His gift.

In the insightful words of Elton Trueblood: "The Christian is joyful, not because he is blind to injustice and suffering, but because he is convinced that these, in the light of the divine sovereignty, are never ultimate. . . . The humor of the Christian is not a way of denying the tears, but rather a way of affirming something which is deeper than tears."

Yes, a few things in life are absolutely tragic, no question about it. First among them, a joyless Christian.

A truly cheerful face comes from a joyful heart,
not from a lack of concern for life's tragedies.

THE POTTER AND THE CLAY

Revelation 3:7–8

*B*y now in our Christian walk we hardly need the reminder that life is not a cloud-nine utopia. It is a terribly unrealistic view to think that Christ helps you live happily ever after; it's downright unbiblical! Most of life is learning and growing, falling and getting back up, forgiving and forgetting, accepting and going on.

We know the sovereign Potter is working with our clay as He pleases. I've watched a few potters at work. And it's a funny thing. I have seen them suddenly mash the clay down and start over again. Each time they do this, the clay comes out looking entirely different. And with gifted potters, they can start over and over—and each time it's better and better.

He is the Potter, we are the clay. He is the one who gives the commands; we are the ones who obey. He never has to explain Himself; He never has to ask permission. He is shaping us over into the image of His Son, regardless of the pain and heartache that may require. Those lessons are learned a little easier when we remember that we are not in charge, He is.

Daniel Webster was asked,
"What is the greatest thought that can occupy a man's mind?"
He said, "His accountability to God."

GIVING YOURSELF PERMISSION

❧ *Galatians 1:6–10* ❧

*B*ack when I was in grade school, it was always a special treat when the teacher gave the class permission to do something unusual. I remember one hot and humid Houston afternoon when she gave everyone permission to go barefoot after lunch. We got to pull off our socks, stick 'em in our sneakers, and wiggle our toes all we wanted to. During the afternoon recess that extra freedom added great speed to our softball game on the playground.

Isn't it strange then, now that you and I are grown and have become Christians, how reluctant we are to give ourselves permission to do . . . to think . . . to say . . . to buy and enjoy . . . or to be different and not worry about who may say what?

Even though our God has graciously granted us permission to be free, to have liberty, to break the chains of rigidity, and to enjoy much of this life, many in His family use such strange reasoning: "I mean, after all, what would people say?" or "Well, I wasn't raised to enjoy life; I was taught to be more conservative, more responsible and serious than that." So goes the persuasion of an oversensitive conscience trained in the school of negativism.

Tragic. No, worse than that, it is downright unbiblical.

Have we forgotten the promise, "where the Spirit of the Lord is, there is liberty" (2 Cor. 3:17)? Let that sink in.

The Spirit of the Lord has provided long-awaited liberty. Give yourself permission to lift those wings and feel the exhiliration of a soaring lifestyle.

*Allow the green light of grace to shine brighter
than the amber light of caution or the red light of don't.*

THINK IT OVER

❧❧ ❧❧

A bazaar was held in a village in northern India. Everyone brought his wares to trade and sell. One old farmer brought in a whole covey of quail. He had tied a string around one leg of each bird. The other ends of all the strings were tied to a ring which fit loosely over a central stick. He had taught the quail to walk dolefully in a circle, around and around, like mules at a sugarcane mill. Nobody seemed interested in buying the birds until a devout Brahman came along. He believed in the Hindu idea of respect for all life, so his heart of compassion went out to those poor little creatures walking in their monotonous circles.

"I want to buy them all," he told the merchant, who was elated. After receiving the money, he was surprised to hear the buyer say, "Now, I want you to set them all free."

"What's that, sir?"

"You heard me. Cut the strings from their legs and turn them loose. Set them all free!"

With a shrug, the old farmer bent down and snipped the strings off the quail. They were freed at last. What happened? The birds simply continued marching around and around in a circle. Finally, the man had to shoo them off. But even when they landed some distance away, they resumed their predictable march. Free, unfettered, released . . . yet they kept going around in circles as if still tied.

Until you give yourself permission to be the unique person God made you to be . . . and to do the unpredictable things grace allows you to do . . . you will be like that covey of quail, marching around in vicious circles of fear, timidity, and boredom.

A NECESSARY CHANGE

❧ *Psalm 121* ❧

*T*here is a sign along an Alaskan highway that has brought a smile to many a motorist: "Choose Your Rut Carefully . . . You'll Be in It for the Next 150 Miles."

Author Henri Nouwen, in his book *In the Name of Jesus,* admits to being in one for well over twenty years. Judging from externals, he had it made; the University of Notre Dame, Yale, and Harvard were on his résumé . . . not too shabby. And his field of study was equally impressive: theology mixed with courses in pastoral psychology and Christian spirituality. Nothing wrong with that, but the rut got so deep he began to churn internally. Listen to his honest admission: "After twenty-five years of priesthood, I found myself praying poorly, living somewhat isolated from other people, and very much preoccupied with burning issues. . . . Something inside was telling me that my success was putting my own soul in danger. . . . I woke up one day with the realization that I was living in a very dark place and that the term 'burnout' was a convenient psychological translation for a spiritual death."

Nouwen asked the Lord to show him where He wanted him to go and he would follow. The Lord made it clear to him that he should leave his prestigious role as a distinguished professor at an Ivy League university and join the L'Arche communities for mentally handicapped people.

The lessons awaiting Nouwen were numerous: some painful, a few humiliating, but all of them necessary. Slowly, almost imperceptibly, he experienced a change deep within his own being. The master teacher learned to be the humble servant . . . the self-confident, proud individualist became a compassionate, caring friend.

Most of us have no idea how deeply entrenched we are in the rut of routine. Externally, everything looks fine. Our activities often revolve around the church and Christian friends we love. Unfortunately, this rut of religious activity can numb our souls until we find ourselves in need of spiritual refreshment—a fresh touch from God.

It's then that we need to slow down, pull out of that rut, and take a different path. Sometimes this means just getting away from it all—literally—a place where there are no demands on our time, where we can find spiritual renewal.

Slow down, be quiet, watch the squirrels, gaze at a sunset, and think through your life. GET OUT OF YOUR RUT.

Filter out the essentials from the incidentals and reestablish your walk with Christ.

THEM BONES, THEM BONES

❧ *Acts 16:19–25* ❧

*D*uffy Daugherty, a colorful Michigan State football coach in years past, used to say that you needed only three bones to journey successfully through life: a wishbone, to dream on . . . a backbone, for strength and courage to get through the tough times . . . and a funny bone, to laugh at life along the way. Not bad advice.

When I think of these three bones, the apostle Paul immediately springs to mind. Though under arrest and facing an uncertain tomorrow, his wishbone was in healthy shape. His dream of spreading the gospel far and wide was being realized. "Now I want you to know, brethren, that my circumstances have turned out for the greater progress of the gospel . . . and that most of the brethren, trusting in the Lord because of my imprisonment, have far more courage to speak the word of God without fear" (Phil. 1:12–14).

How about Paul's backbone? Need I repeat the dark side of his résumé? "Five times I received from the Jews thirty-nine lashes. Three times I was beaten with rods, once I was stoned, three times I was shipwrecked, a night and a day I have spent in the deep. I have been on frequent journeys, in dangers from rivers, dangers from robbers, dangers from my countrymen, dangers from the Gentiles, dangers in the city, dangers in the wilderness, dangers on the sea, dangers among false brethren; I have been in labor and hardship, through many sleepless nights, in hunger and thirst, often without food, in cold and exposure" (2 Cor. 11:24–27).

Curiously, though, all this did not embitter or sour the Apostle of Grace. His funny bone stayed intact. In fact, no other writer of Scripture mentions joy or rejoicing more often. Remember when he and Silas were seized by a hostile mob, beaten mercilessly, then dumped into a dungeon with their feet fastened in stocks? It was around midnight at the end of that same day, while their sores were oozing and their bruises throbbing, that he and Silas were praying and singing a few duets of praise (Acts 16:19–25).

What exceptional dreams . . . what relentless courage . . . what contagious joy!

History is still being written. And we're still on the journey from here to eternity. The destination's sure for the Christian, but the trip isn't easy.

Dream big . . . don't let anybody or anything break your *wishbone*. Stay strong, full of faith, and courageous . . . keep that *backbone* straight. And along the way, don't forget to laugh and enjoy the journey.

Your funny bone isn't merely a nice option;
it's part of your survival gear for the trip to glory.

SEEING ABOVE THE CLOUDS

❧ *Nahum 1* ❧

*S*torm clouds gather. Problem is, they're the wrong kind. We need rain desperately, but these clouds hold no rain. These clouds are depressing, not unlike the kind Winston Churchill described in his first volume on World War II, which he titled *The Gathering Storm*. I cannot forget his terse, apt description of those months prior to the Nazi blitzkrieg that ultimately leveled much of London: "the future was heavy with foreboding."

Storm clouds without rain. War clouds without relief.

Such clouds not only cast ominous shadows of uneasiness, they breed pessimism. And unless I miss my guess, many of you are paying more attention to the bad news according to CNN than you are to the Good News according to Christ Jesus, our Lord. You're better students of world geography, public polls, and the *Wall Street Journal's* analysis of our times than you are of God's sovereign hand in world affairs and His prophetic plan.

Lest you forget, He is still in charge. As the prophet Nahum stated so confidently: "The LORD is slow to anger and great in power; the LORD will not leave the guilty unpunished. His way is in the whirlwind and the storm, and clouds are the dust of his feet" (Nah. 1:3, NIV).

Stop. Read that again, only more slowly this time.

When God is in clear focus, His powerful presence eclipses our fears. The clouds become nothing more than "the dust of His feet."

Seeing above the clouds won't just happen, however. Not as long as we keep feeding our minds on daily doses of media madness and political pessimism. We need to release our fears and refresh our souls as we spend time in the quiet presence of the living Lord.

When we do, we are then able to get on with life with a lighter heart, better sight, and calmer spirit. We discover again how beautifully the truth can set us free.

I can't promise that the clouds will be gone, but I can assure you, you won't be the same. Gathering storm clouds don't change overnight . . . but by learning to see above them, you'll change. And in the final analysis, that's what counts, isn't it? Not removing the clouds, but seeing above them.

When we have God in clear focus, His powerful presence eclipses our fears.

BEWARE OF HEIGHTS!

1 Corinthians 10:31

*W*hile cleaning out my study at home last Monday, I came across a book I had read several years ago. It's one of those volumes that stays with you— resourceful, insightful, and timeless. One particular line about halfway through the book jumped off the page: "A time to be careful is when one reaches his goals. . . . It is then, with all his resources spent and his guard down, that an individual must watch out for dulled reactions and faulty judgment."

In other words, vulnerability accompanies achievement. After the long haul, energy drained, dreams realized, enthusiasm peaked, desire accomplished—watch out!

Maybe that is the best explanation for the rarity of repeating champions. Back in the mid-1980s, the Chicago Bears cleaned everyone's plow. They won it all. The Windy City had waited so long, many were sure their team had what it took to do a repeat performance. How wrong they were! Before the taste of victory became stale, the erosion of self-destruction was underway.

What happens in sports can happen as readily in a ministry. During the difficult years, the watchword is survival, and the battle cry is sacrifice. Hard times bind people together. Goals are set. Prayers are offered. Every week is a new adventure in faith. By and by, the pieces fall into place, and the goals are finally reached. It is there—on the perilous pinnacle of accomplishment—that the adversary lurks with his corrupting influence.

The same can happen to an individual. My thoughts return to the man whose heart followed hard after God. Jesse's youngest son preferred the rugged solitude of the wilderness . . . but Jehovah's plan was that he occupy the throne of Israel. Years of hardship and humiliation under Saul's incessant assault preceded his promotion. Even when he became the king, the thirty-year-old monarch conducted himself with unselfish, untarnished integrity. The nation flourished because David's magnificent obsession was the glory of God.

Then came that infamous day in early spring—the morning David chose to sleep in rather than accompany his men to battle. Who knows why? Could it be that his impressive record of successes made him soft? Only a brief spell of passionate indulgence, yet it changed everything. His peace vanished. His character blasted irretrievably. His family life destroyed.

Alas, he was not the last to fall prey to the peril of past victories. The paths of history are strewn with the litter of heroes who forgot to walk carefully along the narrow ledges of the heights. How have the mighty fallen!

Resting on your laurels is a synonym for flirting with disaster.
Write that reminder down where you can see it frequently.

STAYING YOUNG

❧ *Proverbs 16:31* ❧

*T*like the question once asked by Satchel Paige, that venerable alumnus of baseball: "How old would you be if you didn't know how old you were?" An honest answer to that question depends on an honest admission of one's attitude. It has nothing to do with one's age. As someone young at heart has written:

I have become a little older since I saw you last, and a few changes have come into my life since then. Frankly, I have become quite a frivolous old gal. I am seeing five gentlemen every day.

As soon as I wake up, Will Power helps me get out of bed. Then I go to see John. Then Charlie Horse comes along and when he is here he takes a lot of my time and attention. When he leaves Arthur Ritis shows up and stays the rest of the day. He doesn't like to stay in one place very long, so he takes me from joint to joint. After such a busy day I'm really tired and glad to go to bed with Ben Gay. What a life!

P.S. The preacher came to call the other day. He said at my age I should be thinking about the hereafter, I told him, "Oh, I do all the time. No matter where I am—in the parlor, upstairs, in the kitchen, or down in the basement—I ask myself what am I here after?"

Five tips for staying young:

Your mind is not old, keep developing it.

Your humor is not over, keep enjoying it.

Your strength is not gone, keep using it.

Your opportunities have not vanished, keep pursuing them.

God is not dead, keep seeking Him.

Remember, old folks are worth a fortune——they have silver in their hair,
gold in their teeth, stones in their kidneys, lead in their feet,
and gas in their stomachs.

PROMISES, PROMISES

❧ Look up the promises listed in the words below ❧

God's Book is a veritable storehouse of promises—over seven thousand of them. Not just eloquently worded thoughts that make you feel warm all over, but verbal guarantees in writing, signed by the Creator Himself, in which He declares He will do or will refrain from doing specific things.

But, are all seven thousand-plus promises ours to claim? I mean, am I free to choose any one of them and believe it's for me here in my situation today?

Many—dare I say most?—of the scriptural promises are ours to claim. But all? Hardly. To claim "every promise in the Book" could be disillusioning at best, disastrous at worst.

To begin with, some promises are uniquely historical in nature. They were made to specific individuals in a particular era and fit only that unique combination. Take this one for example: "Your wife shall have a son." I can just see some well-meaning husband "claiming the promise" of Genesis 18:10. After all, "It's in the Book!"

At the risk of being a party pooper, I recommend a closer look at that promise. It was given specifically to Abraham, and it came as a direct fulfillment of God's earlier covenant with Abraham (Gen. 12:1–3) in which He promised to make of him "a great nation." That promise of a son was uniquely Abraham and Sarah's to claim.

There are also conditional promises . . . words of assurance offered to those who first fulfill their part of the arrangement. The promise is absolutely reliable, but it is linked to a condition. An example? You claim God's promise to direct your steps to lead you clearly into His will. After all, Proverbs 3:6 says, "He will make your paths straight," plain and simple.

Wait a minute. Check out the context: "Trust in the LORD with all your heart . . . do not lean on your own understanding. In all your ways acknowledge Him *[our part]*, and He will make your paths straight *[God's promise]*."

Why do I make such a big deal of all this? Because there are numerous, pure-hearted, trusting people in the Body who latch on to such promises and build their hopes high, only to suffer great pain later in the backwash of disillusionment.

In case all this is making you feel a little shaky, I need to reaffirm that most of those seven thousand promises are still ours to count on. Need a few classic examples? Isaiah 26:3–4; Romans 8:32, 38–39; Galatians 6:9; Psalm 37:7, 23, 28; 2 Corinthians 4:16–18; Hebrews 6:10. Look 'em up.

Take your stand on the promises of God. Thousands of 'em are right there, waiting to be used.

Make sure you're standing on the promises and not outside the premises.

THINK IT OVER

❦❦❦

*H*ere's another promise many try to claim . . . without the condition. "God has offered me His peace, and I'm claiming it now. After all, Philippians 4:7 promises,

> And the peace of God, which surpasses all comprehension,
> shall guard your hearts and your minds in Christ Jesus.

But such peace escapes you as you continue to be besieged by worry and fear.

Why? Because peace isn't dropped in a bundle from heaven by parachute. Peace is a by-product—the promised result following our fulfilling our part of the process. And what is that?

When answering such questions, always go back to the context in which you found the promise, in this case Philippians 4. Notice that just before the promise of peace is the condition on which that promise is based:

"Be anxious for nothing [in other words, stop worrying about anything], but in everything by prayer and supplication [in addition, start praying about everything] with thanksgiving [and don't forget to be thankful in all things] let your requests be made known to God. And . . .

The equation would look like this:

Absence of worry + Prevalence of prayer + Spirit of gratitude = Peace of God

Don't be afraid of God's not keeping His promises.
He has and He will continue to do so. But make an intelligent and careful
study of the one(s) you choose to claim. Be certain they are rightfully yours.

ADMITTING NEED

❧ *Exodus 17* ❧

A prayer to be said
When the world has gotten you down,
And you feel rotten,
And you're too doggone tired to pray,
And you're in a big hurry,
And besides, you're mad at everybody . . .
Help!

*A*sking for help is smart. So why don't we? You want to know why? Pride. Which is nothing more than stubborn unwillingness to admit need. The result? Impatience. Irritation. Anger. Longer hours. Less and less laughter. No vacations. Inflexibility. Longer and longer gaps between meaningful times in God's Word. Precious few (if any) moments in prayer and prolonged meditation.

My friend, it's time to declare it: No way can you keep going at this pace and stay effective year after year! Give yourself a break! Stop trying to cover all the bases! Relax!

Once you've put it into neutral, crack open your Bible to Exodus 18:18–27, the account of a visit Jethro made to his son-in-law Moses. Jethro wasn't impressed as he watched Moses dash from one person to another, one need to another. "What is this thing that you are doing for the people?" he asked. Moses was somewhat defensive (most too-busy people are) as he attempted to justify his schedule. Jethro didn't buy it. He advised Moses against trying to do everything alone and reproved him with strong words: "The thing that you are doing is not good. You will surely wear out" (vv. 17–18).

In other words, he told Moses: CALL FOR HELP.

The benefits of shifting and sharing the load? Read verses 22–23: "It will be easier for you. . . . You will be able to endure." Isn't that interesting? We seem to think it's better to have that tired-blood, overworked-underpaid, I've-really-got-it-rough look. Among Christians, it's what I call the martyr complex that announces, "I'm working so hard for Jesus!"

The truth of the matter is, that hurried, harried appearance usually means, "I'm too stubborn to slow down" or "I'm too insecure to say no" or "I'm too proud to ask for help." Since when is a bleeding ulcer a sign of spirituality . . . or a seventy-hour week a mark of efficiency?

The world beginning to get you down? Too tired to pray? Ticked off at a lot of folks? Let me suggest one of the few four-letter words God loves to hear us use: HELP!

Efficiency is enhanced not by what we accomplish but by what we relinquish.

KNOCK, KNOCK

❧ *Luke 21* ❧

*W*e preachers receive some hilarious stuff in the mail, which helps compensate for the periodic blasts that come our way (usually unsigned). I'm particularly grateful for a friend of mine who never fails to lift my spirits by passing on something he has read or heard that I might be able to use.

One item I found especially fascinating was a series of statistics from a book by Daniel Weiss titled *One Hundred Percent American,* in which the author sets forth a sequential series of percentages (from 1% to 100%) that tell us some interesting facts about Americans. For example:

1% of Americans read the Bible more than once a day;

15% of American married men say they do most of the cooking in the household;

30% of Americans smoke cigarettes;

42% of Americans cannot name a country near the Pacific Ocean;

67% of Americans believe files are being kept on them for unknown reasons;

70% of Americans own running shoes but don't run;

84% of Americans believe heaven exists;

94% of American men would change something about their looks if they could;

96% of American school children can identify Ronald McDonald (who is second only to Santa Claus);

99% of American women would change something about their looks if they could.

I remember the old saying that "statistics usually lie and liars use statistics," so I'll not press the point on any of Mr. Weiss's figures. Instead, I'll refer to another item from my friend: a Frank and Ernest cartoon where the two characters are standing before a priest and Frank asks, "How come opportunity knocks once, but temptation beats at my door every day?"

Frank is right: Temptation beats at our door every day. But when it comes to opportunity, who can say how rare it is? Less than 10%? Less than 5%? Probably so.

Looking back over your shoulder, you probably cannot name one opportunity that lingered, gathering dust. The age-old aphorism remains true: "Four things come not back: the spoken word; the speeding arrow; time past; the neglected opportunity."

Time is short. Opportunity is knocking. Please answer it.
One hundred percent of those who do find themselves blessed.

STRESSES THAT FRACTURE

❧ *Psalm 23* ❧

*S*tress: that confusion created when one's mind overrides the body's desire to choke the living daylights out of some jerk who desperately needs it. No, you won't find that definition in the dictionary, but right now, I think it should be. It's been one of those weeks. Know what I mean?

Overcommitment. Deadlines. Unrealized expectations. People problems. A stack of phone calls to return. A couple of major interruptions. Not to mention an enormous bill from the vet after he treated our dog, telling us she has some profound, exotic inner itch or something. My in-box resembles the Leaning Tower . . . and then one of my grandsons asks innocently, "Bubba, how come you yell when you talk?" On top of all that I receive a six-page letter from a pious soul who feels "led of God" to correct my position on the day Christ died, my too-liberal view of eschatology, and my extravagance for owning two cars. Page after page. From a guy who doesn't even know me.

I know, I know. I should "turn the other cheek." I really ought to "see the good in it." On some other day I'd probably not give his words a second thought. But when you suffer from stress fractures, the soft cushion of tolerance gets deflated, leaving nerves raw and feelings bloody.

A recent *Sports Illustrated* article painted a vivid picture: "A stress fracture begins when the shocks and strains of playing game after game create microscopic cracks in the outer layers of bone—usually in the legs and feet. If the pounding continues and those tiny crevices, which often go undetected, aren't allowed to heal, they can enlarge. When the cracks become large enough to cause pain, they are stress fractures."

Stress fractures aren't limited to athletes. Microscopic cracks in bones are painful, but can they match the hurt of a stress-fractured spirit . . . an aching heart? That's a pain like none other, isn't it? It's deep. It throbs. It lingers in the day and haunts you through the night.

So, what do we do to stop the pounding? Ah, that's the question. "Lighten up" is a start. Try not to make a federal case out of everything that happens. Then, laugh more. Admit those imperfections. Let some stuff go. Don't try to be Wonder Woman or the all-powerful Mr. Fix-It.

Above all, turn it over to God. Tell Him everything. He has no problem hearing about our hurts. Furthermore, He can keep any secret you tell Him. He can even handle it when you yell.

As the pounding lessens, so will the pain.

Don't let stress fracture you.

THE FINAL TOLL

❧ *Romans 14:7–9* ❧

*S*leep came hard for me last night. Earlier that evening, Cynthia and I had read together a letter from our long-time friend Wally Norling, who had just returned from the bedside of Betty, his "loving partner in life for forty-two years." Betty is dying of cancer of the liver, and Wally's letter, written in the midst of that, was a gracious, understated masterpiece of faith.

I lay there wide awake, reviewing the forty-plus years Cynthia and I have had together. I thought about those innocent early years, which seemed so tough back then. Years of enforced separation (thanks to the military), of a career change, of graduate school, of financially lean times, of learning and growing closer together.

Then came our child-bearing years—wonderful years, so incredibly surprising to both of us. The loss of two precious children by miscarriage, the healthy births of four. Yes, four! The simple joys of tent camping, of early schooling, of struggling with "finding myself" in pulpit style. Discovering much of what "being a pastor" meant. All the while, Cynthia was right there . . . understanding, affirming, being mother to our children and partner with me, assuring me that it was worth all the effort. Though she never bragged about it, I know she prayed me through many a sermon. As I improved, I got the credit, but she deserved the applause. As the song goes, she was the wind beneath my wings . . . and boy, did I need healthy gusts at times! Still do.

Before dropping off to sleep, I did a quick recap of the balance of our years together. Wow! Giant steps through big-time changes. Two people so different, yet so close.

As I remembered all this, I realized anew the enormity of Wally's loss, and that reminds me of what John Donne wrote in 1624: "No man is an island, entire of itself; every man [or woman] is a piece of the continent, a part of the main . . . any man's [or woman's] death diminishes me, because I am involved in mankind; and therefore never send to know for whom the bell tolls; it tolls for thee."

Last night, in the arms of my wife, I couldn't help but imagine the night that ominous final bell might toll on our marriage. I tried to picture life without my loving partner . . . that dark era when the other side of my bed will be empty and lonely memories will replace the warmth of reality. And, sadly, I fell asleep.

"In the hour of need, the grace of God is more than adequate" (Wally Norling).

HEALING TAKES TIME

✿ *Ecclesiastes 3:1–4* ✿

*H*ippocrates was a Greek physician considered by many to be "the Father of Medicine." It is he, you may recall, who wrote the immortal Hippocratic Oath still taken by those entering the practice of medicine.

This ancient physician lived somewhere between 450 B.C. and 375 B.C. He wrote much more than the famous oath that bears his name. Other pieces of fine literature flowed from his pen, many of which still exist. Most of his works, as we might expect, deal with the human anatomy, medicine, and healing.

In a piece titled "Aphorisms," for example, he wrote: "Extreme remedies are very appropriate for extreme diseases." On another occasion he authored "Precepts." These words appear in the first chapter: "Healing is a matter of time."

While reading those thoughts recently, it occurred to me that one might connect them in a paraphrase full of significance and relevance for our own time: "Recovering from extreme difficulties usually requires an extreme amount of time."

In our microwave culture, that statement may not sound terribly encouraging. "Slow" finds little place in our accepted vocabulary. We have very little patience for activities or enterprises that compel us to wait.

But more often than not, real recovery is slow. It takes time. And the deeper the wound, the more extensive the damage or trauma, the greater amount of time may be required for us to recover.

Wise counsel, Hippocrates! We tend to forget your insightful advice.

A solid grasp of God's Word will help you wait through the amount of time needed for your recovery.

A SURVIVAL SECRET

❦ *1 Thessalonians 4:1–8* ❦

*O*ne winter day while a Chilean peasant was tending his cattle along a long, deep gorge in a remote area of the Andes, he saw two gaunt, bearded figures across the chasm. Thinking they were terrorists, he ran and hid. The next day he returned and saw they were still there. He quickly gathered a pencil, some paper, and a stone, wrapped them in a handkerchief, and heaved them across to the strangers.

When the package came back, thirteen hand-scribbled words said it all: "We came from a plane that fell in the mountains. We are Uruguayan."

Out of forty-five members of an amateur rugby team, sixteen had survived an indescribable ten-week ordeal. They did so because they were willing to do the unthinkable. They committed cannibalism, eating from the dead bodies of their companions. Critics came out of the woodwork, especially from their church. But the fact is, because they were willing to take such drastic measures, sixteen survived.

If you and I hope to survive this transition into the twenty-first century, it will require some drastic measures on our part, too. It will require a willingness to change.

To describe our times as intense is to state the obvious. And to complicate matters, the intensity is on the increase. We thought times were wicked when we were growing up, but compared to today, the situation forty or fifty years ago seems idyllic.

While struggling with all that recently, I found encouragement from a statement in Paul's final letter: "Nevertheless, the firm foundation of God stands, having this seal, 'The Lord knows those who are His,' and, 'Let everyone who names the name of the Lord abstain from wickedness'" (2 Tim. 2:19).

Isn't that great! The foundations God has laid won't be destroyed. No matter how bad it gets, no matter how intense the wickedness, God's standard is not subject to change.

So, then where do all these drastic changes take place? Within you and me, of course! Remember, that last part of 2 Timothy 2:19 is a command. It calls for obedience. He is telling us to make whatever changes are necessary so that we might "abstain from wickedness." Yes, *abstain*.

Surviving times as intense as ours will not occur easily or automatically. Furthermore, it is not something we do corporately or, for that matter, publicly. It's an "inside job," and it calls for increased discipline in the private realms of our lives. It's a survival secret being overlooked by many.

Whatever changes you need to make, start today. Survival requires change. Sometimes, drastic change.

Drastic times call for drastic measures.

THINK IT OVER

❧❧ ❧❧

*H*ere are several very personal questions to help you know how severe we need to be with ourselves in order to "abstain from wickedness." Answer each one honestly.

- Are you regularly with a person of the opposite sex in inappropriate situations?
- Are you completely above reproach in all your financial dealings, including your taxes?
- Do you expose yourself to explicit sexual material?
- If you have a family, do you invest sufficient time with them?
- Do you tell the truth? How often do you lie (don't forget to count the little white ones)?
- How quickly do you say "I am wrong; I am genuinely sorry" when you have said or done something that hurts another?
- Do you hold grudges?
- Are you knowingly compromising in some area of your life, refusing to acknowledge the consequences that you will surely have to face?
- Have you formed a habit that is detrimental to your health or your job or your walk with Christ?
- Are you proud, selfish, arrogant?
- Have you taken credit for something that someone else did and should have been rewarded for?
- Do you return things you borrow?
- Have you failed to confess something to someone who should know of your wrong-doing?
- Are you abusing your mate or your children—physically or emotionally?
- Do you allow abuse to happen without seeking help?
- Do you regularly spend time in prayer and in the Scriptures?

WITNESSING

❧ *Acts 8* ❧

*V*arious methods are employed to communicate the good news of Christ to the lost. Take the Eager-Beaver Approach, for example. "The more scalps, the better." This numerical approach is decision-centered, and little (if any) effort is directed toward follow-up or discipleship or cultivating a relationship.

The Harvard Approach is quite different: "Let's all discuss the world's religions." While this reason-centered approach is educational and occasionally quite stimulating, it suffers from one mild drawback—*no one ever gets saved!* Being sophisticated is more important than telling the truth about sin or heaven or hell. Discussion is in . . . decisions are out.

Perhaps the most popular is the Mute Approach: "I'm just a silent witness for God." Somewhere along the line this person has swallowed one of Satan's tastiest tidbits: "Just live a good Christian life. Others will ask you about Christ if they are really interested, so relax." "Faith," please remember, "comes from hearing" (Rom. 10:17).

What we need, I submit to you, is the Philip Approach. This Christ-centered method is set forth in a series of seven principles drawn from Acts 8:26–40.

Philip was engaged in an evangelistic crusade in Samaria when the Lord instructed him to go south to the desert road that ran from Jerusalem to Gaza. Faithful Philip "arose and went." He was *available* (Principle 1). On the road he encountered an Ethiopian statesman traveling home from Jerusalem. And the Spirit of God prompted Philip to approach the traveler. Philip was *led by the Spirit* (Principle 2). He sensed that God was clearly opening the door.

Philip cooperated, for *obedience* (Principle 3) is essential. He heard the man reading Isaiah aloud and asked, "Do you understand what you are reading?" A *proper opening* (Principle 4) is so important. Philip didn't barge in and start preaching.

The man invited Philip to sit with him and assist him in his quest for understanding. Philip responded with great *tactfulness* (Principle 5). Even though he had his foot in the door, he remained sensitive to when he should speak of salvation. When that moment came, he "opened his mouth" and became *specific* (Principle 6). No vague dialogue about religion. He spoke only of the Savior, the main issue. The last few verses then describe the *follow-up* (Principle 7) Philip employed.

As you rub shoulders with hungry, thirsty humanity, keep the Philip Approach in mind. I can't think of a place I'd rather be at the moment Christ returns than riding shotgun in a twenty-first-century chariot, speaking openly about faith in the Savior.

As we become alert to those empty chariot seats God wants us to occupy, we may even begin to feel comfortable in them.

New Hope

🐾 *Psalm 13* 🐾

*F*loundering with my father is among my most cherished childhood memories. Armed with a beat-up Coleman lantern, two gigs, a stringer . . . we'd head to the water. When the sky got nice 'n' dark, we'd wade in about knee-deep and stumble off into the night.

By and by we'd round the point about a mile away from the bay cottage where the other members of the Swindoll tribe were. And here we were—knee-deep in muddy, cold salt water, with nothing but thick darkness in front of us. To this day I remember looking back wistfully over my shoulder toward that ever-so-tiny light in the distance.

Soon I began asking myself why. Why in the world had I agreed to come? And if I asked him once, I must have asked a dozen times, "How much longer, Daddy? When are we gonna turn around?"

While he was searching for flounder, I was listening for those marvelous words, "Well, Son, this is far enough. Let's turn around." Instantly, I found myself wading on tiptoes, caring nothing about finding some poor flounder—only that light, that tiny signal in the distance that assured me my dad really knew the way. Once spotted, my entire personality changed. My anxieties were relieved. My questions were answered. Hope lit the darkness like a thousand lanterns . . . Hope—how powerful is its presence.

Take from us our wealth and we are hindered. Take our health and we are handicapped. Take our purpose and we are slowed, temporarily confused. But take away our hope and we are plunged into deepest darkness . . . stopped dead in our tracks, paralyzed. Wondering, "Why?" Asking, "How much longer? Will this darkness ever end? Does He know where I am?"

Then the Father says, "That's far enough," and how sweet it is! Hope revives and washes over us.

Are you ready for a light at the end of your tunnel? Look! There it is in the distance. It may be tiny, but it's there. You made it! Your Father knew exactly where He was going. And why. And for how long. That cottage in the distance? You'll soon be there, laughing and singing again with the family. One day your journey into darkness may be one of your most cherished memories.

There is nothing like light, however small and distant,
to put us on tiptoes in the darkness.

LOW TIDES

🍃 *Psalm 55* 🍃

The smoky tones of Peggy Lee's voice occasionally blow across my mind: "Is that all . . . is that all there is . . . ?" With no bitterness intended, I ask that haunting question in the backwash of certain situations.

How much like the tide we are! When our spirits are high, we are flooded with optimism, hope, and expectation. But when low, our jagged barnacles of disappointment, discouragement, and disillusionment are exposed. We struggle to maintain an even keel as the rough winds jerk our sails.

Like the pull of the sea, some of our low tides are almost predictable.

Is that all . . . is that all there is to victory?

Elijah asked that. And he was fresh off a great victory at Carmel! It's hard to believe 1 Kings 18 and 19 are connected. Vulnerable and frightened, he suffered the low tide that often follows victory, perhaps the cruelest dart in the devil's quiver.

Is that all . . . is that all there is to vision?

Paul asked that. Having taken gigantic strides into the vast regions of Asia, he was caught at low tide. He freely admits this to his friends at Corinth: "For we do not want you to be unaware, brethren, of our affliction which came to us in Asia, that we were burdened excessively, beyond our strength, so that we despaired even of life" (2 Cor. 1:8).

Is that all . . . is that all there is to valor?

David asked that when, after proving himself a dedicated warrior, unmatched for bravery in Israel's ranks, he was forced to flee from Saul. Reeling in fear and despair, David even disguised himself as insane before the king of Gath. The once-exalted warrior now "scribbled on the doors of the gate, and let his saliva run down into his beard" (1 Sam. 21:13).

Low tide . . . how painful yet how essential. Without it, we cannot have high tide. Without it, there would be no need for Elishas to minister to victoryless Elijahs . . . no need for visionaries to fall in dependence on their faces before God . . . no need for the valiant to be reminded of their Source of strength.

Is that all . . . is that all there is to low tides?

No, there is more, much more, most of which can never be described . . . only discovered.

When it seems like that's all there is, remember all you have in Him.

JOYFUL GENEROSITY

❧ *2 Corinthians 9* ❧

houghts disentangle themselves . . . over the lips and through the fingertips. I learned that saying over thirty years ago, and just about every time I put it to the test, it works! Whenever I have difficulty comprehending the complicated or clarifying the complex, I talk it out or write it out.

Take the importance of giving joyfully to God, for example. Second Corinthians 9:7 says: "Let each one do just as he has purposed in his heart; not grudgingly or under compulsion; for God loves a cheerful giver." The original meaning of the word translated here as "cheerful" is "hilarious," and this is the only time it's found in the New Testament. It's the hilarious giver God prizes.

Now, how does this translate into daily life? How do these thoughts disentangle themselves to become meaningful parts of our lives? I'd like to make the following four suggestions for ways we can bring joy into our giving.

Reflect on God's gifts to you. Hasn't He been good? He certainly has to me. Better than I deserve! In light of God's magnificent grace, a cheerful heart and openhanded generosity seem the most natural responses.

Remind yourself of His promises regarding generosity. Call to mind a few biblical principles that promise a bountiful harvest to those who sow bountifully. Jesus Himself spoke of how much more blessed it is to give than to receive. Bumper crops are God's specialties, so we have nothing to restrain us from dropping maximum seed.

Examine your heart. Nobody knows the combination to your private vault. Only you can probe its contents by asking the hard questions: Do I really believe God's promises on giving generously? Am I responding as I do because I care or because I feel guilty? Is my giving proportionate to my income? Have I prayed, or is my giving impulsive? Am I a consistent giver or more hot 'n' cold?

Glorify God by becoming generous. He prizes generosity, especially joyful generosity. Perhaps we need to break the habit of being so conservative, so careful. Maybe we even need to "scare" ourselves with acts of generosity . . . going out on a limb, as it were, and genuinely trusting God to honor our financial faith.

Well, that's it. Just a little lips-and-fingertips clarification. All of us would be wise to address our reluctance to sacrifice financially for the cause of Christ. After all, our goal is joyful generosity, isn't it?

Do you qualify as a "hilarious giver"? If not, why not?

THE NEED FOR INTEGRITY

❧ *1 Thessalonians 2:3* ❧

*L*eaders with power and brains are common. So are leaders with riches and popularity. But a competent leader full of integrity and skill, coupled with sincerity, is rare indeed.

Deception creates suspicion. Once the leader's followers begin to suspect motives or find that what is said publicly is denied privately, the thin wire of respect that holds everything in place snaps. Confidence drains away. All of us have suffered disappointment and no little fear as we watched President Clinton's secret life exposed to the public in the last several years. With each revelation of lies, our respect and confidence in our leader dwindled.

The late President Dwight Eisenhower stated his opinion with dogmatism: "The supreme quality for a leader is unquestionably integrity. Without it, no real success is possible, no matter whether it is a section gang, on a football field, in an army, or in an office. If his associates find him guilty of phoniness, if they find that he lacks forthright integrity, he will fail. His teachings and actions must square with each other."

I can think of few ingredients more foundational to being a good leader than knowing oneself—and accepting oneself—and feeling secure about oneself inside one's own skin.

"The first great need, therefore, is integrity and high purpose."
— Dwight D. Eisenhower

TRUTH OR CONSEQUENCES

❧ *Galatians 6:1–10* ❧

*F*rom all those I have confronted, dealt with, or heard about who have fallen into sexual impurity, two paths led them astray. The first is *subtle deception.* This is an almost passive series of thoughts which include rationalization, ignoring the warnings of a sensitive conscience, the consistent erosion of one's walk with Christ, and tolerating things that were once intolerable.

The Scriptures include direct warnings against deception. In fact, we are frequently commanded not to be deceived. For just a few examples, see 1 Corinthians 6:9–10, 15:33; Galatians 6:7–8; and 1 John 1:8. Interestingly, nearly all these warnings about being deceived are found in a context of sexual and/or moral impurity.

Second, there is the path of *deliberate action.* Once the mental roadblocks are cleared away, the excitement of "stolen waters" becomes sweet to the transgressor's taste. Make no mistake about it, the pleasures of sin—those erotic excursions into secret experiments with forbidden escapades—are both enjoyable and stimulating. They may yield only temporary delights, but they are enough to make one's carnal appetites crave more.

Again, God's Word addresses the issue head-on: "Flee immorality" (1 Cor. 6:18). "Flee" means just that. Get out! Don't let yourself get cornered. Counteract those weak and vulnerable places in your psyche by taking practical steps of resistance.

Let's return to a few pertinent scriptures. They are to the point; therefore, they will sting. But hopefully that will help get your attention. Whatever you do, don't excuse sinful behavior by claiming you are "addicted" or "victimized." Those terms only help you escape responsibility.

"Can a man take fire in his bosom, and his clothes not be burned? Or can a man walk on hot coals, and his feet not be scorched? So is the one who goes in to his neighbor's wife; whoever touches her will not go unpunished. . . . The one who commits adultery with a woman is lacking sense; he who would destroy himself does it. Wounds and disgrace he will find, and his reproach will not be blotted out" (Prov. 6:27–29, 32–33).

Burned. Scorched. Punishment. Wounds and disgrace. Reproach. Forgiveness may come. The affair(s) may end. Restoration may occur. But the consequences will not go away.

God's simple formula is truth or consequences.

Think It Over

✺✺✺✺

*F*ollowing is an incomplete list of what you have in store after your immorality is found out

Your mate will experience the anguish of betrayal, shame, rejection, heartache, and loneliness. No amount of repentance will soften those blows.

Your mate can never again say that you are a model of fidelity. Suspicion will rob her or him of trust.

Your escapade(s) will introduce to your life and your mate's life the very real probability of a sexually transmitted disease.

The total devastation your sinful actions will bring to your children is immeasurable. Their growth, innocence, trust, and healthy outlook on life will be severely and permanently damaged.

The heartache you will cause your parents, your family, and your peers is indescribable.

The embarrassment of facing other Christians, who once appreciated you, respected you, and trusted you, will be overwhelming.

If you are engaged in the Lord's work, you will suffer the immediate loss of your job and the support of those with whom you worked. The dark shadow will accompany you everywhere . . . and forever. Forgiveness won't erase it.

Your fall will give others license to do the same.

The inner peace you enjoyed will be gone.

You will never be able to erase the fall from your (or others') mind. This will remain indelibly etched on your life's record, regardless of your later return to your senses.

The name of Jesus Christ, whom you once honored, will be tarnished, giving the enemies of faith further reason to sneer and jeer.

INTIMATE COMMUNICATION

🌸 *Deuteronomy 6* 🌸

*S*ome frightening facts have been released by the Planned Parenthood Federation. Their growing concern? Increasing sexual activity among preteen girls.

"Agency counselors throughout the country are overwhelmed by these kids," states Dr. Gerry Oliva, medical director for the federation in San Francisco. Consequently, the agency is developing a special program just for girls nine to twelve who are "sexually active and need advice." The simple fact is this: Telling a girl the facts of life when she's ten or eleven may be too late!

You who are parents need to think it over . . . to come to terms with this business of communicating openly, tactfully, and intelligently with your children in the areas of intimacy. It's a parental task that must be handled with great care and wisdom—but it must be handled. Obviously, it is not to be directed only toward the girls, but boys as well. Nor should it be communicated only by mothers, but by both parents. God's beautiful plan regarding conception and birth needs to be shared from a balanced perspective.

Allow me to put the reluctant parent at ease. Questions from your children regarding sex are as normal as questions regarding science or sports or God, for that matter. Questions are invitations to step carefully into your child's private thought world.

God has provided you, parents, with the very best teaching model your child needs: affectionate love between you and your mate. No greater influence can mark your child than an honest, warm relationship between you and your spouse that often expresses itself in kisses, embraces, and tenderness.

But that merely prepares the way. Words must accompany actions. Practical, meaningful, accurate information at appropriate times during your child's growing years is absolutely essential if you want him or her to be intimately healthy, confident, and godly.

Believe me, your youngster *will* learn about sex. Society offers raw, profane, distorted classes every day. If you ignore it long enough, you won't have to bother with it at all. In bits and pieces, it will take its own shape . . . the wrong shape, possibly resulting in marital misunderstanding or personal tragedy (dare I say perversion) that could have been prevented.

So before you cop out, it might be wise to blow the dust off that old adage. Something about "an ounce of prevention . . ."

Sometimes silence can be deadly.

STOP THE ELEVATOR

❧ *John 11:1–44* ❧

*E*levators are weird places. You're crammed in with folks you've never met, so you try really hard not to touch them. And nobody talks, except for an occasional "Out, please." You don't look at anyone; in fact, you don't look anywhere but up, watching those dumb floor numbers go on and off.

In a strange sort of way, an elevator is a microcosm of our world today: a crowded, impersonal place where anonymity, isolation, and independence are the norm.

A recently published report by sociologist Ralph Larkin on the crises facing suburban youth underscores several aspects of this new malaise of the spirit. Many children of affluence are depicted as passively accepting a way of life they view as empty and meaningless, resulting in a syndrome that includes "a low threshold of boredom, a constricted expression of emotions, and an apparent absence of joy in anything that is not immediately consumable."

Exit: involvement and motivation.

Enter: indifference; noncommitment; disengagement; no sharing or caring; meals eaten with headsets turned up loud; separate bedrooms, each with a personal telephone, TV, and private bath; and an it's-none-of-your-business attitude.

Dr. Philip Zimbardo, author of one of the most widely used psychology textbooks, addressed this issue in a *Psychology Today* article entitled "The Age of Indifference." "I know of no more potent killer than isolation. . . . It has been shown to be a central agent in the etiology of depression, paranoia, schizophrenia, rape, suicide, mass murder. . . . The Devil's strategy for our times is to trivialize human existence in a number of ways: by isolating from one another while creating the delusion that the reasons are time pressures, work demands, or anxieties created by economic uncertainty."

We must come to terms with all this. The need is urgent! Our Savior modeled the answer perfectly. He cared. He listened. He served. He reached out. He supported. He affirmed and encouraged. He touched as well as stayed in touch. He walked with people . . . never took the elevator.

The only escape from indifference is to think of people as our most cherished resource. We need to work hard at reestablishing family fun, meaningful mealtimes, people involvement, evenings without the television blaring, times when we genuinely get involved with folks in need—not just pray for them.

Stop the elevator. I want to get off.

"Speech is civilization itself. The word, even the most contradictory word, preserves contact—it is silence which isolates" (Thomas Mann).

OUT OF ORDER

🐝 *Proverbs 1:1–7* 🐝

*D*oing all things "decently and in order" applies to a lot more areas than theology. It's remarkable how many guys who have the ability to articulate the most exacting details and nuances of their area of expertise never get their desks cleared off or their workrooms organized. They're brainy enough to rebuild some complex engine, but the trash under the kitchen sink can overflow until it's ankle deep, and they aren't even aware of it. Isn't it amazing how many men have quiz-kid heads and pigpen habits?

And it's not limited to the male species. Some women have the toughest time just keeping a path clear from the front door to the den. I heard last week about a gal who was such a lousy housekeeper that *Good Housekeeping* canceled her subscription! She must have been a friend of Erma Bombeck. She's the one who admitted that her cupboard shelves were lined with newspapers that read "MALARIA STOPS WORK ON THE CANAL." Of course, it's possible to become a "neatness neurotic." Like the fastidious wife of that poor fella who got hungry and got out of bed for a midnight snack. When he came back to bed, she had it made.

Truthfully, however, most of us don't struggle with being too orderly. Our problem is the other side of the coin. And the result is predictable: We burn up valuable energy and lose precious time.

Stop and think that over. Maybe a few questions will help prime the pump of self-analysis:

Do you often lose things?

Are you usually late for appointments and meetings?

Do you put off doing your homework until late?

Are you a time waster . . . like on the phone or with TV?

Are you prompt in paying bills and answering mail?

How many unfinished projects do you have lying around?

Does your desk stay cluttered? How about the tops of tables and counters?

Can you put your hands on important documents right away?

Do you have a will? Is it in a safe place?

Can you concentrate and think through decisions in a logical manner?

We'll talk some more about this tomorrow. For now, think about this: Spending what it takes to become a little more efficient is an investment that pays rich dividends. When we are reluctant to do so, our lives are marked by mediocrity, haphazardness, and disorder.

Time spent on the right things is never wasted.

SLUG THAT SLUGGARD!

❧ *Proverbs 24–27* ❧

*S*tab, stab. Twist, twist. Did yesterday's questions hit below the belt? Maybe so. But they are the kind of questions that reveal the pulse of your efficiency heartbeat.

If you're like I am, life is too busy to add some unrealistic, humongous, impossible-to-achieve-anyway program. Instead, let's deal with the problem in a straightforward and simplified manner. First, admit to yourself that you could stand a change here and there. Try to be specific enough to pinpoint a couple of particular areas that keep bugging you. Don't bite off too much, just one or two trouble spots you plan to deal with first.

Now then, write down the problem. Maybe it would be "I am usually late to a meeting. More often than not, I have to hurry . . . and even then, I am five to ten minutes late."

Once this is done, think about several practical ways you can conquer the habit or pattern you've fallen into. Again, write down the plan for correction.

One final suggestion: Work on only one or two projects at a time. If you try to shoot at too many targets at once, you won't hit any. This will frustrate you and may cause you to give up. And, by the way, don't forget to pray and read a brief portion of God's Word. You'll certainly find help there.

For example, the Book of Proverbs puts a high priority on orderliness. You can't read it without getting motivated . . . and convicted! Take 26:13–16, where inefficiency is personified as a sluggard: 'The sluggard says, 'There is a lion in the road! A lion is in the open square!' As the door turns on its hinges, so does the sluggard on his bed. The sluggard buries his hand in the dish; he is weary of bringing it to his mouth again. The sluggard is wiser in his own eyes than seven men who can give a discreet answer."

The syndrome is painfully clear:

We see danger . . . but we don't care (the lion).

We are concerned . . . but are too lazy to change (the bed).

We become victims of habit (the dish).

We rationalize our failures.

"Decently and in order." That's our goal, remember. Most of us are a lot more decent than we are orderly. Which means we qualify as highly moral, well-behaved sluggards.

*An orderly life is like an orderly closet;
it looks good and it serves its intended purpose.*

PREDESTINED FOR SERVICE

❧ *Romans 8:28–29* ❧

ainful though it may be for us to admit it here in this great land of America, we're losing touch with one another. The motivation to help, to encourage, yes, to serve our fellow-man is waning. People have observed a crime in progress but refused to help so as not to be involved. Even our foundational values are getting lost in these confusing days. And yet, it is these things that form the essentials of a happy and fulfilled life.

Maybe you've never before stopped to consider that God is committed to one major objective in the lives of all His people: to conform us to "the image of His Son." Well, rather than getting neck deep in tricky theological waters, I believe the simple answer is found in Christ's own words. Listen as He declares His primary reason for coming:

"For even the Son of Man did not come to be served, but to serve, and to give His life a ransom for many" (Mark 10:45).

No mumbo jumbo. Just a straight-from-the-shoulder admission. He came to serve and to give. It makes sense, then, to say that God desires the same for us. After bringing us into His family through faith in His Son, the Lord God sets His sights on building into us the same quality that made Jesus distinct from all others in His day. He is engaged in building into his people the same serving and giving qualities that characterized His Son.

Whoever wishes to become great among you shall be your servant.

SECOND-GENERATION FALLOUT

🐾 *2 Kings 18–21* 🐾

A curious phenomenon has plagued families for as long as there have been families. It's that age-old problem of second-generation fallout that breaks the hearts of godly moms and dads.

The scenario goes something like this. A man and woman fall in love and get married. They also love Christ and desire to serve Him with all their hearts. As their children come along, they teach and train and pray that God will get hold of their little lives and use them for His glory.

But what about the now-grown kids? Ah, there's the rub. Somewhere along the way God got pushed way down on their list of priorities. Disciplines like prayer, church attendance, tithing, serving, and serious Bible study got lost in the shuffle.

I recently stumbled upon one of those father-son stories that still speaks volumes. The dad was Hezekiah, a king who took the throne when he was twenty-five and reigned until he was fifty-four. All the while, his heart remained warm toward his God, and God prospered him. What a man! When Hezekiah was forty-two, he and his wife, Hephzibah, had a son, Manasseh. But you'd never know he came from Hezekiah stock. According to the inspired historian's account, he seduced the people of Judah "to do evil more than the nations whom the LORD destroyed" (2 Kings 21:9). What went wrong? Why didn't Hezekiah's righteousness and passion pass to his son? I believe there are at least three reasons:

First, Manasseh had a will of his own—as we all do—and with that will he stubbornly and deliberately refused to respond to the Lord (2 Chron. 33:10). Second, he was weak-willed and overly influenced by ungodly and wicked associations (2 Kings 21:3, 6). And third, he was neglected by his preoccupied, busy father. The king was at the zenith of his reign when Manasseh was born, and there is every indication that the prince saw little of his father during the formative years of his life. Hezekiah simply never took the time.

Sound familiar at all? While you still have your children under your roof, take time to talk together, to play together, to relax together . . . just to be together.

It is amazing how powerful first-generation presence can be
when it comes to curing the second-generation plague.

THINK IT OVER

❧❧❧

*T*hose three reasons we discussed yesterday cause me to reserve my concluding thoughts for you parents who still have your children under your roof. Let me be painfully and firmly honest with you as I offer three suggestions:

First, teach personal responsibility. "Son, even though you are the only one, do what's right. Don't be afraid to stand alone." Then explain how it can be done. Or, "Sweetheart, even though others may be involved, take responsibility for your part in any wrongdoing." Ours is an era where passing the buck is an art form, where seeing oneself as an innocent victim is in vogue. Help your child face up to the hard facts . . . to tell the truth, regardless.

Second, emphasize the erosion principle. Evil is getting increasingly worse but also more cleverly disguised. Point that out. Explain how easy it is to get used to it . . . to shrug it off, rather than identify it and confront it.

Gary Bauer tells the shocking yet true story of a teacher who, twenty-five years ago, used to walk into her fourth grade class and greet them. "Good morning, children," to which they would respond, "Good morning, Miss Jones." She left teaching for many years to have her own family and rear them. She returned recently to the classroom and began the day in her usual way, "Good morning, children." To which a young thug on the front row responded, "Shut up, bó!" That's what I mean by the erosion principle. If your youngster isn't alert, he or she will get swept up in it.

Third, take time. Not just to eat together, or work together around the house, or do homework together or go to the athletic games together, although those are important, too. Take time to talk together and walk together. To play together. To relax together. To do fun stuff together . . . just to be together.

Want a tip? Start today.

GOD'S DELIVERY SERVICE

❧ *1 Corinthians 2* ❧

I don't know where you are today, but I have a sneaky suspicion that you, like me, might have a few intruders crowding into your life and could use some divine reinforcements. If so, don't hesitate to call for help. Tell your Father that you are running out of hope and energy and ideas . . . that you need "not . . . words taught by human wisdom, but . . . those taught by the Spirit, combining spiritual thoughts with spiritual words. . . . For who has known the mind of the Lord, that he should instruct him? But we have the mind of Christ" (1 Cor. 2:13, 16).

You may have cancer. So what can you do? You dial Heaven 911 and you tell God you have an emergency need: "I have cancer, Lord, and I need wisdom." And at that very moment He will begin to make His deliveries.

Amazingly, you soon discover that your greatest enemy is not the disease but subtle, slippery feelings of despair, the thief of peace. And so you rely on God's daily delivery service to get you through that one day. And then the next.

When Dan Richardson, an enthusiastic believer in Christ, lost his battle with cancer, the following piece was distributed at his memorial service.

Cancer is limited . . .

> It cannot cripple love,
> It cannot corrode faith,
> It cannot eat away peace,
> It cannot destroy confidence,
> It cannot kill friendship,
> It cannot shut out memories,
> It cannot silence courage,
> It cannot invade the soul,
> It cannot reduce eternal life,
> It cannot quench the Spirit,
> It cannot lessen the power of the resurrection.

You cannot deny that you have the disease, but you can deny despair from taking control. Wherever you are, whatever your circumstances, call for God's daily delivery of wisdom, strength, and grace.

Each morning, slam the door on despair. If you don't, it will slip in and rob you. And you'll soon find a peace missing.

JUST DO IT

❧ *James 1:22–25* ❧

*W*e Christians have too many meetings! Where did we get the idea that our goal in the family of faith should be seeing who can absorb the most information? Since when do we equate spirituality with a numb posterior?

Now, don't jump to the conclusion that I'm questioning the value of meeting together. Some of the most helpful and meaningful times in my life have taken place in a gathering of believers. But when I review our Lord's style of instruction, I cannot help but see how different it was from ours. He never suggested that the Twelve write anything down or repeat His words verbatim. And when He did exhort them, He used simple words, vivid illustrations, everyday examples, and easily understood applications—prompting them to action.

Words. Words. Words. We have become "too wordy" in our faith, which explains our excessive interest in meetings. When did we get the idea that more information leads to deeper consecration?

Jesus' arch enemies, the Pharisees, were great on loud, dogmatic commands, lengthy requirements, and drawn-out demands. Oh, how they loved the sound of their own words! But when it came to doing, they struck out.

James exhorts us to be "doers of the word, and not merely hearers who delude themselves" (James 1:22). In other words, don't talk compassion; lend a hand. Don't pound a pulpit about generosity; give. Just do it.

We won't be met at the portals of heaven by some angel with a clipboard who asks, "And how many meetings did you attend in your lifetime on earth?" But while we're on earth, there is a question we do need to answer: "Why call ye Me, 'Lord, Lord,' and do not the things which I say?"

What do you think would happen if, instead of going to some meeting or conference, you spent that time alone with the Father?

SOMETHING OLD

❧ *Isaiah 40* ❧

*T*here is something grand about old things that are still in good shape. Old furniture, rich with the patina of age and history, is far more intriguing than the modern stuff. When you sit on it or eat off it or sleep in it, your mind pictures those in previous centuries who did the same in a world of candlelight, oil lamps, buggies, and potbelly stoves. Each scrape or dent holds a story you wish you knew.

Old hardback books are far more fascinating than today's slick paperbacks. I find it therapeutic to hold in my hands pages that have endured the ages, to pore over lines that other eyes have pondered and other fingers have marked. The authenticity of antiquity thrills me.

Old churches affect me the same way. As you settle into the creaking oak pew, you can hear the pipe organ filling the sanctuary with one of Bach's masterworks. The thunderous voice of the preacher is in the woodwork, and the altar beckons you to be still and know that God is God.

Strangely, such sights and sounds equip us to face our own battles with renewed vigor, for it's the old things—things that have outlived fashions and fads, that have endured wars and recessions, presidents and plagues—that remind us to pause and encourage us to strengthen our roots. These do more than prompt nostalgic feelings; they remind us that we are not alone in this adventurous pilgrimage from earth to heaven. By standing on the shoulders of yesterday, the view into tomorrow is not nearly so frightening.

The Bible is old also—ancient, in fact. Its timeless stories have for centuries shouted, "You can make it! Don't quit . . . don't give up!" Its truths, secure and solid as stone, say, "I'm still here, waiting to be claimed and applied." Whether it's a prophet's warning, a patriarch's prayer, a poet's psalm, or a preacher's challenging reminder, the Book of books lives on, offering us new vistas. It still speaks as it did in the days when reformers heralded hope from strong pulpits, when rough-hewn revivalists pleaded for souls in open-air campaigns, when faithful expositors taught saints and lived lives of uncompromising integrity, when rugged missionaries left the comforts of home to carry its message to hostile tribes and foreign climes.

The truths of this old Book have endured in spite of the attacks of its critics and the attempts of the Adversary to silence its message—like an ageless anvil wearing away the hammers.

Though ancient, it has never lost its relevance. Though battered, no one has ever improved on its content. Though old, it never fails to offer something pure, something wise, something new.

By touching something old, something new is stirred within us.

DON'T WAIT

❧ *2 Corinthians 6:1–10* ❧

*R*emember me? I'm the guy who promotes waiting. Allowing the Lord to open the doors, clear the way, smooth the path, shove you through. You know, all the stuff you expect a preacher to say.

But I do think we can get so good at waiting that we never act. We yawn and passively mutter, "Maybe, someday" as we let opportunities slip away. Like having friends over for ice cream or going on a picnic. Like using the fine china or celebrating a birthday . . . or slipping away for a weekend of relaxation and romance . . . or sailing for a day . . . or spending a week away with the family. "Not this year . . . but maybe, someday . . ."

Don't wait! If you continue such passivity, someday will never come—and you'll regret it for the rest of your days. I realized this anew when I read the following in the *Los Angeles Times*. Ann Wells writes:

> My brother-in-law opened the bottom drawer of my sister's bureau and lifted out a tissue-wrapped package. . . . He discarded the tissue and handed me the slip. It was exquisite; silk, handmade and trimmed with a cobweb of lace. The price tag with an astronomical figure on it was still attached.
>
> "Jan bought this the first time we went to New York, at least eight or nine years ago. She never wore it. She was saving it for a special occasion. Well, I guess this is the occasion."
>
> He took the slip from me and put it on the bed with the other clothes we were taking to the mortician. His hands lingered on the soft material for a moment, then he slammed the drawer shut and turned to me.
>
> "Don't ever save anything for a special occasion. Every day you are alive is a special occasion."
>
> I remembered those words through the funeral and the days that followed when I helped him and my niece attend to all the sad chores that follow an unexpected death. . . .
>
> I'm still thinking about his words, and they've changed my life. . . . I'm not "saving" anything; we use our good china and crystal for every special event—such as losing a pound, getting the sink unstopped, the first camellia blossom. . . .
>
> "Someday" and "one of these days" are losing their grip on my vocabulary. If it's worth seeing or hearing or doing, I want to see and hear and do it now. . . . I'm trying very hard not to put off, hold back, or save anything that would add laughter and luster to our lives. And every morning when I open my eyes I tell myself that it is special.

Every day is that special day you've been waiting for. Seize it!

DEVELOPING HUMILITY OF MIND

✸❧ *2 Corinthians 4:5* ✸❧

*Y*ourself, yourself, yourself. We're up to here with self! Do something either for youself or with yourself or to yourself. How very different from Jesus' model and message. He offers rather a fresh and much-needed invitation to our "me-first" generation. There is a better way, Jesus says: "Be a servant, give to others!" Now that's a philosophy that anybody can understand. And, without question, it is attainable. Just listen: "Do nothing from selfishness or empty conceit, but with humility of mind let each of you regard one another as more important than himself; do not merely look out for your own personal interests, but also for the interests of others" (Phil. 2:3–4).

Know what all that means? Well, for starters, "nothing" means just that. Stop permitting two strong tendencies—selfishness and conceit—to control you! Let nothing either of them suggests win a hearing. Replace them with "humility of mind." But how? By regarding others as more important than yourself. Look for ways to support, encourage, build up, and stimulate the other person. And that requires an attitude that would rather give than receive.

"Humility of mind" is really an attitude, isn't it? It's a preset mentality that determines ahead of time that I will care about others' needs more than my own.

The decision to give ourselves to others is a daily taking up of the cross.

Things That Strangle Us

❧ *Mark 4* ❧

*W*hile reading through Mark's Gospel recently, I was drawn into the scene of chapter 4. You remember, it's that time Jesus sat down in a little boat by the seashore and talked about a farmer who dropped seeds into the dirt. Same seed, different soil, different results. Four to be exact.

Some seeds fell beside the road . . . the birds gobbled them up. A few seeds fell on rocky ground . . . the sun scorched the rootless growth, and they withered and died. Other seeds fell among thorns . . . which choked out the growth so severely there was no crop to harvest. Still other seeds fell into good soil . . . bumper crop. Then Jesus explained each point.

First, He said, the seed represents "the word." I believe we're safe in saying that "the word" refers to truth. God's truth. Second, the different soils represent people's varied responses to that "word." All four "hear," but not all reap a harvest. That's significant. Hearing guarantees nothing. Next, the results are directly related to the condition of the soil . . . not the quality of the seed. If you look closely, you'll see that the first two groups lack roots. Only with the last two groups does Jesus mention fruit.

I think it's obvious that the first two groups of people are without spiritual life. No roots, no fruit, no growth, no change whatsoever. The third group hears, but only the fourth group "hears the word and accepts it," resulting in strong, healthy growth. It's the third group that intrigues me. These people hear everything the fourth group hears. But those truths are not really accepted, allowed to take root, and grow. Instead, the thorns "choke the word and it becomes unfruitful."

Thorns that choke? What are they? Jesus doesn't leave us in the dark. They are "the worries of the world, and the deceitfulness of riches, and the desires for other things" (Mark 4:19).

The term "worry" is derived from the old German word *wurgen,* which means "to choke." By extension, the word came to denote "mental strangulation" and, finally, to describe the condition of being harassed with anxiety. Worry begins as a thin stream trickling through our minds. If entertained, it cuts a deeper channel into which other thoughts are drained.

But the third species of thorns is the killer: "the desires for other things." It's the picture of discontentment, the plague of pursuit: pushing, straining, stretching, relentlessly reaching, while our minds become strangled with the lie "enough just isn't enough."

Jesus closed off His brief talk with that familiar line, "He who has ears, let him hear" (Mark 4:9).

When the thorns of life scratch us, we need the pruning shears of the Word.

THINK IT OVER

❧❧❧

$\mathcal{T}$ he bad news is this: Listening won't make the thorns go away, no matter how much we concentrate and welcome Jesus' teachings. Thorns come with the territory called depravity.

But the good news is this: Listening—I mean really giving heed to the seed—results in deeper roots and greater fruit . . . and thorns can't strangle such healthy growth.

Jesus is still communicating, but if we're not careful, we'll let our mental strangulation drown out His voice. Things that strangle us grow well in comfortable surroundings even when we look like we're listening.

In what way might these thorns be encroaching in your life?

Worries?

The deceitfulness of riches?

The desires for other things?

EXPECTING THE UNEXPECTED

✇ *Isaiah 43:15–19* ✇

*I*t had been a long time since Horace Walpole smiled. Too long. Life for him had become as drab as the weather in dreary old England. Then, on a grim winter day in 1754, while reading a Persian fairy tale, his smile returned. He wrote his longtime friend, Horace Mann, telling him of the "thrilling approach to life" he had discovered from the folk tale.

The ancient tale told of three princes from the island of Ceylon who set out on a pursuit of great treasures. They never found that for which they searched, but en route they were continually surprised by delights they had never anticipated. While looking for one thing, they found another.

The original name of Ceylon was Serendip, which explains the title of this story—"The Three Princes of Serendip." From that, Walpole coined the wonderful word "serendipity." And from then on, his most significant and valued experiences were those that happened to him while he was least expecting them.

Serendipity occurs when something beautiful breaks into the monotonous and the mundane. A serendipitous life is marked by "surprisability" and spontaneity. When we lose our capacity for either, we settle into life's ruts. We expect little and we're seldom disappointed.

Though I have walked with God for several decades, I must confess I still find much about Him incomprehensible and mysterious. But this much I know: He delights in surprising us. He dots our pilgrimage from earth to heaven with amazing serendipities.

Isaiah's words make me smile every time I read them because I have seen their truth come to pass time and again. God still stands behind this promise:

> See, I am doing a new thing!
> Now it springs up; do you not perceive it?
> I am making a way in the desert
> and streams in the wasteland. (Isa. 43:19, NIV)

Your situation may be as hot and barren as a desert or as forlorn and meaningless as a wasteland. You may be tempted to think, "There's no way!" when someone suggests things could change. All I ask is that you read that verse one more time and be on the lookout. God may very well be planning a serendipity in your life.

God has been doing "a new thing" in drab deserts
and wintry wastelands for centuries.

GLORY BEYOND THE GRIND

❧ *Exodus 15:2* ❧

*E*ven though the song was composed before I was born (which makes it a real oldie), I often find myself humming it in the shower at the beginning of a busy day, between appointments and assignments in the middle of a hectic day, and on the road home at the end of a tiring day. Somehow it adds a soothing touch of oil to the grind: "Without a song the day would never end . . . without a song. . . ."

True, isn't it? The right combination of words and melody seldom fails to work its magic. And given the pressures and demands we are forced to cope with on a daily basis, we could use a little magic.

The homemaker with children at her feet who faces fourteen or more hours a day in the grind of an endless list of chores. The professional who deals with the grind of people, people, people. The truck driver who heads into the grind of traffic snarls and monotonous miles. The athlete who lives with the grind of unending hours of practice. Students and faculty who face the cyclical grind of daily preparation and assignments, exams and papers.

Fact is, no matter who you are or what you do, the grind ain't gonna go away! The sales person has quotas. The performer has rehearsals. The therapist can't escape one depressed soul after another. The preacher is never free of sermon preparation. The broadcaster cannot get away from the clock any more than the military person can escape the hassle of red tape. Days don't end . . . roads don't bend . . . help!

The question is, how do we live beyond the daily grind? The answer is, a song. But not just any song! Certainly not some mindless, earsplitting tune yelled into a microphone. No, not that. I have in mind some songs that are really old. We're talking ancient here. In fact, they are the ones inspired and composed by our Creator-God-the original Rock music, with a capital "R." They're called psalms.

These are the timeless songs that have yielded delicious fruit in every generation. Not silly ditties, but strong melodious messages specially designed to help us live beyond the grind. That's right, *beyond it.* "We'll get along as long as a *psalm* is strong in our souls."

Those age-old compositions drip with the oil of glory that enables us to live beyond the grind. Songs of victory, affirmation, and encouragement, of confidence-giving strength, of hope, of compassion.

Without God's song in our soul, our long days will never end and those wearisome roads will never bend.

God's Book is full of songs—150 of them.
Let's sing them frequently and allow their time-tested lyrics to oil our days.

GO FOR IT

❧ *Luke 5:1—10* ❧

*I*n his fine little book *Fully Human, Fully Alive,* author John Powell relates an experience of a friend who was vacationing in the Bahamas. The friend was sightseeing when he noticed a crowd gathered toward the end of a pier. He walked down to investigate the commotion. Powell says:

> . . . he discovered that the object of all the attention was a young man making the last-minute preparations for a solo journey around the world in a homemade boat. Without exception everyone on the pier was pessimistic. All were actively volunteering to tell the ambitious sailor all the things that could possibly go wrong. . . .
>
> When my friend heard all these discouraging warnings to the adventurous young man, he felt an irresistible desire to offer some optimism and encouragement. As the little craft began drifting away from the pier towards the horizon, my friend . . . kept shouting: "BON VOYAGE! You're really something! We're with you. We're proud of you!"

How few are those who see beyond the danger . . . who say to those on the edge of some venture, "Go for it!" Funny, isn't it? I suppose it's related to one's inner ability to imagine, to envision, to be enraptured by the unseen, all the hazards and hardships notwithstanding.

How glad I am that certain visionaries refused to listen to the crowd on the pier. I'm glad . . .

- that Edison didn't give up on the light bulb
- that Luther refused to back down
- that Michelangelo kept painting
- that Lindbergh kept flying
- that Papa Ten Boom said "yes" to frightened Jews

Almost every day—certainly every week—we encounter people who are in their own homemade boat, thinking seriously about setting forth. The ocean of possibilities is enormously inviting, yet terribly threatening. Urge them on! Dare to say what they need to hear the most, "Go for it!" Then pray like mad. How much could be accomplished if only there were more brave souls on the end of the pier smiling and affirming.

Most of the time it's not a matter of having the goods, but of hearing the bads.

NOSTALGIC MUSINGS

❦ *Jeremiah 6:14; 8:11; Matthew 24:6–7, 11* ❦

*F*or over an hour the other day I strolled down Nostalgia Lane with a September 4, 1939, copy of *Time* magazine. What a journey! Pickups sold for $465 and best-selling books cost $2. Big news in the music world was Bing Crosby, whose records sold for 35 cents a platter. What was most intriguing, however, was the international scene, as presented by the staff writers. The threat of war was a slumbering giant, and Adolf Hitler's name appeared on almost every page of the Foreign News section. President Franklin Roosevelt was busy calming the troubled waters of our nation's fear of war, speaking openly of his "lovely hope for peace." In spite of the Nazi war machine that had already consumed Italy, Sicily, Albania, and was primed to pounce on Poland, Hungary, Belgium, and France, the talk in America was amazingly casual—a smug, business-as-usual attitude.

How naive we were! Little did we know that within months the insane führer would unleash a hellish nightmare from which we could not escape. Before his screams were silenced, acres of soil would be covered with small white crosses, and thousands of American homes would have their tranquil plans for peace invaded by the brutal enemy of grief.

Every so often when we enter such a relatively calm era, it is easy to forget the prophet's warning to beware of those who superficially heal the brokenness of a nation by announcing "peace, peace" when "there is no peace" (Jer. 6:14; 8:11). And if we feel sufficiently comfortable and relaxed, it's mighty easy to block from our minds the Savior's prediction of "wars and rumors of wars" and His warning that "many false prophets will arise and mislead many" (Matt. 24:6–7, 11).

Who knows? Fifty years from now another preacher could be leafing through a *Time* magazine yellow with age, feeling a nostalgic twinge and smiling at what we consider modern times. He will no doubt notice the business-as-usual look on our faces, only to be seized with the realization that we had no idea what a ragged edge we were living on in our relaxed American culture.

If indeed there is an America fifty years from now.

We need to be alert.
Sometimes the best of times may be a breeding ground for the worst of times.

RESTORING COMPASSION

❧ *Matthew 25:34–36* ❧

*A*s one understanding soul expressed it: "Compassion is not a snob gone slumming. It's a real trip down inside the broken heart of a friend. It's feeling the sob of the soul. It's sitting down and silently weeping with your soul-crushed neighbor."

Parceling out this kind of compassion will elicit no whistles or loud applause. In fact, the best acts of compassion will never be known to the masses. Nor will fat sums of money be dumped into your lap because you are committed to being helpful. Normally, acts of mercy are done in obscurity with no thought (or receipt) of monetary gain.

Compassion usually calls for a willingness to humbly spend oneself in obscurity on behalf of unknowns. How few there are in our fast-paced, get-rich-quick society who say to such a task, "Here am I, use me." Truly compassionate people are often hard to understand. They take risks most people would never take. They give away what most people would cling to. They reach out and touch when most would hold back with folded arms. Their caring brings them up close where they feel the other person's pain and do whatever is necessary to demonstrate true concern.

If God's people are to be living examples of one thing,
that thing ought to be—it must be—compassion.

PROVIDENCE

❧ *Genesis 50* ❧

I've been giving a lot of thought these days to the subject of God's will. While engaged in a study of that issue recently, I came across a term we rarely use or read these days: providence.

The root meaning of providence is "foresight . . . to see in advance" or "to provide for." But those definitions could leave us with too shallow an understanding. Providence contains far more than a passive reference to God's foreknowledge.

Back in the seventeenth century, the Westminster divines hammered out a much more thorough statement: "God, the great Creator of all things, doth uphold, direct, dispose, and govern all creatures, actions, and things from the greatest event to the least, by His most wise and holy providence, according to His infallible foreknowledge, and the free and immutable counsel of His own will, to the praise of the glory of His wisdom, power, justice, goodness and mercy."

Make no mistake about it, "He's got the whole world in His hands." From the greatest to the least, nothing is beyond the scope of His sovereign power and providential care. He makes the rain fall, the sun shine, the stars twinkle—in this and all other galaxies. He raises up people and kingdoms and He brings down both. He numbers the hairs on our heads and determines the days of our lives. In doing so, He weaves everything together into His design. Ultimately, the tapestry of His handiwork will be something to behold!

"But wait," I hear someone say, "don't you and I possess a will? We're not robots, are we?" R. C. Sproul addresses this well in *Essential Truths of the Christian Faith:* "We are creatures with a will of our own. We make things happen. Yet the casual power we exert is secondary. God's sovereign providence stands over and above our actions. He works out His will through the actions of human wills, without violating the freedom of those human wills."

God's redemptive providence is always at work, even through the most diabolical schemes and actions. Classic illustration? The betrayal of Jesus Christ by Judas. Strange as it may seem, Judas's worst act of wickedness helped to bring about the best thing that ever happened: the Atonement.

So, take heart, my friend. God is in full control. Nothing is happening on earth that brings a surprise to heaven. Nothing is outside the scope of His divine radar screen as He guides us safely home. Things that seem altogether confusing, without reason, unfair, even wrong, do indeed fit into the Father's providential plan.

Nothing touches us that has not first passed through His hands.

THINK IT OVER

After a lengthy bout with despair, severe depression, and suicide attempts, writer and poet William Cowper (1731–1800) discovered comfort in God's providence, which led him to write "Shining out of Darkness":

God moves in a mysterious way,
His wonders to perform;
He plants his footsteps in the sea
And rides upon the storm.

Deep in unfathomable mines
Of never failing skill,
He treasures up his bright designs,
And works his sovereign will.

Judge not the Lord by feeble sense,
But trust him for his grace;
Behind a frowning providence,
He hides a smiling face.

Can you think of instances in your own life, with the advantage of 20–20 hindsight, wherein someone or something meant evil against you, "but God meant it for good"? Thank and praise Him for it—and for His continual providence.

A Little Courtesy, Please

❧ *Ephesians 4:29–32* ❧

*S*pring has sprung. Longer days are before us. And baseball, that grand old American game, is upon us. One hundred and sixty-two regular-season games, to be specific.

That's a lot of strikeouts and double plays, hot dogs and Cokes, relaxed conversations and fun memories. Families can hang out and spend the whole evening doing really nothing. It's great! While all those men are out there playing a kid's game, nobody has any reason to get uptight.

Funny thing about baseball, though. The guys who have more reason than anyone else to get nervous and uneasy are on the field, but they're not on a team. They're the guys in uniform, affectionately referred to as "the umps" . . . or stuff much worse than that.

The horror stories they tell never cease to sadden and sometimes shock me. If it wouldn't mean my loss of limb or life, I'd like to take some fans who delight in insults and say, "Hey, let's remember that those fellows are doing a lot better job than we could do. Show a little courtesy, please!"

I would especially like to see some changes at Little League games. This is supposed to be a pleasant setting where boys have the opportunity to learn more about the game of life than the game of baseball. That was driven home to me recently when I read the words of Donald Jensen, who was struck in the head by a thrown bat while umpiring a Little League game in Terre Haute, Indiana. He continued to work the game but later that evening was placed in the hospital. While being kept overnight for observation, Jensen wrote an eloquent letter. At one point he says:

> The purpose of Little League is to teach baseball skills to young men. Obviously, a team which does not play well in a given game, yet is given the opportunity to blame that loss on an umpire for one call or two, is being given the chance to take all responsibility for the loss from their shoulders. A parent or adult leader who permits the younger player to blame his failures on an umpire . . . is doing the worst kind of injustice to that youngster. . . . This irresponsibility is bound to carry over to future years.

What Donald Jensen wrote that night was absolutely right. Next time you're tempted to insult an umpire, remember him—the late Donald Jensen. The following morning he died of a brain concussion.

How we play often reveals how we live.

I PROMISE

❧ *1 Kings 3:5–15* ❧

*R*ecently a friend dropped by my study to chat. This man is a true friend, and he also speaks the truth in love, which brings me to the most important part of our visit.

As he closed his folder, he tilted his head and took a deep breath, obviously gathering courage to say something.

"Go ahead . . . tell me what's eating away at you," I urged.

"Well, I don't know how I should say these things, Chuck, but I can't just ignore them either. The fact is, I'm concerned."

"Concerned about what?" I probed.

He then went on to tell me, his dark eyes fixed squarely on mine, that he was concerned about the number of responsibilities I had been taking on of late. "I don't think you'll fall morally or ethically," he said. "What does worry me is that you could be tempted to let your time with God and your time in the study of the Scriptures become less important to you. I want to urge you: *Do not let that happen.*"

Ours is a day of superficiality. If you can fake it, you're often admired as being clever, rather than being criticized for being phony. And mediocrity can mark the ministry just as easily as it can mark other callings and vocations. We're all depraved. The difference is that some of us are better at cover-up.

So, after my friend left, I made a few promises. Maybe these are promises you should make, too, adapting them to your own situation.

I promise to keep doing original and hard work in my study. Those to whom I am called deserve my best efforts.

I promise to maintain a heart for God. That means I will pray frequently and fervently and stay devoted to Him and to my calling.

I promise to remain accountable. Living the life of a religious Lone Ranger is not only unbiblical, it's dangerous.

I promise to stay faithful to my family. My wife deserves my time, affection, and undivided attention. Our now-grown children deserve the same.

I promise to be who I am. Just me. I plan to keep laughing, saying things a little off the wall, being a friend.

Do you need to "tell the truth in love" to someone?
Do you need to make a few promises yourself?

RELEVANCE OF REFORMING

❧ *1 Corinthians 15:58; 1 Peter 5:8–11* ❧

*E*very time you pick up a daily paper or watch the news you see someone protesting something. When I think of "protest," however, my thoughts often turn to that small band of men who had the guts to protest a religious system that had become corrupt to the core.

Godless church prelates paraded their carnality, indulging in shameless acts of the flesh. Bibles, banned from the common people, were chained to ornate pulpits and printed only in Latin, the "secret language" of the clergy. Instead of demonstrating compassion, unselfishness, grace, and other servantlike characteristics, those who led were anything but models of Christ.

"Enough!" thought a few straight-thinking souls. Men like Wycliffe, Tyndale, Zwingli, Knox, Calvin, and Luther refused to sit back, smile, and stay quiet. Their zeal became contagious, and they led thousands of others who joined their band of "protestants." And protest they did!

Luther's philosophy could be summed up in his own timely words: "If you preach the gospel in all aspects with the exception of the issues which deal specifically with your time— you are not preaching the gospel at all."

In other words, the gospel isn't to be changed. But it is to cut into each generation, like a flashing sword sharpened on the stone of Scripture, tempered in the furnace of reality, relevance, and need.

Jesus Christ met people where they were. His words touched nerves. There was a lot more here-and-now than then-and-there in His talks. His attack on the hypocrisy and prejudice of religious phonies came through loud and clear. He met people as they were, not as they "ought to" be. Angry young men, blind beggars, proud politicians, loose-living streetwalkers, ignorant fishermen, naked victims of demonism, and grieving parents were as clearly in His focus as the Twelve who sometimes hung on His every word.

His enemies misunderstood Him, but they couldn't ignore Him. They hated Him, but were never bored around Him. Jesus was the epitome of relevance. Still is.

It is we who have hauled the cross back out of sight. It is we who have left the impression that it belongs beneath the soft shadows of stained glass and marble statues.

And so . . . let's never lose relevance as we continue our work of reforming. Let's never bore people with the gospel. Let's never think that Christianity is something we must keep to ourselves and fearfully protect. Let's stay in the trenches of real-world involvements.

*"Jesus was not crucified in a cathedral between two candles,
but on a cross between two thieves" (George MacLeod).*

DISCIPLINES OF DURABILITY

❧ *Hebrews 11* ❧

*T*ucked away in the folds of Hebrews 11 is a two-word biography worth a second glance: "he endured" (11:27). The "he" refers to Moses. Moses was the one who hung tough, who refused to give in or give up, who decided that no amount of odds against him would cause him to surrender. He had staying power. He possessed the disciplines of durability.

He endured, despite the contempt of Pharaoh, the mightiest monarch of that era. He endured, despite the stubbornness of the Hebrews who grumbled, blamed, complained, and rebelled. He endured, despite the criticism of Miriam and Aaron, his own sister and brother. When ten out of twelve spies came back with their nay-sayings, Moses stood fast. When Korah and Dathan and Abiram led a cold, cunning conspiracy against him, Moses remained "resolute."

Maybe the great Apostle of Grace had such things in mind when he introduced his classic essay on the armor of God by saying, "and having done everything . . . stand firm" (Eph. 6:13).

Stand firm when the wicked appear to be winning. Stand firm in times of crisis. Stand firm even when no one will know if you compromised. Stand firm when big people act contemptibly small. Stand firm when people demand authority they don't deserve. Stand firm . . . keep your head . . . stay true . . . endure!

I have no idea where this finds you. For all I know, you are stronger than ever, pressing on with a full tank of resolve. That's great. However, you may be getting shaky. Your normally thick hide of moral purity and ethical integrity may be wearing thin. It's possible you've begun to listen too closely to your critics or need others' approval too much. Maybe you've started giving in to the kids in little areas you once resisted because you're tired, sort of shrugging off your better judgment.

Moses endured—even in his eighties. How? The same verse tells us: by focusing his attention on "Him who is invisible." He fixed his heart and soul on the One who, alone, judges righteously. He continually reminded himself that his sole purpose in life was to please the Lord . . . to obey Him . . . to glorify Him . . . to gain His approval at all cost.

Whatever it is you're facing, stand strong. Walk in quiet confidence, not veiled pride. Be sure without being stubborn . . . firm without being unteachable . . . enduring but not discourteous . . . full of truth balanced with grace.

Exacting indeed are the disciplines of durability.

"To be torn unmercifully by external forces, and still to preserve one's inward integrity, is to know the discipline that endures" (V. Raymond Edman).

"Permission Granted"

❧ *2 Corinthians 3:17* ❧

*P*aul jumped all over the Galatians for allowing a handful of legalistic Judaizers to invade their lives and clip their wings. Remember his rebuke? "It was for freedom that Christ set us free; therefore keep standing firm and do not be subject again to a yoke of slavery. . . . For you were called to freedom, brethren." (Galatians 5:1, 13).

In other words, "Permission granted." Enjoy! Go after it! Be who you are. Give yourself the okay to break the mold and exercise your God-given freedom. Chase those goals with all your heart.

It may take awhile. And you will have to train yourself to care less and less about what a few may say. It will help if you'll remind yourself that when they criticize you, they simply want you to be as miserable as they are. Since they cannot give themselves permission, who do you think you are to get away with it? If you keep that maverick thought in mind, it will help you soar like an eagle instead of standing around with all the turkeys.

Do you know your biggest hurdle?

You.

It's giving yourself permission, plain and simple. If you fail to press on while the light is green, you will spend so much of your life in the amber zone waiting for "just the right moment." Christ has literally set you free.

Give yourself permission to soar...then jump!

THE SIGNIFICANCE OF ONE

🌺 *Esther 1–10* 🌺

*I*n our overpopulated, impersonal world, it is easy to underestimate the significance of one. With so many people, most of whom seem so much more capable, more gifted, more prosperous, more important than I, who am I to think my part amounts to much?

Aren't you glad Patrick Henry didn't think that way? And Henry Ford? And Martin Luther King Jr.? And Walt Disney? And Martin Luther? And Winston Churchill? And Jackie Robinson? And Irving Berlin? And Abraham Lincoln? And Charles Wesley? And Marian Anderson?

"But it's a different world today, man. Back then, there was room for an individual to emerge, but now, no way!"

Wrong. God has always underscored individual involvement . . . still does.

How many did it take to help the victim who got mugged on the Jericho Road? One Good Samaritan.

How many were chosen by God to confront Pharaoh and lead the Exodus? One.

How many sheep got lost and became the object of concern to the shepherd? One.

How many did the Lord use to get the attention of the land of Palestine and prepare the way for Messiah? One.

Never underestimate the power of one!

Many centuries ago a woman almost did. She thought things were too far gone. And she certainly didn't think there was anything *she* could do. It was only a matter of time before all the Jews would be exterminated.

Her name was Esther. She was the Jewish wife of a Persian king, the man who was about to be tricked into making an irrevocable, disastrous decision. All Jews would be exterminated.

But the tide could be turned by . . . guess how many? You're right, one.

One woman—only one voice—saved an entire nation.

As is true of every person who stands in the gap, she was willing to get personally involved, to the point of great sacrifice. Or, as she said, "If I perish, I perish" (Esther 4:16).

Please, put aside all excuses and ask yourself, "What should I be doing?"

Yes, you alone can make a difference. The question is, will you?

If you don't do your part, who will?

Think It Over

🎞🎞

*A*ren't we glad somebody has always believed in the significance of one?

Like back in—

1645 . . . when one vote gave Oliver Cromwell control of England.

1776 . . . when one vote gave America the English language instead of German.

1845. . . when one vote brought the state of Texas into the union.

1868 . . . when one vote saved President Andrew Johnson from impeachment.

1875 . . . when one vote changed France from a monarchy to a republic.

1941 . . . when one vote saved the Selective Service System just twelve weeks before Pearl Harbor was attacked.

And did you know that in 1923, one vote gave Adolph Hitler control of the Nazi Party?

Ah, the power of one! Never underestimate it.

You, alone, can make a difference!

APPLAUSE

🐾 *Matthew 6:1—18* 🐾

*I*f a modern Rip van Winkle were to awaken from twenty years' slumber and stumble into today's world, I suspect he'd be amazed. Some of the changes, even in worship, would make the old gentleman wonder about us.

Picture him sitting on a pew, connecting with his God in worship. Then to his amazement, he hears folks clapping! Frowning, he feels suddenly and strangely interrupted. Why are these people applauding? Wasn't that music an offering of praise to the One they have gathered together to worship? Isn't silence—just the awesome sound of silence—sufficient?

Continuing to observe, he finds inconsistency in it all. Why don't these people applaud everything? How come a singer receives applause and the one who reads Scripture never does? And why don't they applaud the sermon?

Besides, he concludes, he prefers to do his applauding in his mind and heart.

But, then, doesn't the Bible talk about God's people clapping their hands? Yeah, it does. Several times in the psalms. But it also mentions shouting and dancing and groaning and playing on instruments we don't even have today. Obviously, God doesn't want us to be stoic and grim all the time. There have to be occasions when such spontaneous bursts are prompted by the Spirit within us. To cap off all such expressions would not only be unfair, it would be unbiblical.

Maybe, then, what these people need is to be sure that their responses in corporate worship are prompted by the Spirit and not by a small group of people who are ready to clap at anything . . . for any reason.

What I would tell our visitor is that it all has to do with the spirit of God's truth rather than the letter of the Law. If anyone can show me *from Scripture* the up-tight, air-tight guideline for putting a stop to all spontaneous applause, I'm ready to listen. But let's also remember that when we come together to worship we're not an audience watching a show where entertainers expect applause.

And no offense, but I tend to agree with old Rip. I've never seen a group of people applaud a snowcapped mountain range or an exquisite, priceless painting or a breathtaking sunset.

Silence befits the profound, the awesome.

Think before you applaud. Is it the best way to give God your praise?
Is it appropriate? Is it necessary? Would silence be better?

His Workmanship

❧ *1 Kings 5–6* ❧

ometimes fundamentalists can be the ugly ducklings of Christendom. We
sometimes clothe the infinite riches of Christ in unattractive rags! As a result,
the treasure of Truth is tainted and cheapened by the way it is presented to the
public.

Pick most any town and drive to the church which announces that it preaches Christ
and embraces the fundamentals of the faith. Chances are (with, thankfully, some exceptions)
you will find an unattractive structure surrounded by pathetic landscaping. The sign is either
out of date, obscure, unattractive, or big as a battleship.

Inside, you will find that the cheapest possible grade of lumber, paint, carpet, musical
instruments, and furnishings were used. The piano is out of tune. The hymnals are worn out
and dog-eared, some of them literally held together with Scotch tape.

Several years ago a man told me that his first contact with a Christian was so offensive
he "never wanted to hear about Jesus again." He said the person who witnessed to him had
bad breath and body odor, never once smiled, was dressed in clothing completely out of
date, and angrily closed his remarks with, "Don't blame Jesus if you go to hell."

Meanwhile, I've just finished reading the account in First Kings where God worked
through Solomon in the building of the temple. What quality! What attention to details!
What exacting requirements! What fabulous beauty! No one could ever say that God didn't
care how attractive His workmanship was. All you have to do is look at the beauty and intri-
cacy of the world He created.

As Christians, we represent the magnificent King of kings. So does our church. We may
not have a fortune, but whatever we do or build or sing or print or teach or type or promote
or present certainly ought to be attractive and appealing. The same is true for us individually. Our wardrobe may be limited, but it can always be neat and clean. We Christians have
enough barriers to overcome in this society without increasing the friction by sloppy dress,
poor workmanship, and offensive habits that repel rather than attract.

Let's not change our message. But it will be worth it to change our appearance from the
ugly duckling to the swan. We are His workmanship, and all we do should reflect that
beauty and grace.

Sometimes people can't see past us to hear our message.
We never have a second chance to leave a first impression.

ACCOMMODATING

❧ *1 Peter 1:13–2:3* ❧

I don't know anyone who would build a summer home at the base of Mount Vesuvius, and it would be tough trying to get campers to pitch their tents where Big Foot had been spotted. No family I know is interested in vacationing in a houseboat up the Suez Canal.

And yet there are Christians running loose today who flirt with risks far greater than these. And they do so with such calm faces you'd swear they had ice water in their veins.

Who are they? They are the ones who rewrite the Bible to accommodate their lifestyle. Whenever they run across Scripture verses or principles that attack their position, they alter them to accommodate their practice. That way, two things occur: 1) All desires (no matter how wrong) are fulfilled. 2) All guilt (no matter how justified) is erased.

Here is a sampling of accommodating theology:

God wants me to be happy. I can't be happy married to her. So I'm leaving . . . and I know He will understand.

There was a time when this might have been considered immoral. But not today. The Lord gave me this desire and wants me to enjoy it.

Look, nobody's perfect. So I got in deeper than I planned. Sure, it's a little shady, but what's grace all about, anyway?

Hey, life's too short to sweat the small stuff. We're not under law, you know.

If that's true . . . if that's right, then what in the world does it mean to be *holy?*

"Like the Holy One who called you, be holy yourselves also in all your behavior" (1 Pet. 1:15). Or *pure?*

"For this is the will of God, . . . that you abstain from sexual immorality" (1 Thess. 4:3). Or under *grace?*

"Shall we sin because we are not under law but under grace? May it never be!" (Rom. 6:15).

The simple fact is this: If we sow a lifestyle that is in direct disobedience to God's revealed Word, we ultimately reap disaster.

The consequences of sin may not come immediately . . . but they will come eventually. And when they do, there will be no excuses, no rationalization, no accommodation. God doesn't compromise with consequences.

When the bill comes due, the wages of willful sin must be paid in full.

How Could It Be?

✻ *Isaiah 64:6–7* ✻

*W*hoever is soft on depravity should go see *Schindler's List*. It's not for the fainthearted, I warn you. It is a raw, harsh, shocking exposé of unbridled prejudice, the kind of anti-Semitic prejudice spawned in hellish hate among the Nazis prior to and during World War II.

Many of the scenes are absolutely chilling. Trainloads and truckloads of horrified men, women, and precious children being hauled like helpless cattle to their deaths. The inhuman condition of the work camps, the "showers," the ovens, the smokestacks belching human ashes. Worst of all, the ability of human beings to carry all that out with hardly a shrug.

As everyone filed out, including my oldest son and one of my sons-in-law, we noticed that nobody said a word. You could have heard the proverbial pin fall to the carpet. We drove home, all caught in the grip of the same question: *How?*

How could such hatred, such extreme, vicious hatred, fill the minds of those wearing swastikas? How could they walk back into their barracks or offices or homes and smile or carry on their duties or forget what they had just done?

I believe I know. Really, the answer is simple. One word will do. *Depravity.* It's not a sickness. It's death. Living death. It's the filthy cesspool of the unregenerate heart.

And let's not feel so smug about it. Born spiritually dead and diseased by sin from our mother's womb, we have the roots of wickedness deep within us. You do. I do. Every human does, including children. The psalmist admits: "Behold, I was brought forth in iniquity, and in sin my mother conceived me" (51:5).

Read these words from the pen of the apostle Paul: "There is none righteous, not even one; there is none who understands, there is none who seeks for God. All have turned aside . . . there is none who does good, there is not even one" (Rom. 3:10–12).

Which brings us back to the same question we asked in the car that night: *How?* How could God possibly give His Son for such hopelessly lost sinners? How could He look past the hate and horror of our depravity? How could you and I have found our name on the *Savior's List?* Again, the answer is simple. One word will do. *Grace.*

"There is no man so good that if he placed all his actions and thoughts under the scrutiny of the laws, he would not deserve hanging ten times in his life"
(Montaigne).

WHAT VICTORY IS NOT

✷ *1 Corinthians 15:57* ✷

*V*ictory is not a once-for-all, automatic inheritance. Christians need to be reminded that the life God provides—the abundant life—is not a continuous, unbroken chain of victories. Victory is available, but not automatic. The strength we need is there to be claimed but we should never think of the Christian life as "instant success."

Victory is not an emotional high.

Christians do not gain victory by psyching themselves up or getting in the mood or waiting till it "feels right" to act.

Victory is not a dream reserved for supersaints.

Unlike the lonely runner on the track, the Christian who conquers does so "through Him who loved us." Jesus is always with us and we have His promise He will not leave us.

Victory does not happen to us while we passively wait.

Many today peddle a spiritual-sounding version of the "sit and wait" philosophy, but a victorious Christian is deliberately and personally involved in a process that leads to victory. If you are to achieve your goals, you must be involved to the maximum extent.

The victory we desire is never automatic.

AN ADVOCATE

❧ *1 John 2* ❧

*T*he Book of Job drips with mystery. The sobs of the man and the silence of his God form a strange combination. From the start, there are surprises and anomalies. Job is portrayed for us as "blameless, upright, fearing God, and turning away from evil" (1:1) . . . and yet the bottom drops out of his world. He loses everything except his life and his wife. How strange of God to permit one of His own to become the victim of a devil-inspired plot to reduce him to putty.

The man's misery knew no bounds, but his integrity remained intact, which amazed his wife—not one of the most helpful of mates. To top things off, a handful of frowning fellows gathered around Job to "preach at him," but the truth is, they came to condemn. One after another, time after time, Job's "counselors" pointed long fingers of accusation and cut him down.

Finally . . . there was no place to look but up; however, even then he felt shut out. He longed to approach God and pour out his woes, but he couldn't. At least he couldn't do so on his own. Why? Listen to Job's answer to that question: "He is not a man as I am that I may answer Him, that we may go to court together. There is no umpire between us, who may lay his hand upon us both" (9:32–33).

What did he need? What was it Job longed for? An advocate. Job called him "an umpire," someone who could stand in his stead and represent him, a suffering sinner, before God, the Holy One. The Hebrew term from which "umpire" is translated is YAH-KAAK, which in verb form means "to decide, to prove, convince, reason, to argue." Job wished for someone who would understand his predicament, take up his cause, and argue his case.

An advocate is someone who has authority, someone who will be heard and respected, where we would be ignored. The more passionate and complicated the issue, the more vital is our need for a qualified go-between. Someone to carry our torch. Someone who understands the issues and is able to articulate the salient points of the argument.

There is one Advocate we all need—one who represents sinners like us in the highest of all places—the presence of God: "And if anyone sins, we have an Advocate with the Father, Jesus Christ the righteous" (1 John 2:1).

What a great promise! "We have an advocate." He is there and, like a good "umpire," He is not silent.

The next time you start feeling like Job—alone, accused, deserted by friends, misunderstood, ripped off—turn to Him, your own "Advocate with the Father."

THINK IT OVER

❧❧

*G*race frees us to fly. So, fly! Dare I give a few illustrations? Aw, why not? You've had your eye on that sailboat or catamaran or sports car for some time. Why not? You've thought a lot about a cruise or a trip to Europe but never permitted yourself to do more than think. Why not?

Your hairdo has looked the same for three decades. You've wondered about trying something really chic. Why not?

You long to get your degree, but everybody tells you to give up that dream; it's too late. Should you press on? Why not?

You were raised to play it safe, never risk to think of all the missionaries who have it so tough . . . so you've never given yourself permission to skydive or bungee jump or hop into a pair of roller blades or let your hair blow in the breeze with the convertible top down Why not? (If it helps, most missionaries I know wouldn't hesitate to do any of those things at a second's notice. So don't use them as your excuse!)

Your kids are still around and you realize it won't be many more years and they will all be gone . . . so why not build some great memories? Take them out of school for the day and go to Disneyland. Or how about a fishing trip or a drive up into the mountains for an overnight out under the stars? Or plan a big family reunion this summer? Why not?

You're an adult. But your mom or dad still maintains too much control over you. You long to be strictly on your own, free of those manipulative "hints" and guilt trips. It's time to break away and get unstuck. Why not?

You'd love to throw a big, crazy party with a few happy-go-lucky folks who know how to have fun. Why in the world not?

Grace frees us to fly. So, fly!

GOING ON

🌺 *1 Samuel 30:1–6* 🌺

*F*lying ace Chuck Yeager has written a book with an inviting title: *Press On!* A guy with his adventurous background, plus a chest full of medals to prove it, probably has a lot to say about "pressing on." Few will ever know the thrill of breaking sound barriers, but all of us live with the daily challenge of pressing on. The question is how?

How does the patient go on after the physician breaks the news about the dreaded biopsy? How does the divorcée go on after the divorce is final? How does anyone press on when the bottom drops out?

I have recently discovered some principles from Scripture that have certainly come to my rescue. They emerge from the life of David when he and his fellow warriors were returning from battle. Exhausted, dirty, and anxious to get home, they came upon a scene that took their breath away. What was once their own quiet village was now smoldering ruins; their wives and children had been kidnapped by the same enemy forces that had burned their homes to the ground.

As if that were not bad enough, David's own men turned against him, and talk of mutiny swirled among the soldiers.

If ever a man felt like hanging it up, David must have at that moment. But he didn't.

What did he do instead? Read this very carefully: "But David strengthened himself in the LORD his God" (1 ⸱ n. 30:6).

He got alone and poured his heart before the Lord . . . got things squared away vertically, which helped clear away the fog horizontally. He did not surrender to hard times.

Why not? How did he go on?

By refusing to focus on the present situation only.

What happens when we stay riveted to the present misery? One of two things: Either we blame someone (which can easily make us bitter), or we submerge in self-pity (which paralyzes us).

Instead of retaliating or curling up in a corner and licking his wounds, he called to mind that this event was no mistake. The Lord wasn't absent. On the contrary, He was in full control. Bruised and bloody, David faced the test head-on and refused to throw in the sponge.

When we get things squared away vertically,
it helps clear away the fog horizontally.

LIFE'S ARROWS

❧ *2 Samuel 16:10–12* ❧

*H*aving just held a memorial service for a friend several years younger than I who had died with liver cancer, I have been thinking about how to respond when struck by an arrow of affliction. Not a little irritating dart, but an arrow plunged deeply.

My friend chose not to curl up in a corner with a calendar and put Xs on days. On the contrary, the news of his malignancy only spurred him on to drain every ounce out of every day. His physician had told him he would probably be gone before last Thanksgiving. "Says who?" he mused. Not only did he live through Thanksgiving, at Christmas he threw a party, the following Easter was delightful, a fun picnic on the Fourth of July was a gas . . . and he had a special celebration in the planning stage for this Thanksgiving! A close friend of his told me that the last time they talked he had made an appointment to have his teeth fixed.

I love that kind of spunk! It underscores one of my unspoken philosophies of life: When struck by an arrow, don't seek more days in your life but more life in your days. Forget quantity; pursue quality. Look beyond the pain and you'll find incredible perspective.

When the thorn punctured Paul's balloon, he refused to wallow in self-pity and whine away the balance of his days. He learned to glory in his weaknesses. He discovered a contentment, even a joy, in the midst of "distresses . . . persecutions . . . difficulties" (2 Cor. 12:10). In weakness he found inner strength.

In spite of his brothers' cruel mistreatment, subsequent slavery in Egypt, false accusations from Mrs. Potiphar (resulting in being dumped into a dungeon for years), Joseph steered clear of bitterness. As a matter of fact, he ultimately told his brothers, "God turned into good what you meant for evil" (Gen. 50:20, TLB). Talk about incredible perspective regarding life's arrows!

Arrows don't change a person's direction. They merely deepen his or her character; they help the afflicted rediscover certain values before achieving even greater things—if we let them.

So, which arrow has struck you recently? News of an alleged "terminal" illness? Physical pain? Unfair treatment? False accusations? Struggles at home? Somebody throwing rocks? An accident that's left you scarred? Don't waste time licking your wounds or wondering why. Make a decision to do what you were doing even better than ever. Life's arrows are nothing more than momentary setbacks that help us regroup, renew, and reload—so, what are you waiting for?

Don't seek more days in your life but more life in your days.

ASKING WHY

✇ *Job 2:9–10* ✇

*T*he sound was deafening. Although no one was near enough to hear it, ultimately it echoed around the world. None of the passengers in the DC-4 ever knew what happened—they died instantly. That was February 15, 1947, when the Avianca Airline flight bound for Quito, Ecuador, crashed into the 14,000-foot-high peak of El Tablazo not far from Bogota, then dropped—a flaming mass of metal—into a ravine far below.

Before leaving the Miami airport earlier that day, a passenger named Glenn Chambers had written a note to his mother on a piece of paper he picked up in the terminal. The paper was a piece of an advertisement with the single word WHY? sprawled across the center. In a hurry and preoccupied, he scribbled his note around that word, folded it, and stuffed it into an envelope addressed to his mother.

The note arrived after the news of his death. When his mother received it, there, staring up at her, was that haunting question: WHY?

Of all questions, this is the most searching, the most tormenting. It accompanies every tragedy.

Consider Job . . . imagine his feelings! He lost everything. Shortly thereafter he broke out in boils—from head to toe. Grief-stricken. Stunned. Bankrupt. In excruciating pain, both in body and spirit. But he wisely stated, "Shall we accept only good from God and never adversity?"

Notice very carefully what Job claimed that day. Don't miss the thing that carried him through. Job grabbed one great principle and held on: God is too kind to do anything cruel . . . too wise to make a mistake . . . too deep to explain himself.

That's it! Job rested his case there.

It's remarkable how believing that one profound statement erases the "Why?" from earth's inequities.

All other sounds are muffled when we claim His absolute sovereignty. Even the deafening sound of a crashing DC-4.

When we know Who, we can stop asking "Why?"

BENEFITS OF BREAKDOWNS

❧ *1 Samuel 18* ❧

*W*ho would've ever guessed it? Out of the blue came this nobody. He had spent his youth working for his dad in the quiet, rugged outdoors. Now, suddenly, he was the most famous man in the country. But he couldn't wait to retreat to the hills where life was simple and uncluttered.

That first night back under the stars must have been a restless one as he recalled the frightening scene of battle . . . the intimidating sound of the giant's voice as it echoed across the chasm . . . the feel of those five smooth stones . . . the deadening thud as rock struck forehead . . . the shout of triumph . . . the admiring look of dismay from the tall Israelite king. Now, silence.

Little did the lad know that God would lead him to more valleys—deeper than he could have dreamed possible. The events that followed the giant killing defied logic.

Even though David conducted himself with humility, loyalty, and grace, the man whose face—and life!—he had saved turned against him. Displeased by the boy's popularity, insecure over his own eclipsed public image, King Saul became a savage, driven mad by suspicion and jealousy.

In spite of this tragic twist in their relationship, David prospered. Three times in the biographical account we read that fact (1 Sam. 18:5, 14, 15). In addition, "he behaved himself more wisely than all the servants of Saul" (18:30). This led to growing popularity, increased favor in the eyes of Saul's inner circle, military victories, and enormous praise from the public. David found himself sandwiched between public applause and private horror.

It is easy to forget that two magnificent, lasting benefits were born out of that womb of woe: first, the deepening of much of David's character; and second, the composing of many of David's psalms. The traits we remember and admire as being worthy of emulation were shaped, honed, and polished while he lived like a fugitive in the wilderness, and the psalms we turn to most often emerged from a broken heart.

Where are you today? Has there been a recent breakdown? A trust no longer there? A friend no longer near? A dream no longer clear? A future no longer bright?

Take heart! It is in that precise crucible that God can (and often does) do His best work!

Some of your best traits and some of your finest works will grow out of the incredibly painful periods in your life.

MY STRESS—GOD'S STRENGTH

❧ *Psalm 46* ❧

*L*et me give you three very practical thoughts regarding this matter of God's strength through stress, as found in Psalm 46.

First, His strength is immediately available. Our trials are not superficial or irrelevant. They are vehicles of grace that God uses to bring us growth. Superficial problems call for superficial solutions. But real life isn't like that; its headaches and stresses go deeper, right down to the bone. They touch the nerve areas of our security. But God says He is a present help in trouble. He is immediately available. Do you realize that wherever you travel, whatever the time of day, you can call and He will answer? He's a very present and immediate help.

The second thing I observe about God's power in this psalm is that it is overpowering! It's a tent that can stretch over any stress—in fact it's tailor-made for stress. Furthermore, His power is not dependent on our help. You're weak, remember? Have you felt that weakness lately? Maybe it's time to say, "Lord, I love You. Through Your strength I will not be moved. I will stop running, stop striving. I will not fear. I will hold on to You. I will count on You to build that tent around me and protect me from the blast."

God says, "Cease striving, and know that I am God."

Beautiful! Really?

Isaiah 29:13–16

Fresh-fallen snow blanketed the range of mountains on the northeast rim of the Los Angeles basin. When I caught my first glimpse of it in the distance, I found myself smiling and saying aloud, "Beautiful!" Seventy-five miles away, it was beautiful. Up close, well, that was an entirely different matter.

About the time we reached 4,500 feet, narrow Highway 18 began to gather white dust. The temperature was right at freezing, the clouds were thick, and the wind had picked up considerably. I could have turned back then—and should have—but we were only fifteen or so minutes from our destination. So we pressed on.

The freak storm, however, made it increasingly obvious that things weren't going to get better, so we decided to cut short our visit. By now the wind was howling and the snow was swirling across the asphalt. Disappointed, we began a journey we shall never forget. And for the next several miles a brief conversation haunted me. It had occurred before we left:

"Shouldn't we buy tire chains?" she asked.

"Naw, this won't be any problem," he answered.

"Are you sure? It's downhill all the way back," she reminded him.

"Don't worry, hon. We'll be outa this in no time," he said.

An hour and a half—which seemed more like a decade—later, we reached San Bernardino. Between 6,000 feet and sea level, only the Lord knows for sure what happened.

There was no sin—mortal or venial, thought, word, or deed—I didn't confess. No prayer I didn't use. No verse I didn't claim. You know how folks say that when you are drowning your entire life passes before your eyes? Well, I can assure you the same is true as you fishtail your way down a glazed, winding, narrow, two-lane mountain highway.

Now there's a lesson I will think of every time I see any beautiful snowcapped mountain range. It may seem beautiful from a distance, but when you get real close, the scene is entirely different. It's a lot like life. Behind that beauty are bitter cold, screaming winds, blinding snow, icy roads, raw fear, and indescribable dangers. Distance feeds fantasy.

But the comforting fact is that as we journey through life, we have a Guide who knows all about those places. He knows our way, and He will get us through.

The Lord is our spiritual road atlas. When we rely on Him, we'll never get lost.

THINK IT OVER

❧❧ ❧❧

*F*rom a distance we in the church often look like beautiful people. We're well-dressed. We have nice smiles. We look friendly. We appear cultured, under control . . . at peace.

But what a different picture comes in view when someone gets up close and in touch!

What appeared so placid is really a mixture of winding roads of insecurity and uncertainty . . . maddening gusts of lust, greed, and self-indulgence . . . and pathways of pride glazed over with a slick layer of hypocrisy. All this is shrouded in a cloud of fear of being found out.

From a distance, we dazzle; up close, we're tarnished. Put enough of us together and we may resemble an impressive mountain range. But when you get down into the shadowy crevices . . . the Alps we ain't.

That's why our Lord means so much to us. He is intimately acquainted with all our ways. Darkness and light are alike to Him. Not one of us is hidden from His sight. All things are open and laid bare before Him: our darkest secret, our deepest shame, our stormy past, our worst thought, our hidden motive, our vilest imagination . . . even our vain attempts to cover the ugly with snow-white beauty.

He comes up so close. He sees it all. He knows our frame. He remembers we are dust.

Best of all, He loves us still.

WE HOPE . . . WE WAIT

🐟 *Romans 8:18–27* 🐟

*R*ome wasn't built in a day." If I heard that once, I heard it a hundred times while I was growing up. I was young and impatient, anxious to reach the goals I felt were important. But there was always this irksome reminder that good things take time and great things take even longer.

Now, however, at long last, I am discovering that stuff about Rome is true. And Paul's words to the century-one Christians who lived there are also truer than ever: "But if we hope for what we do not see, with perseverance we wait eagerly for it" (Rom. 8:25).

Four words jump out at me as I chew on that thought—"we hope . . . we wait." And sandwiched between—"what we do not see"—are the things that take so long. Several examples flash across my mind.

Rearing children. Few processes require more patience. Time and again we parents repeat cautions or instructions until we are blue in the face. We wonder if our words will ever sink in.

So "we hope . . . we wait." Take it by faith—one day you'll find that it sank in . . . and you'll be so glad you persevered.

Accepting defeats. Ours is a winner-oriented world. But isn't it strange that the best lessons are invariably learned from defeat? Pain remains a strict but faithful teacher, and the crucible produces much more character than waving the winner's flag. We know that theoretically. But let some defeat hit us squarely in the chops, and we drop like a two-ton anchor. Job's question—"Shall we indeed accept good from God and not accept adversity?"—seems to take a lifetime to answer with "yes, we willingly accept both" (Job 2:10).

And so—"we hope . . . we wait."

Appreciating aging. I am amused at the extent to which some folks will go to hide or deny the presence of age. Now, I'm all for keeping one's mind young and body strong and perceptions keen, but the last time I checked, the Scriptures honored age and spoke of gray hair with respect. Besides, it means we are all that much nearer to seeing our Lord face to face . . . a truth for which "we hope . . . we wait."

The good news is that in the process we're gaining wisdom.

And so, fellow Romans, we're in it together . . . we keep hoping and we keep waiting.

Whether you're rearing children or accepting defeat or simply facing the truth that you're getting older, take heart! Better still, relax! You, like ancient Rome, are still being built.

BEING NORMAL

❧ *Ephesians 4:1–7* ❧

*E*ver felt weird because you were "normal"? I remember the first time I had that feeling. I was a teenager surrounded by other teenagers in a testimony meeting. One girl, with tears running down her face, told of an alcoholic father who beat her mother almost every weekend. She described how she would hide in the closet lest she become a target of his drunken rage. Then she told how her friend at school had led her to Christ.

I sat very still. My dad didn't drink, nor had I ever hidden from him or seen him hit my mother. And the only time I'd ever heard him swear was when we had a flat on the way to our two-week vacation at my granddad's cottage.

After the girl sat down, a guy stood up and talked about how he had spent a couple days in jail the past summer for shoplifting.

And then another girl stood up. She looked "fast" (my mother's term)—too much makeup, teased hair, big earrings. In between two dozen "uhs" she struggled to admit that she had gotten pregnant and her folks had kicked her out.

Me? Peace was my everyday partner. I thought everyone had good meals, a comfortable bed, and a happy, harmonious family. Not until I joined the marines several years later did I realize my life was the exception rather than the rule.

Today, however, the "abnormal" is considered the norm. You're a freak unless you've got a ton of trash to unload. If you are not recovering from something, addicted to something, or a victim of something, you feel like I felt sitting in that testimony meeting.

Question: Is there a place where you can feel normal being "normal"? Or, if you're still struggling with something, still trying to come to terms with some heartrending problem, is there a place where you won't feel "weird"?

Well, there should be, and it should be the local church—the Body of Christ. The church is a place for young and old, single and married, broken or healing, happy or sad, truck driver or brain surgeon, student or retiree, saint or seeker, you name it.

Whether we are normal or nearly normal or hoping someday to be normal, we belong. Whatever our situation, our status, our struggle, or our style, we are all looking for the magnificent truths of God, for genuine Christian fellowship and togetherness.

In the Body of Christ we are all the same: forgiven, but not perfect.
Except for One.

OUTSTANDING VS. VALUABLE

Philippians 1:1–11

I remember the year NBA stars Michael Jordan and Earvin "Magic" Johnson were vying for the Most Valuable Player award. That year it was incredibly close, and the final tally resulted in Johnson's winning the award by the narrowest of margins. The choice boiled down to an understanding of the definition of "valuable" as opposed to the definition of "outstanding."

As one sportswriter correctly stated, few people would disagree that Jordan was the single most "outstanding" professional basketball player that year. The leading scorer in the NBA, the man was virtually unstoppable. No one would argue that he alone was the reason the Bulls gave the Pistons a run for their money. Jordan was a wizard in sneakers.

In spite of all this, however, Jordan wasn't voted MVP. Why? Because the MVP not only takes into consideration superb individual performance but also the ability to inspire and involve one's teammates, encouraging and enabling them to excel.

In thinking about this, it occurs to me that the ranks of Christianity include a few "superstars"—extremely capable women and men who have been appointed and anointed by God to occupy significant roles of responsibility. As significant as these outstanding folks may be, however, the greater award goes to the most valuable—those individuals who may not be as impressive or as popular or even as capable on their own, but who can inspire and involve others on the team. Whenever they are engaged in the action, good things happen.

Let me suggest at least eight qualities needed to be valuable:

Initiative—being a self-starter with contagious energy

Vision—seeing beyond the obvious, claiming new objectives

Unselfishness—releasing the controls and the glory

Teamwork—involving, encouraging, and supporting others

Faithfulness—hanging in there, in season and out

Enthusiasm—bringing affirmation, excitement to a task

Discipline—modeling great character regardless of the odds

Confidence—representing security, faith, and determination

Will you accept the challenge of focusing on being a valuable team player?

What qualities do you value and why?

HYPOCRISY'S HIDDEN HORRORS

❧ *Romans 7:14–25* ❧

*I*n his November 11, 1942, report on the war to the British House of Commons, Winston Churchill referred to "the soft underbelly of the Axis." While half the world was intimidated by the powerful blitzkrieg style of Nazi warfare, the perceptive prime minister focused on the other side—the hidden side: the insecurity, the lack of character, the insanity behind the public image of the German dictator. Adolf Hitler may have seemed strong to his adoring public and the goosestepping soldiers who proudly wore their führer's swastika. But the pudgy, cigar-smoking resident of 10 Downing Street was neither impressed nor frightened. He knew it was only a matter of time before the corruption lurking within exposed the soft underbelly of "Corporal Hitler."

Mark Twain used another word picture to convey a similar thought: "Everyone is a moon, and has a dark side which he never shows to anybody."

This dark side can exist for years behind carefully guarded masks.

Most of us remember the Watergate scandal. Like me, many firmly resisted the thought of corruption in the Oval Office till the very end. Such compromise and corruption were unthinkable. As time passed and the truth emerged, however, the soft underbelly of Richard Nixon came to light. Conversations with those who were there at the time and participated in the cover-up and books documenting those events forced me to accept what I once denied.

Life magazine's feature article on Elvis Presley in June 1990 was yet another reminder of how much difference there can be between image and reality. Appropriately titled "Down at the End of Lonely Street," the documented account of how the man existed in private toward the end of his life was nothing short of shocking. The handsome, seemingly happy-go-lucky performer, whose smile and wink melted hearts the world over, existed in a nightmare world of depression, despair, and massive doses of drugs.

The lesson in all this is obvious: The safest route to follow is Authenticity Avenue, walled on either side by Accountability and Vulnerability. The alternate route dead-ends at Lonely Street, whose bleak scenery is best stated in a verse from the ancient Book of Numbers: "be sure your sin will find you out" (32:23). Haunting thought, but oh, so true. I cannot explain how or why, I only know that rattling skeletons don't stay in closets . . . lies don't remain private . . . affairs don't stay secret. It's only a matter of time.

Hidden works of darkness always come to light.

UNCROSSABLE RIVERS OF LIFE

❧ *Luke 18:27* ❧

*W*e often find ourselves bogging down in our spiritual growth simply because the challenges before us look absolutely impossible. Such frustrations are not new. Jeremiah tells us: "Ah Lord God! Behold, Thou hast made the heavens and the earth by Thy great power and by Thine outstretched arm! Nothing is too difficult for Thee" (Jer. 32:17).

Do you realize that whatever thing or things you're calling "impossibilities" could be superimposed over what God says is "nothing" to Him? Nothing!

Close your eyes for a moment. I want you to think about that which seems most impossible. Nothing is impossible with God. That includes your uncrossable river, your mountain, any impossibility. Is it your business? Or your school? Or your marriage? How about keeping the house clean, keeping up with the wash, having a ministry with others, or healing strained relationships with people? Will you ask the Lord to handle that specific impossibility, and then leave it with Him in a faith that simply will not doubt?

Do that right now . . . please!

Remember, the things impossible with men are possible with God.

YOU CAN MAKE A DIFFERENCE

❧ *Mark 6* ❧

*O*verwhelming odds can make cowards of us all. I remember the first time I felt overwhelmed regarding ministry in a vast arena. My life had been quiet and manageable. From my birthplace in a south Texas country town, I moved with my family to Houston, where we lived through my high school years. Our home was small and secure. After marriage, a hitch in the corps, and seminary, Cynthia and I became involved in ministries that were like our past . . . small, pleasant, and fulfilling. Our children were small, our lives were relaxed and rather simple, and our scope of God's work was quite comfortable.

The call to Fullerton, California, in 1971 changed all that. In fact, it was as the plane descended over Los Angeles when we were coming to candidate that I got this overwhelming feeling. I looked out the little window and watched as mile after mile of houses and freeways and buildings passed beneath us. I tried to imagine ministering to this sprawling metropolis of never-ending humanity. I thought, How can I possibly get my arms around this monstrous task? What can I do to reach the multiple millions in Southern California?

Suddenly, God gently reminded me, as He does to this day: *I will never reach them all— that is humanly impossible. But I am responsible for those I come in contact with, and with God's help, I will make a difference in their lives.*

I stopped paying attention to the enormity of the impossible and started pouring my time and energy into the possible—the people and the place where God had called me and my family. Call my vision limited if you will, but it has made all the difference in my peace of mind. I cannot do it all . . . I cannot get my arms around the vast boundaries of our region (no one can!), but I am able to touch those who come into the scope of my "radar screen." Peace of mind comes in knowing that in at least their lives, my touch can make a difference, even if it is only one here and another there.

One person cannot beat the odds. There will always be more to reach than time or energy or commitment can provide. But the truth is that each one of us can touch a few. How wrong we would be to stop helping anyone because we cannot help everyone.

Don't panic. Count on the Lord to honor and multiply even your smallest efforts. Last time I checked, He was still rewarding faithfulness.

Ignore the odds. Even though you cannot do everything, you can do something
You may be only one, but you can still make a difference. So make a difference.

THINK IT OVER

❧❧❧

*C*enturies ago a little boy found himself in the midst of a vast crowd of people—larger than any group he'd ever seen. He had come out of curiosity, having heard that a man named Jesus was nearby.

Not knowing how far he would have to travel or how long he would be gone, the boy had packed a small lunch for himself, a couple of small fish and some bread.

Suddenly a man tapped the lad on the shoulder and asked what he had in his hand. And the next thing the boy knew, his lunch was feeding over five thousand people!

Once Jesus got hold of the boy's simple meal there was no limit to what He could make of it.

Feeling a little overwhelmed? Starting to get the idea that you're surrounded by folks getting giant things done while it's all you can do to make it through the week? Maybe you've fallen into a well of comparison, and you're drowning in discouragement because "compared to____" you're not making nearly the difference he or she is.

To all who feel overwhelmed or who are tempted to take a much too critical look at their lives and feel insignificant . . . take heart! Do what you can!

A HOPE TRANSFUSION

❧ *Job 19:25–26* ❧

*E*aster and hope are synonymous. That special day never arrives without its refreshing reminder that there is life beyond this one. True life. Eternal life. Glorious life. Those who live on what we might call "the outskirts of hope" need a transfusion. Easter gives it.

I think of all those who are battling the dread disease of cancer. Talk about people living on "the outskirts." They fight the gallant battle, endure the horrible reactions of chemotherapy, and anxiously await the results of the next checkup.

And then there are those who still grieve over the loss of a mate, a child, a parent, or a friend. Death has come like a ruthless thief, snatching away a treasured presence, leaving only memories. What is missing?

Hope. Hope has died. There is nothing like Easter to bring hope back to life. Easter has its own anthems. Easter has its own scriptures. And Easter has its own proclamation: "He is not here, for He has risen, just as He said" (Matt. 28:6).

When Christians gather in houses of worship and lift their voices in praise to the risen Redeemer, the demonic hosts of hell and their damnable prince of darkness are temporarily paralyzed.

When pastors stand and declare the unshakable, undeniable facts of Jesus' bodily resurrection and the assurance of ours as well, the empty message of skeptics and cynics is momentarily silenced.

Our illnesses don't seem nearly so final.

Our fears fade and lose their grip.

Our grief over those who have gone on is diminished.

Our desire to press on in spite of the obstacles is rejuvenated.

Our identity as Christians is strengthened as we stand in the lengthening shadows of saints down through the centuries, who have always answered back in antiphonal voice: "He is risen, indeed!"

A hope transfusion awaits us. It happens every year on Easter Sunday.

Alleluia!

Jesus lives and so shall we! Death, where is your victory?

IN YOUR SPRING BONNET

❧ *1 Samuel 16:7; Matthew 5:5* ❧

*T*he clothing industry makes a killing every spring when people come out from under rocks to wrap themselves in new Spring threads, shoes, and hats. It won't be any different this year, I'm sure. Kids will be dragged from store to store as their little frames are fitted with Sunday stuff.

I've been through the apparel torture chamber too many years to ignore the obvious: Most boys never outgrow their shrug-of-the-shoulder attitude toward new clothes . . . and most girls will forever maintain their ecstatic delight for such. Why? Now that's a question worth some thought.

I'm of the opinion that most men buy their clothes for purely functional purposes. A suit of clothes hides your underwear, keeps you warm (or cool), and provides pockets for cash, keys, and a handkerchief. But when a woman buys a garment, she is usually looking for something that will change or enhance her.

Now wait! Before you reject that, listen to what Sydney J. Harris, the syndicated newspaper columnist, says: "What a woman wants in a new dress, or suit, or coat is another facet to her personality."

Frankly, this helps explain three mysteries men often wrestle with: 1) How can a woman stand before a closet full of garments and say, "I don't have anything to wear!"? 2) Why do women's clothes seem to be made in such a flimsy fashion with loosely held snaps and hooks? (As planned, they are not supposed to last eight to ten years!) 3) Why is a woman so distraught when she sees another woman wearing the same garment?

Well, so much for my philosophizing. Maybe it will help some husbands to be more tolerant . . . and perhaps it will help some wives not to feel guilty about having fun in the department store this week. Relax! If clothing helps express another facet of the real you, go to it!

Simon Peter was married too. So he knew what he was talking about when he wrote a reminder to the ladies: "Your beauty should not come from outward adornment. . . . Instead, it should be that of your inner self, the unfading beauty of a gentle and quiet spirit, which is of great worth in God's sight" (1 Pet. 3:3–4).

We cannot substitute outer garb for inner godliness.

Hope in Dark Places

❧ *Isaiah 53* ❧

I love music! Choral music, instrumental music, popular music, classical music . . . folk tunes, ballads, country western and bluegrass . . . the patriotic and romantic. For me, music is a must.

Like you, I have my favorite hymns—the ones that hold some special meaning for me or evoke grand and vivid memories of significant events. Invariably, those things pass in mental review as I become "lost in wonder, love, and praise" in my worship.

While thinking of the glorious message of the Resurrection recently, I found myself suddenly overwhelmed with the music that has accompanied the celebration of the empty tomb for centuries. Various scenes crossed my mind. I saw myself as a lad holding my mother's hand in a little Baptist church in South Texas. I remembered a sunrise service on the island of Okinawa when I fought back tears of loneliness. Another hymn took me to Chafer Chapel on the campus of Dallas Seminary, where 350 young men preparing for ministry stood side by side and sang heartily of the Savior we'd soon be proclaiming.

During my nostalgic pilgrimage, at each geographical spot revisited, I gave God thanks that Job's words were mine as well: "I know that my redeemer liveth" (Job 19:25, KJV).

Gloria Gaither's familiar lyrics then brought me into the seventies: "And because He lives, I can face tomorrow. Because He lives, all fear is gone." It is Jesus Christ—the miraculously resurrected Son of God—who remains the Object of our worship, the Subject of our praise.

That hope has kept believers strong in the darkest places.

"Thus far did I come, burdened with my sin. Nor could ought ease the grief that I was in 'til I came hither. What a place is this! Must here be the beginning of my bliss? Must here the burden fall from off my back? Must here the chains that bound it to me crack? Blest cross! Blest sepulchre! Blest rather be, the Man who was put to shame for me" (John Bunyan).

RISEN, INDEED!

🍃 *Luke 24; John 20* 🍃

*N*o need to prolong the story. Or complicate it. Or embellish it. Or try to explain it. Or defend it. Just declare it. The facts speak for themselves.

Jesus of Nazareth said He would "suffer . . . be killed, and be raised up on the third day" (Matt. 16:21).

Betrayed by Judas, He was seized, placed under arrest, pushed hurriedly through several trials (all of them illegal), and declared guilty . . . first of "blasphemy," next of "treason" (Luke 22:70–23:24).

Alone and forsaken, He endured the torture of scourging, the humiliation of insults and mockery, and the agony of that walk to Golgotha (Mark 15:15–22).

The horrors of crucifixion followed, leaving Him suspended for six excruciating hours . . . the last three of which were spent in eerie darkness that "fell over the whole land" (Mark 15:33).

By three o'clock that afternoon He uttered His final words. "Father, into Thy hands I commit My spirit" (Luke 23:46).

Then . . . He died (Matt. 27:50; Mark 15:37; Luke 23:46; John 19:30).

Two men, Joseph of Arimathea and Nicodemus, took Him down from the cross, prepared the body for burial, and placed it "in the garden in a new tomb" (John 19:38–41).

The chief priests and the Pharisees had the tomb secured by a large stone, a seal set on the stone, and a body of men sent to guard the site (Matt. 27:62–66).

Guarded and sealed, the tomb was silent as He remained lifeless, untouched, and unseen until the early hours of the morning on the first day of the week (Luke 24:1–2).

Before dawn a miracle occurred. Bodily, silently, victoriously, He arose from death. In resurrected form, He passed through the stone, leaving the mummylike wrappings still intact (John 20:1–8).

When astonished people visited the site that morning, they found the stone rolled away and the body gone. Then they were asked by angels, "Why do you seek the living One among the dead? He is not here, but He has risen" (Luke 24:5–6). Christ is risen, indeed!

"And when I saw Him, I fell at His feet as a dead man. And He laid His right hand upon me, saying, 'Do not be afraid; I am the first and the last, and the living One; and I was dead, and behold, I am alive forevermore'" (Rev. 1:17–18).

ENCOURAGEMENT

❧ *Hebrews 10:24–25* ❧

*W*hen you stop to analyze the concept, "encourage" takes on new meaning. It's the act of inspiring others with renewed courage, spirit, or hope. When we encourage others we spur them on, we stimulate and affirm them.

I do not care how influential or secure or mature a person may appear to be, genuine encouragement never fails to help. Most of us need massive doses of it as we slug it out in the trenches. But we are usually too proud to admit it. Unfortunately, this pride is as prevalent among members of God's family as it is on the streets of the world.

It is helpful to remember the distinction between appreciation and affirmation. We appreciate what a person does, but we affirm who a person is. Appreciation comes and goes because it is usually related to something someone accomplishes. Affirmation goes deeper. It is directed to the person himself or herself. While encouragement would encompass both, the rarer of the two is affirmation.

All of us need encouragement—somebody to believe in us. To reassure and reinforce us. To help us pick up the pieces and go on. To provide us with increased determination in spite of the odds.

Even when we don't earn the right to be appreciated
we can still be encouraged and affirmed
Encourage someone today!

DEEP-WATER FAITH

❧ *Luke 4–7* ❧

*E*dith, a mother of eight, came home from a neighbor's house one afternoon and noticed that things seemed a little too quiet. Curious, she peered through the screen door and saw five of her children huddled together. As she crept closer, trying to discover the center of their attention, she could not believe her eyes. Smack dab in the middle of the circle were five baby skunks!

Edith screamed at the top of her voice, "Quick, children . . . run!"

Each kid grabbed a skunk and ran.

Some days are like that, aren't they? Pressures and problems tend to multiply.

Jesus, the Son of God, was not immune from pressures when He was among us. At one point, He sought a place of rest and solitude. Spotting a fishing boat at the water's edge, He stepped in and sat down and "began teaching the multitudes from the boat." When He had finished speaking, He told Simon Peter, "Put out into the deep water and let down your nets for a catch."

Simon said, "Master, we worked hard all night and caught nothing, but at Your bidding I will let down the nets" (Luke 5:4–5).

No one can criticize Peter for being reluctant. He'd been fishing all night and caught zilch. But he wisely surrendered. "And when they had done this, they enclosed a great quantity of fish . . . so that they began to sink" (5:6–7).

When the Master of heaven, earth, sea, and sky calls the shots, things happen . . . which explains Peter's explosive reaction: "But when Simon Peter saw that, he fell down at Jesus' feet, saying, 'Depart from me, for I am a sinful man, O Lord!'" (v. 8).

Then Jesus said to him, "Do not fear, from now on you will be catching men" (v. 10).

Once they heard His invitation, they literally dropped everything. "And when they had brought their boats to land, they left everything and followed Him" (v. 11). Amazing, isn't it? They abandoned their nets, boats, business, and future dreams. Everything!

Perhaps it is time for you to take a mental boat trip out into the deeper waters of faith. And when Jesus says, "Follow Me," do it. Unlike Edith's kids, drop everything and run.

Is your life full of appointments, activities, hassles, and hurry? Are you finding all your security in your work . . . your own achievements? What is your "everything"?

THINK IT OVER

🐝🐝🐝

*W*hy should we be willing to drop everything and follow Jesus Christ? And what happens when we do? I can think of at least six reasons:

1. Jesus chooses not to minister to others all alone. He could, but he deliberately chooses not to. He could have rowed that boat Himself: He could have dropped those nets over the side Himself. He certainly could have pulled up the nets choked with fish. Instead, He had the disciples do it. And He specifically stated, "From now on you will be catching men."

2. Jesus uses the familiar to do the incredible. He came to their turf (lake, boat), their place of work (fishing), and had them use their skills (nets). In a familiar setting, He made them aware of incredible possibilities.

3. Jesus moves us from the safety of the seen to the risks of the unseen. He led them "out into the deep water" where nobody could touch bottom before He commanded, "Let down your nets." Nothing spectacular occurs in shallow water.

4. Jesus proves the potential by breaking our nets and filling our boats. When God's hand is on a situation, nets break, eyes bulge, deck planks groan, and boats almost sink. It's His way of putting the potential on display.

5. Jesus conceals His surprises until we follow His leading. Everything was business as usual on the surface. Boats didn't have a halo; nets didn't tingle at their touch; the lake water didn't glow; a chorus of angelic voices didn't thunder from the sky. No. The divinely arranged surprise came only after they dropped the nets. Remember, it wasn't until he followed Jesus' instructions that Peter changed "Master" to "Lord."

6. Jesus reveals His objective to those who release their security. He could read their willingness in their faces. Then—and only then—did He tell them they would be engaged in "catching men." And guess what—they jumped at the chance!

WANTED: THINKERS

❧ 2 *Peter* 3 ❧

*E*ntertainment is everything today. So important, in fact, that we have television programs and magazines devoted solely to the subject. All of which makes it real difficult to be committed to substance rather than the superficial. This includes reading widely, probing deeply, seeing with discernment, rejecting the false, learning the facts. In short, thinking!

Critic Neil Postman, author of *Amusing Ourselves to Death,* correctly argues that television is converting us from a "word-centered culture" to an "image-centered culture." Even the news broadcasts are under increasing pressure to entertain more than inform.

Ted Koppel, the penetrating host of *Nightline,* calls this "Vannatizing" (after Vanna White, *Wheel of Fortune's* celebrity hostess, whose role on the highly rated game show is a matter of looking cute and saying "hello" and "bye-bye"). Toddler talk. Don't think, just look. Don't question, relax. "There's not much room on television for complexity," says Koppel. "We now communicate with everyone and say absolutely nothing."

I can handle "Vannatizing" a game show. But when it comes to our faith, "Vannatizing" is intolerable. When will we ever learn that sacred things cannot be staged and remain sacred? What will it take to finally convince us of what Muggeridge stated so well, "You cannot present an authentic message by means of an inauthentic medium"?

My hope rests in the remnant of believers who still believe in thinking . . . who have an insatiable hunger for learning . . . who appreciate the hard work that goes into knowing where they stand theologically and yet knowing where they need to bend practically.

What I'm pushing for is more who know what they believe, and why. Folks who can spot phony baloney before it hits the headlines . . . who know some guru is spouting heresy even though his promises sound inviting. Folks who don't wait to be told every move to make, who are challenged within to grow, to study, to learn.

Such discernment never comes automatically. Thinking is hard work, but, oh, so rewarding. And so essential for survival.

Furthermore, you won't feel quite so intimidated the next time some guy who just heard you're a Christian leans over and asks why. Your defense will make better sense.

If you have the opportunity, take a course at a nearby Bible school, Christian college, or seminary. Or perhaps your church offers some in-depth study electives.
You will gain a broader base of knowledge, a wider scope of awareness,
and a deeper commitment to truth.

EXPECT THE UNEXPECTED

❧ *Psalm 8* ❧

*M*ost folks I know like things to stay as they are. You've heard all the sayings that reveal our preference for the familiar: Leave well enough alone. I don't like surprises. If it ain't broke, don't fix it. Stay with a sure thing.

We admire pioneers . . . so long as we can just read about them, not finance their journeys. We applaud explorers . . . but not if it means we have to load up and travel with them. Creative ideas are fine . . . but "don't get carried away," we warn. Plans that involve risks prompt worst-case scenarios from the lips of most who wait in the wings.

Don't misunderstand. Just because the plan is creative is no guarantee that stuff won't backfire. On the contrary, surprises and disappointments await anyone who ventures into the unknown.

But the fact is, the alternative is worse. Can anything be worse than boredom? Is there an existence less challenging and more draining than the predictable? I don't think so.

More importantly, God doesn't seem to think so either. As I read through the biblical accounts of His working in the lives of His people, the single thread that ties most of the stories together is the unexpected. Need some examples?

After aging Abraham finally got the son God had promised to him, after he cultivated a father-son bond closer than words could describe, after fixing his hopes on all that God had said He would do through that boy to whom Sarah gave birth, God told Abraham to sacrifice Isaac on the mountain.

Even though the prophet Hosea had lived righteously before his Lord and had been faithful to his wife, Gomer, she left their home and family and became a harlot in the streets of Israel. God's instructions? Go find her and remarry her.

When it came time for God to send His Son to earth, He did not send Him to the palace of some mighty king. He was conceived in the womb of an unwed mother—a virgin!—who lived in the lowly village of Nazareth.

In choosing those who would represent Christ and establish His church, God picked some of the most unusual individuals imaginable: unschooled fishermen, a tax collector(!), a mystic, a doubter, and a former Pharisee who had persecuted Christians. He continued to pick some very unusual persons down through the ages. In fact, He seems to delight in such surprising choices to this very day.

So, let God be God. Expect the unexpected.

God likes surprises. Breaking molds is His specialty.

SATANIC RIP-OFF

❧ 1 Peter 5:8–9 ❧

A basketball fan at the Portland airport awaited the arrival of the Trailblazers following a victory over the Lakers and attempted to scalp a couple of tickets to the next game. As the shyster wormed through the crowd, he located a well-dressed man who listened to his offer.

"How much?" asked the gentleman.

"One hundred fifty bucks," the scalper replied under his breath.

"Do you realize you're talking to a plainclothes officer of the law?" the man asked. "I'm going to turn you in, fella."

Suddenly the seller began to backpedal. He talked about how large a family he had . . . how much they needed him . . . how he'd never do it again.

"Just hand over the tickets and we'll call it even," said the well-dressed man. "And I'd better never catch you here again!"

But the worst was yet to come. The man was no officer at all. Just a quick-thinking guy who used a little ingenuity to rip off two choice seats to the next playoff game (as he anonymously admitted in the local newspaper several days later).

Satan's strategy is just as ingenious and effective. For example, he hears what we hear from the pulpit on Sunday morning, and in the process he plans his approach. He baits the rip-off trap, then sets it up with just the right hair trigger:

An argument in the car after church over where to go for dinner.

Preoccupation with some worrisome problem during the message.

A personality conflict with another church member.

Silently Satan prowls around, camouflaged in the garb of our physical habits and our mental laziness, seeking to devour. Then, at the precise moment when it will have its greatest impact, he snatches away the very truth we need the most.

Remember that next Sunday morning. Prepare your heart and mind before the service, girding yourself with the armor of God.

Don't let Satan rip you off.

In case you question the effectiveness of Satan's strategy, think back just two or three weeks. Maybe even one will do. Do you remember the sermon title? How about the outline? Do you recall a couple of applicable principles? You see, his plan is working brilliantly.

RECHARGE YOUR BATTERY

❧ *Acts 1* ❧

*M*orale and vision fade fast. This is especially true when the battle is raging. Or when the pace is blistering. Or when the task is boring. Many war veterans tell spine-tingling stories pulsating with heroism and enthusiasm. Without exception, such remarkable acts of bravery were accomplished because the troops felt fresh surges of determination that caused the odds against them to pale into insignificance. Those same veterans can tell of other occasions when the battle was lost due to low morale and fuzzy vision.

Optimism, courage, and faithfulness feed on high morale. The ability to push on, alone if necessary, requires clear vision. In order for goals to be reached, there has to be a stirring up from within . . . a spark that lights the fire of hope, telling us to "Get at it" when our minds are just about to convince us with "Aw, what's the use?" It's called motivation.

Coaches are great at this. We've all seen it happen. The team is getting stomped. They can't get anything going during the entire first half. But then . . . magic!

Back in the locker room, away from the fans, the coach and team meet head-on. What results is nothing short of phenomenal. The players are transformed through the inspiration of a few minutes with one who is a master at building morale and clearing vision.

Christians should have no difficulty identifying with soldiers in the field or athletes in a game. Our ability to accomplish what is expected of us is directly linked to our morale and vision. What we need is a charge of renewal. God understands that. His people have been that way since the beginning.

For Abraham, the place of renewal was Bethel, where he "built an altar to the LORD and called upon the name of the LORD" (Gen. 12:8). For Moses and the Israelites, it was the tabernacle in the wilderness, where God's glory rested. For the Twelve, it was their frequent meetings with Jesus.

All of us need such times and places of renewal, when our morale and vision are reignited and our spiritual batteries are recharged . . . when the Spirit of God can do His masterful work of motivation. When that occurs, a burst of new energy returns and we're back on our feet, winning a second-half victory on the same turf that had earlier spelled defeat.

You may need your inner battery recharged.

We cannot deliver the goods if our heart is heavier than the load.

THE PHYSICAL BODY

❧ 1 Thessalonians 4:1–8 ❧

*V*olumes are written about the mind, our emotional makeup, our "inner man," the soul, the spirit and the spiritual dimension. But by comparison, very little is being said by evangelicals today about the physical body.

- We are to present our bodies as living sacrifices to God (Rom. 12:1).
- We are instructed not to yield any part of our bodies as instruments of unrighteousness to sin (Rom. 6:12–13).
- Our bodies are actually "members of Christ" (1Cor. 6:15).
- Our bodies are actually "temples" literally inhabited by the Holy Spirit (1Cor. 6:19).
- We are expected to "glorify God" in our bodies (1 Cor. 6:20).
- We are to become students of our bodies, knowing how to control them in honor (1 Thess. 4:4).

You see, these bodies of ours can easily lead us off course. It isn't that the body itself is evil; it's just that it possesses any number of appetites that are ready to respond to the surrounding stimuli . . . all of which are terribly appealing and temporarily satisfying.

Let me ask you: Do you know your body? Are you aware of the things that weaken your control of it? Have you stopped to consider the danger zones and how to stay clear of them?

Personal purity is an attainable goal.

WHAT ABOUT FIDELITY?

❧ *Proverbs 6:27–29, 32–33* ❧

I just returned from our nation's capital where I was privileged to spend time with many of the highest ranking officers in the military. If you have ever wondered if there is anyone in the upper echelon of the military who loves Christ, wonder no longer. Many of these men and women are magnificent models of strong Christian commitment who frequently put their faith on the line.

While sitting around a table one morning, the subject of moral purity surfaced. They spoke of the importance of an officer's having a clean record and maintaining strong character traits if he or she hoped to be trusted in larger realms and promoted to higher ranks. Their commitment to personal integrity was expressed so spontaneously and sincerely.

As I listened to them, I was humiliated to think that a standard of high moral character was still of paramount importance among military officers while within the ranks of the clergy an epidemic of impurity rages.

As Christian leaders, we need to reaffirm our commitment to moral purity and to private lives that are absolutely free of secret sins. While forgiveness continues to be the pulse-beat of a grace-oriented ministry, a firm commitment to holiness remains vital. Those who adopt a deceptive, compromising life of hypocrisy are responsible for the damage that occurs when they are found out. Nor are the consequences erased, even though they may repent and seek the Lord's and others' forgiveness.

Often, we are too quick to breeze past the damage that has been done, attempting to hurry the process of forgiveness at the expense of the restoration process. A contrite heart has no expectations and makes no demands; it acknowledges that the deception and the extent of continued sin result in the continued forfeiture of many of the privileges that were once enjoyed. Please read that again. If you've gotten soft on this issue, stop and read the daily reading suggested above. Don't try to explain these verses away. They mean exactly what they say.

The issue here is not a lack of forgiveness; it's the faulty thinking that forgiveness is synonymous with the returning of all rights and privileges.

Never has the truth of Peter's words resounded more clearly: "It is time for judgment to begin with the household of God" (1 Pet. 4:17).

As believers, we need to reaffirm our commitment to moral purity and to private lives that are absolutely free of secret sins.

THINK IT OVER

🙚🙚 🙚🙚

*N*athan then said to David, "You are the man! Thus says the LORD God of Israel, 'It is I who anointed you king over Israel and it is I who delivered you from the hand of Saul. I also gave you your master's house and your master's wives into your care, and I gave you the house of Israel and Judah; and if that had been too little, I would have added to you many more things like these! "Why have you despised the word of the LORD by doing evil in His sight? You have struck down Uriah the Hittite with the sword, have taken his wife to be your wife, and have killed him with the sword of the sons of Ammon. Now therefore, the sword shall never depart from your house, because you have despised Me and have taken the wife of Uriah the Hittite to be your wife. . . . Indeed you did it secretly, but I will do this thing before all Israel, and under the sun.'"

Then David said to Nathan, "I have sinned against the LORD," And Nathan said to David, "The LORD also has taken away your sin; you shall not die. However, because by this deed you have given occasion to the enemies of the LORD to blaspheme, the child also that is born to you shall surely die" (2 Sam. 12:7–14).

David was "a man after God's own heart." Yet, once he crawled into bed with Uriah's wife on that moonlit spring night, never again did he know all the former joys of close family ties, public trust, or military invincibility.

This wasn't his family's fault or the public's fault or the Philistines' fault or the prophet Nathan's fault. It was David's fault, full-on.

COMPASSION IN SLOW MOTION

❧ *Isaiah 30:1–26* ❧

$\mathcal{T}$he timing is as critical as the involvement. You don't just force your way in. Even if you've got the stuff that's needed . . . even if you hold the piece perfectly shaped to fit the other person's missing part of the puzzle . . . you can't push it into place. You must not try.

You must do the most difficult thing for compassion to do.

You must wait.

Even if there is rebellion? Even if there's rebellion.

Even if sin is occurring? Yes, often even then.

Even if others are suffering and disillusioned and going through the misery of misunderstanding, heartache, and sleepless nights? Believe it or not, yes.

There are times (not always, but often) when the better part of wisdom restrains us from barging in and trying to make someone accept our help. The time isn't right, so we wait.

Even the Lord waits, as when Isaiah reported to the nation whom the Lord called "rebellious children" (Isa. 30:1). These people were rife with shame, reproach, unfaithful alliances, oppression, and a ruthless rejection of God's holy Word. Their unwillingness to repent added insult to injury.

But what was Jehovah's response? Hidden away in the first part of verse 18 is the incredible statement: "Therefore the LORD longs to be gracious to you, and therefore He waits on high to have compassion on you."

Instead of storming into the dark alleys of Judah, screaming "Repent!" and shining bright lights to expose the filthy litter of their disobedience, the Lord tapped His foot, folded His arms . . . and waited. Not even the Lord pushed His way in. He waited until the time was right.

Our Lord would love to piece together the shattered fragments of your life. But He is waiting . . . graciously waiting until the time is right.

Until you are tired of the life you are living . . . until you see it for what it really is.

Until you are weary of coping . . . of taking charge of your own life . . . until you realize the mess you are making of it.

Until you recognize your need for Him.

He's waiting . . .

God's timing is always on time.

JUMPING TO CONCLUSIONS

✌ *Exodus 14–15* ✌

HE OPERA AIN'T OVER . . . 'TIL THE FAT LADY SINGS. It was a banner hung over the wall near the forty-yard line of Texas Stadium. The guys in silver and blue were struggling to stay in the race for the playoffs. So some Cowboy fan, to offer down-home encouragement, had splashed those words on a king-size bedsheet for all America to read. It was his way of saying, "We're hangin' in there, baby. Don't count us out."

Sure is easy to jump to conclusions, isn't it? People who study trends make it their business to manufacture out of their imaginations the proposed (and "inevitable") end result. Pollsters do that too. After sampling 3 percent of our country (or at least they say that's what it equates to), vast and stunning statistics are announced.

Every once in a while it's helpful to remember times when those preening prognosticators wound up with egg on their faces. Like when Truman beat Dewey, and England didn't surrender, and the Communists didn't take over America by 1975.

Yes, at many a turn we have all been tempted to jump to "obvious" conclusions, only to be surprised by a strange curve thrown our way. God is good at that.

Can you recall a few biblical examples?

Like when a young boy, armed with only a sling and a stone, whipped a giant over nine feet tall. Or the time an Egyptian army approaching fast saw the sea open up and the Hebrews walk across. Or how about that dead-end street at Golgotha miraculously opening up at an empty tomb three days later?

Anybody—and I mean anybody—near enough to have witnessed any one of those predicaments would certainly have said, "Curtains . . . the opera is over!"

Unless I miss my guess, a lot of you who are reading this page are backed up against circumstances that seem to spell THE END. Pretty well finished. Apparently over. Your adversary would love for you to assume the worst, to heave a sigh and resign yourself to the depressed feelings that accompany defeat, failure, maximum resentment, and minimum faith.

But take heart. When God is involved, anything can happen. The One who directed David's stone and opened that sea and brought His Son back from the dead takes delight in the incredible.

In other words, don't manufacture conclusions. There are dozens of fat ladies waiting in the wings. And believe me, the opera ain't over!

God delights in mixing up the odds as He alters the obvious
and bypasses the inevitable.

THE BLAME GAME

❧ *1 John 1* ❧

*R*emember comedian Flip Wilson's old line, "Da debil made me do it"? Here was this character who had obviously done something bad. But instead of taking the blame, he pointed an accusing finger at "da debil." Why did we laugh? We weren't just laughing at his hilarious routines; we were laughing at ourselves— at one of our favorite indoor games: The Blame Game. And since he is altogether wicked and invisible and unable to challenge our accusation in audible tones, there's no better scapegoat than old Lucifer himself.

But when this practice becomes a daily habit, it stops being funny and starts being phony. It's when we become escape artists, dodging the responsibility of our own disobedience, that we carry the thing too far. Not just blaming Satan for every evil action, but finding him in every nook and cranny . . . thinking he is the subtle force behind all wicked events and encounters. It's the age-old conspiracy mentality.

There are those, for example, who see and hear the devil in certain types of music. They tell us to play the tapes backwards and we can hear the subliminal satanic message . . . which seems a lot like reading a book in a mirror to detect its evil connotation. Strange. They warn us against Proctor and Gamble because the beard of a face in the tiny logo includes 666. Don't laugh. So many believed this that the company was forced to spend a fortune trying to combat fears of a satanic connection.

You and I know there is a devil and a host of demons. There is an authentic "prince of the power of the air," whose sole goal is to infect and influence with evil. He is on the prowl (1 Pet. 5:8), diabolical in nature and deceptive in method (2 Cor. 11:3). He is responsible for much wickedness, but not all of it—there's also the world and the flesh, remember (1 John 2:15–16). If he cannot get us entrapped in one extreme, where he's an imaginary prankster with horns, pitchfork, and red long johns . . . then it's the other, where he's everywhere, in everything, embodying everyone, and we start listening to music backwards and sniffing out signs of 666 in labels, license plates, and leaders.

C'mon, Christian, let's wise up. We look foolish enough in the eyes of the lost without giving them fuel for the fire. Leave the funny stuff for the comedians and the phony stuff for fanatics. We've got our hands full maintaining a sensible balance on the tightrope of truth. For if there's one thing "da debil" can't stand, it's the truth.

Some people spend so much time looking for what isn't there
that they fail to see what is.

A CHEERFUL HEART

🕮 *Ecclesiastes 3:1–13* 🕮

*E*arthquakes! Prison riots! Economic pressures! Divorce! No jobs! Drugs! Disease! Death! Pretty serious scene, isn't it? Yet that is the emotional environment in which we live. No wonder someone has dubbed this the "aspirin age." Small wonder more of us are not throwing in the towel.

In spite of these bleak surroundings—or perhaps because of—I firmly believe we need a good dose of Solomon's counsel. Listen to David's wisest son: "A joyful heart makes a cheerful face, but when the heart is sad, the spirit is broken. . . . All the days of the afflicted are bad, but a cheerful heart has a continual feast. . . . A joyful heart is good medicine [the Hebrew says, 'causes good healing'], but a broken spirit dries up the bones" (Prov. 15:13, 15; 17:22).

Have you begun to shrivel into a bitter, impatient, critical Christian? The Lord tells us that the solution is simple: "A joyful heart" is what we need . . . and if ever we needed it, it is now.

By a sense of humor I mean that necessary ingredient of wit: those humorous, enjoyable, and delightful expressions or thoughts that lift our spirits and lighten our day. When we lose our ability to laugh—I mean really laugh—life's oppressive assaults confine us to the dark dungeon of defeat.

Personally, I think a healthy sense of humor is determined by at least four abilities:

The ability to laugh at our own mistakes.

The ability to accept justified criticism—and get over it!

The ability to interject (or at least enjoy) wholesome humor when surrounded by a tense, heated situation.

The ability to control those statements that would be unfit—even though they may be funny.

James M. Gray and William Houghton were two great, godly men of the Word. Dr. Houghton writes of an occasion when he and Dr. Gray were praying together. Dr. Gray, though getting up in years, was still interested in being an effective witness and expositor. He concluded his prayer by saying: "And, Lord, keep me cheerful. Keep me from becoming a cranky, old man!"

Let's ask our understanding Father to remind us frequently of the necessity of a cheerful spirit and to give us an appreciation for laughter.

ENOUGH IS ENOUGH

❧ *1 Timothy 6:17–19* ❧

*I*f there were one great message I could deliver to those who struggle with not having an abundance of this world's goods, it would be this simple yet profound premise for happiness: Great wealth is not related to money! It is an attitude of satisfaction coupled with inner peace, plus a day-by-day, moment-by-moment walk with God. Sounds so right, so good, doesn't it? In our world of more, more, more . . . push, push, push . . . grab, grab, grab, this counsel is long overdue. In a word, the secret is contentment.

Contentment is something we must learn. It isn't a trait we're born with. But the question is how?

First, it really helps us to quit striving for more if we read the eternal dimension into today's situation. We entered life empty-handed; we leave it the same way.

Second, it also helps us model contentment if we'll boil life down to its essentials and try to simplify our lifestyle: something to eat, something to wear, and a roof over our heads. Everything beyond that we'd do well to consider as extra.

It's foolish to trust in riches for security and they bring no lasting satisfaction. It is God alone who supplies us "with all things to enjoy" which leads to contentment.

ENDANGERED SPECIES

❧ *Psalm 78* ❧

*R*emember when men were men? Remember when you could tell by looking? Remember when men knew who they were, liked how they were, and didn't want to be anything but what they were?

Remember when it was the men who boxed and wrestled and bragged about how much they could bench press?

Remember when it was the women who wore the makeup, the earrings, and the bikinis?

Remember when it was the men who initiated the contact and took the lead in a relationship, made lifelong commitments, and modeled a masculinity grounded in security and stability?

I'm talking about men who are discerning, decisive, strong hearted, who know where they are going and are confident enough in themselves (and their God) to get them there. Men who aren't afraid to take the lead, to stand tall, firm in their principles, even when the going gets rough.

Such qualities not only inspire the respect of women, they also engender healthy admiration among younger men and boys who hunger for heroes. We need clear-thinking, hard-working, straight-talking men who, while tender, thoughtful, and loving, don't feel the need to ask permission for taking charge.

Over the last three decades we have seen a major assault on masculinity. The results are well represented in the arts, the media, the world of fashion, and among those who have become the heroes of our young people.

On the heels of a bloody Civil War, Josiah Holland wrote a passionate prayer on behalf of our country. It begins, "God, give us men. . . ." But the truth is, God doesn't give a nation men; He gives us boys. Baby boys, adolescent boys, impressionable boys, who need to know what becoming a man is all about. God's plan is still as He designed it at creation. And it starts in the home.

Men, are you modeling manhood according to God's Word?
Moms and dads, are you raising your sons to be authentically masculine?
If not, why not? Think it over!

THINK IT OVER

❧❧ ❧❧

*F*uture Shock author Alvin Toffler saw all this happening in his 1980 book, *The Third Wave,* where he announced

> . . . the role system that held industrial civilization together is in crisis. This we see most dramatically in the struggle to redefine sex roles. In the women's movement, in the demands for the legalization of homosexuality, in the spread of unisex fashions, we see a continual blurring of traditional expectations for the sexes.

Toffler is on target but too soft. The separate distinction of male and female is not merely a "traditional expectation"; it's a biblical precept.

"Male and female He created them" (Gen. 1:27).

And it isn't simply a "role system that held industrial civilization together." It is a major foundational block upon which any healthy civilization rests.

When male and female roles get sufficiently blurred, confusion and chaos replace decency and order. When effeminate men begin to flood the landscape, God's longsuffering reaches the length of its tether, ushering in the severest judgment imaginable . . . a la Sodom and Gomorrah.

Romans 1:24–27 is still in the Book.

MAKING MELODY

✺ *Psalm 98* ✺

*G*od's sharp sword stabbed me deeply recently as I was on a scriptural hunt in the Ephesian letter. I was searching for a verse totally unrelated to the one that sliced its way into me. It was another of those verses I feel sorry for (like John 3:17 and 1 John 1:10—look 'em up). This was Ephesians 5:19: "speaking to one another in psalms and hymns and spiritual songs, singing and making melody with your heart to the Lord."

Everybody knows 5:18, where we are told "be filled with the Spirit." But have you ever noticed that verse 18 ends with a comma, not a period? The next verse describes the very first result of being under the Spirit's control: WE SING!

Now let's go further. Ephesians 5 never once refers to a church building. I mention that because we Christians have so centralized our singing that we seldom engage in it once we walk away from a service. Stop and think. Did you sing on the way home last Sunday night? How about Monday, when you drove to work . . . or around the supper table . . . or Tuesday as you dressed for the day? Chances are, you didn't even sing before or after you had your time with the Lord any day of the week. Why?

The Spirit-filled saint is a song-filled saint! Animals can't sing. Neither can pews or pulpits or Bibles or buildings—only you. And your melody is broadcasted right into heaven, where God's antenna is always receptive . . . where the soothing strains of your song are always appreciated.

- Let me offer five suggestions:
- Whenever and whatever you sing, concentrate on the words.
- Make a definite effort to add one or two songs to your day.
- Sing often with a friend or members of your family. It helps break down all sorts of invisible barriers.
- Blow the dust off your tape or CD player and put on some beautiful music around the house. And don't forget to sing along and add your own harmony and "special" effects.
- Never mind how beautiful or pitiful you may sound. You are not auditioning for the choir; you're making melody with your heart. SING OUT!

If you listen closely when you're through, you may hear the hosts of heaven shouting for joy. Then again, it might be your neighbor . . . screaming for relief.

Sing loud enough to drown out those defeating thoughts that clamor for attention.

SPY IN THE SKY

🕮 *Psalm 19* 🕮

*L*et me introduce you to the Hubble Space Telescope (affectionately dubbed "ST"). Says one authority: "It's not hyperbole to say that ST is as much an improvement over the most powerful existing telescope as Galileo's first spyglass in 1609 was over the human eye. . . . It could bring into focus the stars on an American flag at a distance of 3,000 miles. ST will record images . . . via electronic light collectors so sensitive they could detect a flashlight on the Moon."

Thanks to ST, a mind-boggling new dimension will open to us because it will take us back into time. To understand this, think of a bolt of lightning flashing across the sky. Five or six seconds later we hear a thunderclap. In actuality, we are hearing back into time. The sound of the thunder is signaling an event that—thanks to the lightning flash—we know happened five to six seconds earlier.

Astronomer Richard Harms uses this analogy to describe ST's ability to help us view the distant past by virtue of its capacity to see great distances. "Instead of sound waves from thunder," he suggests, "think of light waves traveling from a far galaxy to the space telescope above the earth. Light moves very fast, but the distance is so vast that a certain amount of time has to elapse before the light can get from there to here." A "light year" is the distance light travels in one year, 5.8 trillion miles. Thus, ST should be able to pick up images that have been traveling for as long as twelve billion years.

Are you ready for this? That means we'd be able to see events that transpired when the universe was a dozen billion years younger!

Just this morning, thinking about all this, I read these familiar words: "And God made the two great lights, the greater light to govern the day, and the lesser light to govern the night; He made the stars also. And God placed them in the expanse of the heavens" (Gen. 1:16–17).

Wouldn't it be something if one of ST's most distant signals revealed evidences of the creative hand of God? That should be sufficient to turn goose-pimple excitement into mouth-opening faith, even for the most cynical scientists.

"O world invisible, we view thee, O world intangible, we touch thee,
O world unknowable, we know thee" (The Kingdom of God, *Francis Thompson*).

MEMORIES

🍂 *Acts 20:16–24* 🍂

*T*had just completed a manuscript on Philippians, and my heart was full of joy. Not only because I was through (isn't that a wonderful word?) but because joy, the theme of the inspired letter I had spent weeks studying, had rubbed off. It was as if Paul and I had shared the same room and written at the same desk.

I was smiling and humming the little chorus "Rejoice in the Lord always, and again I say, rejoice!" as I inserted the books I had used back onto my library shelves. As I shoved the last volume in place, my eyes fell upon an old work by a British pastor of yesteryear, F. B. Meyer. It was his work on Philippians, but for some reason I had not consulted it throughout my months of study. Thinking there might be something to augment my now-finished manuscript, I decided to leaf through it before calling it a day.

It was not his words that spoke to me that evening, however, but the words of my mother. For as I began looking through it, I realized the book had once been a part of her library; after her death in 1971 it had found its way into mine. In her inimitable handwriting, my mother had added her own observations, prayers, and related scriptures in the margins throughout the book. Inside the back cover she had written: "Finishing reading this, May 8, 1958."

When I saw that date—1958—memory carried me back to a tiny island in the South Pacific where I had spent many lonely months as a marine. There, in May of '58 I had reached a crossroad in my own spiritual pilgrimage and committed myself to a lifetime of ministry.

Amazingly, it was the same month of that same year that my mother had finished Meyer's book. As I scanned her words, I found one reference after another to her prayers for me as I was far, far away . . . her concern for my spiritual welfare . . . her desire for God's best in my life.

As I slid Meyer's book back on the shelf, I thought of the invaluable role my parents had played during the formative years of my life . . . and how the torch had been passed from them to Cynthia and me to do the same with our children—and they, in turn, with theirs.

I could almost hear Mother's voice saying, "I'm still praying for you, Son. Keep walking with God. Finish strong!"

What treasured legacy has been passed on to you? What prevailing prayers, lasting love, wise warnings, hearty laughter? What are you passing on to your children?

MOTHER'S DAY

❧ *Proverbs 31:10–31* ❧

*I*f there's one attitude families are guilty of more than any other when it comes to mothers, it's presumption . . . taking them for granted . . . being nearly blind on occasion to the load moms carry. This was reinforced in my mind last week as I was thumbing through a row of crazy greeting cards at a local drugstore. Time and again the joke in the card drew its humor from this obvious attitude that pervades a household: *Forget the housework, Mom. It's your day. Besides, you can always do double duty and catch up on Monday!*

But my favorite was a great big card that looked like a third grader had printed it. On it was a little boy with a dirty face and torn pants pulling a wagonload of toys. On the front it read: *"Mom, I remember the little prayer you used to say for me every day . . ."* and inside, *"God help you if you do that again!"*

Jimmy Dean, the country-western singer, does a number that always leaves me with a big knot in my throat. It's entitled "I Owe You." In the song a man is looking through his wallet and comes across a number of long-standing "I owe yous" to his mother . . . which he names one by one.

Borrowing that idea, I suggest you who have been guilty of presumption unfold some of your own "I owe yous" that are now yellow with age. Consider the priceless value of the one woman who made your life possible—your mother.

Think about her example, her support, her humor, her counsel, her humility, her hospitality, her insight, her patience, her sacrifices. Her faith. Her hope. Her love.

Old "honest Abe" was correct: "He is not poor who has had a godly mother." Indebted, but not poor.

Moms, on Mother's Day Sunday we rise up and call you blessed. But knowing you, you'll feel uneasy in the limelight. You'll probably look for a place to hide. True servants are like that.

You're probably going to be taken out to eat (which will add to our indebtedness!). But in all honesty, it won't come anywhere near expressing our gratitude.

So, live it up on Sunday. It's all yours.

My advice? Shake up the family for a change. Order steak and lobster!

Mother's Day should not be just one day a year.

WINNING DISCIPLINE

❧ *1 Corinthians 9:19–27* ❧

*D*iscipline is one of the most hated terms of our times . . . right alongside patience and self-control. But have you noticed how often it comes up in the testimonies of those who win?

The apostle Paul says that he willingly forfeited his apostolic rights for the sake of winning more. That took discipline. Paul says that he endured all things in order to reach his objective; he exercised "self-control in all things."

Here are key uses of discipline:

- No runner completes the training or a race without it.
- No weight-loss program is maintained without it.
- No human body is kept fit without it.
- No mind is sharpened without it.
- No temptation is overcome without it.

If you want to put a stop to mediocrity, to replace excuses with fresh determination and procrastination with tough-minded persevance, you need discipline. Winners know that disciplined persistence must be a major part of their trainiing. That's the only way victory becomes an attainable reality rather than a distant dream.

The undisciplined is a headache to himself and a heartache to others,
and is unprepared to face the stern realities of life. (Wheaton College Bulletin)

THE GREATEST INFLUENCE

❦ *2 Timothy 1:1–5* ❦

*S*everal years ago someone interviewed the contemporary artist Marc Chagall for a PBS program. The young, arty interviewer started the session with a question about influences. His question was very long and involved and exhibited his own learning along the way, giving everybody, including Chagall, a lecture on the nature of influences on the artist.

When the young man finally gave the artist a chance to answer for himself, Chagall said, in the simplest way, that his greatest influence was his mother. It took the poor young man a bit of time to get his bearings after that.

I know of no more permanent imprint on a life than the one made by mothers. I guess that's why Mother's Day always leaves me a little nostalgic. Not simply because my mother has gone on (and heaven's probably cleaner because of it!), but because that's the one day the real heroines of our world get the credit they deserve. Hats off to every one of you!

More than any statesman or teacher, more than any minister or physician, more than any film star, athlete, business person, author, scientist, civic leader, entertainer, or military hero . . . you are the most influential person in your child's life.

Never doubt that fact!

There would never have been an Isaac without a Sarah, a Moses without a Jochebed, a Samuel without a Hannah, a John without an Elizabeth, a Timothy without a Eunice, or a John Mark without a Mary.

A mother's influence is so great that we model it even when we don't realize it, and we return to it—often to the surprise of others.

As I think of my own mother's influence on me, two words come to mind: class and zest. My mother, being a classy lady, was determined to keep our family from being ignorant of the arts or lacking in social graces. I have her to thank for my love of artistic beauty, fine music, which fork to use, and no gravy on my tie. She also possessed such a zest for life. I am indebted to her for my enthusiasm and relentless drive. Her indomitable spirit got passed on, thank goodness.

And so, mothers, don't ever forget the permanence of your imprint. The kids may seem ungrateful, they may act irresponsible, they may even ignore your reminders and forget your advice these days. But believe this: They cannot erase your influence.

Think about how your own mother has influenced your life. Have you ever thanked her? Have you thanked God for your mother's influence in your life?

THINK IT OVER

❧❧

*S*everal years ago I asked the ministry staff at the church I was pastoring to reflect on how their mothers had influenced their lives. Here are a few of the responses I received

"The interest, concern, and care for older people that my mother modeled in a Christlike manner impacted my life to the extent that today I am involved in a ministry with senior adults" (Dave Jobe).

"Trying to define my mother's influence is like trying to talk definitively about clean air, pure water, warm sunshine, and the law of gravity. She consistently modeled faith, patience, love, hard work, and forgiveness" (Paul Sailhamer).

"It was at my mother's knee that I learned many of the values I hold today. A disciplined life of service for the Lord and to the needy stand out in my mind. No job was too big, no sacrifice too great, no circumstance too difficult to serve the Lord. Total trust in an all-powerful God was her guarantee of success. Her unflinching belief in me gave motivation and strength" (Doug Haag).

"My mom is the greatest. I will always remember her for taking time to be with me as a child, praying for me as I wandered away from the Lord as an adolescent, and even now caring about me as an adult. It was through her that I learned the compassionate side of life" (Bruce Camp).

"One of the fondest memories of Mother's influence on my life came in the first grade when I was sent to sit outside the class for talking out of turn. My mother worked as an aide at the school, and I was filled with dread as I saw her walking down the breezeway toward me. As she approached she asked, "Have you been talking aloud in class?" I nodded. She laughed. She never mentioned the incident again . In her own subtle way she was teaching me that I had the responsibility of accepting the consequences for my own actions" (Dean Anderson).

STORMS

❧ *Nahum 1* ❧

*B*low that layer of dust off the Book of Nahum in your Bible and catch a glimpse of the last part of verse three, chapter one: "The way of the Lord is in the whirlwind and in the storm" *(Berkley Version).*

That's good to remember when you're caught in a rip-snortin' Texas frog strangler as I was last week. I reminded myself of God's presence as the rain-heavy, charcoal-colored clouds were split apart by lightning's eerie fingers and the air shook with earth-shattering, ear-deafening reports of thunder. Once again the Lord, the God of the heavens, was having His way in the whirlwind and the storm.

But how about those storms of life? What about the whirlwinds of disease, disaster, and death? What about the storms of interruptions, irritations, and ill-treatment? Well, if Nahum's words apply to the heavenly sphere, they also apply to the earthly—to the heartrending contingencies of daily living.

Life is filled with God-appointed storms. A sheet of paper ten times this size would be insufficient to list the whirlwinds of our lives. But two things should comfort us in the midst of daily lightning and thunder. First, we all experience them. Second, we all need them. God has no method more effective. The massive blows and shattering blasts (not to mention the small, constant irritations) smooth us and humble us and force us to submit to the role He has chosen for us.

William Cowper could take the stand in defense of all I have written. He passed through a period of great crisis in his life. Finally one bleak morning he tried to put an end to it all by taking poison. The attempt at suicide failed. He then hired a coach and was driven to the Thames River, intending to throw himself from the bridge but was "strangely restrained." The next morning he fell upon a sharp knife but the blade broke! He later tried to hang himself but was found and taken down unconscious . . . still alive. Some time later he took up a Bible, began to read the Book of Romans, and was gloriously saved. The God of the storms had pursued him unto the end and won his heart.

After a rich life of Christian experiences, Cowper sat down and recorded his summary of the Lord's dealings in the familiar words: "God moves in a mysterious way / His wonders to perform; He plants His footsteps in the sea, / and rides upon the storm."

Before the dust settles, why not ask God to have His way
in today's whirlwind and storm?

THE PALE HORSE

❧ *Psalm 23* ❧

*T*he path of the pale horse named Death, mentioned in Revelation 6:8, is littered with bitterness, sorrow, fear, and grief. This ashen stallion started his lengthy journey ages ago and races through time with steady beat and dreadful regularity. As long as we exist in the land of the dying, we shall hear the somber knell of his hoofbeats.

Sadly, some people hurry their appointment with death. Painful though it may be to hear and accept, thousands of people will take their own lives during the next twelve months. For in our land, suicide is now almost an epidemic.

Once *every minute* someone in the United States attempts suicide.

In this country, there are 24 percent more deaths by suicide than by murder.

Suicide is the number 9 cause of adult death in the USA. For Americans between fifteen and thirty years of age, it is the number 3 cause of death. It is the number 2 cause among teenagers.

Four out of five people who commit suicide have tried it previously. Those who are unsuccessful usually try again.

Contrary to popular opinion, people who threaten suicide often mean it. Threats should be taken seriously.

Thankfully, suicidal individuals usually communicate their feelings before acting, thus making this irrevocable act preventable if those who are close are wise and sensitive enough to read the signals.

Some of the warning signals or clues you should be aware of are 1) talk about suicide, 2) a sudden change in personality, 3) deep depression, 4) physical symptoms—sleeplessness, loss of appetite, decreased sexual drive, drastic weight loss, repeated exhaustion, 5) actual attempts, and 6) crisis situations—death of a loved one, failure at school, loss of job, marital or home problems, and a lengthy or terminal illness. These are certainly not "sure signs," but if any or several persist, please step in and offer help. Contact your physician or ask advice from your local Suicide Prevention Center's twenty-four-hour crisis line; you may also want to contact one of the spiritual leaders or officers of your church or a member of the pastoral staff. Such situations are often emergencies. To delay could result in tragic consequences.

Those who are strong need to bear the weaknesses of the weak (Rom. 15:1). That may mean blocking the path of the pale horse!

Sometimes if we are to hear what is being said,
we need to listen to what is not being said.

DEFYING THE ODDS

🕸 *1 Samuel 17* 🕸

*R*eader alert: [I wrote this back when Lenny Dykstra was playing for the Mets. But the truth still applies.] No offense, but Lenny Dykstra doesn't look like much of an athlete. He looks more like some team's mascot. Or like the guy who wears that silly chicken suit and does cartwheels around stadiums. The kid can't stand much more than five-seven. That little Dutch boy is the starting center fielder for the National League New York Mets. Nicknamed "Nails"—as in "tough as" and "harder than."

With game three of the 1986 National League Championship Series fairly boring and all but over—bottom of the ninth, Mets losing—veteran Houston Astros' reliever Dave Smith must have smiled inside as the little guy walked up to the plate. Dykstra fouled off Smith's stinging fastball, and then, without hesitation, he slammed the next one over the fence. We're talking Big Apple Explosion!

As *L.A Times* sportswriter Gordon Edes put it: "His you-gotta-believe-it, two-run home run gave the Mets a 6-5 win and transformed Shea Stadium—as polite as Carnegie Hall for most of the overcast afternoon—into a high-fivin', Astro-defyin', bring-on-the-World-Series-jivin' madhouse."

I always sit up and take notice when odds are defied. We all do, don't we? That's why we pull for the underdog. And why we never tire of the David-and-Goliath story. Or the way those walls fell flat at Jericho. Or the crossing of the Red Sea. Or Daniel standing nose-to-nose with a den full of hungry lions.

It's no big deal for huge hunks of humanity to hit homers. But when the little fella smashes one over four hundred feet, that's news.

Why? Because that gives all of us hope. If he can do that, surrounded by all those towering odds stacked against him, then there's hope for me, facing all my odds. It's like getting a shot of fresh motivation in both arms.

Want to defy the odds? Aim high. Forget "I can't."

Or, in baseball parlance, get hold of that bat, step up to the plate, and slam that sucker outa the park!

"But the bravest are surely those who have the clearest vision of what is before them, glory and danger alike, and yet not withstanding go out to meet it"
(Thucydides).

STAYING IN STEP

❧ *Matthew 16* ❧

*B*etter than any other word I can think of, *change* describes our world. Vast, sweeping changes, especially in the last 150 years. Simply to survive requires adjusting, and to make any kind of significant dent calls for a willingness to shift in style and to modify methods.

Consider two of the more pronounced changes in our world.

*Population.*It was not until 1850 that the number of people on this globe reached one billion. By 1930 (a mere eighty years later) the number had doubled. Only thirty years later—1960—it had shot up to three billion.

Speed. Until the early 1800s the fastest any human being could travel was about 20 miles per hour-on the back of a galloping horse. By 1880 the "streamline" passenger train whipped along at 100 miles per hour, an unheard of and fearsome velocity. Today, the supersonic Concorde can cruise at well over 1000 miles per hour and manned space rockets jump the speed to 16,000 miles per hour.

And I haven't even mentioned the technological advancements in the last century, or the enormous changes made in military armament and defense, agricultural processes, housing, modes of transportation, medicine, music, architecture and engineering, luxury items and personal conveniences, computers, clothing, and cars.

Since God is eternally relevant, since none of this blows Him away (omniscience can't be mind-boggled!), He is still in touch, in control, and fully aware. Why He has caused or allowed this radical reshaping of human history, nobody can say for sure. But we can reasonably surmise that God is up to something.

Some would suddenly shout, "These are signs predicting Christ's soon return." Quite possibly. But what about until then? What is essential? We're back where we started, aren't we? Being adaptable, willing to shift and change.

Take communication. We must hammer out new and fresh styles on the anvil of each generation, always guarding against being dated and institutionalized. This calls for creativity, originality, and sensitivity.

More than anything else, I'm convinced, the thing that attracted people to Jesus was His fresh, authentic, original style in a world of tired phrases, rigid rules, and empty religion. Remember the report made to the Pharisees? "Nobody ever spoke like this man." He was in step with the times without ever stepping out of the Father's will.

Though times may change, the Lord is constant.

MARKS OF INTEGRITY

❧ *1 Corinthians 11:28, 31* ❧

*T*hanks to the Word of God, we can list several marks of integrity that God would have us appropriate into our lives. Do you have these marks of integrity?

- An excellent attitude
- Faithfulness and diligence at work
- Personal purity of the highest caliber
- Consistency in your walk with God

You have the scalpel in your hand. Self-examination is up to you. It is not only a good idea, it's a biblical imperative.

A reminder: Only you can do the surgery on your soul, only you. No one else can know the truth. You can cover up, twist the facts in your mind, rationalize, and ignore . . . and no one will know the difference—no one except you. But if you really want to strengthen your grip on integrity, you will come to terms with the whole truth, regardless of the consequences.

Read the Book of Daniel to see the biblical picture of integrity. Daniel refused to compromise and consequently was thrown into the lions' den. Look what God did. He honored Daniel's faithfulness. He'll do the same for you.

Sometimes when you exhibit real, unvarnished integrity,
you get dumped into the lions' den. Remember, God's there, too!

WHATEVER HAPPENED TO HIM?

❧ *John 3:11–17* ❧

*F*or years we Americans have been hung up on records and statistics—particularly in the world of sports. They have become the standards for greatness.

What's really amazing is that once "unreachable" world records now seem reachable. Some, like breaking the four-minute mile, are now so commonplace we hardly notice anymore. And Ukrainian-born Sergei Bubka beat all the competition at the 1983 World Championships with an 18-foot pole vault when he was only nineteen. After that he added one inch after another, until finally he broke the magic barrier by clearing 20 feet. Before long, that twenty-foot standard will be as big a yawner as the four-minute mile.

What I'm looking forward to is the day somebody can clear 1250 feet . . . something over one hundred stories. I mean, at the rate today's athletes are going, they'll probably clear that by the end of this decade, right?

"Wrong," you answer. "In fact, impossible." And you are absolutely correct. The height of the Empire State Building? Get serious. It ain't gonna happen.

Which is exactly the point of a statement that appears in a letter written during the first century: "For all have sinned and fall short of the glory of God" (Rom. 3:23). The spiritual standard God has set for all who wish to measure up is perfection, nothing less. To clear that level calls for a spotless record, a flawless past, impeccable morality, a complete absence of wrong. In plain and simple English, *no sin.*

Whoever qualifies, please step forward . . . line forms to the right. No one?

Oops, wait a second. My mistake. Seems like there was one unusual man who didn't "fall short." As I recall, He claimed to be God, then demonstrated it to perfection. He even promised to draw people to Himself, to forgive their sins, to give them a place in heaven if they would believe in Him.

But didn't He wind up just outside Jerusalem on a cross? Wasn't He crucified? He died, didn't He? Too bad. If He were really God, as He claimed, death would not have stopped Him, right? I mean, He would have come back more alive than ever. And when He did, He certainly wouldn't have had any trouble clearing the Empire State Building, would He? In fact, He would still be alive today, still drawing people to Himself, wouldn't He?

Do you wonder whatever happened to Him?

Have I got some good news for you!

The best news is the good news of the gospel.

THINK IT OVER

🙚🙚🙚

*N*ow if Christ is preached, that He has been raised from the dead, how do some among you say that there is no resurrection of the dead? But if there is no resurrection of the dead, not even Christ has been raised; and if Christ has not been raised, then our preaching is vain, your faith also is vain. Moreover we are even found to be false witnesses of God, because we witnessed against God that He raised Christ, whom He did not raise, if in fact the dead are not raised. For if the dead are not raised, not even Christ has been raised; and if Christ has not been raised, your faith is worthless; you are still in your sins. Then those also who have fallen asleep in Christ have perished. If we have only hoped in Christ in this life, we are of all men most to be pitied.

But now Christ has been raised from the dead, the first fruits of those who are asleep. For since by a man came death, by a man also came the resurrection of the dead. For as in Adam all die, so also in Christ all shall be made alive.

—1 CORINTHIANS 15:12–22

Hallelujah!

VIOLENCE

2 *Timothy* 3:1–5

*L*ike sticks of dynamite taped together with a short fuse, our times are really volatile. Anger is ready to explode into physical violence at the slightest provocation. This entire globe seems brimming with hair-trigger hostility, ready to flare into full-scale disaster.

It's not just a vast global problem, however. It's personal. It's in your neighborhood. Your school. Where you work. Home security systems are no longer considered a luxury for the rich. Even teachers are not safe in the classroom.

But I must confess, the final straw of shock came when I read of the murder of John White in a quiet neighborhood in southwest Cleveland. The killer? A nineteen-year-old hired by White's two kids. That's right. His seventeen-year-old son and fourteen-year-old daughter paid $60 to have their own father killed.

The teenagers paid off the murderer, then hid the body in a back room of the house. After that they used their dad's credit cards to go on a ten-day spending spree. While their father's body was decaying in the utility room, they were cooking meals in the kitchen a few feet away and enjoying themselves in the living room.

After being caught, they openly confessed the entire, bizarre event. When asked why, they answered: "He wouldn't let us do anything we wanted." The dad had angered the kids by trying to enforce an evening curfew and by not allowing them to quit school or "smoke pot." So they had him killed.

Centuries ago, in a stone dungeon, the apostle Paul wrote his last few sentences. Yet, today, they stab us awake with incredible relevance: "But realize this, that in the last days difficult times will come. For men will be . . . arrogant, revilers, disobedient to parents, ungrateful, unholy . . . brutal, haters of good, treacherous, reckless" (2 Tim. 3:1–4).

The Greek term he chose for "difficult times" means, literally, "fierce, harsh, hard to deal with, savage." It is used only one other time in the New Testament, when it describes two demon-possessed men as "exceedingly violent" (Matt. 8:28).

An apt description of our times. Yet there is a glimmer of hope amid this flood of violence. It is this: Christ's coming cannot be far away. These "last days" of pain—though they may seem to pass slowly—are daily reminders that our redemption draws near. And "we shall all be changed, in a moment, in the twinkling of an eye" (1 Cor. 15:51–52).

Like, fast. Really fast. Faster than a short fuse on sticks of dynamite.

When everything looks hopeless, we have the comfort of our eternal Hope.

TOOLS

❧ *2 Timothy 2:15* ❧

*R*emember that time you got ticked off trying to find a verse in the Bible and couldn't? That was almost as bad as the day you decided to read a couple of chapters and got hung up on "Nazirite" . . . or scratched your head over "cubit."

These are like hardened, glazed coverings that suddenly obscure our understanding of God's truth. The pick and shovel of good intentions simply will not cut through. Sharper tools than that are needed, believe me!

Listen, you don't have to be a theological brain to dig into God's riches . . . but you do need some mining equipment. These tools are basic to intelligent, meaningful Bible study. They will enable you to find most of the answers you need, and they are as easy to use as your TV guide. There are at least four you should have on hand.

A Bible concordance. It contains an alphabetical index of all the terms found in the Bible, and it comes in handy when you want to put your finger on a particular verse but can only remember a few words in it. It's also invaluable if you want a complete list of all the verses using the same word.

The best concordances available are Robert Young's *Analytical Concordance to the Bible* and James Strong's *Exhaustive Concordance to the Bible.* I must also add W. E. Vine's *Expository Dictionary of New Testament Words* for you who are serious students, wanting to learn the shades of meaning and theological implications of different New Testament terms.

A Bible dictionary. It is more than a list of words and definitions. It's like a one-volume encyclopedia, containing vital information on people, places, doctrines, customs, and cultural matters. I recommend either *Unger's Bible Dictionary* (well illustrated, scholarly but readable) or *The New Bible Dictionary* (contains longer articles on technical subjects).

A Bible atlas. The most popular is *Baker's Bible Atlas.* Another reliable one is *Macmillan Bible Atlas,* containing over 250 different maps. If you can't afford an atlas, at least purchase a good set of biblical maps.

A Bible commentary. This is a single-volume book that offers comments and insights on every chapter in the Word of God. Hands down, my favorite is *The Wycliffe Bible Commentary* edited by Pfeiffer and Harrison. It is reliable and well arranged.

Don't delay now. Get those tools you need soon . . . and don't let them rust on you!

It's amazing how a few of the right tools,
when used correctly, can open God's treasures.

TRAUMA

❦ *Matthew 11:27–30* ❦

*L*ike potatoes in a pressure cooker, we twenty-first-century creatures understand the meaning of stress. A week doesn't pass without a few skirmishes that beat up on our fragile frames. They may be as mild as making lunches for our kids before 7:30 in the morning (mild?) or as severe as a collision with another car . . . or another person. Makes no difference. The result is "trauma." You know, the bottom-line reason Valium remains the top seller.

The late Joe Bayly, insightful Christian writer and columnist, certainly understood trauma. He and his wife lost three of their children: one at eighteen days (after surgery); another at five years (leukemia); a third at eighteen years (sledding accident plus hemophilia). In my wildest imagination, I cannot fathom the depth of their loss. In the backwash of such deep trauma, Joe and his wife stood sometimes strong, sometimes weak, as they watched God place a period before the end of the sentence on three of their children's lives. And their anguish was not relieved when well-meaning people offered shallow, simple answers amidst their grief.

H. L. Mencken must have had such situations in mind when he wrote: "There's always an easy solution to every human problem—neat, plausible, and wrong."

Eyes that read these words might very well be near tears. You are trying to cope without hope, and there's no relief on the horizon. You're bleeding and you've run out of bandages. You have moved from mild tension to advanced trauma.

Listen carefully! Jesus Christ opens the gate, gently looks at you, and says: "Come to Me, all you who labor and are . . . overburdened, and I will cause you to rest. [I will ease and relieve and refresh your souls]" (Matt. 11:28, *Amplified*).

Nothing complicated. No big fanfare, no trip to Mecca, no hypnotic trance, no fee, no special password. Just *come*. Meaning? Unload. Unhook the pack and drop it in His lap . . . now. Does He know what trauma is all about? Remember, He's the One whose sweat became like drops of blood in the agony of Gethsemane. If anybody understands trauma, He does. Completely.

He's a Master at turning devastation into restoration. His provision is profound, attainable, and right.

Allow Him to take your stress as you take His rest.

SAINTS IN CIRCULATION

✵ *Jeremiah 12* ✵

*D*uring the reign of Oliver Cromwell, the British government began to run low on silver for coins. Lord Cromwell sent his men to the local cathedral to see if they could find any precious metal there. After investigating they reported: "The only silver we can find is in the statues of the saints standing in the corners."

To which the radical soldier and statesman of England replied: "Good! We'll melt down the saints and put them in circulation!"

That brief but direct order states the essence of the practical goal of authentic Christianity. Not rows of silver saints crammed into the corners of cathedrals, but melted saints circulating through the mainstream of humanity. Where life transpires in the raw.

On campuses where students carve through the varnish of shallow answers. In the shop where employees test the mettle of everyday Christianity. At home with a houseful of kids, where R&R means run and wrestle. In the concrete battlegrounds of sales competition, seasonal conventions, and sexual temptations, where hard-core assaults are made on internal character. On the hospital bed, where reality never takes a nap. In the office, where diligence and honesty are forever on the scaffold. On the team where patience and self-control are checked out.

The cost factor of being a saint occurs on Monday and Tuesday and throughout the week. That's when we're "melted down and put in circulation." "Sunday religion" may seem sufficient, but it isn't. And pity the person who counts on it to get him through.

Sure, you can opt for an easier path. You can keep your own record and come out smelling like a rose:

Dressed up and drove to church. Check

Got a seat and sat quietly. Check

Gave money . . . listened to the sermon. Check

Closed my Bible, prayed, looked pious. Check

Shook hands, walked out. Check

Still a saint? A silver one, in fact. Icily regular, cool and casual, consistently present . . . and safely out of circulation . . . until the Lord calls for an investigation of the local cathedral.

Those who successfully wage war with silent heroism under relentless secular pressure—ah, they are the saints who know what it means to be melted.

REQUIREMENTS FOR VICTORY

❧ *1 John 5:4–7* ❧

*A*ccording to Scripture, three things are required for spiritual victory: birth, faith, and truth. In order to enter into the ranks of the victorious, we must be "born of God." It occurs when I accept Jesus Christ as savior.

Then comes faith. I draw upon the power that is in me. I no longer operate on the basis of human strength, but by faith. I rely upon divine power.

Then is truth. Everything is made possible by the truth, by believing the truth, by living the truth. Allow the truth to invade, reshape, and cultivate your life anew.

Tell me, have you had such a birth?

If so, are you operating in faith?

And the truth—is it the truth you are claiming?

If you've answered yes to all three questions, then it's time for action. Quit hiding behind those excuses! Stop telling yourself it's too late! It is never too late to start doing what is right. Start now. Trust me, you can move from the realm of defeat and discouragement to victory and hope if you will simply take action now.

Aim high. Go hard after God. Press on.

Everything is made possible by the truth.

THE ULTIMATE CLASS ACT

❧ *Matthew 18* ❧

*C*lass Action is a class act. It's a film about two lawyers who go head-to-head, both in court and in life. They are father and daughter . . . on opposite sides of a complicated case charged with the full spectrum of emotions.

It is the father-daughter interplay that gives the story its definition. During her early teen years her father was often on the road, busily engaged in various cases and crusades. During that impressionable era of her life, he was not only unfaithful to her mother, he was virtually out of touch with the family. The daughter's resentment of her father's lifestyle festered into full-blown competition, both privately and professionally. Nothing would please her more than winning that class-action suit in the courtroom . . . a perfect place to unleash her rage, to humiliate her father and retaliate on behalf of her mother, whom she idolizes.

Behind this brilliant woman's drive and accomplishments lie demons of bitterness. Unknown to the young woman, her soul awaits that moment when she can finally forgive her father . . . and be free.

What is true in the make-believe world of film is all the more true in the real world of life. Jesus Himself spoke of forgiveness on several occasions. Like the time Peter asked Him if forgiving someone "seven times" was sufficient. After all, that was over twice the going rate according to the Pharisees' teaching. To paraphrase Jesus' terse answer: "Would you believe seventy times seven?" In other words, an infinite number of times . . . no limit.

Jesus then went on to point out that without forgiveness there cannot be freedom, and He told them the story of a man who, after having been forgiven an enormous debt, refused to forgive someone who owed him a measly twenty bucks. The man who would not forgive was called back before the king, who "handed him over to the torturers" (Matt. 18:34). That word means "inquisitors," conveying the idea of personal torment . . . internal torture. Jesus added: "So shall My heavenly Father also do to you, if each of you does not forgive his brother from your heart" (18:35).

We are most like beasts when we kill. We are most like men when we judge. We are most like God when we forgive.

Of all the actions you can carry out, that one is the ultimate class act.

Freedom and forgiveness both begin with the same letter.

THINK IT OVER

🙚🙚

*D*o you need to be set free? Honestly now, is your next step the need to forgive? Do it. Don't let anything or anyone talk you out of it. I know, I know. After all the misery you have had to endure, why should you have to be the one who humbles yourself and forgives?

Christ could have asked the same question at Golgotha. Perhaps He did at Gethsemane. But once He discerned the Father's determination, there was no looking back . . . no turning back.

Remember His cry from the cross? "Father, forgive them . . ." (Luke 23:34).

Look up "forgive" and "forgiveness" in your Bible concordance and read the Scriptures listed. One you will find there is:

"And be kind to one another, tender-hearted, forgiving each other, just as God in Christ also has forgiven you" (Eph. 4:32).

A GIFT FOR DAD

❧ *Proverbs 13* ❧

*I*n an age of equal rights and equal time, it seems only fair to give dads equal attention. Sometimes it seems the only time that happens is during the big commercial buildup for Father's Day, and then it's all buy, buy, buy! Families wonder whether to wrap us in robes, fill us with food, surprise us with skis, tickle us with tools, or just cover us with kisses. If I know dads, most of 'em blush no matter what you do. They are so used to providing, receiving is a little weird.

For the next several minutes, think about your father, okay? Meditate on what that one individual has contributed. Think about his influence over you, his investment in you, his insights to you. Feel his hand wrapped around yours . . . his strong, secure arm across your shoulders. Remember his grip that once communicated a balanced mixture of gentleness and determination . . . compassion and masculinity . . . not only his "I understand" but also his "Now, straighten up!"

Best of all, take time to recall his exemplary character. The word is "integrity." Pause and remind yourself of just one or two choice moments in your past when he stood alone . . . when he stood by you . . . when he stood against insurmountable odds . . . when he provided that shelter in your time of storm . . . when he protected you from the bitter blast of life's harsh consequences . . .

In the wake of such a legacy, which time can never erase, give God thanks. Thank the Giver of every good and perfect gift for the meaningful marks your dad has branded on the core of your character . . . the wholesome habits he has woven into the fabric of your flesh. While meandering through this forest of nostalgia, stop at the great oak named Proverbs and reflect upon the words the wise man carved into its bark long centuries ago: "A righteous man who walks in his integrity—how blessed are his sons [and daughters] after him" (20:7).

How very true! How blessed you are!

Dad is not perfect; he would be the first to admit it. Nor is he infallible, much to his own disappointment. Nor altogether fair . . . nor always right. But there's one thing he is—always—he is your dad . . . the only one you'll ever have. Take it from me, there's only one thing he needs on Father's Day. Plain and simple, he needs to hear you say, "Dad, I love you."

That's the best gift you can give. Nothing you can buy will bring him anywhere near the satisfaction that four-word gift will provide. "Dad, I love you."

Look your dad in the eye or call him on the phone and give him the gift he needs
more than anything. Give him your love.

TIPPING

❧ *Proverbs 22:9* ❧

I feel like starting with the words the nurse says as she approaches your bed with one hand behind her back: "This won't take long, but it may sting a little."

Are you aware of what waiters and waitresses say about the Christians they serve? Do you have any idea how much they dread waiting on our tables in restaurants after church on Sundays? Or any other day when we go in groups with big Bibles under our arms? We gobble up the chow, asking for this favor and that, seldom pausing long enough to smile or say, "Thank you." That's bad enough, but then we leave a tip that is more of an insult than a generous expression of gratitude.

Just last week a waiter informed me that the place where he works has the toughest time getting a full crew to wait tables on Sunday. "We'd all rather work late Friday and Saturday nights week after week than work Sunday afternoons," he said.

When I asked why, he told me.

"Because Christians are usually loud, they often lack good table manners, and they are stingy with the tips."

The waiter who spoke to me is a Christian. He's on our side. And he's embarrassed. Says he has a tough time talking to the crew about Christ after the place closes at night. They give him this cynical "You gotta be kidding!" response that comes after six or eight of Christ's followers walk away, leaving a tract and a dollar bill. Or maybe just a tract. Sometimes, neither.

If you're among the thoughtful, the gracious, the kind who leave a full 15 percent or more, keep it up. May your tribe increase. But if you're the type who falls into the tightfisted and less than thoughtful category, how about thinking of your witness as something more than a Bible in your pocket and words out of your mouth? Sometimes it's what comes out of your pocket after something has gone into your mouth . . . and I'm not referring to a tract. Listen: "It is possible to give away and become richer! It is also possible to hold on too tightly and lose everything. Yes, the liberal man shall be rich! By watering others, he waters himself" (Prov. 11:24–25, TLB).

C'mon, Christian, loosen up. If you can afford to eat out, you can also handle a healthy tip. Maybe all you needed was a shot in the arm.

There's no doubt about it. Actions often speak much louder than words.
What are your actions saying?

TACT

*W*isely labeled "the saving virtue," tact graces life like fragrance graces a rose. One whiff erases any memory of the thorns. It's remarkable how peaceful and pleasant tact can make us. Its major goal is avoiding unnecessary offense, and that alone ought to make us crave it. Its basic function is a keen sense of what to say or do in order to maintain the truth and good relationships, and that alone ought to make us cultivate it. Tact is incessantly appropriate, invariably attractive, incurably appealing, but rare . . . oh, is it rare!

Remember the teacher who lacked tact? Each morning you wondered if that was the day you'd be singled out and embarrassed by some public putdown. Remember the boss who lacked tact? You never knew if he ever understood you or considered you to be a valuable person. And who could forget that tactless physician? You weren't a human being; you were Case Number thirty-six.

But the classic example of tactless humanity, I'm ashamed to declare, is the abrasive Christian (so-called) who feels it his or her calling to fight for the truth with little or no regard for the other fella's feelings. Of course, this is supposedly done in the name of the Lord—"to do anything less would be compromise and counterfeit."

This person's favorite modus operandi is either to overlook or openly demean others. Unfortunately, some preachers are the greatest offenders. They seem to delight in developing a devastating pulpit that scourges rather than encourages, that blasts rather than builds.

"The heart of the righteous ponders how to answer," writes Solomon. "That which turns away wrath is a gentle answer," said he. "The wise person uses his tongue to make knowledge acceptable," he adds. "The tongue of the wise brings healing," and "A man has joy in an apt answer and how delightful is a timely word!" (see Prov. 12:18; 15).

No facts need be subtracted when tact is added, by the way. Years ago, I used to sell shoes. My seasoned employer, with a twinkle in his eye, instructed me never to say, "Lady, your foot is too big for this shoe!" I was taught to say, instead, "I'm sorry, but this shoe is just a little too small for your foot." Both statements expressed the facts, but one was insulting while the other was tactful.

It didn't shrink her foot, but it did save her face . . . and that's what tact is all about.

Look for an opportunity today to bring healing through a tactful answer.

SURPRISES

❧ *Exodus 6:1–8* ❧

*R*emember the words Marine Private Gomer Pyle used to repeat in almost every episode of his television show? *"Surprise, surprise!"* Some surprises *refresh us*. We're low. Under the pile. Then, out of the blue, we receive a letter of affirmation. Those lines, though few, lift our spirits. Maybe it's an unexpected phone call or a hug of reassurance that sends us soaring.

Some surprises *relieve us*. This certainly happened to my brother Orville and his family when they were caught in Hurricane Andrew near Miami. As the wind reached 160 miles an hour, he, his wife, and their loved ones took refuge in the master bedroom. They heard windows crash, doors blow off their hinges, and walls break apart.

Only one room sustained no damage to walls, floor, or roof: *the master bedroom,* where Orville and his family had huddled and prayed for six terrifying hours! And, as Orville told our sister, Luci, something good came out of the calamity. "When all the fences were blown down, we finally met all our neighbors." Surprise, surprise!

Some surprises *rebuke us*. In a recent "Dear Abby" column I read a poignant story. A young man from a wealthy family was about to graduate from high school. It was a custom in their affluent community for parents to give their graduating children a new car, and the boy and his dad had spent weeks visiting one dealership after another. The week before graduation they found the perfect car. The boy was certain it would be in the driveway on graduation night.

On the eve of his graduation, however, his father handed him a small package wrapped in colorful paper. It was a Bible! The boy was so angry he threw the Bible down and stormed out of the house. He and his father never saw each other again.

Several years later the news of the father's death finally brought the son home again. Following the funeral, he sat alone one evening, going through his father's possessions, when he came across the Bible his dad had given him. Overwhelmed by grief, he cracked it open for the first time. When he did, a cashier's check dated the day of his high school graduation fell into his lap—in the exact amount of the car they had chosen together. Rebuked by surprise!

Life is short. God is sovereign. All plans are in His hands, not ours.

*Surprises are part of God's divine plan, designed
to remind us that He is still in charge.*

THE GOOD SAMARITAN

❧ *Luke 10:25–37* ❧

A Greek class was given an assignment to study the story of the Good Samaritan in Luke 10:25–37. As is true in most classes, a couple or three of the students cared more about the practical implications of the assignment than its intellectual stimulation.

The three carried out a plan where one played the Samaritan victim. They tore his clothes, rubbed on mud and catsup to create "wounds," marked up his face and eyes, then placed him along the path that led from the dormitory to the classroom building. While the other two hid and recorded, he groaned and writhed, simulating great pain.

Not one student stopped. They walked around him, stepped over him, and said things to him. Nobody stopped to help.

This incident always reminds me of a scripture that penetrates the surface of our intellectual concerns. "This is how we know what love is: Jesus Christ laid down his life for us. And we ought to lay down our lives for our brothers. If anyone has material possessions and sees his brother in need but has no pity on him, how can the love of God be in him?" (1 John 3:16–17, NIV).

Following the will of the Lord requires wisdom, clear thinking, and yes, action! Those Seminary students were full of the Word and, probably had a great deal of love. But they did not see their fellow man lying beside the sidewalk. They were too full of 'words' to see God's work right in front of their eyes.

You must really want to do the will of God!

GRADUATION THOUGHTS

❧ 2 *Timothy* 3 ❧

*Y*ou—or someone you know—may soon be graduating. I extend my congratulations! Whether you set new academic records or not, you finished. You saw it through. I commend you. Before that happens, however, let me give you four simple commandments that apply to anyone who is graduating. My thoughts grow out of the final four verses of 2 Timothy 3.

1. *Don't stop your learning.* Paul urges his friend Timothy to "continue in the things you have learned" (3:14). It is one thing to take a course, to complete one's work, to earn a diploma or a degree; it's another thing to become a student for the rest of your life: to remain hungry for knowledge, to stay curious, to read widely, to be adventurous, creative, on a never-ending pursuit of truth.

2. *Don't forget your leaders.* As Paul reminds his friend to continue in those things he has learned, he adds, "knowing from whom you have learned them." Timothy needed to remember, to stay near, to thank the teachers who had impacted his life and contributed to his growth.

3. *Don't discount your legacy.* Timothy's heart didn't just happen to be open and sensitive to spiritual things. He was the product of a legacy, a spiritual continuum. His mentor, Paul, affirms, "For I am mindful of the sincere faith within you, which first dwelt in your grandmother Lois, and your mother Eunice" (1:5).

4. *Don't ignore your Lord.* As Paul closes these very personal lines to his younger friend, he returns to "the sacred writings" and assures Timothy that "all Scripture is inspired by God and profitable . . . that the man [and the woman] of God may be adequate, equipped for every good work" (3:16–17). In effect he was saying that God's Word would remain a reliable, profitable source of nutritious food throughout his life and was exhorting him to stay close to the Lord, regardless.

And so, graduate, continue feeding on God's Word. Stay near the only One who can lead you safely on your journey.

For those of you for whom graduation is a dim memory, the admonition remains the same: Don't stop your learning. Don't forget your leaders. Don't discount your legacy. Don't ignore your Lord.

THINK IT OVER

✣ ✣ ✣

*T*his weekend I would challenge you to read through the entire book of 2 Timothy. Then, try to make a list of all Paul's admonitions to his young friend. What examples does Paul give from his own life? How are you living in the light of these?

NOBODIES

❧ 1 Corinthians 12:19–25 ❧

*P*ull a sheet of scratch paper out of your memory bank and see how well you do with the following questions:

Who taught Martin Luther his theology and inspired his translation of the New Testament?

Who visited with Dwight L. Moody at a shoe store and spoke to him about Christ?

Who was the wife of Charles Haddon Spurgeon?

Who was the elderly woman who prayed faithfully for Billy Graham for over twenty years?

Who helped Charles Wesley get underway as a composer of hymns?

Who were the parents of the godly and gifted prophet Daniel?

Okay, how'd you do? Before you excuse your inability to answer these questions by calling the quiz "trivia," better stop and think. Had it not been for such unknown persons—such "nobodies"—a huge chunk of church history would be missing. And a lot of lives would have been untouched.

Nobodies. What a necessary band of men and women . . . servants of the King . . . yet nameless in the kingdom! Men and women who, with silent heroism and faithful diligence, relinquish the limelight and live in the shade of public figures.

As Jim Elliot, martyred messenger of the gospel to the Aucas once remarked: "Missionaries are a bunch of nobodies trying to exalt Somebody."

Praise God! We're among that elite group mentioned in 1 Corinthians 12: "some of the parts that seem weakest and least important are really the most necessary. . . . So God has put the body together in such a way that extra honor and care are given to those parts that might otherwise seem less important" (vv. 22, 24, TLB).

If it weren't for the heroic "nobodies," we wouldn't have any sound or lights or heat or air conditioning in our churches next Sunday. We wouldn't have homes in which high schoolers can meet on Sunday nights to sing and share. We wouldn't have church staff and officers and teachers working together behind the scenes.

Nobodies . . . exalting Somebody.

Are you playing a behind-the-scenes role?
Thank God for giving you that opportunity.

MIND UNDER MATTER

🐾 *Romans 1:18–20* 🐾

*W*hen I was deep in the redwoods some time ago, I lay back and looked up. I mean really up. It was one of those clear summer nights when you could see forever. So starry it was scary. The vastness of the heavens eloquently told the glory of God. No words could adequately frame the awesomeness of that moment. One of my mentors used to say, "Wonder is involuntary praise." That night, it happened to me.

What boggled my mind as I curled up in my sleeping bag that night was this: *Everything I have seen belongs to this one galaxy. Perhaps there are a hundred more beyond our own. Maybe a thousand. Or a hundred thousand . . . each one much larger than ours. Who knows?*

But let's limit our thinking just to this one solar system . . . a tiny fraction of the universe above us. A scientist once suggested an interesting analogy. To grasp the scene, imagine a perfectly smooth glass pavement on which the finest speck can be seen. Then shrink our sun from 865,000 miles in diameter to only two feet . . . and place the ball on the pavement to represent the sun.

Step off 82 paces (about two feet per pace), and to represent proportionately the first planet, Mercury, put down a tiny mustard seed. Take 60 steps more and for Venus put down an ordinary BB. Mark 78 more steps . . . put down a green pea representing Earth. Step off 108 paces from there, and for Mars put down a pinhead. Then take 788 steps more and place an orange on the glass for Jupiter. After 934 more steps, put down a golf ball for Saturn.

Now it gets really involved. Mark 2,086 steps more, and for Uranus . . . a marble. Another 2,322 steps from there you arrive at Neptune. Let a cherry represent Neptune. This will take 2 ½ miles, and we haven't even discussed Pluto!

We have a smooth glass surface 5 miles in diameter, yet just a tiny fraction of the heavens. Now, guess how far we'd have to go on the same scale before we could put down another two-foot ball to represent the nearest star. We'd have to go 6,720 miles! Miles, not feet! And that's just the first star among millions. In one galaxy among hundreds, maybe thousands. And all of it in perpetual motion . . . perfectly synchronized . . . the most accurate timepiece known to man. Phenomenal isn't the word for it.

No God? All by chance? Are you kidding? Listen carefully: "Since the creation of the world God's invisible qualities—His eternal power and divine nature—have been clearly seen, being understood from what has been made, so that men are without excuse" (Rom. 1:20, NIV).

The boggled mind leads to a bended knee.

PHYSICIANS

Matthew 9:10–12

*P*hysician. One upon whom we set our hopes when ill and our dogs when well," defines A. Bierce in *The Devil's Dictionary*.

Of all the professions, that of the physician has to be the most paradoxical. Brilliant and quick-thinking . . . yet unable to write so that anybody (except a pharmacist) can decipher the words. Decisive and disciplined . . . yet more preoccupied than an overworked inventor on the edge of a discovery. He's the only guy I know who can have both hands in your mouth while asking you three questions back to back as he stares up your nose and has his mind on his golf game. Honest and principled . . . yet lies through his teeth every time he says, "This won't hurt a bit . . . you'll hardly feel it."

The physician lives with two unique pressures day and night.

The pressure of life and death. A wrong decision, an unexpected change in a person's body, a drastic reaction to medication, a risk that backfires, a misdiagnosis, a hurried oversight, and a dozen other technical or ethical errors can result in death. What a heavy weight to hang on the thin wire of fallible humanity!

The pressure of success and failure. In a moment of time, years of schooling and decades of a respected practice can crumble and fall. Or, because of "the breaks," the doctor can find himself on the lofty pinnacle of power, prestige, and wealth, dangerously close to the point of idolatry.

If any profession on earth calls for a living, vital, incessant relationship with the eternal God, this one does. And yet therein lies the greatest paradox. Many of those dealing with life-and-death issues are themselves neither prepared to live nor ready to die.

In light of all this, it is interesting to ponder how much we owe to one medical doctor of the first century. His name was Dr. Luke, the beloved personal physician of Paul, the great apostle.

Through Luke's counsel and treatment, Paul was able to live on, fight hard, finish his course, and reach the Roman Empire with the message of hope. Like all great physicians, Luke realized all he could do was diagnose properly, treat the illness correctly . . . and then wait. Only God can heal.

And so, we thank our Lord for every Dr. Luke today—not miracle workers, but mere humans desperately in need of the Divine.

Our Great Physician understands the unique pressures each one of us faces, day and night. Ask for His counsel and diagnosis.

LOOKING AT LIFE

🐾 *James 4:13–15* 🐾

*S*nap a telescopic lens on your perspective for the next few minutes. Pull yourself up close . . . close enough to see the real you. From the reflection in your mental mirror, pay close attention to your life. Try your best to examine the inner "you" on the basis of time.

The only way we can do this, of course, is to look in two directions . . . backward and forward. In many ways what we see in our past and visualize in our future determines how we view ourselves today . . . in that third dimension we call "the present."

As we look back, one overriding thought eclipses all others. It's not new nor very profound, but it's the truth: LIFE IS SHORT. That's not only a valid observation from experience . . . it's biblical.

Psalm 90 is loaded with reminders of the brevity of life. *Life is short . . . like yesterday when it passes by . . . as a watch in the night . . . like grass, it sprouts and withers . . like a sigh, soon it is gone.* Life is indeed short.

As we look ahead, we again see one major message. And it's neither new nor profound, but it sure is true: LIFE IS UNCERTAIN. A single adjective could precede most every event in our future: "unexpected." Unexpected surgery, transfer, change, accomplishment, loss, benefit, sickness, promotion, demotion, gift, death. Life is indeed uncertain.

Well then, since life is so brief and uncertain, how should we view our present?

I suggest there are three words that adequately and accurately describe the present. They do not contradict either lesson we have learned from time, nor do they require rose-colored glasses. Neither do they agree with philosophy's futile meanderings. For as we look at the present, we discover: LIFE IS CHALLENGING.

Because it is short, life is packed with challenging possibilities. Because it is uncertain, it's filled with challenging adjustments. I'm convinced that's much of what Jesus meant when He promised us an abundant life. Abundant with challenges, running over with possibilities, filled with opportunities to adapt, shift, alter, and change. Come to think of it, that's the secret of staying young. It is also the path that leads to optimism and motivation.

With each new dawn, life delivers a package to your front door. When you hear that ring tomorrow morning, try something new. Have Jesus Christ answer the door for you.

Life's most challenging opportunities are often brilliantly disguised as unsolvable problems.

HOW'S YOUR CONSCIENCE?

🐝 *Romans 6:6; 12:13* 🐝

*C*onscience is our moral intuition. It's that part of us that passes judgment on our own state. And it takes away our confidence when something is sour or bad. It takes away our security when it is soiled.

"Let your conscience be your guide." You've heard that. You've said it. Wait a minute. Sometimes that's reliable. But a great deal depends on the condition of your conscience. What if your conscience is seared?

Conscience is like a compass. If a compass is faulty, you'll quickly get off course. A conscience gets its signals from the heart, which can be dulled, hardened, calloused. Furthermore, a conscience can be overly sensitive or can even drive one mad.

Someone who has been reared by legalistic parents who used guilt and shame to manipulate their children often has a conscience that is overly sensitive. Some have consciences so twisted and confused, they need extensive help before they can think correctly. Some need Christian therapists to help them understand their unhealthy consciences. A conscience that is legalistic is not a good guide. A libertine conscience is not a good guide either, nor is a calloused conscience.

In order for one's conscience to be a good guide, one the Spirit can direct, it needs to be healthy, sensitive and capable of getting God's message.

For Men

❧ *Ephesians 6:4–8* ❧

I don't often recommend a volume without reservation, but I think every man should read *Temptations Men Face* by Tom Eisenman. I'm not saying I agree with everything in it, or that you will, but his observations, insights, and suggestions are both penetrating and provocative. In fact, that book got me thinking about the top temptations fathers face.

First, the temptation to give things instead of giving ourselves. Don't misunderstand. Providing for one's family is biblical. First Timothy 5:8 calls the man who fails to provide for his family's needs "worse than an unbeliever." But the temptation I'm referring to goes far beyond the basic level of need. It's the toys vs. time battle: a dad's desire to make up for his long hours and absence by unloading material stuff on his family rather than being there when he is needed.

Second, the temptation to save our best for the workplace. How easy it is for dads to use up their energy, enthusiasm, humor, and zest for life at work, leaving virtually nothing for the end of the day.

Third, the temptation to deliver lectures rather than earning respect by listening and learning. When things get out of hand at home, it's our normal tendency to reverse the order James 1:19 suggests. First, we get mad. Then, we shout. Last, we listen. When that happens, we get tuned out.

Fourth, the temptation to demand perfection from those under our roof. We fathers can be extremely unrealistic, can't we? Fathers are commanded not to exasperate their children (Eph. 6:4).

Fifth, the temptation to find intimate fulfillment outside the bonds of monogamy. Thanks to our ability to rationalize, we men can talk ourselves into the most ridiculous predicaments imaginable.

Sixth, the temptation to underestimate the importance of your cultivating your family's spiritual appetite. Fathers, listen up: Your wife and kids long for you to be their spiritual pacesetter.

Ready for a challenge? Begin to spend time with God, become a man of prayer, help your family know how deeply you love Christ and desire to honor Him.

How about facing the music and then changing the tune?
Say a firm NO to any of these subtle, sneaky, slippery temptations
that have slipped into your life.

THINK IT OVER

❧❧❧

*H*ow have you responded to these temptations mentioned in yesterday's reading in your own life? Do you give things instead of giving yourself, your presence, your personal involvement?

Do you save your best for the workplace?

Do you deliver lectures rather than earning respect by listening and learning?

Do you demand perfection from those under your roof?

Do you try to find intimate fulfillment outside the bonds of monogamy?

Do you cultivate your family's spiritual appetite?

IT'S A CHURCH

❧ *Acts 20:25–38* ❧

A birth is always exciting. Yes, *always.* Whether it is your baby or someone else's, those first cries never fail to make our hearts flutter. Family ties are strengthened as new life extends the roots. Everybody moves in closer and smiles approvingly. What power little babies possess!

What frequently happens in a home occurs all too rarely in a church. Somehow the natural and beautiful drive to reproduce gets lost in the youthful busyness of church life. And if she's not careful, the church begins to grow old, brittle, and inbred, losing interest in giving birth.

The result is tragic: a selfish shell of activity where the *talk* of new life replaces the actual joy of birth. It's a disease, sort of a Laodicean lukewarmness, that causes the once-vibrant, attractive church to turn inward, to become a religious relic, an overweight body lacking vision, passion, and mission. And the terminal verdict (which nobody wants to admit) is ultimately whispered in the hallways of history: *sterility.*

Thankfully, some churches stand in contrast to such a scene, giving birth to new bodies.

Under the watchful eye of a mature church, a young body springs to life. For months the older body gives the baby great prenatal care, resisting the temptation to hurry the birth. They nurture each family member and keep the communication lines open. A teachable spirit coupled with a desire to cultivate its own identity and distinct style of ministry eventually enables the healthy new body to live and breathe on its own.

Then, finally, it's time to cut the cord and detach the new body from the "mother." Smiles brighten faces as the labor is ended . . . and as God witnesses the moment of delight and announces from heaven, "It's a church!"

Being a part of such new life, beginning life anew away from the security and the stability of the parent church, is courageous and, in some ways, sacrificial. But it is right. It is biblical. It is also exciting, as all births are. When I think of all this, I always think of the journeys of the apostle Paul and the delight he took in the various churches he saw come to life and maturity.

If you have not already witnessed such an event in your own church life, I hope you will have the opportunity sometime in the future. When the time is right, you will know it. 'Cause you know how births are. You just can't delay them, even if you try.

Wouldn't you like to contribute to an event that is a part of Christ's own prediction,
"I will build my church"?

EVERYBODY'S TREAT

❧ *Philemon* ❧

*M*y treat!" Nice words to hear, huh? They have flowed into my ears from any number of places. At Thirty-One Flavors on a smoggy, stifling, sweltering August afternoon after I've ordered a double-decker "pralines 'n' cream, dark cone" with a buddy. He digs deeper, faster. I start licking, smilin'. Full of gratitude, I leave wondering why I ordered two scoops. We laugh. I say thanks.

In line for Angel game tickets with another couple, Cynthia and I are looking forward to nine innings of relaxation, when our friends surprise us. "But we said Dutch." "Yeah, well, not this time." Great game. Friendship deepens. Everybody wins (even the Angels!).

Treats are neat. Spontaneous. Unexpected. Pleasant moments that communicate: "You are special . . . loved, appreciated, affirmed, deserving," and a half-dozen other warm fuzzies we need to hear but seldom hand out.

That's one kind of treat—"an act of generosity as an expression of regard or friendship." But treat can also be "an unexpected source of joy, delight, or amusement." Rather than an act, this represents a fact. A happy happening.

I'm thinking of something that never fails to enhance, to encourage, to refresh, to renew. Not every so often, but every single time. The kind of treat where you pick up the tab but the expense is virtually forgotten, thanks to the meaningfulness of the event and the memory that will never be erased. Like time spent on a vacation or at a retreat or at a conference center. A full week or two away from the daily grind. Out where birds still sing and squirrels still run free and nights are still cool and skies are still clear. That's the *where*.

But the essential question is *why?* Because you need a place to relax and get your emotional battery recharged. You need a time to rediscover some of the sparkling gems tucked away in God's Book that have gathered dust, thanks to our fast-paced schedule. You need an opportunity to sing your heart out, to relax.

So, take time out of your too-busy schedule to walk, to play, to nap, to get reacquainted with your loved ones, family, or friends.

Take time to meet with God . . . alone. This is one treat you can't deny yourself.

Tell yourself "my treat," and it will be everybody's treat.

Treat yourself to refreshment for your spirit as well as your body.

MAKING MEMORIES

❧ *Malachi 3:16–17* ❧

*C*all me sentimental, but some tunes really send me reeling. And nobody—I mean nobody—does it any better than Barbra Streisand. Her rendition of "The Way We Were" is pretty close to the ultimate in my book. Remember the words? "Memories . . . light the corners of my mind. . . ."

I don't know what Streisand thinks of when she sings those words, but I know what Swindoll thinks of when he hears them. I think of the lovely teenage girl I married in '55. I think of the paths we've walked together, the smiles and laughter we've shared, the pain we've endured, the decisions we've made, the places we've lived, the four children we've reared . . . yes, especially them. How brightly they light the corners of my mind!

Memories . . .

Those misty, watercolor memories take me back to birthday parties, afternoon picnics, vacation trips, school projects, ball games, graduation excitement, quiet talks, and long walks in the woods. Yeah, those are the memories time can never erase.

Sometimes it seems that things were so much simpler then. Yes, in many ways I think they were. Just pack the kids in the ol' station wagon, lock up the house, and head for family camp. We did that year after year after year.

Memories . . .

There are times this bride of mine and I glance back over our shoulders and ask each other some pretty gutsy questions. Like, "If we had the chance to do it all again, would we?" *You bet.* "Could we?" *No doubt.* Fact is, we still do. We're still building . . .

Memories . . .

And we've noticed that our married kids are starting to do the same thing. And why not? Summer isn't summer for a Swindoll unless it includes a week (or more) of time away from the hassle and the heat, investing ourselves in the lives of a few folks who love the same things . . . who realize if you don't take the time, you won't have the stuff which makes life bearable, like . . .

Memories . . .

Want to have something meaningful to look back on for the rest of your life? Want a scrapbook of scattered pictures filled with smiling faces? Do yourself and your family a favor. Paint some watercolor memories together this summer . . . or fall . . . or winter . . . or spring.

People who do that are not just sentimental . . . they're smart.

Tomorrow's memories come from today's decisions.

WORTH YOUR TIME

🐚 *Revelation 1:1–3; 3:11–12* 🐚

*I*t was Ernest Hemingway who once said, "Time is the least thing we have of." And he was right. How quickly time passes—and how often we lament this. If only we could tack an extra twenty-five or thirty years on to the usual span. There is so much more we want to see, to celebrate, to do. So many places to go, so much to enjoy, to feel, to read, to talk about, to participate in, to encounter. Yet, for each of us, this thing called time is in such short supply.

Our frustration is only compounded by the numerous unimportant, dumb things that steal our minutes and siphon the significance out of our hours. You know what I mean. Stuff like getting gas or a haircut, standing in the eternal line at the DMV, doing the laundry, washing all the dishes after every meal, mowing the lawn, and a dozen other time-consuming things that have to be done but keep you from doing the things that make life so invigorating and fulfilling.

Since "time is the least thing we have of" and since there is no way we're going to escape all the stupid time-traps that accompany our earthly existence, seems to me that we're left with two choices: Either we can fuss and whine about not having enough time, or we can take the time we've got left and spend it wisely. I mean *really* wisely, with our priorities in the right order.

Speaking of that, what are you doing with the rest of your life? I'm talking about cultivating relationships, building memories that will help lift the load of future trials, and the deliberate pursuit of activities that will yield eternal dividends.

Do you have a family? Rather than leaving them the leftovers and crumbs and giving your job your best hours and your most creative ideas, how about rethinking the value of strengthening those ties? And while we're at it, let's not leave out necessary time for quietness, for personal reflection and refreshment.

You say you don't have time to add another week to your squirrel-cage lifestyle. Don't kid yourself. You keep blowin' and goin' like you've been doing most of your adult life, and you'll wind up mumbling to yourself in the twilight years, wondering how you could have stayed so busy yet accomplished so little.

Hey, maybe Hemingway wasn't right after all. You and I have more time than we realize . . . once we get our priority ducks in a row.

Have you ever wondered how you can stay so busy yet accomplish so little?
Think seriously about how you can reorder those priorities.

ON PATTING BIRDS

❧ *Hebrews 6:10* ❧

*I*n a cartoon strip some years ago a little guy was taking heat from his sister and friends for a newly found "calling"—patting birds on the head. The distressed birds would approach, lower their little feathered pates to be patted, sigh deeply, and walk away satisfied. It brought him no end of fulfillment—in spite of the teasing he took from others. "What's wrong with patting birds on the head?" he wanted to know. "What's wrong with it?" his embarrassed friends replied, "No one else does it!"

If your niche is encouraging, please don't stop. If it is embracing, demonstrating warmth, compassion, and mercy to feathers that have been ruffled by offense and bruised by adversity, for goodness' sake, keep stroking. Don't quit, whatever you do.

I think many Christians are dying on the vine for lack of encouragement from other believers. Proverbs 15:23 says, "A man has joy in an apt answer, And how delightful is a timely word." Isn't that true? It's a delightful thing to receive a good word just at your time of need. Encourage someone today.

If God made you a "patter," then keep on patting to the glory of God.

WORKPLACE LESSONS

❧ *Mark 2* ❧

*W*hile traveling across northern California several years ago, I tuned in a radio talk show where the host had just conducted a poll of his listeners regarding job satisfaction. Some sort of questionnaire had been mailed to folks within a broad radius of several cities along the San Francisco peninsula and East Bay region. The show's host had gathered and compiled the answers and was, that day, announcing the results.

To his surprise (and mine) he discovered that well over 80 percent who responded were dissatisfied with their occupations, and when he tabulated the results by cities, some were as high as 84 percent. And the unhappiness he discovered in the workplace was not passive, meek, and mild. Some even responded with intense words like "despise . . . resent . . . dread."

The average worker in the 1940s and 1950s was a male breadwinner with a wife and a houseful of kids to support. He worked full-time and long hours either in an office or a factory—mainly a factory since America was still an industrial society. He was a member of a union, motivated by job security and steady pay, and he looked forward to retirement at age sixty-five. His work was his world.

How things have changed!

Among other changes, today's "average worker" does not belong to a union and would not consider joining one, plans to work past retirement age (many work well into their seventies), and is willing to accept a certain amount of insecurity in exchange for the possibility of being rewarded for superior performance. Maybe that explains why one-third of Americans switch jobs each year.

What's true for the "average worker" in the workplace may also be true for the "average worshiper" in the churchplace, where things are also surprisingly different than in the 1940s and 1950s.

I wonder how many churchgoers, if polled, would be honest enough to admit that frustration mixed with mediocrity also abounds on Sunday. If they had a chance to say so, I wonder if some would respond with intense words like "despise . . . resent . . . dread." And if they did, I wonder if many in the church would care enough to listen or to change.

Be honest now . . . would you?

Not all change is good, but not to change can be bad.

THINK IT OVER

❧❧ ❧❧

A Public Agenda Foundation study, coauthored by Daniel Yankelovich, came up with these top ten qualities that today's workers want in a job:

1. Work with people who treat me with respect
2. Interesting work
3. Recognition for good work
4. Chance to develop skills
5. Work for people who listen if you have ideas about how to do things better
6. A chance to think for myself
7. Seeing the end results of my work
8. Working for efficient managers
9. A job that is not too easy
10. Feeling well-informed about what is going on

Ponder that list. Notice what isn't included in the top ten: job security, benefits, vacation time, and high salary. Yet most companies still operate as though they are the big four—the only ways to motivate and keep their employees.

Ours is a new world. We cannot exist as though it isn't changing.

Now, think about your church. Do you think any of the above might apply? Do any of them apply to you? How is your church meeting the changes and challenges of today?

INJUSTICE

❧ *Amos 5:14–15, 24* ❧

*T*he old prophet Habakkuk wrote relevant words of truth when he put this down in the first chapter of his prophecy: "Yes, destruction and violence are before me; strife exists and contention arises. Therefore, the law is ignored and justice is never upheld. For the wicked surround the righteous; therefore, justice comes out perverted" (Hab. 1:3–4).

The writer of those words died centuries ago, but oh, how his words live on! If you are even slightly aware of everything happening in the world around us, you know how up-to-date his words really are.

The criminal is now the hero, sadly misunderstood and mistreated. The victim is the selfish sadist who decides to press charges because he is bigoted, rash, or confused. The courtroom now resembles a stage peopled by actors vying for starring roles, rather than a dignified chamber of law and order. Judges and juries can be bought, bribed, swayed, or wooed, given sufficient time in the legal pressure cooker. Jury members, who used to be anonymous and sequestered in the name of fairness and objectivity, now appear on talk shows.

Remember that beloved childhood tale of Little Red Riding Hood? Well, if that scenario took place today, here's what would probably happen.

After the heroic woodcutter rescued Little Red Riding Hood by killing the wolf, who had already eaten her grandmother and then tried to kill Little Red, there would be an inquest. At this time, certain "facts" would emerge. First of all, the wolf, prior to his execution, had not been advised of his rights. Then, the ACLU would enter the picture, maintaining that the hungry and needy wolf was merely "doing his thing" and thus did not deserve death.

On this basis the judge would decide that there was no valid legal basis for charges against the wolf and, therefore, *the woodcutter was guilty* of unaggravated assault with a deadly weapon. He would then be arrested, tried, convicted, and sentenced to niney-nine years.

A year from the date of the incident at grandmother's, her cottage would be dedicated as a shrine for the wolf who had bled and died there. Wreaths would be placed there in memory of the brave, martyred wolf. There would not be a dry eye in the whole forest.

If this were not so tragic and true a picture, it would be amusing. But frankly, I'm not laughing. Injustice isn't at all funny.

Sometimes justice truly is blind. Shouldn't we be helping to remove the blindfolds?

SITTING IN THE LIGHT

❧ *1 John 1:5–7* ❧

*Y*ou do not have to sit outside in the dark. If, however, you want to look at the stars, you will find that darkness is required. The stars neither require it nor demand it" (Annie Dillard).

A lot of things in life are like that, aren't they?

A piano sits in a room, gathering dust. It is full of the music of the masters, but in order for such strains to flow from it, fingers must strike the keys . . . trained fingers, representing endless hours of disciplined dedication. You do not have to practice. The piano neither requires it nor demands it. If, however, you want to draw beautiful music from the piano, that discipline is required.

A child plays at your feet, growing and learning. That little one has incredible potential, a hidden reservoir of capability and creativity, but in order for those possibilities to be developed, parents must take time . . . listen, train, encourage, reprove, challenge, support, and model. Moms and dads do not have to do any of that. The child neither requires nor demands that we do so. If, however, we hope to raise secure and healthy offspring, those things are required.

Time spreads itself before us, directionless and vacant. That time can be filled with meaningful activities and personal accomplishments, but in order for that to occur, you must think through a plan and carry it out. You do not have to plan or follow through. Time neither requires it nor demands it. If, however, you hope to look back over those days, weeks, months, and years and smile at what was achieved, planning is required.

What is true of the stars, a piano, a child, and the days ahead is especially true of your mind. It awaits absorption. It will soak up whatever you feed it: imaginary worries, fears, filthy and seductive thoughts, hours of television, and selfish greed . . . *or* good books, stimulating discussions, exciting risks of faith, the memorization of Scripture, and learning a few new skills. You can even take a course or two that will stretch your mental muscles.

You do not have to pay the price to grow and expand intellectually. The mind neither requires it nor demands it. If, however, you want to experience the joy of discovery and the pleasure of plowing new and fertile soil, effort is required.

Light won't automatically shine upon you, nor will truth silently seep into your head by means of rocking-chair osmosis.

It's up to you. It's your move.

If the splendor of the stars is worth sitting outside in the dark, believe me, the joy of fresh discovery is worth sitting inside in the light.

DIVINE RELIEF

❧ *Ephesians 2:1–9* ❧

*W*hat those little Visine drops do for our eyes, *relief* does for our sighs . . . "it gets the red out." Few feelings bring a greater sense of satisfaction than relief, which Webster defines as "the removal or lightening of something oppressive, painful, or distressing."

When we are relieved of physical pain, we breathe easier. Hope returns as pain departs.

When a relationship is strained and we finally work things out, that sense of relief is better than anything money can buy.

When we finally crawl out from under the load of a heavy financial debt, nothing can compare to that sweet relief.

God calls this divine gift of relief "mercy." That's right, *mercy*. It's a twin alongside *grace*.

Grace and mercy are usually seen together, but for some strange reason, mercy seems to live in grace's shadow, eclipsed by her popularity and prestige. Check it for yourself. When the two are named together, grace always comes first. I find the result of that a little unfortunate, because most folks emphasize grace so much that mercy is seldom highlighted.

So, it's time to give mercy her due!

According to Ephesians 2:4, God is "rich in mercy." He is loaded with it! And aren't we glad? If He were not rich in mercy, we might feel secure in God's love and we might be encouraged by His grace, but our lack of relief would hinder the presence of peace. The essential link between God's grace and our peace is His mercy . . . that is, God's infinite compassion actively demonstrated toward the miserable. Not just pity. Not simply sorrow or an understanding of our plight, but divine relief that results in peace deep within.

Paul, after admitting that he was "formerly a blasphemer and a persecutor and a violent aggressor," was allowed to become not only a follower of the Way, but a participant in the service of the King.

How? Read 1 Timothy 1:13 for yourself: "I was formerly a blasphemer and a persecutor and a violent aggressor. And yet I was shown mercy."

In the simplest of terms, revolutionary changes occur in our lives because we were "shown mercy."

What a relief!

The essential link between God's grace and our peace is His mercy.

GOD'S SHEEPDOGS

🐾 *Psalm 32* 🐾

*T*he words of Psalm 23 are very familiar to all of us. Yet, unless we read that psalm through the eyes of a sheep, we will miss its magnificent message. Remember how it concludes? "Surely goodness and mercy shall follow me all the days of my life: and I will dwell in the house of the LORD for ever" (KJV).

Think of goodness and mercy as God's sheepdogs. They stay with us, close by our side, "all the days of our lives." And what helpful companions they are!

The ancient Hebrews had one word they used most often for mercy: *chesed,* pronounced "kesed." It is frequently translated "kindness" and "lovingkindness." While grazing through the Old Testament this past week, I found no less than five different "miseries" to which mercy brings needed relief.

When we're suffering the pain of unfair and unjust consequences (Gen. 39:21–23). Joseph, when dumped into a dungeon because of a false accusation, was given *chesed*—divine relief. It relieved him of the *misery of bitterness,* the companion of unfair treatment.

When we're enduring the grief of a death (Ruth 1:8–9). Shortly after the premature deaths of her sons, Naomi asks the Lord to grant her grieving daughters-in-law *chesed.* God not only gives "dying grace," He also provides "grieving mercy," which relieves us of the *misery of anger* in the backwash of our accepting the loss of a loved one.

When we're struggling with the limitations of a handicap (2 Sam. 9). David extended *chesed* to Mephibosheth, the crippled son of Jonathan, and provided him a place at the king's table for the rest of his days. Mercy relieves the *misery of self-pity* that often accompanies a handicap.

When we are hurting physically (Job 10:12). The Lord gave *chesed* to Job, which strengthened him to go on during his days of intense pain. Divine relief removes the *misery of hopelessness* that would otherwise overwhelm us in times of great affliction.

When we are under a cloud of guilt after we have committed a transgression. Psalms 32 and 51 both speak of David's gratitude for *chesed* after the Bathsheba affair. His sin was not only forgiven, his guilt was taken away. In His mercy and lovingkindness, God relieves the *misery of guilt* . . . the lingering sting of wrongdoing.

No unfair consequence is too extreme for mercy. No grief too deep. No handicap too debilitating. No pain too excruciating. No sin too shameful.

Sheep are often in need, so mercy, our faithful companion, stays near.

"There's a wideness in God's mercy, like the wideness of the sea"
(Frederick W. Faber).

CHANGING CAN'TS TO WON'TS

🕸 *Romans 12:21* 🕸

*C*an't and won't. Christians need to be very careful which one they choose. It seems that we prefer to use "can't."

> "I just can't get along with my wife."
> "My husband and I can't communicate."
> "I can't discipline the kids as I should."
> "I just can't give up the affair I'm having."
> "I can't stop overeating."
> "I can't find time to pray."

Any Christian who takes the Bible seriously will have to agree the word here really should be "won't." Why? Because we have been given the power, the ability to overcome. Literally!

Any good psychiatrist knows that "I can't" and "I've tried" are merely lame excuses.

We're really saying "I won't," because we don't choose to say "With the help of God, I will!"

Now, go back and change all those "can'ts" on that internal list you carry around to "won'ts" and see how that makes you feel about yourself. Not very good, huh? It's the same as "choosing" to disobey. Today you can choose to be an "I will" person.

An excuse has been defined as the skin of reason stuffed with a lie.
(Michael Green, Illustrations for Biblical Preaching).

Time with God

❧ *Exodus 3* ❧

I was raised to believe in the importance of a "quiet time." To the surprise of some, that concept did not originate with the late Dawson Trotman, the founder of the Navigators, but with the Lord Himself.

The Scriptures are replete with references to the value of waiting for the Lord and spending time with Him. When we do, the debris we have gathered during the hurried, busy hours of our day gets filtered out. With the debris out of the way, we are able to see things more clearly and feel God's nudgings more sensitively.

When David wrote, "Wait for the LORD; be strong, and let your heart take courage; yes, wait for the LORD" (Ps. 27:14), he was intimately acquainted with what that meant. When he admitted, "I waited patiently for the LORD; and He inclined to me, and heard my cry" (40:1), it was not out of a context of unrealistic theory. The man was hurting, in great pain.

Time with God? Who experienced its value more than Job after losing it all? Remember his confession? What makes it even more remarkable is that he stated it while surrounded by those who accused him: "But He knows the way I take; when He has tried me, I shall come forth as gold. My foot has held fast to His path; I have kept His way and not turned aside. I have not departed from the command of His lips; I have treasured the words of His mouth more than my necessary food" (Job 23:10–12).

That's it! That is exactly what occurs when we remove ourselves from the fast track and keep our appointment with Him who made us. What great thoughts He has for us, what insights, what comfort, what reassurance!

And the best part of all is that such divine breakthroughs come so unexpectedly. Though you and I may have met in solitude with God morning after morning, suddenly there comes that one day, like none other, when He reveals His plan . . . and we're blown away.

Understand, those phenomenal moments are the exception, not the rule. If God spoke to us like that on an everyday basis, burning bushes would be as commonplace as traffic lights and ringing phones. Fact is, never again in all of time has the voice of God been heard from a bush that refused to be consumed with flames. You see, God is into original works, not duplicated recordings.

But never doubt it: He still longs to speak to waiting hearts . . . hearts that are quiet before Him.

Keep your daily appointment with God.
It's the one meeting you can't afford to miss. Don't be late!

THINK IT OVER

❧❧ ❧❧

*I*f you aren't already doing so, I would strongly urge you to begin keeping a personal journal and write in it daily. This will not only help you focus your thoughts during and after your quiet time with God, but will enable you to look back on His footprints in your life.

Make sure this journal includes your prayer diary. Spend time in prayer every day—every single day.

As David, who knew what it meant to be alone with God, wrote:

Therefore, let everyone who is godly pray to Thee in a time when Thou mayest be found; Surely in a flood of great waters they shall not reach him. Thou art my hiding place; Thou dost preserve me from trouble; Thou dost surround me with songs of deliverance. I will instruct you and teach you in the way which you should go; I will counsel you with My eye upon you (Ps. 32:6–8).

COMING APART

🙠 *Mark 1* 🙠

*I*t was dear old Vance Havner, that venerable, leathery prophet of God, who once declared: "If you don't come apart . . . you will come apart"—wise counsel based on Mark 1:35.

After Jesus' disciples had been slugging it out in the trenches, preaching, counseling, ministering to the needs of others, and skipping meals, our Savior observed their drooping shoulders and said: "'Come away by yourselves to a lonely place and rest a while.' (For there were many people coming and going, and they did not even have time to eat.) And they went away in the boat to a lonely place by themselves" (Mark 6:31–32).

It wasn't planned. Nor was it requested or expected by the men. It was, however, absolutely essential. So the Master interrupted their activities with a brief parenthesis of time. To come apart. So they wouldn't come apart.

There are times when God has to force us to hear His words . . . when He can no longer allow us to ignore His words . . . for our own good.

I can vividly recall a time when this happened to me. A friend who also happened to be a doctor invited me to lunch. During our time together, he warned me about my stress load. That same week a preacher friend called and asked me directly, "Chuck, are you tired . . . really exhausted?" About the same time, my wife and kids were reminding me of some of the very truths I have proclaimed above and had often proclaimed to others. And, most important of all, the Lord God tapped me on my inner man's shoulder and told me, "Come apart."

So for the next several days, I did just that. I ignored the phone calls, postponed my correspondence, disregarded previous plans, and stepped aside for several days.

And you know what? The world didn't come to an end.

And you know what else? When I returned from that "quiet place," my perspective was fresher and my mind was clearer.

Feel someone tapping on your shoulder?

The shortest distance between two points is not always a straight line.

THE TONGUE

❧ *Psalm 39* ❧

*M*any great men and women down through the ages have offered counsel on how to keep our tongues checked and caged. Like Will Noris, the American journalist who specialized in rhymes that packed a wallop. He once wrote: "If your lips would keep from slips, / Five things observe with care: / To whom you speak, of whom you speak, / And how . . . and when . . . and where."

Publius, the Greek sage, put his finger on a technique we tend to forget when he admitted: "I have often regretted my speech, never my silence."

King David put it even more bluntly in Psalm 39:1: "I said, 'I will guard my ways, that I may not sin with my tongue; I will guard my mouth as with a muzzle.'"

That's what it takes, friends and neighbors. A conscious, tight muzzle on the muscle in your mouth. With emphasis on "conscious."

To accomplish that disciplined objective, I offer these three suggestions:

Think first. Before your lips start moving, pause ten seconds and mentally preview your words. Are they accurate or exaggerated? Kind or cutting? Necessary or needless? Wholesome or vile? Grateful or complaining?

Talk less. You increase your chances of blowing it if you talk too much. Furthermore, compulsive talkers find it difficult to keep friends. Conserve your verbal energy!

Start today. Fit that muzzle on your mouth now. It's a project you've put off long enough.

Johann Wolfgang von Goethe, the brilliant German poet and playwright, stated a practical guideline worth remembering: "One ought, every day at least, to hear a little song, read a good poem, see a fine picture, and, if it were possible, to speak a few reasonable words."

Think first. Talk less. Start today.

ADJUSTMENTS

❧ *James 1* ❧

*E*ver made a mental list of things that irritate you? Here are a few I've got on mine: traffic jams, long lines, misplaced keys, stuck zippers, interruptions, late planes, squeaking doors, incompetence, and flat tires.

One of these days it should dawn on us that we'll never be completely free of irritations as long as we are on this planet. Never. Upon coming to this profound conclusion, we would then be wise to consider an alternative to losing our cool. The secret is adjusting.

Sounds simple . . . but it isn't. Several things tend to keep us on the edge of irritability. For one thing, we develop habit reactions, wrong though they may be. Also, we're usually in a hurry—impatient. Add to that the fact that our daily expectations are unrealistic; there's no way we can possibly get it all done anyway. All this increases the level of pressure within us. And when you increase the heat to our highly pressurized system by a fiery irritation or two (or three) . . . BOOM! Off goes the lid and out comes the steam.

When it comes to irritations, I've found that it helps if I remember that I am not in charge of my day . . . God is. And while I'm sure He wants me to use my time wisely, He is more concerned with the development of my character and the cultivation of the qualities that make me Christlike within. One of His preferred methods of training is through adjustments to irritations.

A perfect illustration? The oyster and its pearl. An irritation occurs when the shell of the oyster is invaded by an alien substance—like a grain of sand. When that happens, all the resources within the tiny, sensitive oyster rush to the irritated spot and begin to release healing fluids that otherwise would have remained dormant. By and by the irritant is covered—by a pearl. Had there been no irritating interruption, there could have been no pearl.

No wonder our heavenly home has pearly gates to welcome the wounded and bruised who have responded correctly to the sting of irritations.

J. B. Phillips must have realized this as he paraphrased James 1:2–4: "When all kinds of trials and temptations crowd into your lives, my brothers, don't resent them as intruders, but welcome them as friends! Realize that they come to test your faith and to produce in you the quality of endurance. . . . let the process go on until that endurance is fully developed, and you will find you have become men [and women] of mature character."

How many pearls have you made this week?

BE FORGETFUL

❧ *Matthew 18:21–35* ❧

T'll forgive . . . but I'll *never* forget. We say and hear that so much that it's easy to shrug it off as "only natural." That's the problem! It is the most natural response we can expect. Not *supernatural*. It also can result in tragic consequences.

In his book *Great Church Fights,* Leslie B. Flynn tells of two unmarried sisters who lived together, but because of an unresolved disagreement over an insignificant issue, they stopped speaking to each other. They continued to use the same rooms, eat at the same table, use the same appliances, and sleep in the same room . . . all separately . . . without one word. A chalk line divided the sleeping area into two halves, separating doorways as well as the fireplace. Each would come and go, cook and eat, sew and read without ever stepping over into her sister's territory. Because both were unwilling to take the first step toward forgiving and forgetting the silly offense, they coexisted for years in grinding silence.

After I spoke at a summer Bible conference meeting one evening, a woman told me she and her family had been camping across America. In their travels they drove through a town and passed a church with a name she said she would never forget—THE ORIGINAL CHURCH OF GOD, NUMBER TWO.

Whether it is a personal or a public matter, we quickly reveal whether we possess a servant's heart in how we respond to those who have offended us.

And it isn't enough simply to say, "Well, okay—you're forgiven, but don't expect me to forget it!" That means we have erected a monument of spite in our mind, and that isn't really forgiveness at all.

Servants must be big people. Big enough to go on, remembering the right and forgetting the wrong.

Perhaps Amy Carmichael put it best when she wrote in her book *If:* "If I say, 'Yes, I forgive, but I cannot forget,' as though the God, who twice a day washes all the sands on all the shores of all the world, could not wash such memories from my mind, then I know nothing of Calvary love."

Forgetting an offense means being, in the true and noble sense of the term, self-forgetful.

MASTERING HABITS

❧ *1 Corinthians 6:12* ❧

*T*used to bite my fingernails right down to the quick. I'd bite them off just as soon as the first signs of new growth would appear. Research shows that it takes only three or four weeks for an activity to become a habit.

Not a person who reads this is completely free from bad habits. It's the price we pay for being human. Let's focus on five suggestions that will help us overcome bad habits.

Stop rationalizing. Refuse to make comments like: "Oh, that's just me. I've always been like that." Such excuses take the edge off disobedience and encourage you to diminish or completely ignore the Spirit's work of conviction.

Apply strategy. Approach your target with a rifle, not a BB gun. Take on one habit at a time, not all at once.

Be realistic. It won't happen fast. It won't be easy. Nor will your resolve be permanent overnight. Periodic failures, however, are still better than habitual slavery.

Be encouraged. Realize you're on the road to ultimate triumph, for the first time in years! Enthusiasm strengthens self-discipline and prompts an attitude of stick-to-it-iveness.

Start today. This is the best moment thus far in your life. To put it off is an admission of defeat and will only intensify and prolong the self-confidence battle.

One day at a time, attack one habit at a time.

FUNNY TRUTH

❧ *1 Kings 18* ❧

*M*aybe I'm weird, but there are times the Bible makes me laugh. I mean really laugh. The older I get and the more comfortable I feel in the Book, the more I find times when a smiling response is not only appropriate, it's expected.

Like that time when the main event at Mount Carmel brought out 450 idolatrous prophets on one side and Elijah, all alone, on the other. You remember the story (1 Kings 18). Baal vs. Jehovah. Big altar, prayer for fire. The One who "answers by fire" . . . that's the One to follow.

From morning 'til noon those prophets of Baal called on their deity. Those guys got so anxious that they "leaped about the altar which they had made."

Elijah became amused at their antics and started mocking them: "Call out with a loud voice, for he is a god; either he is occupied or gone aside, or is on a journey, or perhaps he is asleep and needs to be awakened" (18:27). And to amplify the humor, some scholars believe that the Hebrew idiom rendered "gone aside" suggests that Baal may have "gone to the bathroom." Come on, smile; it's okay.

There are many more incidents that add a touch of humor to God's truth. Just the other day while I was digging through the dark days in David's life, I came upon a choice piece of humor. Saul's jealousy had grown into murderous rage, which forced David to run for his life. Suddenly, surrounded by a bunch of strangers from Gath, he didn't know what else to do but fake insanity. "So he disguised his sanity before them . . . and scribbled on the doors of the gate, and let his saliva run down into his beard" (1 Sam. 21:13).

Now, that was anything but funny. But when you read the next couple of verses, you can't help laughing. Upon witnessing this strange phenomenon, the people of Gath hauled the stranger up to their king's front door. And it's his response that's so funny: "Behold, you see the man behaving as a madman. Why do you bring him to me? Do I lack madmen, that you have brought this one to act the madman in my presence? Shall this one come into my house?" In other words, King Achish was up to his ears with more than enough nuts in his kingdom!

Truth is not only stranger than fiction, it's often funnier. When it is, we don't insult God by laughing; we honor Him. It's our way of expressing appreciation for His desire to touch us where we live and to keep His truth interesting, appealing, and, yes, real . . . for so much of life is funny. *Really* funny.

God sets His truth in picture frames of life.

THINK IT OVER

❧❧ ❧❧

*D*o you teach the Bible? If so, that's great. No other calling is more needed or carries with it greater responsibility. My advice?

Study hard.
Pray for insight.
Be accurate with facts.
Be clear in your delivery.
Take your time. Relive and imagine those scenes.
Try not to blot out the color.
Guard against running a marathon with only seriousness setting your pace.

When you happen upon those scenes where the lighter side appears, slow down and call attention to it.

Those you teach will not only appreciate it, they will also learn that among all His glorious attributes, God has a marvelous sense of humor. And they'll be much more interested in the other things He says that aren't at all funny.

I've noticed that those who are free enough to laugh when something is funny are better equipped not to laugh when nothing is funny.

· Deep Grief

🐾 *1 Corinthians 10:11–13* 🐾

*T*he past couple of weeks have been some of the toughest of my life. My emotions have spanned the spectrum: shock, sorrow, horror, intense anger, disillusionment, disappointment, and utter bewilderment. I have prayed—without much benefit. I have read the Scriptures from the Psalms and Proverbs to the words of Jesus and various sections of the letters from Paul, Peter, James—without much peace.

I feel like Job, who admitted, "If I speak, my pain is not lessened and if I hold back, what has left me? . . . He has exhausted me. . . . My spirit is broken" (Job 16:6–7; 17:1).

It occurred to me around 4:20 this morning that perhaps the late, great Spurgeon might have understood my grief better than any other when he wrote over a century ago in his *Lectures to My Students,* in a chapter entitled "The Minister's Fainting Fits":

> Who can bear the weight of souls without sometimes sinking to the dust? . . . To see the hopeful turn aside, the godly grow cold, professors [and pastors] abusing their privileges, and sinners waxing more bold in sin—are not these sights enough to crush us to the earth? . . .
>
> The lesson of wisdom is, be not dismayed by soul-trouble. Count it no strange thing, but a part of ordinary ministerial experience. . . . Live by the day, by the hour. . . . Be not surprised when men fail you; it is a failing world. . . . Be content to be nothing, for that is what you are.

No longer should we be saying that "perilous times will come." They have arrived, fellow pilgrim; they are *now.* And we must face them head-on, doing whatever is necessary to stand firm.

As Carl Henry wrote so eloquently in *Twilight of a Great Civilization:*

> We may even now live in the half generation before all hell breaks loose, and if its fury is contained we will be remembered, if we are remembered at all, as those who used their hands and hearts and minds and very bodies to plug the dikes against impending doom.

The secret of standing in treacherous times is being willing to "take heed"
lest we also fall.

WHO, INDEED, KNOWS?

❧ *Psalm 139* ❧

I grew up in the heyday of radio. (Fact is, I didn't even see a television set until I was a teenager.) If we got our homework done, we could listen to various weeknight radio shows. Remember that spooky line the announcer always gave just before *The Shadow* came on: "Who knows what evil l-l-lurks in the hearts of men? The Shadow knows!" Then there would be a blood-curdling laugh, which faded away into the distance. I always liked all the lights on when we listened to that program.

Many years have passed since those simple and innocent days of my childhood, but that single line remains a haunting question to this day: Who, indeed, knows what wickedness lurks in the hearts of men and women?

We think we do. But how wrong we usually are. The heart houses secrets we can never see. People are awfully good at cover-up. Smiling masks often camouflage breaking hearts. About the time we think we've got somebody figured out, we're stunned to discover how much was hidden from view. Lurking in many a life is pain beyond belief.

In our world of superficial talk and casual relationships, it is easy to forget that a smile doesn't necessarily mean "I'm happy" and the courteous answer "I'm fine" may not be at all truthful. Just because it's Christmas, we can't assume everybody's merry. Even the closest family members can be blindly unaware of each other's pain.

I'm not suggesting that everyone is an emotional time bomb or that masks are worn by all who seem to be enjoying life. But I've lived long enough to know that many a heart hides agony while the face reflects ecstasy.

There is Someone, however, who fully knows what lurks in our hearts. And knowing, He never laughs mockingly and fades away. He never shrugs and walks away. Instead, He understands completely and stays near.

Who, indeed, knows? Our God, alone, knows. He sympathizes with our weaknesses and forgives all our transgressions. To Him there are no secret struggles or silent cries. He hears. He sees. He stays near. He accepts us and loves us unconditionally. He is "the Father of mercies and the God of all comfort."

He who loves us most knows us best. He who knows us best cares the most.

DEPRAVITY ON DISPLAY

❧ *Romans 1* ❧

*P*aul's exposé of depravity in Romans 1:18–32 is a chilling account of human wickedness, a vivid pen-portrait of unleashed unrighteousness, unashamed godlessness, and unnatural lust. Reaching the final argument of his prosecution, the teacher from Tarsus twists the accusing knife with cruel eloquence: "and, although they know the ordinance of God that those who practice such things are worthy of death, they not only do the same, but also give hearty approval to those who do them" (Rom. 1:32).

This came home to me anew as I read about a scam that took place in New York City when some con men decided to make some extra cash by feeding on the depravity of humanity. Naturally, they made a killing.

They got a pile of cardboard boxes, newspapers, stickers that read "Factory Sealed," a roll of bubble plastic, and a stack of stolen shopping bags from Macy's. They stuffed each box with bricks and newspapers until it weighed enough, then wrapped everything in bubble stuff and affixed the stickers. As the evening rush-hour traffic backed up at the Holland Tunnel, the con artists started wandering the curb, carrying the bogus boxes inside the Macy's shopping bags. When they spotted a potential buyer stranded in traffic, they walked up to the car window and started fast-talking a cash deal.

"Hey, man, I got a Sony Handicam here . . . just got if off a FedEx truck." He lifts the box out of the bag, saying, "Macy's sells 'em for $999." Then, jerking his head around nervously, he says, "I'll take 90 bucks, cash."

The cars start to edge forward and the other drivers start yelling. The thief delivers his final pitch: "Okay, man, I'll let you have it for $45. Take it or leave it."

And the driver takes it, knowing it's hot merchandise.

When asked about how it feels to rip people off, selling them empty boxes, one of the men said, "Hey, man, I'm not beating an honest man. No one buys hot unless they've got larceny in their heart."

I must admit . . . the guy's got a point! The fella who grabbed the box and sped off into the night was just as guilty as the thief on the street, and, along with that, his money gave "hearty approval" to the one who ripped him off.

Happens all the time. The details change, but it's still depravity on display. Furthermore, no one is immune. In fact, the possibilities of appealing to our old nature are endless.

What kind of deals do you make when no one is looking?
Are you, right now, aware of wrong and giving hearty approval to another's sin?

BACK-DOOR BLESSING

❧ *James 1* ❧

I had lunch recently with a businessman who runs his own company. As we talked, the subject of wisdom kept popping up in our conversation. So I asked, "How does a person get wisdom? I realize we are to be men of wisdom, but few people ever talk about how it is acquired."

His answer was quick and to the point: "Pain."

I paused and looked deeply into his eyes. Without knowing the specifics, I knew his one-word answer was not theoretical. He and pain had gotten to know each other rather well.

It was then I quoted from the first chapter of James: "When all kinds of trials and temptations crowd into your lives, my brothers, don't resent them as intruders, but welcome them as friends! Realize that they come to test your faith and to produce in you the quality of endurance. But let the process go on until that endurance is fully developed, and you will find you have become men of mature character with the right sort of independence" (James 1:2–4, *Phillips*).

There is no shortcut, no such thing as instant endurance. The pain brought on by interruptions and disappointments, by loss and failure, by accidents and disease, is the long and arduous road to maturity. There is no other road.

But where does wisdom come in? James explains in the next verse: "And if, in the process, any of you does not know how to meet any particular problem he has only to ask God—who gives generously to all men without making them feel foolish or guilty—and he may be quite sure that the necessary wisdom will be given him" (1:5).

As I see it, it is a domino effect. One thing bumps up against another, which, in turn, bumps another, and in the long haul, endurance helps us mature. Periodically, however, we will find ourselves at a loss to know what to do or how to respond. It's then we ask for help, and God delivers more than intelligence and ideas and good old common sense. He dips into His well of wisdom and allows us to drink from His bucket, whose refreshment provides abilities and insights that are of another world. Perhaps it might best be stated as having a small portion of "the mind of Christ."

When we have responded as we should to life's blows, enduring them rather than escaping them, we are given more maturity that stays with us and new measures of wisdom, which we are able to draw upon for the balance of our lives.

By accepting life's tests and temptations as friends,
we become men and women of mature character.

MANUAL LABOR MOTIVATION

Ephesians 4:28

ome collegians think manual labor is the president of Mexico—until they graduate. Suddenly the light dawns. Reality frowns. And that sheltered, brainy scholar who has majored in medieval literature and minored in Latin comes of age. He experiences a strange sensation deep within two weeks after framing his diploma. Hunger. Remarkable motivation accompanies this feeling.

His attempts at finding employment prove futile. Places with openings don't really need a guy with a master's in medieval lit. They can't even spell it. When employers are looking for people, they want someone who can put to use the knowledge that's been gained whether the field is geology or accounting, engineering or plumbing, barbering or welding.

Just now finishing school? Looking for a job? Remember this—dreams are great and visions are fun. But in the final analysis, when the bills come due, they'll be paid by manual labor, hard work forged in the furnace of practicality.

Even the great apostle Paul worked with his hands to support himself.

BURIED LONG ENOUGH

❧ *Daniel 6* ❧

*S*olomon once wrote: "He who walks in integrity walks securely, but he who perverts his ways will be found out" (Prov. 10:9). Job became "the greatest of all the men of the east." People respected him because he was "upright, fearing God, and turning away from evil" (Job 1:1–3). Job walked securely.

Similar things were said of Joseph. Whether managing workers or handling large sums of money or all alone in the home with Mrs. Potiphar, Joseph could be trusted.

Daniel also distinguished himself among his peers because "he possessed an extraordinary spirit." His enemies "could find no ground of accusation or evidence of corruption" anywhere (Dan. 6:1–4).

What did these men have in common?

Perfection? These men were far from perfect.

Easy times? Hardly.

How about slick rhetoric? Wrong again.

What they had in common was *character*—high moral character. They walked securely; they didn't fear being "found out."

Call me dated or old-fashioned or idealistic if you wish, but my passionate plea is that we unearth and restore the concept of character. It's been buried long enough.

Character belongs first on our list when searching for employees of excellence in the workplace. It must be a nonnegotiable among those we place into leadership positions in our schools, our churches, our nation. Character is what wholesome parents strive to cultivate in their children. It is *the* foundational quality all of us expect from the circle of professionals and laborers who serve us up close and personal.

We have every right to expect of ourselves and others virtue, dignity, self-mastery, resoluteness, determination, strength of will, moral purity, and personal integrity—in public and in private. The fact that many fail to live up to the minimal daily requirement does not change the ideal.

If men like Job and Joseph and Daniel could demonstrate character in the worst of times, you and I can do so now. And because we can, we must.

Think about the people you admire and respect most. Does character figure into that assessment? What qualities do you look for in a leader . . . in an elected official? Do you need to revise your priorities in light of this?

THINK IT OVER

༜ ༜

*U*nfortunately, we have grown accustomed to shrugging off lapses in moral character, manifested in secretive and deceptive lifestyles. We are frequently told that trying to find people who value honesty and model responsibility, who promote fairness, accountability, loyalty, respect for others, and who hold to strong, upright convictions is not at all realistic.

"Such people don't exist . . . we need to stop requiring personal purity," we are told. Or, as one air-headed soul said during the last presidential campaign, "We're voting for president, not pope."

To such an analogy, I reply "Nonsense!" That kind of logic (or rather, lack of logic) gives me the jitters. Such reasoning reminds me of a piece of nonsense I learned in elementary school.

Why Are Fire Engines Red?

They have four wheels and eight men;
Four plus eight is twelve;
Twelve inches makes a ruler;
A ruler is Queen Elizabeth;
Queen Elizabeth sails the seven seas;
The seven seas have fish;
The fish have fins;
The Finns hate the Russians;
The Russians are red;
Fire engines are always rushing;
So that's why they're red.

Just think about it.

REAPING THE WHIRLWIND

❧ *Ephesians 5* ❧

*E*ver get the feeling that you have a simple answer to a problem, but you wonder why nobody else has mentioned it? Maybe you don't understand all the facts, you think. Or maybe your answer is too simple. Then again, perhaps they've made the thing too complicated.

Well, that's the way I feel about the tragic problem of AIDS.

Now, I realize there are exceptions, that some people contract AIDS who were not promiscuous. Because they are innocent victims and in the great minority, I need to make it clear that I do not include them in the thoughts I'm sharing here. My comments are directed toward those who deliberately participate in sexual activities outside the God-ordained bonds of heterosexual marriage.

There is only one, simple, twofold solution to the problem of AIDS. It isn't novel or easy. And it certainly isn't original with me.

The twofold answer is *marital fidelity* or *sexual abstinence.*

I am always stunned when I hear about more requests for federal funds to promote "AIDS education." How much education is needed to shake your head and say the simplest word in the English language? We don't need to educate folks on how to hop in the sack safely. No big deal. "Just say no."

Are "morality," "chastity," "virginity," and "decency" forgotten words? Have we totally forgotten the fact that centuries ago God established strict codes of moral conduct because He knew that sexual promiscuity spread disease and caused death? Are we so blinded by rationalization that we have blocked out of our minds the calamitous demise of societies that tolerated illicit practices—Sodom and Gomorrah, ancient Greece, debauched Rome?

God's message still speaks with forceful and insightful relevance: "For this is the will of God, your sanctification . . . that you abstain from sexual immorality" (1 Thess. 4:3). "Flee immorality" (1 Cor. 6:18). "Let marriage be held in honor . . . let the marriage bed be undefiled; for fornicators and adulterers God will judge" (Heb. 13:4).

The problem of AIDS is horrible, but understanding the ultimate cause is not complicated. To borrow from the prophet Hosea (who knew the tragic consequences of sexual impurity), our land has sown the wind and we are now reaping the whirlwind. The storm will not subside unless we return to marital fidelity and sexual abstinence.

The total cure is repentance.

God's moral codes never go out of fashion.

REALITY CHECK

❧ *John 8:1–11* ❧

*T*he older I get, the less excited I am about theory . . . and the more I care about reality. Who cares if the stuff that flows from my pen stimulates the intellect and gives folks fodder for philosophizing? So what if these words tickle ears and answer questions nobody is asking? Provocative, relevant, issue-related writing with enough creativity and honesty to keep the reader reading is what interests me . . . not much else. And so every once in a while I frown, squint, and peer objectively at a page and ask hard questions: Am I in touch? Is this worth mentioning? Does it scratch an itch? Will it make any difference?

I did that after I wrote a column on an "affair." Just decided to face the facts, say it straight, and risk being bold rather than subtle. Another risk is being overzealous and offensive. There's a fine line between being necessarily straightforward and needlessly blunt. Jesus, who never once compromised with sins of the flesh, had a remarkable way of keeping the sinner's dignity intact, à la John 8. I love that about Him as much as anything He modeled.

Anyway, the upshot of all this is a letter that I received in response to my "affair" column. The person who wrote it reinforced my hope that my words would indeed connect and communicate. Here are a few excerpts.

> I rarely write letters like this! But I feel so strongly about what you've written. . . . I was the unfaithful partner in a marriage. Although it was many years ago, it is still a painful memory. It did happen before I knew the Lord, and it has been His grace that has healed and sustained our marriage. My point in writing at all is really to commend and encourage you to continue to address these very difficult subjects. A stand must be taken and too many evade the confrontation. . . . Thank you for your convictions and the courage to speak on them.

So I include this here to ask, again, if this speaks to anyone out there. Perhaps you are still on the fence. Still trying to break off an illicit relationship and come back to your original commitment. Wondering if you dare. If you can. If it's worth it.

You do the same. Walk back into your mate's arms and never walk away again.

As Jesus said, "Go and sin no more."

Telling the truth in love can uncover the lie of sin.
Examine your own life with this in mind.

ANOTHER CHANCE

❧ *Ecclesiastes 12* ❧

*I*nstant replays have become old hat. Whether it's an impressive backhand or a slam dunk or a touchdown pass, we never have to worry about missing it the first time around. It'll be back again and again, and probably again. In slow motion at least once. Every coordinated movement, every graceful or powerful motion returns to be analyzed by fan and announcer alike.

It occurred to me recently that I'd enjoy (for lack of a better title) *delayed* replays of some of the more significant times in my life. I'm fantasizing the possibility of having a chance to relive a particular experience that could have been handled differently. More wisely. With greater tact. In better taste. You know, all those "If I had that to do over again" thoughts. Wouldn't that be neat?

Just think of all the things you'd refrain from saying that you blurted out the first time around. It would be a whole other story the second time around, wouldn't it?

Even everybody's friend, Erma Bombeck—the gal you'd think never regretted a moment—agreed. However, she admitted:

> If I had my life to live over again, I would have waxed less and listened more. Instead of wishing away nine months of pregnancy and complaining about the shadows over my feet, I'd have cherished every minute of it and realized that the wonderment growing inside me was to be my only chance in life to assist God in a miracle. . . . I would have cried and laughed less while watching television . . . and more while watching life. . . . There would have been more I love yous . . . more I'm sorrys . . . more I'm listening . . . but mostly, given another shot at life, I would seize every minute of it . . . and never give that minute back until there was nothing left of it.

Unfortunately, life doesn't offer "delayed replays." Second times around don't happen. "You mean God won't forgive?" You know better than that. "And people can't overlook my failures?" Come on, now. That's not the issue at all. Most people I know are amazingly understanding. Our biggest task is forgiving ourselves.

The main message is clear: Think before you speak. Pause before you act. Make every minute count.

Another chance? No chance. Today is memory in the making, a deposit in the bank of time. Let's make it a good one!

Today is tomorrow's yesterday. How do you want to remember it?

BLIND SPOTS

❧ *1 Timothy 3–4* ❧

*A*ll of us played follow-the-leader as kids. But even then, when the guide in front was too daring or foolish, we would step aside. There were definite limits on how far we would follow.

Sadly, this is not always true in the spiritual realm, where leaders unworthy of the name sometimes command blind devotion. (Remember Jonestown and Waco and those fallen tel-evangelists?)

No one ever defined that follow-no-matter-what syndrome better than our Lord in Matthew 15:14: "Let them alone; they are blind guides of the blind. And if a blind man guides a blind man, both will fall into a pit."

Remember now, Jesus warned us against blind guides, not *all* guides. God still uses strategic, trustworthy, dedicated leaders, and they deserve our respect.

But how can we tell when "blindness" starts to set in? What are the symptoms to look for in strong, natural leaders that tell us trouble is brewing? After thinking about this for quite a while, I am ready to suggest six blind spots we dare not overlook.

Authoritarianism. Take care when a leader begins repressing your freedom. If there is the lack of a servant's heart, of a teachable spirit, pride is in control. Be especially wary of one who seems to have all the answers.

Exclusiveness. Watch out for the "we alone are right" and the "us four and no more" atti-tudes. They reveal themselves in an encouragement to break commitments with your mate, family members, and long-standing friends.

Greed. Moneygrubbing is another telltale sign. Especially if funds wind up in the leader's pocket and become "nobody's business."

Sensuality. Moral purity is a must if the leader claims God's hand is on his life. A holy life is never optional.

Unaccountability. Leaders who refuse to be accountable to anyone forfeit the right to be trusted and followed. Every leader needs counsel and occasional confrontation.

Rationalization. When wrong is justified with a defensive spirit, when inappropriate actions are quickly glossed over, when scriptural truth is twisted to fit a sinful lifestyle, when gray-black facts are whitewashed, stop your support.

Take Christ's advice: "Let them alone"!

If you're going to follow the leader, look where you're going.

PEER PRESSURE

❧ 1 Peter 2:20–24 ❧

*O*nce a spider built a beautiful web in an old house. He kept it clean and shiny so that flies would patronize it. The minute he got a "customer" he would clean up after him so the other flies would not get suspicious.

Then one day this fairly intelligent fly came buzzing by the clean spiderweb. Old man spider called out,"Come in and sit." But the fairly intelligent fly said, "No sir, I don't see other flies in your house, and I am not going in alone!"

Presently the fly saw on the floor below him a large crowd of flies dancing around on a piece of brown paper. He was delighted! He was not afraid if lots of flies were doing it. So he came in for a landing.

Just before he landed, a bee zoomed by, saying, "Don't land there, stupid. That's fly-paper!" But the fairly intelligent fly shouted back, "Don't be silly. Those flies are dancing. There's a big crowd there. Everybody's doing it. That many flies can't be wrong!" Well, you know what happened. He died on the spot.

Some of us want to be in the crowd so badly we end up in a mess because we didn't listen or search out a situation.

What does it profit a fly (or a person) if he escapes the web
only to end up in the glue?

LEAVE IT TO GOD

❧ *Luke 10* ❧

*P*hilip Melanchthon and Martin Luther were once deciding on the day's agenda. The former was disciplined, intellectually gifted, serious, and goal-driven; the latter was equally intelligent but much more emotional, risky, even playful.

Melanchthon said, "Martin, this day we will discuss the governance of the universe."

To which Luther responded, "Philip, this day you and I will go fishing and leave governance of the universe to God."

What wise counsel!

I love Jesus' model of balance. He arrived on the planet with a mission more important than any soul who has drawn a breath of earth air. Yet He didn't really get started until He turned thirty. What about all those "wasted" years? He left them to God.

There's a great scene in Luke when a bunch of His disciples returned from their practical work project. They were all excited about their success, especially that "even the demons are subject to us in Your name."

Ever so graciously Jesus offered this mild rebuke: "Do not rejoice . . . that the spirits are subject to you, but rejoice that your names are recorded in heaven" (Luke 10:20). They felt good about themselves because they had done well. Whereas Jesus implied, "Leave all that to God . . . you have nothing to prove; you are approved. Your names are in the Book and that's what really matters."

I used to feel driven and drained by the never-ending demands of ministry. If folks weren't changing, I felt responsible. If some drifted, I felt at fault. If there wasn't continual growth, I ached as if I needed to make it happen. If a sermon failed to ring with clarity and power, I struggled all of Monday and half of Tuesday. Talk about wasted energy. I've learned to place those cares in the hands of One who can handle them.

Let's declare today the day you and I give ourselves permission to relax without being afraid or feeling guilty . . . and leave the stuff we cannot handle or change to God. Is it a deal? Great! But what shall we do about the person who thinks we are slacking off too much? You guessed it. Just leave it to God!

THINK IT OVER

❧❧❧

*C*an't seem to get where you want to go fast enough?
Leave it to God.
Worried about your kids?
Leave it to God.
Living in a place you'd rather not be?
Leave it to God.
Looks like you won't graduate with honors?
Leave it to God.
No matter how hard you try, your life's partner simply is not responding?
Leave it to God.
Found a lump and you see the doctor tomorrow?
Leave it to God.
You've said the right words to that friend who is lost, and you've been all you know to be; still, zip?
Leave it to God.
Haven't got a date for the prom?
Leave it to God.
A mid-career change seems scary?
Leave it to God.
You did the job but someone else got the credit?
Leave it to God.
Getting older, alone?
Leave it to God.

THE DEPTHS

❧ *Romans 11:33—36* ❧

*A*nyone who loves the sea has a romance with it as well as a respect for it. The mind moves into another gear as the primeval rhythms of the seashore erode tidy resolutions and hectic deadlines.

Anne Morrow Lindbergh beautifully describes this in her classic *Gift from the Sea* . . .

> The mind . . . begins to drift, to play, to turn over in gentle careless rolls like those lazy waves on the beach. One never knows what chance treasures these easy unconscious rollers may toss up, on the smooth white sand of the conscious mind; what perfectly rounded stone, what rare shell from the ocean floor. . . .
>
> But it must not be sought for or—heaven forbid!—dug for. No, no dredging of the sea-bottom here. That would defeat one's purpose. The sea does not reward those who are too anxious, too greedy, or too impatient. To dig for treasures shows not only impatience and greed, but lack of faith. Patience, patience, patience, is what the sea teaches. Patience and faith. One should lie empty, open, choiceless as a beach—waiting for a gift from the sea.
>
> What is hidden in the sea is also hidden in God's wisdom.
>
> We speak God's wisdom in a mystery, the hidden wisdom, which God predestined before the ages to our glory, the wisdom which none of the rulers of this age has understood; for if they had understood it, they would not have crucified the Lord of glory; but just as it is written, "THINGS WHICH EYE HAS NOT SEEN AND EAR HAS NOT HEARD, AND WHICH HAVE NOT ENTERED THE HEART OF MAN, ALL THAT GOD HAS PREPARED FOR THOSE WHO LOVE HIM." For to us God revealed them through the Spirit; for the Spirit searches all things, even the depths of God.
>
> (1 Cor. 2:7–10)

Those fathomless truths *about* Him and those profound insights *from* Him produce within us a wisdom that enables us to think *with* Him. Such wisdom comes from His Spirit who, alone, can plumb the depths and reveal His mind.

The hurried, the greedy, the impatient cannot enter into such mysteries. God grants such understanding only to those who wait in silence . . . who respect "the depths of God." It takes time. It calls for solitude.

Get alone with God and gain a new respect for His wisdom. It won't come in a hurry. Don't be afraid to seek the depths. Ideally, find a beach where you can stroll, a weather-beaten bench where you can sit and think . . . where you can be still and know . . .

Find your own "seashore" of solitude and reflection.

A MIDSUMMER-DAY'S DREAM

❧ *Isaiah 26:3* ❧

The thermometer registers in the nineties. The air is still and heavy. The dog is panting, the sun is high, and the birds are silent. It is the middle of summer. Long, hot days . . . uneventful, unguarded, uncomplicated.

Somewhere, miles away, crops push their way toward harvest and waves roar and tumble onto shore. Windswept forests sing their timeless songs, and desert animals scurry in the shadows of cactus and rock.

Within a matter of hours night will fall, the dark sky will glitter with moon and stars, and sleep will force itself upon us. Life will continue on uninterrupted. Appreciated or not, the canvas of nature will go on being painted by the fingers of God.

In the midst of the offensive noise of our modern world—the people, the cars, the sounds, the smog, the heat, the pressures—there stand those reminders of His deep peace. The running wave, the flowing air, the quiet earth, the shining stars, the gentle night, the healing light . . . and from each, the blessing of the deep peace of Christ to you, to me.

Have you such peace, or is it nothing more than a midsummer-day's dream? If you must confess an absence of such peace, may I suggest a simple change of scenery? Visit the seashore and hear the running wave. Take a drive out to the country, roll the windows down, and feel the air flowing through your hair. Walk out into the night and look up at the stars. Be still and discover anew that He is God. The longing of one's heart for deep peace is somehow recaptured in such settings.

Jim Elliot, the martyred missionary, eloquently expressed his own discovery of such peace in this journal entry:

> I walked out on the hill just now. It is exalting, delicious, to stand embraced by the shadows of a friendly tree with the wind tugging at your coattail and the heavens hailing your heart, to gaze and glory and give oneself again to God—what more could a man ask? Oh, the fullness, pleasure, sheer excitement of knowing God on earth! I care not if I never raise my voice again for Him, if only I may love Him, please Him. . . . If only I may see Him, touch His garments, and smile into His eyes.

May the deep peace of our God cool and quiet our overheated souls.

THANKS FOR THE MEMORIES

❧ *Deuteronomy 8* ❧

hile jogging early this morning, I found myself humming the tune Bob Hope immortalized during several wars. I can still remember his tailor-made lyrics, fitted to each occasion. He sang them to lonely soldiers, sailors, airmen, and marines from steamy jungles to frozen reservoirs . . . from the decks of aircraft carriers to makeshift platforms on windswept sand dunes. As guys and gals in uniform laughed and cried, screamed and sipped Coke, they always anticipated Hope's finale as he took the mike and crooned, "And thanks for the memories. . . ."

I remember it well: Christmas of '58 on Okinawa. I was homesick, missing my wife, and counting the days. So when the veteran entertainer sang his closing song, I sang along with him in a flood of memories. I recall how grateful I was for that tour of duty: the lessons I had learned, the disciplines I had begun to employ (thanks to the Navigators), the books I had read, the missionaries I had met, the places I had visited, the journal I had kept, the letters I had written, the verses I had memorized, even the things I had witnessed inside a Marine Corps barracks! And, most importantly, the call I had received from God to enter ministry.

Looking back now, all I can do is smile . . . and sing, "Thanks for the memories." I'm doing that a lot these days as I recall the various things God has done in me and through me and for me—and sometimes in spite of me! And I can't help but give Him praise in my heart.

Pastoring a church has to be the highest of all callings. In this position, one has the privilege of touching life at its tenderest points . . . of walking with pain through its darkest valleys . . . of proclaiming truth in its purest form . . . of confronting sin in its ugliest scenes . . . of modeling integrity through its hardest extremes—while everyone is watching as well as when no one is looking. It is no wonder to me why it requires a God-given calling before one enters it or why such a struggle accompanies resignation from it.

And after all these years I say a resounding, "Thanks for the memories!" For the conversions that have occurred, the addictions that have been conquered, the marriages that have been restored, the fractured lives that have been mended. These memories stay with me and revisit me often as I thank Him for His faithfulness.

Who knows what other surprises God has over the horizon? I do not know what lies ahead, but for today I pause and praise Him . . . and thank Him for the memories.

We know who holds the future . . . as we thank Him for the past.

BAD VIBES

🦋 *Psalm 62* 🦋

*M*ost noises in church don't bug me. I've heard 'em all. People snoring. Babies crying. Rain falling. Crickets chirping. Sound systems popping. Toilets flushing. Offering and communion plates dropping. Sirens screaming and cars speeding outside. Kids yelling and phones ringing inside. Hymnals hitting a bunch of piano keys. Organists standing up on a foot full of bass notes. Coughing. Sneezing. Blowing. Laughing. Crying. Shouting. Whispering. Gasping. Yawning. Clapping.

It's no big deal . . . noises really come with the territory. Even some "joyful noises" are part of the package. I've heard some guys sing so badly they sounded like a bull moose with its hind legs caught in a trap as they bellow the baritone part to "Wonderful Grace of Jesus." And I've heard a few sopranos who really needed to be put out of their misery. (I've often been thankful that stained glass doesn't shatter.) But their motives were right, so they will receive their reward. (I hope it includes heavenly voice lessons or we're all in for an awfully long eternity.)

There is one shrill noise, however, unique to this electronic age, that I find both irritating and irresponsible. It's those plagued digital watches! It's bad enough to have 'em chime and dong and zip and blip and bzzzt and ting every hour on the hour, but since they're not synchronized to go off exactly at the same time, it's fifteen to twenty seconds of every conceivable tone. It's enough to make a hound lift his head and holler.

I'm not alone, believe me. You can't imagine the bulletin stubs, postcards, verbal comments, threats, and letters I've received pleading that somebody say something.

So I think I'll make this suggestion to pastors everywhere: Tell your congregation that if they promise to be more thoughtful with their hourly chimes, you'll be more punctual with your closing time. But warn them that for every weird blip . . . blip . . . blip you hear, you'll add another ten minutes to the sermon.

Won't it be fun watching everybody glare at the guys who turn the meeting into a marathon? Come to think of it, while I've heard lots of sounds and seen lots of sights in churches, I've never seen a Sunday morning congregational mutiny. We could make history!

We cannot watch the clock and at the same time worship the Lord
in the beauty of holiness.

PRAYING TO YOUR FRIEND

Matthew 6:7–13

F rancois Fenelon, a seventeenth-century Roman Catholic Frenchman, said this about prayer:

Tell God all that is in your heart, as one unloads one's heart, its pleasures and its pain, to a dear friend. Tell Him your troubles, that He may comfort you; tell Him your joys, that He may sober them; tell Him your longings, that He may purify them; tell Him your dislikes, that He may help you to conquer them; talk to Him of your temptations, that He may shield you from them; show Him the wounds of your heart, that He may heal them; lay bare your indifference to good, your depraved tastes for evil, your instability. Tell Him how self-love makes you unjust to others, how vanity tempts you to be insincere, how pride disguises you to yourself and others.

If you thus pour out all your weaknesses, needs, troubles, there will be no lack of what to say. You will never exhaust the subject. It is continually being renewed. People who have no secrets from each other never want for subject of conversation. They do not weigh their words, for there is nothing to be held back; neither do they seek for something to say. They talk out of the abundance of the heart, without consideration they say just what they think.

Blessed are they who attain to familiar, unreserved intercourse with God.

HELPING

❧ *Hebrews 10* ❧

*W*ell, it's mid July. Time to make a mad dash for the pool or at least a tall, frosty glass of iced tea. But while you're swimming or sipping, think about helping. Yeah, *helping.*

Think about being of assistance . . . your arm around the hunched shoulders of another . . . your smile saying "try again" to someone who's convinced it's curtains . . . your cup of cool water held up to a brother's cracked lips, reassuring and reaffirming.

Every time I pick up my pen, the thought of helping urges me to push ink into words.

There are enough—more than enough—specialists in body blocks, pass defenses, and tackling. There are more than enough causing fumbles, bruises, and injuries. I'd much rather run interference. I'd much rather slap someone on the back and say, "You can do it. Now git at it!"

I wholeheartedly agree with Philip Yancey, a man who models his own advice: "C. S. Lewis once likened his role as a Christian writer to an adjective humbly striving to point others to the Noun of truth. For people to believe that Noun, we Christian writers must improve our adjectives."

Whether in the sweltering heat of summer or the bitter blast of winter, I'd like to think that some carefully selected turn of a phrase, some pointed story, even the choice of a single word I used might reach out with a grip of fresh hope.

It's all part of helping folks. For, as His Word mandates: "Let us hold fast the confession of our hope without wavering, for He who promised is faithful; and let us consider how to stimulate one another to love and good deeds" (Heb. 10:23–24).

Attractive adjectives plus unselfish verbs equal faith in the Noun of truth.

THINK IT OVER

❧❧

*M*y own concept of God can never remain static after coming into contact with the fictional output of a man driven by such near-spiritual forces, a writer with such a dynamic view of the God who leads man toward scientific maturity. Bradbury, at his best, is not only a prophet for a depressed people; he is a kind of deliverer, awakening our sensibilities.

—Calvin Miller speaking of the writings of Ray Bradbury

Tolkien set out to entertain with his stories—his own children first, and then others. But in the telling, the stories grew into something far grander than anything he himself imagined when he began. That is always the best way. The writer begins with little more than the thread of an idea and the desire to follow it and see where it will go. But as he works at his creation, his labor becomes a sacrifice, of his time if nothing else (but most often, of much else besides). And if he is faithful to the High Quest, God, I believe, accepts the sacrifice and enters into it in ways unforeseen by even the author himself.

—Stephen R. Lawhead speaking of the works of J. R. R. Tolkien

Think about the truth you have seen through the words of others, in both the written word and the spoken word.

Do your own words speak hope, encouragement, and truth to those around you?

CRICKET PLACES

❧ *Psalm 148* ❧

There was once a cricket on the loose in my former church. When things were quiet and still, his wings sang at top volume . . . like at weddings. And funerals. And during long prayers. And very early on Sunday morning before the place started jumpin' with cars and microphones and organ preludes.

I looked all around for that critter. About the time I thought I'd found him, I was wrong. So, early one Sunday morning, I decided to let the cricket stay. Who knows? I thought. Maybe there are times crickets need to be in people places just as there are times people need to be in cricket places.

Like out of doors. Surrounded by the sights and sounds and smells of solitude. And rhythmic running streams. And skies so blue it hurts when you stare. And fragrant, wild blossoms that smell of violet. And awesome, jagged cliffs. And soaring hawks. And field mice playing hide 'n' seek. And funny little lightning bugs. And the shrill screams of whippoorwills on misty mornings. You know, cricket stuff . . . so familiar to them they hardly notice anymore.

I've got to hand it to my church-visiting insect friend: He knew the value of variety. The vast majority of his ilk are in a rut. They hang around the familiar, identify with millions of other Jiminys, run with the swarm, and never know what the rest of the world is like. Think of all the things "our" cricket heard and felt that most of the world's crickets won't experience in a lifetime! I tell you, the guy had spunk. He was willing to risk whatever to break with the predictable.

Are you? If you're like most, the answer, unfortunately, is no.

Unless you plan ahead, life will come and go without your making any break with boredom. Not even for a week. Entire seasons and years will pass without a single significant memory being added to your mental museum . . . unless you determine to split from the swarm.

Isn't it about time you made plans to add some variety to your life? To spend time in a completely different setting? Maybe sneak away for a week to the mountains or the desert or maybe near a lake or alongside the crashing surf . . . you know, cricket stuff!

> *Sometimes crickets need to be in people places,*
> *and sometimes people need to be in cricket places.*

CALLING SIN, SIN

❦ *Proverbs 14* ❦

A bomb exploded in our nation some years ago. In mid-America, of all places. The fuse was lit first in the mind of Karl Menninger, but its effect was not felt until his pen detonated the blasting cap. Suddenly—without prior warning— BOOM! His book *Whatever Became of Sin* stunned and shocked his colleagues.

Most of Menninger's peers had put that hated word to bed decades ago. But now, *the* Karl Menninger, M.D., the Freud of America, whose book *The Human Mind* had introduced psychiatry to the American public back in 1930, that respected, competent, pioneer of the profession, actually had the gall to reintroduce SIN to the vocabulary!

All had been relatively quiet on the Western front. America was still licking its wounds from the riots, campus rebellions, and political assassinations of the sixties. We were biting the bullet of a prolonged war in Southeast Asia. We were hearing rumblings with strange names back then—ecological concerns, energy crises, and "do your own thing." Most of us sensed trouble was brewing . . . *something* was wrong. But none dared call it SIN.

Maybe our president would admit it. Lincoln did, way back in 1863. Eisenhower did, borrowing his words from Lincoln, when the Day of Prayer rolled around exactly ninety years later: "It is the duty of nations as well as of men to own their dependence upon the overruling power of God, to confess their sins and transgressions in humble sorrow, yet with assured hope that genuine repentance will lead to mercy and pardon."

But Eisenhower's subsequent calls to prayer never mentioned that explosive term again. In fact, in 1972, Frederick Fox of Princeton University stated in a compelling article entitled "The National Day of Prayer": "Since 1953, no President has mentioned sin as a national failing. Neither Kennedy, Johnson, nor Nixon. To be sure, they have skirted the word. . . . I cannot imagine a modern President beating his breast on behalf of the Nation and praying, 'God, be merciful to us sinners.'"

"As a nation," admitted one wag at the time, "we officially ceased 'sinning' some twenty years ago."

Then came Menninger, who was gutsy enough to declare the truth. Was what he said new? No, not new. It had been there all the time. It just needed to be declared.

May we all have the courage to say that—to call sin, SIN.

Some words need to be deleted from our vocabulary; others need to be reinstated.

CAPABILITIES

❧ 1 Corinthians 12—slowly and aloud! ❧

*H*ave you ever noticed how uniquely adapted each animal is to its environment and its way of life? On land, a duck waddles along ungainly on its webbed feet. In the water, it glides along smooth as glass. The rabbit runs with ease and great bursts of speed, but I've never seen one swimming laps. The squirrel climbs anything in sight but cannot fly (unless you count great airborne leaps from limb to limb), while the eagle soars to mountaintops.

What's true of creatures in the forest is true of Christians in the family. God has not made us all the same. He never intended to. He planned that there be differences, unique capabilities, variations in the Body. So concerned was He that we realize this, He spelled it out several times in His Word. I charge you to take the time to read 1 Corinthians 12 slowly and aloud. Those thirty-one verses tell us about His desires and designs—which are more attractive than any thirty-one flavors!

The subject is commonly called "spiritual gifts," and it is as helpful as any truth the believer can ever know. In a nutshell, here's the scoop.

God has placed you in His family and given you a certain mixture that makes you unique. No mixture is insignificant!

That mix pleases Him completely. Nobody else is exactly like you. That should bring you pleasure, too.

When you operate in your realm of capabilities, you will excel and the whole Body will benefit . . . and you will experience incredible satisfaction.

When others operate in their realm, then balance, unity, and health automatically occur in the Body. It's amazing!

But when you compare . . . or force . . . or entertain expectations that reach beyond your or others' God-given capabilities, then you can expect frustration, discouragement, mediocrity, and, in the long run, defeat.

If God made you a duck saint—you're a duck, friend. Swim like mad but don't get bent out of shape because you wobble when you run. Furthermore, if you're an eagle saint, stop expecting squirrel saints to soar . . . or rabbit saints to build the same kind of nests you do.

Accept your spiritual species. Cultivate your capabilities. Stop comparing. Enjoy being you!

No one else is exactly like you. Cultivate your capabilities.
Refuse to compare or control.

CAUGHT, NOT TAUGHT

🌭 *1 Corinthians 4* 🌭

*S*ome things are better felt than telt," say our Scottish friends. And that is so true. Take insight, for example—that elusive weave of intuition, perception, alertness, and sensitivity. You just can't teach it. You can, however, nurture it. You can even expand it. But there's no one-two-three process that suddenly makes one insightful. Yet insight is essential in things like teaching or counseling or writing. When insight is present, those skills literally come alive. Insight makes the simple profound and the difficult understandable. Those who have it were not taught it; they caught it. From God.

Another example? Touch. We refer to a gifted musician as having the right "touch"— that sixth sense that lifts sterile black notes off white pages and transforms them into the colorful and moving strains of a masterpiece. Give some pianists the score and you get harmony and rhythm played with proper timing. Place the same piece before one with touch—and there is no comparison. One plays music. The other experiences it, feels it, is moved by it, understands, is lost in it . . . and helps us do the same.

Touch is somehow caught from God, not taught by man. Either you got it or you ain't!

These two extremes pose a practical problem, however: Either we feel deprived . . . or we get stuffy because we got it and they ain't.

Hey, let's once and for all put this frustration to bed. If you've "got it," you caught it. You didn't earn it or learn it or deserve it, nor can you preserve it. God sovereignly marked you out and equipped you with that unique ingredient to reflect His glory. That's the reason. "And what do you have that you did not receive? But if you did receive it, why do you boast as if you had not received it?" (1 Cor. 4:7).

And what if you're among the so-called have-nots? You're gifted, but it's not one of those abilities that seem so enviable. Your particular gift or ability or capability is just as significant, just as deliberately planned by God, as any other. It pleased Him to make you like you are for His glory.

And on top of the responsibility that's yours to contribute your part, you have the added joy of receiving the benefits from those individuals uniquely gifted with things like insight and touch. Those moments come to us on rare occasions in life, not to frustrate us but to refresh us . . . like the soft rush of wind from the flapping of angels' wings.

I don't know how else to describe it. Some things are better felt than telt.

Have you been envious or jealous of another's gift?
Just stop and think of what the world would have missed had you not been in it.

A HOLY LIFE

❦ Leviticus 11:44–45 ❦

As Christians we live a life that is different—morally excellent, ethically beautiful. It's called a holy life. And God honors that. Because it's like He is. And according to Ephesians 5:1, we are to mimic God, living as He lives.

All of our Christian lives we have sung the old hymn "Take Time to be Holy." Those words are true. It does take time to be holy. It certainly takes time to be mature. It takes time to cultivate a walk with the Lord that begins to flow naturally because the enemy is so much more assertive and powerful than we . . . and so creative, so full of new ideas on how to derail us and demoralize us.

We need to lock onto that power that comes from God's presence and invite Him to cleanse our thoughts, to correct our foul speech, to forgive us completely, and make us holy vessels who, like those winged seraphim, spend our days bringing glory to His holy name.

Take a really honest look at your walk. Are there any areas where old sins have begun to take control again? This would be a wonderful time to allow Him to bring fresh order out of longstanding chaos.

God has called us to be holy, so let's be holy.

GOD INCOMPREHENSIBLE

❧ *Job 38:1—40:4* ❧

*L*ost in the silent solitude of recent days, I have been impressed anew with the vast handiwork of our incomprehensible God. The psalmist was correct: The heavens *do* indeed tell of the glory of God . . . their expanse *does* indeed declare the work of His hands (Ps. 19:1).

At a time when one-upmanship and human intimidation have become an art form, it is delightful to be reminded anew that "Our God is in the heavens" and that "He does whatever He pleases" (Ps. 115:3).

Old Zophar was right on target when he asked, "Can you discover the depths of God? Can you discover the limits of the Almighty? They are high as the heavens, what can you do? Deeper than Sheol, what can you know? Its measure is longer than the earth, and broader than the sea. If He passes by or shuts up, or calls an assembly, who can restrain Him?" (Job 11:7–10).

We need that reminder, we who are tempted to think we're capable of calling the shots. We need to be brought down to size, we who feel we've got a corner on our own destiny.

Not only do we feel capable of declaring His overall plan for our own lives, we think we have the ability to discern each detail of His panoramic plan across the centuries. What a joke! We're doing well to "trust and obey" on a day-to-day basis.

Author Annie Dillard, in her prize-winning work *Pilgrim at Tinker Creek,* writes: "In making the thick darkness a swaddling band for the sea, God 'set bars and doors' and said, 'Hitherto shalt thou come, but no further.' But have we come even that far? Have we rowed out to the thick darkness, or are we all playing pinochle in the bottom of the boat?"

Such questions do what they're supposed to do: make us uncomfortable. But in our discomfort an essential change takes place. God becomes what and who He should be to us, namely God Incomprehensible.

We need to discipline ourselves to think on these things! We need to refocus our minds from the horizontal to the vertical. We need to rise above the nonsense of human viewpoint and tedious worries about non-eternal issues. We need to get on with thoughts that really matter.

It's time we got reacquainted with our Maker. It's time we got closer to His thick darkness. Sure beats playing pinochle in the bottom of the boat.

"Teach us to know that we cannot know, for the things of God knoweth no man. . . .
Let faith support us where reason fails, and we shall think because we believe, not in
order that we may believe" (A. W. Tozer).

THINK IT OVER

❧❧❧

*W*hat are the benefits of realizing God Incomprehensible? We no longer reduce Him to manageable terms. We are no longer tempted to manipulate Him and His will . . . or defend Him and His ways Like the grieving prophet, we get new glimpses of Him "lofty and exalted," surrounded by legions of seraphim who witness Him as the Lord of hosts" as they shout forth His praises in antiphonal voice (Isa. 6:1–2). All this gives new meaning to the psalmist's ancient hymn:

> O Lord, our Lord,
> How majestic is Thy name in all the earth. . . .
> When I consider Thy heavens, the work of Thy fingers,
> The moon and the stars, which Thou hast ordained;
> What is man, that Thou dost take thought of him? (Ps. 8:1, 3–4).

"What is man . . . ?" What a great question!

In a world consumed with thoughts of itself, filled with people impressed with each other, having disconnected with the only One worthy of praise, it's time we return to Theology 101 and sit silently in His presence. It's time we catch a fresh glimpse of Him who, alone, is awesome yea, incomprehensible. He is our infinite, inexhaustible God. Any serious study of Him takes us from an unconscious to conscious awareness of our ignorance.

The One we worship defies human analysis.

CHANCE

🐝 *Psalm 19:1–6* 🐝

*W*ith the help of a telescope or a microscope we are ushered into a world of incredible, infinite design. Take your choice: astronomy or biology . . . "the infinite meadows of heaven" (Longfellow) or the diminutive microbes of earth . . . and sheer, unemotional intelligence will force you to mumble to yourself, "Behind all this was more than chance. This design is the result of a designer!" His name? God, the Creator.

To deny that these worlds are the result of God's design is to defy all mathematical calculations of chance. Let me prove that by borrowing the following illustration from a noted scientist and former president of the New York Academy of Sciences, Dr. A. Cressy Morrison. Suppose I would take ten pennies and mark them 1 to 10 and give them to you to put in your pocket. I'd ask you to give them a good shake. Then I'd say, "I'm going to reach into your pocket and draw out penny number 1." My chance of doing this would be 1 in 10 . . . and you would be surprised if I accomplished it. Now, let's go further. I would put number 1 back in your pocket, have you shake them again, and I'd say, "I will now draw out number 2." Now my chances are much slimmer—1 in 100. If I were to draw out number 3 in the same way, the chance would be 1 in 1000. If I drew out each number in successive order, following the identical process, the ultimate chance factor would reach the unbelievable figure of 1 chance in 10 billion!

If I performed that act before your eyes, you would probably say, "The game is fixed," and you would be correct. That's exactly what I am saying about the galaxies and the germs—and, far more importantly, your life and mine on this earth. The arrangement is fixed . . . there is a Designer—God—and He declares His presence twenty-four hours a day. How? Listen to Psalm 19:1: "The heavens are telling the glory of God; they are a marvelous display of his craftsmanship" (TLB).

This planet was designed by God to support one thing: life. Why life? Because only through life can matter understand God and glorify its Maker! Only through faith in the Lord Jesus Christ can the designed know and glorify the Designer.

If you are making no attempt to know and glorify your Designer, you're taking the greatest chance possible. Correction—that's no chance at all. That kind of life has definite consequences and a fixed destiny: eternity in hell . . . lasting separation from your Designer.

Any possibility that you may be the exception? Not a chance.

Telescopes and microscopes can display the design,
but only the eyes of faith can see the Designer.

SAYING GRACE

❧ *Luke 11:1–10* ❧

*M*ost of us did not learn to pray in church. Nor were we taught at school . . . nor even beside our bed at night. If the truth were known, we've done more praying around the kitchen table than anywhere else on earth. From our earliest years we've been programmed: If you don't pray, you don't eat. It started with Pablum and it continues through porterhouse. A meal is incomplete without it.

For some strange reason, at one point as I was growing up, prayer before the meal became the "comedy hour." In spite of parental frowns, glares, and threats, we simply could not keep from laughing. I remember one time my sister and I giggled so long and so loud that Mother finally joined in. My older brother was praying (he usually remembered every missionary from Alaska to Zurich) and never let up. He finished by praying for the three of us!

As we grew older, however, we began to realize how good it is to cultivate this healthy habit. In fact, "asking the blessing" is a sweet, needed, refreshing pause during any hectic day.

But since it occurs so often, an easy trap to fall into is sameness—meaningless, repetitious clichés that might even be boring to God! (Remember, our Lord Jesus warned against the kind of empty verbosity that characterized the Pharisees.)

I haven't got all the answers, but you might start with these suggestions.

Think before you pray. What's on the table? Call the food and drink by name. What kind of day are you facing . . . or have you faced? Pray with those things in mind. Be specific.

Involve others in prayer. Try sentence prayers involving everyone at the table. Or, ask for their requests.

Sing your blessing. The doxology, a familiar hymn, or a chorus of worship offers a nice change of pace. Holding hands adds a lot.

Keep it brief, please. There's nothing like watching a thick film form over the gravy while you plow through all five stanzas of "And Can It Be?"

Occasionally pray after the meal. An attitude of worship is sometimes easier to maintain when stomachs are full.

In case you wonder if your "grace time" is losing its punch, here's a way to find out. When the meal is over, ask if anyone remembers what was prayed for. If they do, great. If they don't, sit back down and discuss why. You've got a lot more to be concerned about than a stack of dishes.

Prayer is truly the pause that refreshes.

THE RIGHT PHILOSOPHY

ᏽᏽ *Ephesians 4* ᏽᏽ

*I*t was one of those days. Demands. Deadlines. Decisions. Endless interruptions mixed with a nagging headache that Tylenol wouldn't erase and positive thinking wouldn't help.

Right in the middle of the mess, a guy poked his head in the door, smiled, and (among other things) dropped a real gem on me: "The person who knows *how* will always have a job . . . and he will always work for the person who knows *why.*"

People who *know how* are on the front lines and in the trenches, selling the product, teaching the students, fixing the cars, typing the letters, swinging the bats, getting the job done. They will always be the largest in number among the work force.

But there must also be those who *know why.* Those who can harness the energy and give direction, those who can manage and motivate and generate enthusiasm among those who know how.

The difficulty comes when those who know why spend too much time doing things that ought to be done by those who know how, or when those who know how do not know the why behind what they are doing, and when those who should know why do not know (or care) why!

Jesus Christ—our ultimate Leader—has clearly declared our philosophy: "And He gave some as apostles, and some as prophets, and some as evangelists, and some as pastors and teachers, for the equipping of the saints for the work of service, to the building up of the body of Christ" (Eph. 4:11–12).

Don't just scan those words; study them. They form the philosophy of the local church, but they have been virtually ignored in this day of maddening activity.

Why has the Lord given leadership? To equip saints.

Why are the saints to be equipped? To serve.

Why is it so important to serve? To build up the Body.

Who is the major target of our ministry? The Christian. What is the major need in his/her life? Being equipped to serve . . . in the home, in the community, in the world. Everything we do, everything we promote and finance and endorse, should relate directly to equipping and/or serving.

It's invaluable that people in the church know why and how. Once they do, it's amazing how involved they become in reaching out to the lost.

Are you equipped to serve? Do you know why and how?

That Dreaded "D" Word

❧ *1 Corinthians 6:12–20* ❧

*O*kay, folks . . . it's that time again. I'm down to two suits, one sports coat, and only a couple of pants that I can squeeze into. No more excuses. I'm tired of good intentions, secret promises to myself, groans and grunts as I roll out of bed in the morning, and especially those well-meaning comments from first-time visitors at our church: "You look . . . uh . . . different than I expected." I suppose that's better than "You look . . . uh . . . fat."

Funny thing about being overweight . . . it's impossible to hide it. So the alternatives are (a) ignore it and lie to yourself by saying nobody notices, (b) make jokes about it, (c) try to solve the problem overnight—which is tempting but dumb, or (d) face the music and get underway with a long-range plan that works.

For me, it's an intelligent diet (ugh!) mixed with a program of regular exercise and a do-or-die mind-set that is determined to see it through, followed by a from-now-on game plan that is realistic, workable, and consistent.

Personally, I don't need a shrink to shrink. But what I do need is discipline with a big *D*. (It might also help me a lot to think of rewards other than a strawberry sundae.) You know what I'm getting at, don't you? If I intend to avoid great widths, I need to go to great lengths to make that happen. And if you are put together somewhat like I am, you do too.

So why am I telling you all this? It would be much easier and certainly less embarrassing for me to say nothing, eat little, exercise in obscurity, and start to shrink. I did that once before and it worked. Problem was, when I got down to my desired weight, a rumor spread that I had cancer. Cynthia even got a sympathy card or two. So . . . none of that.

I'm mentioning it because I need to be accountable and we need to be reminded of the importance of our physical appearance. While there is an overemphasis on this in the secular world, for some strange reason, we Christians tend to underestimate its importance. Yet our bodies are indeed the "temple of the Holy Spirit" and we are to "glorify God" in those bodies (1 Cor. 6:19–20).

So, let's get serious about something we've ignored or excused or joked about long enough. As for me, I've got about forty pounds to go. How about you?

Have you looked in the mirror lately?
Could the Spirit's temple stand a little attention to get it back where it ought to be?

TURNING TURMOIL INTO PEACE

❧ *Philippians 4* ❧

When Christians are up against a wall, it's interesting that they finally turn to prayer. The only thing that will work is the last thing we try. Take a look at this: "Be anxious for nothing, but in everything by prayer and supplication with thanksgiving let your requests be made known to God. And the peace of God, which surpasses all comprehension, shall guard your hearts and your minds in Christ Jesus (Phil. 4:6–7).

Most Christians are so familiar with those words, I fear they may have lost their punch. To guard against that, let's read them from another translation—*The Amplified Bible*: "Do not fret or have any anxiety about anything, but in every circumstance and in everything, by prayer and petition (definite requests) with thanksgiving, continue to make your wants known to God. And God's peace [shall be yours, that tranquil state of a soul assured of its salvation through Christ, and so fearing nothing from God and content with its earthly lot of whatever sort that is, that peace] which transcends all understanding shall garrison and mount guard over your hearts and minds in Christ Jesus."

Now that's a mouthful! If I understand this correctly, the anxiety that mounts up inside me, the growing irritation and the struggles that make me churn, will be dissipated and, in fact, replaced with inner peace if I will simply talk to my God. Prayer is the single most significant thing that will help turn inner turmoil into peace. Prayer is the answer.

Fear nothing!

THANKFUL FOR ANGELS

✣ *Psalm 91* ✣

*H*ave you counted your blessings lately? Let me suggest one you might have overlooked. Let's be thankful for angels—those unseen guardians who work overtime, who never slumber or sleep.

Angels exist as supernatural creatures in and about heaven, and they are frequently dispatched to earth in human form to bring encouragement and assistance. If you have ever encountered the sudden appearance and/or departure of an angel after receiving one's help, you are never quite the same.

Several years ago some high school fellas from the church I pastored in Southern California went on a mountain-climbing excursion, along with their youth leader. While taking in the breathtaking sights, however, the leader realized he had lost the trail. A heavy snowfall had completely covered the path, and he didn't have a clue where they were or how they could get back to the main camp. Sundown was not far away, and they were not equipped to spend the night on the craggy, windblown slopes where the temperature would soon drop even lower.

While trudging through the snow, entertaining thoughts just this side of panic, they suddenly heard someone on the slopes above them yell down: "Hey—the trail is up here!" They glanced up and to their relief saw another climber in the distance. Without hesitation, they began to make their way up to the large boulder where the man was sitting. The climb was exhausting, but their relief in finding the way gave their adrenaline a rush.

Finally, they arrived . . . but to their surprise the man who had yelled at them was nowhere to be found. Furthermore, there were no traces in the snow that anyone had been sitting on the boulder, nor were there footprints around the rock. The trail, however, stretched out before them, leading them to safety. The boys not only learned a valuable lesson about the wilderness but also firmed up their belief in encountering "angels without knowing it."

God's special messengers are often invisible but never impotent. As the psalmist has written: "He will give His angels charge concerning you, to guard you in all your ways. They will bear you up in their hands, lest you strike your foot against a stone" (Ps. 91:11–12).

Can you think of occasions in your own life when you had what you would consider "a close call"? How about one of your kids or friends? Can you remember a time or two when, through some incredible manner, they were shielded from harm or delivered from danger?

THINK IT OVER

❧❧ ❧❧

any years ago one of my mentors told me a story I have never forgotten. A missionary was home on furlough, traveling by car from church to church. Late one rainy evening, facing a long and lonely all-night journey, he asked the Lord to help him stay awake and make it safely to the next place he would minister.

A few minutes later he came upon a man off to the side, thumbing a ride. Although he rarely picked up hitchhikers, he felt sorry for the man out in the rain and offered him a lift. As the two of them began to visit, the missionary was thrilled to discover that the stranger was a believer and that they also had many mutual friends engaged in the Lord's work.

Time passed rapidly as the two of them laughed and shared stories. The fellowship was so rich that the missionary hated to see the early light of dawn and hear his new-found friend say, "Well, here's where I get off." Before saying good-bye, the missionary invited him to have a cup of coffee at a roadside cafe. As they parted, they promised to pray for each other.

The rain had stopped by now, and a bright sun-drenched sky warmed the missionary's soul. Then, a couple of minutes down the road, he realized that he had failed to get the man's address and phone number, so he quickly returned to the cafe. There was no sign of the man. When he asked the cook if he'd seen which way the other fella had gone, he was shocked to hear him respond, "What other fella? You came in here alone . . . I wondered why you ordered two cups of coffee."

The missionary glanced at the table where the two had sat and noticed that the other cup was still full to the brim . . . and the coffee was cold.

As he returned to his car, another surprising realization came to his mind. He remembered that when he had picked up the hitchhiker in the rain the night before, the man had gotten in the car but he wasn't wet!

PREDICTABILITY

❧ *Joshua 14* ❧

*J*ohn Gardner, a United States cabinet member under President Johnson, once pointed out that by their mid-thirties most people have stopped acquiring new skills and new attitudes in any aspect of their lives.

Does that jolt you? Stop and think, you who are over thirty. How long has it been since you acquired a new skill? How many new attitudes have you adopted? Are you compelled to approach a problem the same way every time? Does a maverick (even wild) idea challenge you or make you retreat into your shell? Have you lost that enthusiastic zest for discovery or adventure? Are you becoming addicted to predictability?

I'll let you in on a secret: Living and learning go hand in hand; existing and expiring do too. The constant curiosity and probing inquisitiveness of preschoolers make every day completely fresh and exciting. To them learning is natural; to many adults it's a nuisance. I find that amazing.

If you are saying to yourself, "Well, that's just the way I am; I can't change," then you are limiting God, discounting His power and denying His presence. He's offering you an "abundant life," and you're settling for a bland diet of tasteless existence.

Now I'm not suggesting you go out and do stupid stunts to prove your unpredictability. However, why not turn your everyday problems into creative projects? Why not take life by the throat and achieve mastery over a few things that have haunted and harassed you long enough? Why not broaden yourself in some new way to the greater glory of God?

Remember Caleb? He was eighty-five and still growing when he grabbed the challenge of the future. At a time when the ease and comfort of retirement seemed predictable, he fearlessly faced the "invincible" giants of the mountain. His story is told in Joshua 14. There was no dust on that fella. Every new sunrise introduced another reminder that his body and a rocking chair weren't made for each other. While his peers were yawning, he was yearning.

If you are determined and work quickly, you can keep the concrete of predictability from setting up around you. But if the risks of sailing your ship in the vast ocean of uncertainty make you seasick, you'd better stay near the shallow shores of security. Concrete sinks fast, you know.

I challenge you: This week do something totally unpredictable, even if it's only taking a different route to work. A change of scenery could change your outlook . . . but you'll never know until you try.

PASSIVE MEN, WILD WOMEN

❧ *Ephesians 5:22–33* ❧

hose words aren't original with me. They came from a shrink living in Marin County, California—Pierre Mornell, who wrote a book that bears that title. The issue that concerned Dr. Mornell is found in Christian marriages just as often as in non-Christian ones.

It's the problem of the husband who is "inactive, inarticulate, lethargic, and withdrawn at home. In his relationship to his wife he is passive. And his passivity drives her crazy." He's not necessarily incompetent and dull. At work he may be extremely successful and articulate. And she's not necessarily rebellious and overactive. She may be a good mother, talented, and well-respected by her peers.

At home, however, the husband says, in a dozen different ways, "I'm tired . . . just leave me alone." She makes requests; he ignores them. She gets louder; he retreats further. She adds pressure; he lapses into sullen silence. Ultimately he withdraws; she goes "wild."

Numerous, often complex, reasons lie behind such standoffs, but a couple of extremely important factors stand out.

First, men and women are different, and these differences don't decrease or disappear once people get married. (I've discovered that they gain momentum!) It helps immensely to try to put oneself in the partner's shoes (albeit an extremely tough thing to do) and to realize the other's needs and viewpoint. If you fail to do that, you wind up on the sofa.

Second, harmonious partnerships are the result of hard work; they never "just happen." I don't know of anything that helps this process more than deep, honest, regular communication. Read those last four words again, please. That's not just talking; it's also listening. And not just listening, but also hearing. Not just hearing, but also responding, calmly and kindly.

The "hard work" also includes giving just as much as taking, modeling whatever you're expecting, forgiving as quickly as confronting, putting into the marriage more than you ever expect out of it. Yes, more. In one word it means being *unselfish*.

Few things are better for breaking the passive-wild syndrome than taking off for a couple of days together. Without the kids. Without the briefcase. Without an agenda.

This will go a long way toward keeping you off a counselor's couch . . . or, for that matter, off your own sofa.

On a scale of 1 to 10, how well are you and your spouse communicating?

220

OUTGOING LOVE

🎙 *Romans 14* 🎙

*H*is face was covered with a full beard. His hair fell almost to his shoulders. When he smiled, his white teeth flashed in contrast to the blanket of brown that concealed his skin. His eyes were blue, clear, and alert. His laughter was strong and familiar to my ears. It reminded me of the times we sat together as friends in seminary, wrestling with reason and trying to unscrew the inscrutable.

He's now working at a restaurant, playing bluegrass in a four-piece combo. He also has an exciting ministry in a small church where he works with couples. As we had in the old days, we kicked around all sorts of subjects: his marriage, John Denver, the "Body concept" of the local church, banjos and fiddles . . . and the spiritual hunger on university campuses today. That's what we *talked* about, but we *communicated* more, much more.

Despite the separation of the years and the difference in our current lifestyles, we were inseparably linked as one in the bond of love. It seems so stupid to me that fellowship must be limited to the narrow ranks prescribed by a grim-and-narrow mind-set. Just because I prefer a certain style or attire doesn't mean that it's best . . . nor that it's for everyone . . . nor that the opposite taste is any less pleasing to God.

This gross intolerance of those who don't fit our mold reveals itself in a stoic stare or a caustic comment. Such legalistic and prejudiced reactions will thin the ranks of the local church faster than fire in the basement or flu in the pew.

If you question that, take a serious look at Paul's letter to the Galatians. His pen flowed with heated ink as he rebuked them for "deserting" Christ (1:6), "nullifying the grace of God" (2:21), becoming "bewitched" by legalism (3:1), and desiring "to be enslaved" by this crippling disease (4:9).

Sure there are limits to our freedom. Grace doesn't condone license. Love has its biblical restrictions. The opposite of legalism is not "do as you please." But listen! The limitations of liberty are far broader than most of us realize.

So, the next time you're in Dallas you might want to look up my friend Larry. He plays great mandolin in a top-notch bluegrass combo. He still loves Christ, but he never forces it on you. If you can get beyond his hairy face, you'll find a humble heart.

The bonds of love that bind us are greater than the boundaries that separate us.

LOOKING BACK

❧ *Isaiah 51* ❧

*M*arian Anderson, the great contralto who won worldwide acclaim, didn't simply grow great; she grew great simply. In spite of her fame, she remained a beautiful model of humility.

A reporter interviewing Miss Anderson once asked her to name the greatest moment in her life. She had had so many big moments to choose from. For example:

There was the night conductor Arturo Toscanini announced, "A voice like hers comes once in a century."

In 1958 she became a U.S. delegate to the United Nations.

Then there was that private concert she gave at the White House for the Roosevelts and the king and queen of England.

And in 1963 she was awarded the coveted Presidential Medal of Freedom.

Which of those big moments, among many, did she choose? None of them. Miss Anderson quietly told the reporter that the greatest moment of her life was the day she went home and told her mother she wouldn't have to take in washing anymore.

Unlike Marian Anderson, some of us go to great lengths to hide our humble origins. The truth is, when we peel off our masks, others are usually not repelled; they are drawn closer to us. Frequently, the more painful or embarrassing the past, the greater the appreciation and respect.

The prophet Isaiah mentions this very thing as he reminds us to: "Look to the rock from which you were hewn, and to the quarry from which you were dug" (Isa. 51:1). That sounds much more noble and respectable than its literal meaning, for in the Hebrew text the word "quarry" actually refers to "a hole." Or, as the old King James Version translates it: "Look unto . . . the hole of the pit whence ye are digged."

What excellent advice! Before we get all enamored with our high-and-mighty importance, it's a good idea to take a backward glance at the "hole of the pit" from which Christ lifted us. In fact, let's not just think about it; let's admit it.

Why, some of the greatest saints have crawled out of the deepest, dirtiest, most scandalous "holes" you could imagine. And it was that which kept them humble, honest men and women of God, unwilling to be glorified or idolized.

The next time we're tempted to believe our own stuff, let's just look back to the pit from which we were dug. It has a way of shooting holes in our pride.

Remembering the depths from which we have come
has a way of keeping us all on the same level: recipients of grace.

KNOWING GOD/BEING STILL

❧ *Ephesians 5:1* ❧

*B*e imitators of God, therefore, as dearly loved children" (Eph. 5:1, NIV). Maybe you never realized such a statement was in the Bible. What a strange command: "Be imitators of God"!

But to do that, to be an imitator of God, requires that we come to terms with the value of quietness, slowing down, coming apart from the noise and speed of today's pace, and broadening our lives with a view of the eternal reach of time. It means saying no to more and more activities that increase the speed of our squirrel cage. Knowing God requires that we "be still" (Ps. 46:10).

It means if I'm a pastor, I do more than tend the sheep. The same applies if I'm a businessman or a homemaker. It means I refuse to be driven by guilt and unrealistic demands on my time and my priorities. It means I must draw away from what's going on and seek solitude with my Father.

We'll be criticized, of course, for taking time away to "be still," but it's not a take-it-or-leave-it luxury. It is necessary for survival. Our minds must be liberated from the immediate, the necessary stuff in the mainstream of our world, so we can gain perspective. We have to have "still" times so we can imitate Jesus and lift ourselves away from the grit and grind of mere existence.

Tell yourself right now and throughout today, that it's okay to draw away from the maddening crowd. Jesus did; so can you.

Fatigue is not next to godliness.

SHARING 101

❧ *Philippians 2:1–11* ❧

*A*s our world is getting smaller, our minds seem to be following suit. Our level of selfishness is increasing by the day. Suddenly, nobody wants you to invade his or her "space." Sharing may be the major subject in a kindergarten class, but somewhere on the way to adulthood the lessons get erased.

How easy it is to forget that thinking first of the other person did not originate with Dale Carnegie. It comes straight from the Lord our God, who led Paul to write: "Do nothing from selfishness or empty conceit, but with humility of mind let each of you regard one another as more important than himself; do not *merely* look out for your own personal interests, but also for the interests of others" (Phil. 2:3–4).

If you think most people follow that counsel, see what happens the next time you're driving into the mall and you slip into a parking spot, not realizing someone else was waiting to occupy it. We're talking borderline homicide.

This selfish attitude is also alive and well on airplanes. I remember one in particular: I was sitting on a 727 about halfway back in the coach section (three-plus-three configuration) when a family of three came aboard. Apparently they had purchased their tickets late and were unable to secure reserved seating in the same row. The airline attendant assured them that there were several empty seats . . . surely someone would be willing to swap.

Just in front of me were two empty seats, middle and window . . . and on the other side, same row, the middle and aisle seats were open. The family—all of them friendly and courteous—asked the gentleman on the aisle if he would be willing to move from the right side aisle seat to the left side aisle seat. That's all . . . just stand up, take two steps to the left, then sit back down. Just swap seat 17D for seat 17C.

Do you think he'd do it? No way. He wasn't even courteous enough to answer verbally. Just stared straight ahead as he shook his head firmly.

Just remember this the next time someone cuts in front of you, the next time you are patiently (or impatiently?) waiting your turn in the line or at the light and someone charges ahead of you.

Make it an opportunity to practice Sharing 101. "Therefore however you want people to treat you so treat them for this is the Law and the prophets" (Matt. 7:12).

Watch for an opportunity to share "your" space.

THINK IT OVER

❧❧❧

A lady took my seat in church a while back. It's not that important really. She is a very nice lady, kind and considerate. A good friend, in fact. There were several other seats available. I can sit any place. The people in our congregation are as friendly and caring as you will find any place in the world. A person should be comfortable sitting any place. It's no big deal.

My seat is in the seventh row back from the front of the church. I'm sure she didn't intend to take my seat. She just wouldn't do that. Nor would anybody else in our fine church. It doesn't make that much difference.

My seat is on the end of the pew, on the north side by the windows. On your left as you come into the sanctuary. I can rest my left arm on the end of the pew. It's a good seat. But I would never raise a fuss about a seat. . . . She probably didn't intend anything personal by taking my seat. I would never hold a grudge. . . .

Actually, it was about three months ago when she took my seat. I really don't know why she took it. I've never done anything to her. I've never taken her seat. I suppose I'll have to come an hour early now to get my seat. Either that or sit on the south side.

She really took it because it's one of the best seats in the house. That's why she took it. She had no business taking my seat. . . . And I'm not going to go to church two hours early to get what was rightfully mine from the beginning.

This is the way great social injustices begin: abusive people taking other people's seats in church. This is the way the seeds of revolution are sown. A person can only stand so much. Where is it going to end? If somebody doesn't stand up and be counted, nobody's seat will be safe. People will just sit any place they please. And the next thing they'll do is take my parking place, too. World order will be in shambles. . . .

—ZEAN CARNEY, EDITOR, *The Banner-Press*
David City, Nebraska, May 9, 1991

WHOSE TEAM?

❧ *Joshua 24:14–15; 1 Corinthians 6:9–11* ❧

W hen the death of Richard Nixon and the twentieth anniversary of his resignation were strangely juxtaposed only a few months apart, the networks
were overloaded with revisits to and retrospectives on Watergate.

I was intrigued by a book by Leo Rangell, M.D., a psychiatrist who explores what he
calls "the compromise of integrity" in his careful, articulate analysis of the inner workings in
the head and psyche of Richard M. Nixon and several of his closest confidants. It's called,
appropriately, *The Mind of Watergate*. Within the book is the transcript of a verbal investigation between Senator Howard Baker and young Herbert L. Porter. Here is just a small
portion of it.

Baker: "Did you ever have any qualms about what you were doing? . . . Did you ever
think of saying, 'I do not think this is quite right.' . . . Did you ever think of that?"

Porter: "Yes, I did."

Baker: "What did you do about it?"

Porter: "I did not do anything."

Baker: "Why didn't you?"

Porter: "In all honesty, probably because of the fear of the group pressure that would
ensue, of not being a team player."

Porter's answer keeps coming back to haunt me these days. How much of that whole,
ugly nightmare could have been prevented if only someone had had the courage to stand
alone? If only the fear of doing wrong had been greater than "the fear of group pressure"?

It's terribly hard to stand pat and buck the tide . . . alone.

All this strikes much closer to home than a break-in in D.C. or a breakdown in the Oval
Office. It's a major motivation behind experimentation with drugs or sexual promiscuity or
wholesale commitment to some cult or cooperation with an illegal financial scheme. Group
pressure is terribly threatening.

So be on guard! When push comes to shove, think independently. Think biblically. If
you fail to do this, you'll lose your ethical compass.

Watergate is a timeless lesson: It is not as hard to know what is right to do as to do what
you know is right.

If being a team player requires doing what is wrong, you're on the wrong team.

LAUGH IT OFF

❧ *Psalm 35* ❧

*E*ver get the feeling that life's a little too tight—like an ill-fitting shoe? Commitments are piling up and you're taking things much too seriously? You either can't get to sleep or you wake up at two in the morning and spend the next three hours rehearsing everything you have to do and can't possibly get done? It's enough to make a grown man or woman scream.

So, instead of blaming others or feeling sorry for myself or planning a jump from the Golden Gate Bridge, I'm gonna laugh for a while. If you don't feel like laughing with me, close the book or turn the page. Far be it from me to force you to smile. But if you, too, think it seems appropriate to laugh at some of the stuff that drives us nuts, here are a few groaners.

- If you try to please everybody, nobody will like it.
- The chance of the bread falling with the peanut butter and jelly side down is directly proportional to the cost of the carpet.
- When a broken appliance is demonstrated for the repairman, it will work perfectly.
- Not until you get home from the party will you realize you have a string of spinach in your teeth.
- There's a committee somewhere right now planning your future, and you were not invited to the meeting.
- No one's life, liberty, or property are safe while the legislature is in session.

There are hundreds more, but that's enough for now. I feel better already, don't you? Truly, laughter is often the best medicine.

Don't sweat the small stuff; in fact, the big stuff isn't worth the sweat either.

PREVENTING DRY ROT

✣ *2 Corinthians 4* ✣

*N*ot everybody gets "turned on" over management concepts, but most of us can profit from such information at home or church or school. Even as individuals we may find some of these principles coming in handy.

If organizations are not to become stagnant, they must renew themselves—stay continually fresh. Some years back I found some excellent guidelines for this shared by John W. Gardner in a *Harper's* article entitled "How to Prevent Organizational Dry Rot." I've condensed some of his thoughts here.

1. No Number 1 provided!
2. Don't kill the spark of individuality.
3. Cultivate a climate where comfortable questions can be asked.
4. Don't carve the internal structure in stone. Most organizations have a structure that was designed to solve problems that no longer exist.
5. Have an adequate system of internal communication.
6. Don't become prisoners of procedures. The rule book grows fatter as the ideas grow fewer.
7. Combat the tendency toward the vested interest of a few. In the long run, everyone's vested interest is in the continuing vitality of the organization.
8. The organization must be more interested in what it is going to become than in what it has been.
9. An organization runs on motivation, conviction, and morale. Each person has to believe that his or her efforts as an individual will mean something for the whole and will be recognized by the whole.
10. The profit-and-loss statement is not a clear measure of present performance.

Any of this sound familiar?

Any of it sound helpful?

Any of this reminiscent of those familiar words of the apostle Paul? "But let all things be done properly and in an orderly manner" (1 Cor. 14:40).

And what about your personal renewal? To paraphrase my earlier statement: If individuals are not to become stagnant, they must renew themselves—stay continually fresh.

You think it over. Go back and look at those ten statements in that light . . . then try them on for size.

We should be more interested in what we are going to become
than in what we have been.

OVERSIMPLIFICATION

❧ *Psalm 26* ❧

*I*n my younger years I had a lot more answers than I do now. Things were absolutely black or white, right or wrong, yes or no, in or out—but a lot of that is beginning to change. The more I travel and read and wrestle and think, the less simplistic things seem. I now find myself uncomfortable with sweeping generalities, neat little categories, and well-defined classifications.

We evangelicals are good at building rigid walls out of dogmatic stones . . . cemented together by the mortar of tradition. We erect these walls in systematic circles then place within each our oversimplified, ultra-inflexible "position." Within each fortress we build human machines that are programmed not to think but to say the "right" things and respond the "right" way at any given moment. Our self-concept remains undisturbed and secure since no challenging force is ever allowed over the walls.

Occasionally, however, a strange thing happens: A little restlessness springs up within the walls. A few ideas are challenged. Questions are entertained. Alternative options are then released. Talk about threat! Suddenly our superprotected, cliché-ridden answers don't cut it. The stones start to shift as the mortar cracks.

We can react in one of two ways. One, we can maintain the status quo "position" and patch the wall by resisting change with rigidity. Two, we can openly admit "I do not know" and let the wall crumble. Then we can do some new thinking by facing the facts as they actually are. The more popular, naturally, is the first. We are masters at rationalizing around our inflexible behavior. We imply that change always represents a departure from the truth of Scripture.

Now some changes do pull us away from Scripture, and these must definitely be avoided. But let's be absolutely certain that we are standing on scriptural rock, not on traditional sand. We have a changeless message—Jesus Christ—but He must be proclaimed in a changing, challenging era. That calls for a breakdown of stone walls and a breakthrough of fresh, keen thinking based on scriptural insights.

No longer can we offer tired, trite statements that are as stiff and tasteless as last year's gum beneath the pew. The thinking person deserves an intelligent, sensible answer, not an oversimplified bromide mouthed by insensitive robots within the walls.

All I ask is that you examine your life. For, as Socrates said, "The unexamined life is not worth living."

If you've stopped thinking and started going through unexamined motions,
you've really stopped living and started existing.

THE IMPORTANCE OF ATTITUDE

🎗️ *Philippians 2:3–5* 🎗️

This may shock you, but I believe the single most significant decision I can make on a day-to-day basis is my choice of attitude. It is more important than my past, my education, my bankroll, my successes or failures, fame or pain, what other people think of me, or say about me, my circumstances, or my position. The attitude I choose keeps me going or cripples my progress. It alone fuels my fire or assaults my hope. When my attitudes are right, there's no barrier too high, no valley too deep, no dream too extreme, no challenge too great for me.

Yet we must admit that we spend more of our time concentrating and fretting over the things that can't be chnged—than we do giving attention to the one that we can change, our choice of attitude. Stop and think about some of the things that suck up our attention and energy, all of them inescapable: the weather, the wind, people's action and criticisms, who won or lost the game, delays at airports or waiting rooms, x-ray results, gas and food costs.

Quit wasting energy fighting the inescapable and turn your energy to keeping the right attitude. Those things we can't do anything about shouldn't even come up in our minds; the alternative is ulcers, cancer, sourness, depression.

Let's choose each day and every day to keep an attitude of faith and joy and belief and compassion.

Take charge of your own mind!

CHRIST'S RETURN

❧ *1 Corinthians 15:50–58* ❧

*C*ynthia and I were enjoying a quiet evening at home. The house was unusually still, and we were sitting there sipping freshly perked coffee and having a quiet conversation. You know, one of those priceless moments you wish you could wrap up and bring out again when you really need it.

For some reason our discussion turned to the subject of Christ's return. Our comments ranged from chuckling over letting the folks in the Tribulation worry about cleaning out our garage to contemplating the joys that will be ours as we share eternity with family and friends in the Body of Christ.

Later that evening, however, I found myself returning again and again to the thought, *He is coming back. What a difference it will make!*

Is it a waste of time to focus on the Lord's return? Quite the contrary. It's *biblical;* it's the very thing Titus 2:13 says we ought to do: "looking for the blessed hope and the appearing of the glory of our great God and Savior, Christ Jesus."

This Bible of ours is full and running over with promises and encouragements directly related to the return of our Lord Jesus Christ. It's not just hinted at; it's *highlighted.* You can't read very far without stumbling upon it, no matter which book you choose. In the New Testament alone the events related to Christ's coming are mentioned over 300 times.

"Okay, swell. But what do I do in the meantime?" I can hear all pragmatists asking.

First, it might be best for you to understand what you don't do. You don't sit around, listening for some bugle call or looking for the rapture cloud. You don't quit work. And you don't try to set the date because "the signs of the times" are so obvious!

You do get your act together.

You do live every day (as if it's your last) for His glory.

You do work diligently on your job and in your home (as if He isn't coming for another ten years) for His Name's sake.

Other than that, I don't know what to tell you. Except, maybe, if you're not absolutely sure you're ready to fly, get your ticket fast. As long as they are available, they're free. But don't wait. About the time you finally make up your mind, the whole thing could have happened, leaving you looking back instead of up.

He is coming! What a difference it will make!

THINK IT OVER

❧❧

*A*re you living every day (as if it's your last) for His glory? Do you work diligently at your job and in your home (as if He isn't coming for another ten years) for His name's sake?

Do you shake salt and shine the light every chance you get?

Do you remain balanced, cheerful, winsome, and stable, anticipating His return?

> But we do not want you to be uninformed, brethren, about those who are asleep, that you may not grieve, as do the rest who have no hope. For if we believe that Jesus died and rose again, even so God will bring with Him those who have fallen asleep in Jesus. For this we say to you by the word of the Lord, that we who are alive, and remain until the coming of the Lord, shall not precede those who have fallen asleep. For the Lord Himself will descend from heaven with a shout, with the voice of the archangel, and with the trumpet of God; and the dead in Christ shall rise first. Then we who are alive and remain shall be caught up together with them in the clouds to meet the Lord in the air; and thus we shall always be with the Lord. Therefore comfort one another with these words. (1 Thess. 4:13–18)

Might be a good idea to commit these six verses to memory. You never know when you're going to need to comfort someone with these words.

FACING THE FACTS

❦ *Psalm 127* ❦

*H*ow's it going with you and the kids? Maybe that question doesn't apply to you. You may be single, or you may not have children, or you may have already raised your brood. If so, bear with me while I address those of you who are still in the process of training and rearing.

So, how's it going? What word(s) would you use to describe your overall relationship with your offspring? Challenging? Strained? Pleasant? Impossible? Angry? Threatening? Adventurous? Heartbreaking? Impatient? Exciting? Fun? Busy?

If you want to get your eyes opened to the facts, at the supper table tonight ask your kids to describe their feelings about you and their home. I'd better warn you—it may hurt! But it could be the first step in the right direction . . . the first step toward the restoration of harmony and genuine love under your roof.

Needless to say, having a Christian home is no guarantee against disharmony. The old nature can still flare up, habits set in concrete can lead to broken communication lines, and biblical principles can be ignored. So face the truth, my friend. Stop right now and think about your home.

An evaluation is no good if all it leads to is guilt and hurt. To stop there would be like a surgeon stopping the operation immediately after making his incision. All it would leave is a lot of pain and a nasty scar.

Take time to get next to your children . . . to come to grips with barriers that are blocking the flow of your love and affection (and theirs) . . . to face the facts before the fracture leads to a permanent, domestic disease.

Three biblical cases come to my mind:

Rebekah, who favored Jacob over Esau and used him to deceive his father, Isaac, which led to a severe family breakdown (Gen. 27).

Eli, who was judged by God because of his lack of discipline and failure to stand firm when his boys began to run wild (1 Sam. 3:11–14).

David, who committed the same sin against his son Adonijah by never disciplining him during his early training (1 Kings 1:5–6).

You see, no one is immune . . . not even you. So move ahead. Refuse to pamper your parental negligence any longer.

Take time to evaluate the present condition of your home.
Then take the steps needed to strengthen the weaknesses you uncover.

WOUNDS AND SCARS

🍂 *Psalm 147* 🍂

*T*ucked away in a quiet corner of Scripture is a verse containing much emotion: "From the city men groan, and the souls of the wounded cry out" (Job 24:12).

The scene is a busy metropolis. Speed. Movement. Noise. Rows of buildings. All that is obvious, easily seen and heard by the city dweller.

But there is more. Behind and beneath the loud splash of human activity there are invisible aches. Job calls them "groans." That's a good word. The Hebrew term enlarges it as it suggests that this groan comes from one who has been wounded. Perhaps that's the reason Job adds the next line in poetic form, "the souls of the wounded cry out." In that line, "wounded" comes from a term that means "pierced." But he is not referring to a physical stabbing, for it is "the soul" that is crying out.

You may be "groaning" because you have been misunderstood or treated unfairly. The wound is deep because the blow came from one whom you trusted and respected. It's possible that hurt was brought on by someone's stabbing remark. People are saying things that simply are not true, but to step in and set the record straight would be unwise or inappropriate. So you stay quiet . . . and bleed. Perhaps a comment was made only in passing, but it pierced you deeply.

Others of you are living with the memories of past sins or failures. Although you have confessed and forsaken those ugly, bitter days, the wound stays red and tender. You wonder if it will ever heal. Although it is unknown to others, you live in the fear of being found out . . . and rejected.

Tucked away in a quiet corner of every life are wounds and scars. If they were not there, we would need no Physician. Nor would we need one another.

> Hast thou no wound? . . .
> No wound, no scar?
> Yet, as the Master shall the servant be,
> And, pierced are the feet that follow Me;
> But thine are whole: can he have followed far
> Who has no wound nor scar? (Amy Carmichael)

Only the Great Physician can turn our ugly wound into a scar of beauty.

WINGS

❧ *Mark 6* ❧

*G*rab here, amigo." I grabbed. "Hold on tight, por favor." I held on. "When you come back toward the shore and I blow whistle, you pull cord pronto!" Within seconds I was airborne. A loud "whoosh," a long strong jerk, and I was three hundred feet or so above the picturesque beach at Puerto Vallarta.

You guessed it . . . my first try at parasailing. Four-and-a-half minutes of indescribable ecstasy sandwiched between a few seconds of sheer panic. Talk about fun!

Above me was the bluest, clearest sky you could imagine. Behind me was a full-blown dazzling red-and-white parachute. Down in front, attached to my harness and a long yellow rope, was a speedboat at full throttle. Below, the turquoise sea, various sailing vessels, a long row of hotels, sun bathers the size of ants, and one beautiful lady wondering if she would soon be a widow.

I must confess, for those few minutes I forgot everything else. Never, since childhood, have I felt quite so free, so unencumbered, so completely removed from others' expectations and my own responsibilities.

I like to think that might be the true, authentic, carefree kind of leisure and relaxation Jesus had in mind when He encouraged His twelve to come apart and rest awhile.

How easily we forget the necessity of recreation; how quickly we discount its value! In our neurotic drive for more, more, more, we become all roots and no wings.

Life closes in and takes the shape of a chore instead of a challenge. Fun and laughter, originally designed by God to remove the friction of monotony from the machinery of existence, begin to be viewed as enemies instead of friends. Intensity, that ugly yet persuasive twin of hurry, convinces us we haven't the right to relax . . . we must not take time for leisure . . . we can't afford such rootless, risky luxury. Its message is loud, logical, sensible, strong, and wrong.

We all need roots and wings. But most of us are long on the former and short on the latter.

Expand your world, free your mind, and calm your nerves. Don't wait! Quit worrying about the risk or complaining about the cost.

Take time to soar!

Sometimes say out loud to yourself:
"This is for my good and for God's glory, even though I cannot begin to explain it."

WHO CARES?

❧ *Hebrews 13:1–3* ❧

*W*ho really cared? His was a routine admission to busy Bellevue Hospital. A charity case, one among hundreds. A drunken bum from the Bowery with a slashed throat. The Bowery . . . last stop before the morgue.

The derelict's name was misspelled on the hospital form, but then what good is a name when the guy's a bum? The age was also incorrect. He was thirty-eight, not thirty-nine, and looked twice that. Somebody might have remarked, "What a shame for one so young," but no one did. Because no one cared.

His health was gone and he was starving. He had been found lying in a heap, bleeding from a deep gash in his throat. A doctor used black sewing thread to suture the wound. Then the man was dumped in a paddy wagon and dropped off at Bellevue Hospital, where he languished and died. But nobody really cared.

A friend seeking him was directed to the local morgue. There, among dozens of other nameless corpses, he was identified. When they scraped together his belongings, they found a ragged, dirty coat with thirty-eight cents in one pocket and a scrap of paper in the other. All his earthly goods. Enough coins for another night in the Bowery and five words, "Dear friends and gentle hearts." Almost like the words of a song, someone may have thought.

Which would have been correct, for once upon a time that man had written the songs that literally made the whole world sing. Songs like "Camptown Races," "Oh! Susanna," "Beautiful Dreamer," "I Dream of Jeanie with the Light Brown Hair," "Old Folks at Home," "My Old Kentucky Home," and two hundred more that have become deeply rooted in our rich American heritage.

Thanks to Stephen Collins Foster.

Today, some of these forgotten souls are in prison. Some in hospitals. Some in nursing homes. And some silently slip into church on Sunday morning, confused and afraid.

Do you care? Enough "to show hospitality to strangers," as Hebrews 13:2 puts it? It also says that in doing so, we occasionally "entertain angels without knowing it."

Angels who don't look anything like angels. Some might even look like bums from the Bowery, but they may have a song dying in their hearts because nobody knows and nobody cares.

Deep within many a forgotten life is a scrap of hope,
a lonely melody trying hard to return.

RELEASING IMPOSSIBILITIES

❧ *Matthew 6:25–34* ❧

*W*hen you face an impossibility, leave it in the hands of the Specialist! Refuse to calculate. Refuse to doubt. Refuse to work it out by yourself. Refuse to worry or encouage others to worry. Stand against that.

Instead, say, "Lord, I'm carrying around something I cannot handle. Because You are not only able but also willing, take this off my hands. It's impossible to me, but is as nothing with You." Persevering through the pressures of impossibilities calls for that kind of confidence.

Now, our problem is that we hold on to our problems. If your Swiss watch stops working, you don't sit down at home with a screwdriver and start working on it yourself. You take it to a specialist.

The problem is that the Lord gets all the leftovers after we try to fix things ourselves. We make all the mistakes and get things tied into granny knots, then dump it in His lap and say, "Here, Lord."

No! Right at first, say, "It's impossible; I can't handle it, Lord. Before I foul it up, it's Yours." He is able to handle it. But we don't usually give God those chances to "fix" it. We are so totally (and sinfully) confident in ourselves that we don't give God the chance to do what He is a real Specialist at doing.

If something is humanly impossible,
then what in the world are we doing trying to pull it off?

YA GOTTA HAVE HEART!

❧ *Deuteronomy 31* ❧

*G*etting a big job done calls for heart. Having a high IQ is not essential. Neither is being a certain age. Or possessing a particular temperament. You don't even need the backing of the majority. History books are full of incredible stories of men and women who accomplished remarkable feats in the face of unbelievable odds.

While reading through the exciting story of Nehemiah recently, I was reminded again of this principle. You remember Nehemiah, the Jewish leader whose passion for Jerusalem drove him to leave the security of his home and job in Persia to superintend the building of a protective wall around Zion. What a project! And what obstacles stood against him! But the job got done in record time. Why? Nehemiah stated the reason in his journal entry: "So we built the wall . . . for the people had a mind to work" (Neh. 4:6).

Check the margin of your Bible. The term translated "mind" is the Hebrew word for "heart." Another word for it might be "courage." In fact, they are related.

In an early copy of Webster's dictionary (1828), the author points out that courage comes from *coeur,* the French word for heart: "Courage is the quality that enables one to face difficulty and danger with firmness, without fear or depression." And then, as Webster (a born-again Christian) often did in those days, he concluded his definition with a Scripture reference: Deuteronomy 31. That chapter includes Moses' final speech to the children of Israel shortly before his death and Joshua's taking up the torch of leadership. At 120 years of age, Moses tells 'em, "Ya gotta have heart!"

Since the children of Israel were not people of great courage (they'd been slaves in Egypt for over four hundred years), Moses knew how easy it would be for Joshua and his troops to lose heart.

I'm not suggesting that all of us must be Nehemiahs or Joshuas. Sometimes that may be necessary, but I have observed over the years that some of the greatest demonstrations of courage occur in private places. Sometimes just staying with something over the long haul— maintaining the vision year after year—is magnificent proof of a courageous heart.

You may or may not be a leader. But chances are good that you are influencing others in some measure. Don't just watch things happen. Get in there with both feet. Risk, for a change. Make some waves. Cut a new swath. Quit waiting for the other guy. You get the job done! One reminder: Ya gotta have heart.

"Great deeds are usually wrought at great risks" (Herodotus).

THINK IT OVER

🕮❧ 🕮❧

*L*eaders must go beyond analysis to action. One cannot lead without energy, motion, risk. Leaders are pathfinders, road makers, action takers.

Cowardice, to put it bluntly, is an ungodly trait. God is not passive in the face of evil, nor is He indecisive.

The Psalms are full of powerful lyrics that give us a clear portrait of the Lord God. Never is He portrayed as a mild-mannered, passive Deity, hoping and waiting for things to happen. Always He is aggressively engaged in an all-out war against injustice and inequity.

Righteousness and truth are causes to be fought for. If left to fend for themselves, they can't withstand the overpowering huns of heathenism.

In every generation, then, conflict is inevitable. And the ammunition for such conflicts? You guessed it. Heart.

Do you have it?

Do you take courageous action in the face of wrong?

Will you stand alone, if necessary, and embrace a principle, even though it means you lose votes or friends or prestige . . . or whatever?

Are you an intellectual analyzer of wrong, a mere advocate of achievement, a person who enjoys discussions of issues to the point of getting bogged down in unproductive semantics . . . or do you translate ideas into action?

I have a close friend who spent a day at San Diego's Seaworld. While he and his wife were near the main mall, they saw something unusual in the distance: a bunch of ducks coming toward them . . . on roller skates! They could do it, my friend said, but as they got closer, he could tell that they didn't have their hearts in it.

Some folks are ducks on roller skates; they can do what they do, but they don't have their hearts in it.

A HIGH CALLING

❧ *Ephesians 4:11—16* ❧

*M*any professions draw public attention like warm watermelon draws flies. Those who practice them are constantly in the news. If it isn't the money they make, it's the company they keep or the trends they set or the controversy they spawn. Their notoriety is somewhere between amazing and appalling.

There is one profession, however, that is neither notorious nor controversial. Although essential to our future as a nation, being inseparably linked to the home as few other professions are, it has been treated like a stepchild.

Those who make their living in this field press on against overwhelming odds. They live with criticism they usually don't deserve. They invest extra hours for which they are never compensated. They maintain a standard of excellence regardless of resistance. They remain enthusiastic in spite of daily discouragements. They apply creativity and every motivational technique they can muster without applause or thanks from their recipients.

Fueled by hope, these brave men and women shape minds, stretch imaginations, challenge thinking, and model consistency. They have one major enemy they fight with tireless energy: ignorance.

Who are the relentless, courageous heroes I'm describing?

By now you know. They are those who teach.

The tools of their trade may not seem that impressive—a piece of chalk, a book, an overhead projector, a homework assignment, a smile of encouragement, a nod of affirmation, a strong word of warning, a question to answer, a problem to solve. How powerful are those adept with such tools!

Teachers. Tough-minded, clear-thinking, ever-learning educators who gave me their time and their attention, who early on overlooked my immaturity, who saw raw material behind my boredom, overactivity, and mischievousness, who held my feet to the fire and dared me to grab the challenge, who had enough wisdom to drop the bait in just the right places to hook me for life.

So to all of you who teach, hats off. Yours is an invaluable profession, a calling sure and high and noble, a model we cannot live without if we expect to remain strong and free.

Don't quit. If ever we needed you, we need you today.

Think about those who taught you.
Thank God for them and the lifelong value of their investment in you.

To All Teachers

❧ *James 3:1–12* ❧

I've never had a strong desire to be a teacher. Don't get me wrong. I admire tremendously those who teach. It was a teacher in junior high who taught me to love science. It was a teacher in high school who got me hooked on history. Another teacher helped me overcome stuttering and learn how to speak in public . . . how to think on my feet . . . how to pace the delivery of words . . . how to use humor. And it was yet another teacher who passed along the practical techniques I still use in digging pearls out of scriptural oysters.

So, let me firmly establish this fact: I am deeply indebted to several teachers. If you teach, be encouraged! You probably have no idea how great a contribution you are making.

If I were to teach, however, I think I would keep a personal journal of the funny things my students said.

Actually, Richard Lederer must have had the same brilliant idea. In fact, he even published the mistakes in a book cleverly titled *Anguished English,* in which he sort of pastes together the "history" of the world from genuine student bloopers collected by teachers throughout America, from eighth grade through college level.

Here are a few examples. Hold on tight . . . there's a lot to be learned that you may have missed in your years in school.

For example, did you know that Ancient Egypt was inhabited by mummies who wrote in hydraulics? They lived in the Sarah Dessert and traveled by Camelot. Certain areas of that dessert were cultivated by irritation.

Then we learn that in the first book of the Bible, Guinessis, Adam and Eve were created from an apple tree. One of their children, Cain, asked, "Am I my brother's son?"

After that, Pharaoh forced the Hebrew slaves to make bread without straw, and Moses went up on Mount Cyanide to get the ten commandments. He died before he ever reached Canada.

Later we learn that David was a Hebrew king skilled at playing the liar. He fought with the Finkelsteins. Solomon, one of his sons, had 300 wives and 700 porcupines.

See why I have no compelling desire to be a teacher?

> *"A teacher affects eternity; he can never tell where his influence stops"*
> *(Henry Brooks Adams).*

EXCUSES

❧ *Hebrews 10:23–25* ❧

I'm a sports fan. I'm sure that comes as news to no one! For some strange reason, even when I was growing up, I could remember the most amazing details—okay, maybe "trivia" is a better word—about different ball players. You know, stuff nobody really cares to hear, but nevertheless sticks in my head . . . the way it does with most sport fans.

Another characteristic of a fan is an indomitable sense of commitment or determination—okay, okay, maybe "addiction" is a better word! Against incredible odds, sound logic, and even medical advice, sports fans will persevere to the dying end! Difficulties are viewed as a challenge . . . never an excuse to stay away!

I've often wondered what would happen if people were as intense and committed and determined about church as they are about sports—or any number of other pastimes. This was reinforced some years back in a *Moody Monthly* piece that illustrated twelve excuses a fella might use for "quitting sports." The analogy isn't hard to figure out.

> Every time I went, they asked me for money.
> The people with whom I had to sit didn't seem very friendly.
> The seats were too hard and not comfortable.
> The coach never came to call on me.
> The referee made a decision with which I could not agree.
> I was sitting with some hypocrites—they came only to see what others were wearing.
> Some games went into overtime, and I was late getting home.
> The band played numbers that I had never heard before.
> The games are scheduled when I want to do other things.
> My parents took me to too many games when I was growing up.
> Since I read a book on sports, I feel that I know more than the coaches anyhow.
> I don't want to take my children, because I want them to choose for themselves what sport they like best.

I've come up with a few more:
The parking lot was awful . . . I had to walk six blocks to the stadium.
Nobody came up and introduced himself to me . . . very impersonal, also loud!
The public address and lighting systems don't suit me.
It's always too hot (or cold) in the stadium.
Enough said. Think it over.

What would happen if we approached church responsibilities with the same enthusiasm we give to our hobbies, sports, and other extracurricular activities?

US AND WE, NOT I AND ME

❧❧ *Romans 12* ❧❧

*N*obody is a whole chain. Each one is a link. But take away one link and the chain is broken.

Nobody is a whole team. Each one is a player. But take away one player and the game is forfeited.

Nobody is a whole orchestra. Each one is a musician. But take away one musician and the symphony is incomplete.

We need each other. You need someone and someone needs you. Isolated islands, we're not.

To make this thing called life work, we gotta lean and support. And relate and respond. And give and take. And confess and forgive. And reach out and embrace. And release and rely.

Especially in the God family . . . where working together is Plan A for survival. And since we're so different (thanks to the way God built us), love and acceptance are not optional luxuries. Neither is tolerance. Or understanding. Or patience. You know, all those things you need from others when your humanity crowds out your divinity.

In other words:

> Love each other with brotherly affection and take delight in honoring each other. Never be lazy in your work but serve the Lord enthusiastically. Be glad for all God is planning for you. Be patient in trouble, and prayerful always. When God's children are in need, you be the one to help them out. And get into the habit of inviting guests home for dinner, or if they need lodging, for the night. (Rom. 12:10–13, TLB)

Why? Because each one of us is worth it. Even when we don't act like it or feel like it or deserve it.

Since none of us is a whole, independent, self-sufficient, supercapable, all-powerful hotshot, let's quit acting like we are. Life's lonely enough without our playing that silly role.

The game's over. Let's link up.

"No man is an island, entire of itself; every man is a piece of the continent . . ."
(John Donne).

CHOOSING JOY

❧ *Philippians 4* ❧

I have discovered that a joyful countenance has nothing to do with one's age or one's occupation (or lack of it) or one's geography or education or marital status or good looks or circumstances. Joy is a choice!

Joy is a matter of attitude that stems from one's confidence in God—that He is at work, that He is in full control, that He is in the midst of whatever has happened, is happening, and will happen. Either we fix our minds on that and determine to laugh again, or we wail and whine our way through life, complaining that we never got a fair shake. We are the ones who consciously determine which way we shall go. To paraphrase the poet:

> One ship sails east
> One ship sails west
> Regardless of how the winds blow.
> It is the set of the sail
> And not the gale
> That determines the way we go.
> (Ella Wheeler Wilcox)

Regardless of how severely the winds of adversity may blow,
we set our sails toward joy.

VERITAS MINUS CHRISTO

✣✣ *Proverbs 9:9–12* ✣✣

*I*f you're ever in Boston, you owe it to yourself to drive to nearby Cambridge and visit the Harvard campus. This, our nation's first institution of higher learning, was founded in 1636 and was named after John Harvard, a minister of the gospel. His untimely death a year later resulted in his library of 400 volumes and a gift of 780 pounds sterling being contributed to the fledgling college in Cambridge. Appropriately, those treasures were to help in the training of upcoming generations of Christian ministers.

These facts help explain the original Harvard seal: a shield including three opened books, two facing up, the third facing down, and the Latin words *Veritas Christo et Ecclesiae*—"Truth for Christ and the Church."

The distinguished seal reminded students that truth and freedom are found only in Jesus Christ, and the display of three books represented the importance of knowledge—yet with one turned down, emphasizing the limits of human reason.

Tragically, with the passing of time, that godly philosophy of education has eroded. Harvard's new seal carries no reference to Christ or the church. And the book facing down has now been turned *up*. We can now know it all, this symbol says. There are no divine mysteries. Intellect is everything.

There is a nasty fly in this humanistic ointment, however. It's the D word: Depravity. The sinfulness of the human heart is not altered by the pursuit of knowledge. This explains why a century-one Christian, Saul of Tarsus, warned his friends in Corinth, "Knowledge makes arrogant."

In public schools where prayer is banned and where the teaching of morality is shunned, all that is left is sterile academic knowledge. *Veritas* minus *Christo*. The result? Students today cannot tell right from wrong.

If there is any remaining harbor of hope, it's the family and the church. Moms and dads, stay at it! Pastors and teachers, don't let up!

Uphold the importance of knowledge, but don't forget to address biblical values, godly character, personal integrity, fear of the Lord, moral absolutes, ethical standards, and the value of virtues like love, faith, discernment, self-control.

As Solomon put it: "The fear of the LORD is the beginning of wisdom, and the knowledge of the Holy One is understanding" (Prov. 9:10).

Veritas plus *Christo is the motto to model.*

THINK IT OVER

❧❧ ❧❧

*T*ake away the necessary constraints which Christ alone provides, and the raging beast of depravity within the human heart—no matter how intelligent the mind may be—will growl, crouch, claw, and occasionally attack.

Thus, when academic humanity and unrestrained depravity collide, depravity will win the battle.

Sometimes, the scene is shocking, as in the case of the "Honor Roll Murder" of Stuart Tay. Had it happened in some dark alley, it probably wouldn't have made the evening news—at least not in more than a sentence or two. But this occurred among an upscale, financially prosperous, politically conservative, academically gifted group of young men.

Tough thugs did not kill Stuart Tay. He was murdered by youths headed for Princeton, Yale, and Harvard. Valedictorian types. Quick-minded, bright computer whizzes whom anyone would have picked for tomorrow's leaders. These guys had academic knowledge in abundance. What they didn't have was the ability to restrain the raging beast within.

As it was reported in *Time*, "the victim was brutally beaten with baseball bats before they poured rubbing alcohol down his throat and forced his mouth shut with duct tape. Tay died within minutes from his own vomit."

Horrible. Yet, to be painfully honest, predictable in a sophisticated, politically correct society that idolizes knowledge while it ignores moral standards.

Truth minus Christ.

A NEEDED PIT STOP

❧ *Hebrews 12:1–2* ❧

*I*s time passing faster, or am I just getting older? Can this really be the last hurrah of the summer? School can't actually be starting already, can it? I feel like swapping my calendar for a stopwatch.

Today I have decided to slow down long enough to stop the blur and look. Not just to look, but to see. As Yogi Berra once said, "You can observe a lot just by watching."

Sometimes it helps to open life's door slowly and secretively take a long gaze inside. On other occasions, it's better to jerk it open unannounced, slam on the light, and get a quick read. I've been doing the latter today, and I don't like what I see. My sudden glance has flushed out all sorts of critters.

- Too many involvements
- Intensity level much too high
- Time to pray, to think, to plan, to play is still too rushed
- Midget worries turning into imaginary monsters
- Living life too predictable . . . not enough creativity
- Days off interrupted by needless, low-priority stuff
- Skating across relationships—need to dig deeper
- Extracurricular reading not sufficiently stimulating

I know of no better strategy for stopping such an ugly, rat-infested existence than deliberately pulling off the racetrack and taking periodic pit stops to refuel, renew, refresh, and recover. Let me level with you. Your pace is your problem and my pace is mine. We got ourselves into this maddening race, and each one of us is personally responsible for the speed at which we're driving ourselves.

If you can say, "I've sinned. The pace I'm keeping is not healthy—spiritually, mentally, or physically. It's not what I want, but it's my own doing," then I urge you to do so—and then do something about changing it.

I can't promise instant and total transformation, but I can assure you of this: It will be the most unusual pit stop you'll ever make. You'll not only get your tank filled, you'll also get your rats killed!

Do you think you should take that needed pit stop to refuel, renew, refresh, and recover so you can reenter the race and run with diligence?

SUFFERING

❧ *2 Corinthians 1* ❧

*O*f all the letters Paul wrote, Second Corinthians is the most autobiographical. In this letter Paul records the specifics of his anguish, tears, affliction, and satanic opposition. He spells out the details of his persecution, loneliness, imprisonments, beatings, feelings of despair, hunger, shipwrecks, sleepless nights, and that "thorn in the flesh"—his companion of pain. How close it makes us feel to him when we see him as a man with real, honest-to-goodness problems, just like ours!

It is not surprising, then, that he begins the letter with words of comfort, especially verses 3 through 11. Ten times in five verses (vv. 3–7) Paul uses the same root word, *Parakaleo,* meaning literally, "to call alongside."

This word involves more than a shallow pat on the back. This word involves genuine, in-depth understanding . . . deep-down compassion and sympathy. This seems especially appropriate since it says that God, our Father, is the "God of all comfort" who "comforts us in all our affliction." Our loving Father is never preoccupied or removed when we are enduring sadness and affliction!

There is another observation worth noting in 2 Corinthians 1. No less than three reasons are given for suffering, each one introduced with the term *that:* "that we may be able to comfort those who are in any affliction"; "that we should not trust in ourselves"; "that thanks may be given" (vv. 4, 9, 11). Admittedly, there may be dozens of other reasons, but here are three specific reasons we suffer.

Reason #1: God allows suffering so that we might have the capacity to enter into others' sorrow and affliction.

Reason #2: God allows suffering so that we might learn what it means to depend on Him. Over and over He reminds us of the danger of pride, but it frequently takes suffering to make the lesson stick.

Reason #3: God allows suffering so that we might learn to give thanks in everything. Now, honestly, have you said, "Thanks, Lord, for this test"? Have you finally stopped struggling and expressed to Him how much you appreciate His loving sovereignty over your life?

How unfinished and rebellious and proud and unconcerned we would be without suffering!

May these things encourage you the next time God heats up the furnace!

Years ago I heard two statements about suffering that I have never forgotten: "Pain plants the flag of reality in the fortress of a rebel heart." And, "When God wants to do an impossible task, He takes an impossible individual—and crushes him."

A TERMINAL MOLE

❧ *1 Corinthians 5* ❧

*M*any years ago I broke my left hand. It happened while I was working as an apprentice in a machine shop in Houston. The result was a trip to the hospital and a surgical procedure, during which the doctor inserted a stainless steel pin from my knuckle to my wrist to hold the bone in place while it healed.

During one of my follow-up visits, after the surgeon examined my hand, he mentioned that he'd not be there when I returned to have the pin removed, but he said his associate was well able to handle everything. Curious, I asked if he was planning to take some well-earned vacation time.

"Yes," he sighed, "I'm feeling a little drained these days, so I think I'll escape for a couple of weeks, play some golf, and relax." Then he added, "Also, I've got this little mole on my belly I need to have removed—no big deal, but while I'm away, I'll have that taken care of."

When I returned to have the pin removed, I inquired about my physician. The nurse stared blankly as the associate cleared his throat. Without looking up, he said, "Didn't you hear? He died last week." I was absolutely stunned. My mind whirled. I choked out, "He *what?*"

"It was cancer. When his surgeon made the incision to remove a mole, then probed deeper, he discovered that his entire abdomen was laced with malignant tissue. He never had a clue, just a slight yet steady drain in energy. Actually, the only thing on the surface was that innocent-looking little mole. He didn't live a week after they sewed him up."

Through the years I've often remembered that incident when I look at the slight scar on my wrist. And I am reminded that sin is a lot like that little mole. It starts "small," but soon it is draining and devouring our spiritual energy, like cancer in a body.

Because there may be little evidence on the surface to attract anyone else's attention or arouse suspicion, no one bothers to probe and investigate the devastation these sins are causing beneath the surface.

All the while, however, these silent and relentless killers are sucking motivation, draining energy, and blurring vision.

Don't wait. Before such sin eats deeper into our souls, we need to ask the Great Physician to excise it—to cut it away so that we can become spiritually sound and healthy.

While the mole of sin may appear small, its tentacles reach deep.

Too Fast, Too Soon

❧ *1 Corinthians 13:11* ❧

oo good. That's the only way to describe my early childhood. Lots of friends in the neighborhood. Sandlot football down at the end of Quince Street in East Houston or shooting hoops against the garage backboard. There were family reunions at my granddaddy's little bay cabin, plus fishing, floundering, crabbing, swimming, and eating.

But best of all, we were given room to be kids. Just kids. Listen, I went to school barefoot until the fourth grade, and I was still playing cops and robbers into junior high. Scout's honor. Nobody pushed me to grow up. Life was allowed to run its own course back then.

No longer, it seems. There is a new youngster in our city streets. Have you noticed? Perhaps I'm overly sensitive because I've finished reading David Elkind's splendid book *The Hurried Child,* with the provocative subtitle "Growing Up Too Fast Too Soon." On the cover is a little girl, not more than eleven, with earrings, plucked eyebrows, carefully applied cosmetics, teased and feathered hair, and exquisite jewelry.

Music, books, films, and television increasingly portray the young as precocious and seductive. "Such portrayals," writes Elkind, "force children to think they should act grown up before they are ready."

Emotions and feelings are the most complex and intricate part of a child's development. They have their own timing and rhythm, which cannot be hurried. Growing up is tough enough with nobody pushing.

Am I overreacting to suggest that the unique traumas among today's children are somehow tied to all this? Younger and younger alcoholics. Increased promiscuity among preteens. Higher crime rate than ever involving the very young. And the all-time high suicide rate among children and adolescents is certainly telling us something . . . if nothing else, at least for those kids, it's telling us we're reacting too late.

Scripture clearly states, "There is an appointed time for everything" (Eccles. 3:1). How about time to be a child? How about time to grow up slowly, carefully—yes, even protected, naive? Otherwise, it is too far, too fast, too soon.

Allow your children the joys of childhood.

THE SECRET OF LIVING

❧ *Philippians 1* ❧

*W*hen money is our objective for happiness, we must live in fear of losing it, which makes us paranoid and suspicious. When fame is our aim, we become competitive lest others upstage us, which makes us envious. When power and influence drive us, we become self-serving and strong-willed, which makes us arrogant. And when possessions become our god, we become materialistic, thinking enough is never enough, which makes us greedy. All these pursuits fly in the face of contentment and joy.

Only Christ can satisfy, whether we have or don't have, whether we are known or unknown, whether we live or die. And the good news is this: Death only sweetens the pie! That alone is enough to make you laugh again.

The Living Bible states: "For to me, living means opportunities for Christ, and dying— well, that's better yet!" (Phil. 1:21). The New Testament in Modern English, J.B. Phillips's paraphrase, reads: "For living to me means simply 'Christ,' and if I die I should merely gain more of Him."

What is the sum and substance of all this? The secret of living is the same as the secret of joy: Both revolve around the centrality of Jesus Christ. In other words, the pursuit of happiness is the cultivation of a Christ-centered, Christ-controlled life.

When Christ becomes our central focus,
contentment replaces our anxiety as well as our fears and insecurities.

TIME TO TOUGHEN UP

🕮 *2 Corinthians 11–13* 🕮

*T*here are 1,130 frostbitten miles, mountain ranges, blizzards, hungry beasts, and frozen seas between Anchorage and Nome. This awful trek is the scene of the ultimate endurance test known as the Iditarod Sled Dog Race, where twelve huskies pull a sled and its driver through the most grueling, inhuman conditions one can fathom. The most frequent champion of recent years is a woman named Susan Butcher, whose tough-minded fixation on winning earned her the nickname Ayatollah Butcher.

The secret, she will tell you, is her own mind-set and the training of those dogs, which gives new meaning to the word "serious." Her 150-dog kennel is a thing to behold. Shortly after each pup's birth, while it is still blind, she holds it in her hands and breathes her breath into its nose. That way, she claims, each one will associate her smell with comfort and encouragement. The rapport begins with that breathing-into-the-nose routine. She personally feeds, trains, massages, and—on a rotation basis—sleeps with each dog. She personally nurses them to health when they are injured. She is infinitely patient with them, talks to them, believes in them, even sings to them (old folk songs by Bob Dylan and Joan Baez, plus a few Irish lullabies). The objective? To bond with them. It pays. They have saved her life on the trail more than once. Back in 1979, she led her dog team to the 20,320-foot summit of Mount McKinley. It took forty-four days.

What a woman! One reporter described her as having "a stiff spine . . . a stubborn mind-set," which is what is needed to endure moose attacks, blizzards so severe that one time for five hours she couldn't see the lead dog, and a sudden plunge into icy water (Granite and Maddie, the mushers, pulled her out).

The Christian life isn't an eleven-day race. It's a lifetime journey full of more dangers and pitfalls than a hundred Iditarods. So it's foolish to think we can enter it half-heartedly or sustain it easily. To survive it calls for help from above and toughness from within. If Susan Butcher is willing to give that kind of effort to win a race that is incredible in the eyes of the world, seems to me we should be capable of conquering the marathon from earth to heaven.

A combination of two ingredients is essential: the capacity to accept and the tenacity to endure.

I move that we toughen up. All in favor say, "Mush."

"We could never be brave and patient if there were only joy in the world"
(Helen Keller).

THINK IT OVER

❧❧❧

*T*ake time this weekend to read again, slowly and carefully, through Friday's Scripture reading—2 Corinthians 11–13. List the hardships the apostle Paul endured.

Try putting yourself and your own particular circumstances and trials into Paul's constant affirmations of faith.

Start with . . .

I have been in labor and hardship, through many sleepless nights, in hunger and thirst, often without food, in cold and exposure.

Apart from such external things, there is the daily pressure upon me of concern for all the churches. . . .

If I have to boast, I will boast of what pertains to my weakness.

The God and Father of the Lord Jesus, He who is blessed forever, knows that I am not lying. . . .

Can you do that . . . honestly?

TM

✤ *Genesis 3* ✤

The word is out. TM is "in." Ask any number of celebrities or government leaders or public school officials . . . or thousands of college kids who endorse it. All are oohing and aahing over a Hindu monk with a name that looks like a misprint. Maharishi Mahesh Yogi.

Transcendental Meditation is his bag.

Devotees around this gullible globe have developed a vast network of International Meditation Society centers, declaring them to be the cure for physical and emotional ills and a splendid way to elevate the individual.

Testimonies accompany the propaganda: A professional basketball player claims it helps him make his foul shots. Mothers announce it gives them patience with small children. Merchants experience prosperity by practicing it. Politicians enjoy increased public approval. Teens get dates. Writers get ideas. Salesmen get orders. Habits are conquered. Marriages are saved.

Hold it! Beneath TM's surface rests a philosophy that is worse than dangerous. It's demonic. Behind the guru's smile is a set of teeth whose fangs spread the venom of the Vedas, ancient Indian writings linked directly with hard-core Hinduism. Vedic literature includes sacrificial incantations, formulas used by magicians who practice the black arts. TM is witchcraft wrapped in a clean, white bedsheet.

How does TM work? A client at a TM center pays the fee and receives instructions. This includes the giving of a "mantra" with simple directions. A mantra is a secret, individualized word that is to be used repeatedly during "meditation sessions." Vedism and Hinduism both refer to the mantra. The repeating of the mantra is a signal, asking assistance from the spirit world. Through rigid, disciplined practice, the TM disciple develops the ability to make contact with spirits and thereby gain the so-called assistance he/she desires.

Will you get results if you practice TM? Yes, indeed. Will things happen if you consistently apply the mystical formula? Like you won't believe! Chances are, you'll get more than you bargained for. You'll get much more than assistance. You'll get a glimpse of the guru's guru.

But he won't be smiling . . . and before long, neither will you.

Satan doesn't come to us with horns and pitchfork.
He often comes wrapped in attractive and innocent guise.

TIMING

❧ *Psalm 31:14–15* ❧

*I*n September, Terry Shafer was strolling the shops in Moline, Illinois. She knew exactly what she wanted to get her husband, David, for Christmas. A little shop on Fifth attracted her attention, so she popped inside. Her eyes darted toward the corner display. "That's it!" she smiled as she nodded with pleasure. "How much?" she asked the shopkeeper.

"Only $127.50."

Her smile faded into disappointment as she realized David's salary as a policeman couldn't stand such a jolt. Yet she hated to give up without a try, so she applied a little womanly persistence. "Uh, what about putting this aside for me? Maybe I could pay a little each week, then pick it up a few days before Christmas?"

"No," the merchant said, "I won't do that." Then he smiled. "I'll gift-wrap it right now. You can take it with you and pay me later," he said. Terry was elated.

Then came Saturday, October 1. Patrolman David Shafer, working the night shift, got a call in his squad car. A drugstore robbery was in progress. David reacted instantly, arriving on the scene just in time to see the suspect speed away. With siren screaming and lights flashing, he followed in hot pursuit. Three blocks later the getaway vehicle suddenly pulled over and stopped. The driver didn't move. David carefully approached the suspect with his weapon drawn. In a split second, the door flew open as the thief produced a .45-caliber pistol and fired at David's abdomen.

At seven o'clock in the morning a patrolman came to the door of the Shafer home. Calmly and with great care, he told Terry what had happened.

Stunned, Terry thought how glad she was that she had not waited until Christmas to give her husband his present. How grateful she was that the shopkeeper had been willing to let her pay for it later. Otherwise, Dave would have surely died. Instead, he was now in the hospital—not with a gunshot wound, but with only a bad bruise. You see, David was wearing the gift of life Terry could not wait to give—his brand-new bulletproof vest.

Within the movement of events is the Designer, who plans and arranges the times and the seasons, including the minutest detail of life. You question that? Many do.

But unless I miss my guess, David and Terry Shafer don't. It's funny . . . people who survive a calamity don't have much struggle with sovereignty.

Behind the maze is the Master.

TIGHTWADS

❧ *Matthew 6:19–21* ❧

*M*rs. Bertha Adams, 71 years old, died alone in West Palm Beach, Florida, on Easter Sunday. The coroner's report read: "Cause of death . . . malnutrition." She had wasted away to fifty pounds.

When the state authorities made their preliminary investigation of Mrs. Adam's home, they found a veritable "pigpen . . . the biggest mess you can imagine." The woman had begged food from neighbors' back doors and gotten what clothing she had from the Salvation Army. From all outward appearances she was a penniless recluse. But such was not the case.

Amid the jumble of her unclean, disheveled belongings, the officials found two keys to safe-deposit boxes at two different local banks. In the first box were over 700 AT&T stock certificates, plus hundreds of other valuable certificates, bonds, and solid financial securities, not to mention a stack of cash amounting to nearly $200,000. The second box contained $600,000. Adding the net worth of both boxes, they found well over a million dollars.

Charles Osgood, reporting the story on CBS radio, announced that the estate would probably go to a distant niece and nephew, neither of whom dreamed their aunt had a thin dime to her name.

Don't you wonder about this woman? Why, oh, why would anybody salt away all that bread in two tiny boxes, month after month, year after year, and refuse to spend even enough for food to stay alive?

Fact is, Bertha Adams wasn't saving her money; she was worshiping it . . . hoarding it . . . gaining a twisted satisfaction out of watching the stacks grow higher as she shuffled along the streets wearing the garb of a beggar.

I'm a firm believer in saving, investing, intelligent spending, and wise money management. But I have trouble finding one word of scriptural support for being a tightwad! Never have I seen one who could dream broad dreams or see vast visions of what God can do *in spite of* man's limitations.

Give me a handful of "greathearts" . . . generous, openhanded, visionary, spiritually minded givers . . . magnanimous giants with God who get excited about abandoning themselves to Him. The name of the game is not CAUTION—it's still VISION, isn't it? Seems like I read somewhere that those without it perish.

And speaking of that, when they buried Bertha Adams, she didn't take a penny with her.

Some folks serve the almighty dollar far more faithfully than the Almighty God.
They get greater delight out of balancing the budget
than watching the Lord multiply the loaves and fishes.

THOUGHTS

❧ *Philippians 4:8* ❧

*T*houghts are the thermostat that regulates what we accomplish in life. If I feed my mind upon doubt, disbelief, and discouragement, that is precisely the kind of day my body will experience. If I adjust my thermostat forward to thoughts filled with vision, vitality, and victory, I can count on that kind of day. Thus, you and I become what we think about.

Neither Dale Carnegie nor Norman Vincent Peale originated such a message. God did. "For as [a man] thinks within himself, so he is" (Prov. 23:7). "Therefore, gird your minds for action" (1 Peter 1:13).

The mind is a "thought factory," producing thousands, perhaps hundreds of thousands, of thoughts each day. Production in your thought factory is under the charge of two foremen. One we shall call Mr. Triumph, the other Mr. Defeat.

Mr. Triumph specializes in producing reasons why you can face life victoriously, why you can handle what comes your way, why you're more than able to conquer. Mr. Defeat is an expert in the opposite. He develops reasons why you cannot succeed, why you're inadequate, why you should give up and give in to worry, failure, discouragement, and inferiority.

Give a positive signal, and Mr. Triumph will see to it that one encouraging, edifying thought after another floods your mind. But Mr. Defeat is always standing by, awaiting a negative signal (which he would rather you call "reality" or "common sense!"), and when he gets it, he cranks out discouraging, destructive, demoralizing thoughts that will soon have you convinced you can't or won't or shouldn't.

Thoughts, positive or negative, grow stronger when fertilized with constant repetition. That may explain why so many who are gloomy and gray stay in that mood . . . and why those who are cheery and enthusiastic continue to be so.

What kind of performance would your car deliver if every morning before you left for work you scooped up a handful of dirt and put it in your crankcase? The engine would soon be coughing and sputtering. Ultimately it would refuse to start. The same is true of your life. Thoughts that are narrow, self-destructive, and abrasive produce needless wear and tear on your mental motor. They send you off the road while others drive past.

You need only one foreman in your mental factory: Mr. Triumph is his name. He is eager to assist you and available to all the members of God's family.

His real name is the Holy Spirit, the Helper.

If Mr. Defeat is busily engaged as the foreman of your factory, fire yours and hire ours! You will be amazed at how smoothly the plant will run under His leadership.

GETTING PRIORITIES IN ORDER

Philippians 1:27–30

*M*aking right decisions amidst dilemmas forces us to rethink our priorities. Choosing right priorities forces us to reconsider the importance of Christ in our lives.

There are many voices these days. Some are loud, many are persuasive, and a few are downright convincing. It can be confusing. If you listen long enough you will be tempted to throw your faith to the winds, look out for number one, let your glands be your guide, and choose what is best for you. Initially you will get a rush of pleasure and satisfaction, no question. But ultimately you will wind up disappointed and disillusioned.

I am going to challenge you to keep an eternal perspective even though you are surrounded by a host of success-oriented individuals who are urging you to ignore your conscience and grab all you can now. You want joy? You really want what is best? Simply consider yourself having different priorities than your associates and go God's way. His is the most reliable route to follow when life gets complicated. It will have its tough moments, but you will never regret it.

*God will reward you for pressing on, for your faithfulness,
and you will forget the pain, and, like never before, you will laugh!*

COMPASSION

🕮 *Colossians 3:12–14; James 5:11* 🕮

*I*t was one of those backhanded compliments. The guy had listened to me talk during several sessions at a pastors' conference. All he knew about me was what he'd heard in the past few days: ex-marine . . . schooled in an independent seminary . . . committed to biblical exposition . . . noncharismatic . . . premil . . . pretrib . . . pro this . . . anti that.

Toward the end of the week, he decided to drink a cup of coffee with me and risk saying it straight. It went something like this: "You don't fit. You've got the roots of a fundamentalist, but you don't sound like it. Your theology is narrow, but you're not rigid. You take God seriously, but you laugh like there's no tomorrow. You have definite convictions, but you aren't legalistic and demanding." Then he added: "Even though you're a firm believer in the Bible, you're still having fun, still enjoying life. You've even got some *compassion!*"

"You've even got some compassion!" Like, if you're committed to the truth of Scripture, you shouldn't get that concerned about people stuff—heartaches, hunger, illness, fractured lives, insecurities, failures, and grief—because those are only temporal problems. Mere horizontal hassles. Leave that to the liberals. Our main job is to give 'em the gospel. Get 'em saved!

Be honest now. Isn't that the way it usually is? Isn't it a fact that the more conservative one becomes, the less compassionate?

I want to know why. Why either–or? Why not both–and?

I'd also like to know when we departed from the biblical model. When did we begin to ignore Christ's care for the needy?

Maybe when we realized that one is much easier than the other. It's also faster. When you don't concern yourself with being your brother's keeper, you don't have to get dirty or take risks or lose your objectivity or run up against the thorny side of an issue that lacks easy answers.

And what will happen when we traffic in such compassion? The Living Bible says, "Then the Lord will be your delight, and I will see to it that you ride high, and get your full share of the blessings I promised to Jacob, your father" (Isa. 58:14).

If you really want to "ride high, and get your full share of the blessings," prefer compassion to information. We need both, but in the right order.

Come on, let's break the mold and surprise 'em. That's exactly what Jesus did with you and me and a whole bunch of other sinners who deserved and expected a full dose of condemnation, but got compassion instead.

Others won't care how much we know until they know how much we care.

THINK IT OVER

❧❧❧

*T*he nation to whom the prophet Isaiah wrote was going through the empty motions of a hollow religion. All the right words, all the right appearances, but zero results. They even fasted and prayed. I suppose we could say they looked and sounded orthodox, but they missed God's favor. They observed the external Sabbath, but they lacked the internal Shalom. Why? Don't hurry through the answer (Isa. 58:6–12). It's worth reading aloud, perhaps more than once.

> Is this not the fast which I choose, to loosen the bonds of wickedness, to undo the bands of the yoke, and to let the oppressed go free, and break every yoke? Is it not to divide your bread with the hungry, and bring the homeless poor into the house; when you see the naked, to cover him; and not to hide yourself from your own flesh? Then your light will break out like the dawn, and your recovery will speedily spring forth; and your righteousness will go before you; the glory of the LORD will be your rear guard. Then you will call, and the LORD will answer; you will cry, and He will say, "Here I am." If you remove the yoke from your midst, the pointing of the finger, and speaking wickedness, and if you give yourself to the hungry, and satisfy the desire of the afflicted, then your light will rise in darkness, and your gloom will become like midday. And the LORD will continually guide you, and satisfy your desire in scorched places, and give strength to your bones; and you will be like a watered garden, and like a spring of water whose waters do not fail. And those from among you will rebuild the ancient ruins; you will raise up the age-old foundations; and you will be called the repairer of the breach, the restorer of the streets in which to dwell.

CRITICISM

❧ *Nehemiah 6:1–14* ❧

*O*ne of the occupational hazards of being a leader is receiving criticism (not all of it constructive, by the way). In fact, I firmly believe that the leader who does anything that is different or worthwhile or visionary can count on criticism. In this regard, I appreciate the remarks made by Theodore Roosevelt:

> It is not the critic who counts; not the man who points out how the strong man stumbled or where the doer of deeds could have done them better. The credit belongs to the man who is actually in the arena; whose face is marred by dust and sweat and blood; who strives valiantly; who errs, and comes short again and again, because there is no effort without error and shortcoming; who does actually try to do the deed; who knows the great enthusiasm, the great devotion and spends himself in a worthy cause; who, at the worst, if he fails, at least fails while daring greatly.
>
> Far better is it to dare mighty things, to win glorious triumphs even though checkered by failure, than to rank with those poor spirits who neither enjoy nor suffer much because they live in the gray twilight that knows neither victory nor defeat.

To those words I add a resounding AMEN and add the following advice: A sense of humor is of paramount importance to the leader. Many of God's servants are simply too serious! They must have the ability to laugh at themselves.

Equally important, of course, is the ability to sift from any criticism that which is true, that which is fact. We are foolish if we respond angrily to every criticism. Who knows, God may be using those very words to teach us some essential lessons, painful though they may be.

Isn't this what Proverbs 27:5–6 is saying? "Better is open rebuke than love that is concealed. Faithful are the wounds of a friend, but deceitful are the kisses of an enemy."

And let me call to your attention the word "friend" in these verses. Friendship is not threatened by honest criticism. It is strengthened.

Leaders are not the only ones who receive criticism, of course. We all do. So just remember: When you are criticized by someone who hardly knows you, filter out what is fact . . . and ignore the rest!

Read today's Scripture passage and notice how Nehemiah handled criticism.
He kept his cool, he considered the source, he refused to get discouraged,
he went to God in prayer, and he kept building the wall!

SERVANT-HEARTED

🐝 *2 Corinthians 4:1–7* 🐝

*I*n his fine little volume *In the Name of Jesus,* Henri Nouwen mentions three very real, albeit subtle temptations any servant of Christ faces. They correspond with the three temptations our Lord faced before He began His earthly ministry. They also fit with three observations the apostle Paul mentions in his letter to the Corinthians (2 Cor. 4:1–7).

First Temptation: To be self-sufficient and self-reliant. Instead of being so self-assured, we need to be open, unguarded, and vulnerable.

Second Temptation: To be spectacular . . . a celebrity mentality. In Nouwen's words, "Jesus refused to be a stunt man. . . . He did not come to walk on hot coals, swallow fire or put His hand in a lion's mouth to demonstrate He had something worthwhile to say."

Third Temptation: To be powerful . . . in charge. To lead is appropriate, necessary, and good. But to push, to manipulate, to be in full control . . . never! To say it simply, one God is sufficient.

Servanthood implies diligence, faithfulness, loyalty, and humility. Servants don't compete . . . or grandstand . . . or polish their image . . . or grab the limelight. They know their job, they admit their limitations, they do what they do quietly and consistently.

Servants cannot control anyone or everything, and they shouldn't try.

Servants cannot change or "fix" people.

Servants cannot meet most folks' expectations.

Servants cannot concern themselves with who gets the credit.

Servants cannot minister in the flesh or all alone.

Let me suggest five practical guidelines for cultivating the right kind of servant habits.

Whatever we do, let's do more with others. Ministry is not a solo, it's a chorus.

Whenever we do it, let's place the emphasis on quality, not quantity. Excellence, not expansion, is our goal.

Whenever we go to do it, let's do it the same as if we were doing it among those who know us the best. Not only will this keep us accountable, it'll guard us from exaggeration.

Whoever may respond, let's keep a level head. If someone criticizes, don't allow it to get you down. If someone idolizes, don't tolerate or fantasize such foolishness.

However long we minister, let's model the Master . . . a servant-hearted and a grace-oriented style.

Let's serve . . . in the name of Jesus.

A servant-hearted attitude keeps us from self-minded altitude.

An Appraisal

❧ *Mark 6:30–32* ❧

*W*ell, we are nine months into the year. Throughout the past months we've reaffirmed the significance of pacing ourselves and not allowing the tyranny of the urgent to blind us to the value of the important.

Well . . . how's it going? Pause long enough to review and reflect as you answer these questions.

Is my pace this year really that different from last year?

Am I enjoying most of my activities or just enduring them?

Have I deliberately taken time on several occasions this year for personal restoration?

Do I give myself permission to relax, to have leisure?

Would other people think I am working too many hours and/or living under too much stress?

Do I consider my body important enough to maintain a nourishing diet, to give it regular exercise, to get enough sleep, to shed those excess pounds?

How is my sense of humor?

Is God being glorified by the schedule I keep . . . or is He getting the leftovers of my energy?

Renewal and restoration are not luxuries; they are essentials. Being alone and resting for a while is not selfish; it is Christlike (see Mark 6:30–32). Taking your day off each week and rewarding yourself with a relaxing, refreshing vacation is not carnal; it's spiritual. Nor is an ultra-busy schedule necessarily the mark of a productive life.

If you are courageous enough to make needed changes, you will show yourself wise. But I should warn you of three barriers you will immediately face.

First, by saying no to the people to whom you used to say yes, you'll feel twinges of guilt. Ignore them! Second, most folks won't understand your slower pace, especially those who are in the sinking boat you just stepped out of. Stick to your guns. Third, by not filling every spare moment with activity, you will begin to see the real you, and you'll not like some of the things you observe, things that once contaminated your busy life. But within a relatively brief period of time, you will turn the corner and be well on the road to a happier, healthier, freer, and more fulfilling life.

My desire is that all of us remain "in." In balance. In our right minds. In good health. In the will of God.

Are you?

Don't allow the tyranny of the urgent to blind you to the value of the important.

BEING HOLY

❧ *Psalm 42* ❧

*O*ur fast-lane living these days does not lend itself to the traits we have traditionally attached to godliness. Remember the old hymn we sang in church years ago? "Take time to be holy, speak oft with Thy Lord; abide in Him always and feed on His Word. . . . Take time to be holy, the world rushes on."

We read those words, believe them, and would even defend them, but we sigh as we confess that more often than not we are strangers to them. The idea of taking the kind of time "to be holy" that our grandparents once did is rather dated.

Does this mean, then, that we cannot be holy? Does an urban lifestyle force us to forfeit godliness? Must we return to the "little house on the prairie" in order to be godly?

Obviously, the answer is no. If godliness were linked to a certain culture or a horse-and-buggy era, then most of us would be out of luck! As much as we might enjoy a slower and less pressured lifestyle, God has not called everyone to such a role or place.

Which brings us to a bottom-line question I seldom hear addressed these days: What exactly does it mean to be holy . . . to be godly?

Godliness cannot be confused with how a person looks (hard as it is for us to get beyond that) or what a person drives or owns. As tough as it is for us to be free of envy and critical thoughts, it is imperative that we remind ourselves that "God looks on the heart" (1 Sam. 16:7); therefore, whatever we may say godliness is, it is not *skin* deep.

Godliness is something below the surface of a life, deep down in the realm of attitude . . . an attitude toward God Himself.

The longer I think about this, the more I believe that a person who is godly is one whose heart is sensitive toward God, one who takes God seriously. This evidences itself in one very obvious mannerism: The godly individual hungers and thirsts after God. In the words of the psalmist, the godly person has a soul that "pants" for the living God (Ps. 42:1–2). What matters is the individual's inner craving to know God, listen to Him, and walk humbly with Him.

Godly people possess an attitude of willing submission to God's will and ways. Whatever He says, goes. And whatever it takes to carry it out is the very thing the godly desire to do.

The godly soul "pants" and "thirsts" for God.

The godly take God seriously.

ANALYZING UNSELFISHNESS

🕮 *Philippians 2:1—4* 🕮

To be "humble in heart" as Christ stated He was, is to be submissive to the core. It involves being more interested in serving the needs of others than in having one's own needs met.

Someone who is truly unselfish is generous with his or her time and possessions, energy and money. As that works its way out, it is demonstrated in various ways, such as thoughtfulness and gentleness, an unpretentious spirit, and servant-hearted leadership.

Ours is a day of self-promotion, defending our own rights, taking care of ourselves first, winning by intimidation, pushing for first place, and a dozen other self-serving agendas. That one attitude does more to squelch our joy than any other. So busy defending and protecting and manipulating, we set ourselves up for a grim, intense existence.

In our selfish, grab-all-you-can-get society, the concept of cultivating an unselfish, servant-hearted attitude is almost a joke to the majority. But, happily, there are a few who genuinely desire to develop such an attitude. I can assure you, if you carry out that desire, you will know the secret to a happy life.

Unselfishness is the stuff of which Christlikeness is made!

QUESTS

❧ *Colossians 1* ❧

> My first direct view of *Titanic* lasted less than two minutes, but the stark sight of her immense black hull towering above the ocean floor will remain forever ingrained in my memory. My lifelong dream was to find this great ship, and during the past thirteen years the quest for her had dominated my life. Now, finally, the quest was over.

So wrote Robert Ballard after discovering the ghostly hulk of the R.M.S. *Titanic* in her lonely berth more than two miles deep in the North Atlantic. For nearly three-quarters of a century, since early April 1912, the great ship had been celebrated in legend, along with the 1,522 souls who had disappeared with her beneath the icy waters hundreds of miles off the coast of Newfoundland.

On several occasions, the explorer used the same word to describe his lifelong dream: "quest." It means a pursuit, a search, or, as Webster colorfully adds, "a chivalrous enterprise in medieval romance usually involving an adventurous journey."

What is your "quest"? Do you have a "lifelong dream"? Anything "dominating your life" enough to hold your attention for thirteen or more years?

Without a quest, life is quickly reduced to bleak black and wimpy white, a diet too bland to get anybody out of bed in the morning. A quest fuels our fire. It refuses to let us drift downstream, gathering debris. It keeps our mind in gear, makes us press on.

God is forever on a quest, too. Ever thought about that? In fact, His adventurous journey is woven throughout the fabric of the New Testament.

One thread is in Romans 8:29, where He mentions that He is conforming us to His Son's image: "For whom He foreknew He also predestined to become conformed to the image of His Son."

Another is in Philippians 1:6, where we're told that He began His "good work" in us and He isn't about to stop.

Elsewhere He even calls us His "workmanship" (Eph. 2:10).

Peter's second letter goes so far as to list some of the things included in this quest: "faith . . . moral excellence . . . knowledge . . . self-control . . . perseverance . . . godliness . . . brotherly kindness . . . love" (2 Pet. 1:5–7).

Character *qualities* in His children—that's His quest. And He won't quit until He completes His checklist.

When will that be? When we rest in peace . . . and not one day sooner. Thanks, Lord.

If you think you've arrived, then you probably haven't even started.

THINK IT OVER

❧❧❧

*A*ll of us are surrounded by and benefit from the results of someone's quest. Let me name a few.

Above my head is a bright electric light. Thanks, Tom.

On my nose are eyeglasses that enable me to focus. Thanks, Ben.

In my driveway is a car ready to take me wherever I choose to steer it. Thanks, Henry.

Across my shelves are books full of interesting and carefully researched pages. Thanks, authors.

Flashing through my mind are ideas, memories, and creative skills. Thanks, teachers.

Tucked away in the folds of my life are discipline and determination, a refusal to quit when the going gets rough, a love for our country's freedom, a respect for authority. Thanks, marines.

Coming into my ears is beautiful music—a wonderful mix of melody and rhythm and lyrics that linger. Thanks, composers.

Deep inside me are personality traits, strong convictions, a sense of right and wrong, a love for God, an ethical compass, a commitment to my wife and family. Thanks, parents.

At home is a peaceful surrounding of eye—pleasing design, colorful wallpaper, tasteful and comfortable furnishings, hugs of affirmation—a shelter in a time of storm. Thanks, Cynthia.

My list could go on and on. So could yours.

Because some cared enough to dream, to pursue, to follow through and complete their quest, our lives are more comfortable, more stable.

That is enough to spur me on. How about you?

KEEP IT SIMPLE

🍂 *Micah 6:6–8* 🍂

*M*icah isn't exactly a household word. Too bad. Though obscure, the ancient prophet had his stuff together. Eclipsed by the much more famous Isaiah, who ministered among the elite, Micah took God's message to the streets.

Micah had a deep suspicion of phony religion. He saw greed in the hearts of the leaders of the kingdom of Judah, which prompted him to warn the common folk not to be deceived by religious pretense among nobility. In true prophetic style, Micah comforted the afflicted and afflicted the comfortable. He condemned sin. He exposed performance-based piety. He championed the cause of the oppressed. He predicted the fall of the nation. And he did it all at the risk of his own life.

But Micah didn't just denounce and attack, leaving everyone aware of the things he despised but none of the things he believed. Like rays of brilliant sunlight piercing charcoal-colored clouds after a storm, the prophet saved his best words for a positive message to the people, and I am pleased to say that he did it with simplicity: "With what shall I come to the LORD and bow myself before the God on high? Shall I come to Him with burnt offerings, with yearling calves? Does the LORD take delight in thousands of rams, in ten thousand rivers of oil? Shall I present my first-born for my rebellious acts, the fruit of my body for the sin of my soul?" (Mic. 6:6–7).

Micah's words state exactly what many, to this day, wonder about pleasing God. Teachers and preachers have made it so sacrificial . . . so complicated . . . so extremely difficult. To them, God is virtually impossible to please. Therefore, religion has become a series of long, drawn-out, deeply painful acts designed to appease this peeved Deity in the sky who takes delight in watching us squirm.

Micah erases the things on the entire list, replacing the complicated possibilities with one of the finest definitions of simple faith: "He has told you, O man, what is good; and what does the LORD require of you but to do justice, to love kindness, and to walk humbly with your God?" (Mic. 6:8).

God does not look for big-time, external displays. He does not require slick public performances.

What is required? Slow down and read the list aloud: to do justice . . . to love kindness . . . and to walk humbly with your God. Period.

Faith is not a long series of religious performances or a pile of pious things.
All God asks is simple faith.

PROGRESSIVENESS

❧ *Psalm 103* ❧

*W*e salute visionaries of yesteryear. We shake our heads in amazement as we imagine the herculean courage it took to stand so confidently when the majority frowned so sternly. Looking back, we laud those who refused to take no for an answer. We quote them with gusto. We even name our children after them. Yesterday's progress earns today's monuments of stone.

But today? What do we do with such creatures today? We brand them as irritating malcontents, reckless idealists who simply won't sit down and be quiet. Today's progressive dreamers are seen as wild-eyed extremists. Since they hate the status quo mold, most of them have a tough time going along with the system. They, in fact, loathe the system. But what they lack in diplomacy they make up for in persistence. Cooperative they're not. Resilient they are.

Give most of them a couple hundred years and they'll be admired, lauded, and knighted. But at the present moment, they just seem nuts.

I can scarcely think of a half-dozen churches, for example, that would even consider having Martin Luther candidate for the pulpit. And it's doubtful that any businesses would hire Thomas Edison or Leonardo da Vinci. Which evangelical seminary would chance turning over its students majoring in systematic theology to a firebrand like John Knox? And who, today, would choose to go into battle with a blood-and-guts, straight-shooting commanding officer like George Patton? For that matter, how many votes would a crusty, outspoken, overweight visionary like Winston Churchill or a rugged Andrew Jackson get in our day of slick government and made-for-TV bureaucrats and politicians? You think we'd respect their progressiveness and value their vision? Don't bet on it. People didn't in their day, either.

Are you an eagle-type, soaring high beyond your peers? Do you find yourself bored with the maintenance of the machinery . . . yawning through the review of the rules . . . restless to cut a new swath . . . excited rather than intimidated by the risks? If so, don't expect pats on the back or great waves of applause. Chances are you may even lose a few jobs, fail a few courses, ruffle tons of feathers, and be the subject of the town gossip. Mavericks who don't color within the lines are also notorious for not staying within the fences. And that makes folks terribly uncomfortable.

But take heart! You're in good company!

Today's alleged heretic may well be tomorrow's hero.

·

CONFLICTS

❧ *Ephesians 6:18; Philippians 4:6* ❧

*P*aul found himself between a rock and a hard place. He wanted to be in heaven but needed to be on earth. In a temporal sort of way, I share the same frustration. "But I am hard pressed from both directions, having the desire to depart and watch the Super Bowl . . . yet to remain in the pulpit is more necessary for your sake" (Phil. 1:23–24, *Swindoll paraphrase*).

Now don't get me wrong. I love to preach. It's one of the few things I'd rather do than eat—as my wife can testify. But I also love football. With only minor adjustments, both of these "loves" can be maintained without much difficulty . . . except for one Sunday a year. Super Bowl Sunday. On that particular day I freely admit, I have a conflict.

I've thought of all sorts of alternative plans:

> Place a tiny TV on the pulpit shelf and bow in silent prayer several times (to check the score).
> Put a Walkman in my suit coat and wear an earphone.
> Ask an usher to signal the score periodically.

Conflicts are common. Unfortunately, they are seldom as lighthearted as this one. Some are, in fact, desperately serious.

What is a conflict? A conflict is an emotional collision. It is stress caused by incompatible desires or demands. It is what occurs when we have two or more impulses in competition with one another. The stronger the impulse, the greater the tension. The greater the tension, the louder the collision.

Conflicts come in many packages, such as when a mother wants to walk with God, raise her children to love the Lord and honor His name. But her husband is turned off to spiritual things. That woman has a conflict between her "mother impulses" and her "wife impulses." She lives with an emotional collision.

I have no quick, easy solutions to complex conflicts. But I know this much: Our Lord cares for His own. Knowing our limitations, He urges us to "cast all our anxieties on Him" (1 Pet. 5:7) and to replace worry with active, specific prayer (Phil. 4:6). Prayer may not stop the collision, but, like seat belts, it sure can protect us from serious damage.

Subtract the power of Christ, the wisdom of His Word, the calming presence of the Holy Spirit, and you have unbearable collisions that lead to unbelievable tragedies.

STANDING FIRM

❧ *1 Corinthians 15–16* ❧

I heard a statistic the other day that blew my mind. Anna Sklar, the author of a book called *Runaway Wives,* was a guest on a local talk show. In the course of the discussion, she cited that ten years ago, for every wife or mother who walked away from her home and responsibilities, six hundred husbands and fathers walked out. Today for each man who walks away, two women do.

Pause and let that sink in.

Understand, I'm not advocating either, nor am I taking sides. I'm just amazed at the unbelievably rapid rise in the number of women who choose escape as the favorite method of coping.

Contrary to our great American heritage, many of today's citizens would rather quit than stick. That which was once not even an option is now standard operating procedure. Now, it's "if you start to sink, *jump,* don't bail" . . . or "if it's hard, *quit,* don't bother."

Every achievement worth remembering is stained with the blood of diligence and scarred by the wounds of disappointment. To quit, to run, to escape, to hide—none of these options solve anything. They only postpone the acceptance of, and reckoning with, reality.

Churchill put it well: "Wars are not won by evacuations."

No, battles are won in the trenches . . . in the grit and grime of courageous determination . . . in the arena of life, day in and day out, amidst the smell of sweat and the cry of anguish.

The apostle Paul, the man who bore on his body "the brandmarks of Jesus" (Gal. 6:17), was a living example of his own counsel: "Therefore, my beloved brethren, be steadfast, immovable, always abounding in the work of the Lord, knowing that your toil is not in vain in the Lord. . . . Be on the alert, stand firm in the faith, act like men, be strong" (1 Cor. 15:58; 16:13).

Giving thought to giving up?

Considering the possibility of quitting?

Looking for an easy way out?

Entertaining the idea of running away . . . stopping before it's finished . . . escaping from reality?

Don't! The Lord never promised you a Disneyland. In fact, the only time He ever used the word "easy" was when He referred to a yoke.

Every journey is accomplished one step at a time. Don't stop now.

THE COST OF GIVING

❦ *2 Corinthians 8:7–8* ❦

Can you recall Jesus' radical philosophy: "Be a servant, give to others." The basis of that statement is tucked away in Luke 9:23. Following Christ is a costly, unselfish decision. He says: "If anyone wishes to come after Me, let him deny himself, and take up his cross daily, and follow me."

When you look closely at Jesus' statement, a couple of things seem important. First, those who desire to follow Him closely must come to terms with self-denial. And second, this decision to give ourselves to others (taking up our cross) has to be a daily matter.

Some questions we must ask and answer ourselves are:

- Am I serious about being a follower of Jesus Christ?
- Do I think of others to such an extent that self-denial is becoming the rule rather than the exception in my life?
- Is my walk with Him a daily thing?
- A thorough self-examination is one of the requisites for following closely. Paul tells us to abound in generosity, be givers, be people who excel in unselfishness. That's costly stuff, terribly expensive. Can you pay the price?

Don't kid yourself; where your treasure is, your heart will be also.

INTRUSIONS

❧ *Romans 3* ❧

*I*f you question your depravity, check your attitude toward intrusions. Having a French origin, "intrude" emerges from two terms, meaning "to thrust in." An intrusion, therefore, is someone or something that thrusts itself into our world without permission, without an invitation, and refuses to be ignored.

Like the constant needs and demands of a child. I watched a young mother in a waiting room just last week. She was pregnant and had a toddler, plus one in diapers in her arms. Was she busy! Yet with incredible patience, that mother hung in there. *Her whole world is one gigantic intrusion,* I thought. *I sure hope she's got a husband who understands . . . and helps her out!*

I also wondered if that young mother realized that she was modeling an unforgettable display of Christ's message. Remember His words in Matthew 18:1–6? He flatly declares that receiving children is tantamount to receiving Him. Obviously, He believes they are worth it all, no matter how many intrusions they cause.

Not all agree. Bob Greene, a syndicated columnist based in Chicago, mentioned one such person in a recent article. Greene tells of meeting a smartly dressed twenty-seven-year-old woman about to be married to a man who had a five-year-old son by a previous marriage. Her attitude toward the boy?

"If I had $10,000 I would have the boy killed. . . . I've asked around and $10,000 is about what it costs to hire someone to kill someone else."

Thinking she might be trying to shock him with a sick joke, Greene told her that her alleged humor was way off base.

"It's not a joke," she said. "I want him dead."

When Greene asked her why she was saying those things, it boiled down to intrusions. "The boy disrupts my life."

The columnist assumed that this was only a vicious fantasy. She really didn't have $10,000, did she? "No," she sighed, "I don't have the $10,000." But as she turned to leave, she added, "But I won't always not have the $10,000!"

Can you imagine the treatment she will give that bright, busy, five-year-old boy?

Intrusions prove what the Bible has taught for centuries. Depravity is a universal disease . . . because sin has "thrust itself in."

Because sin "thrust itself in," God sent His Son into the world.

THINK IT OVER

❧❧ ❧❧

*H*ow do you feel about intrusions? Like an early-morning knock at your door? Like a talkative passenger next to you on a packed-out flight? Like an in jury or illness that strikes at the wrong time?

Like the piercing ring of the telephone?

Like the relentless, endless demands of small children?

Like. . . ?

Check your attitude.

IT'S MORE THAN A JOB

🥨 *2 Thessalonians 3* 🥨

A young fella rushed into a service station and asked the manager if he had a pay phone. The manager nodded, "Sure, over there." The boy pushed in some change, dialed, and waited for an answer. Finally, someone came on the line. "Uh, sir," he said in a deep voice, "could you use an honest, hardworking young man to work for you?" The station manager couldn't help overhearing the question. After a moment or two the boy said, "Oh, you already have an honest, hardworking young man? Well, okay. Thanks just the same." With a broad smile stretched across his face, he hung up the phone and started back to his car, humming and obviously elated. "Hey, just a minute!" the station manager called after him. "I couldn't help but hear your conversation. Why are you so happy? I thought the guy said he already had somebody and didn't need you?" The young man smiled. "Well, you see, I am the honest, hardworking young man. I was just checking up on my job!"

Honest, hardworking employees are tough to find, and when you toss in competence, a positive attitude, teachability, punctuality, proper attire, a team spirit, loyalty, confidentiality, honesty, and an ability to get along well with others, wow! No wonder every boss I talk to answers my question "What is the key ingredient of your organization?" the same way: PERSONNEL.

What kind of employee are you? Do a little one-to-ten appraisal (ten being the best) on the following characteristics from the Book of Proverbs: diligent, thoughtful, skillful, loyal, teachable, humble, thorough, fair, cooperative, honest, positive.

Contrary to popular opinion, work is not the result of the curse. Adam was given the task of cultivating and keeping the Garden before sin ever entered (Gen. 2:15).

Then what was the curse? It was the addition of "thorns and thistles" that turned work into a "toil" and made the whole thing a sweaty hassle. But work itself is a privilege, a high calling, a God-appointed assignment to be carried out for His greater glory.

Today, it isn't literal briars and stinging nettles that give us fits; it's thorny people whose thistlelike attitudes add just enough irritation to make the job . . . well, just a job.

The difference is people. No, let's get specific. The difference is you.

The place you work will never be better than you make it.

Give your boss an imaginary phone call,
and listen to His response with an open mind.

KEEP IT FUN!

🍂 *Ecclesiastes 3:4* 🍂

*E*ven though I don't like it, I'm tempted to stand back, shrug, and agree with Virginia Brasier, who wrote "Time of the Mad Atom":

> This is the age of the half-read page.
> And the quick hash and the mad dash.
> The bright night with the nerves tight.
> The plane hop and the brief stop.
> The lamp tan in a short span.
> The Big Shot in a good spot.
> And the brain strain and the heart pain.
> And the cat naps till the spring snaps—
> And the fun's done!

When my wife turned fifty, our younger daughter, Colleen, and I decided it called for a celebration. While running together one morning, Cols and I came up with a surprise birthday party-boat ride down at the Newport Harbor. We communicated this to the family and several of Cynthia's friends. Everyone who came was told to bring "fifty of anything wrapped in black." Cols and Charissa coordinated final plans to meet out-of-town guests at the airport in complete secrecy. The way we synchronized our activities, you'd have thought we were planning the Normandy Invasion.

Finally, B-Day arrived. My excuse to get Cynthia to the dock was a boat show that was in progress. Fifteen minutes prior to our arrival, all the gang had slipped on board. Cynthia and I leisurely walked along the dock where I casually asked an individual, who was really in on the plot, if she happened to know where the *Lyn Dee Belle* was docked. "Sure do," she said. "Be happy to show her to you."

As Cynthia stepped on deck, fifty family members and friends jumped up and screamed, "SURPRISE!" For the next three hours we motored around the harbor, took pictures, laughed, ate, sang, opened the craziest bunch of gifts you ever saw, celebrated, and had nothing but fun. None of us will ever forget that party!

In this day of demands and deadlines, fun's often the first thing to go. Don't let that happen. Because when the fun's gone, the brain strains and the heart pains.

Solomon was right: Happiness and laughter do us good "like a medicine."

MEAN WHAT YOU SING

🌸 *Revelation 5:9—10* 🌸

Nothing touches the human heart deeper than music. This is never more true than when a group of Christians sings heartily unto their Lord. Many a cold heart on skid row has melted as the strains of some old hymn lingered in steamy streets and sleazy alleys surrounding a gospel mission. When congregations sing the praises of the King, even the demonic hosts stand at attention. "The powers of darkness fear when this sweet chant they hear, May Jesus Christ be praised!"

Such moving melodies hold out a warm welcome to strangers, comfort to the broken, refreshment to the lonely, and affirmation to the discouraged. Great music from God's people instructs and reproves, blesses and relieves.

Charles Wesley, perhaps the most prolific hymnist of all time, realized the value of corporate singing as he wrote, "Oh, for a thousand tongues to sing my great Redeemer's praise." There is nothing to compare to that sound. Nothing.

But have you noticed the fly in our melodic ointment? It is not a lack of beauty or harmony, nor is it insufficient volume or intensity. It is, plain and simple, the presence of words with an absence of meaning. We sing well, but we fail to heed the message hidden behind the bars.

Stop and think. There's a line in "Take My Life and Let It Be" that always makes me pause as the words stick in my throat: "Take my silver and my gold, not a mite would I withhold." Imagine! Not even "a mite"! We all sing that with such ease, yet I have known few who wouldn't withhold something. Including me.

Last Sunday after the service our congregation sang "I Give All My Witness to You" . . . and then we left. We all got into our cars, drove away, and most of us have not seen one another since. What's been happening? Has He had our witness? Have the days that passed been that much different than two weeks earlier? A month? Those thoughts haunt me.

Think of each song or hymn as a promise to God, a binding statement of your commitment. Picture the results of this commitment as you sing it with gusto. Then, after the song has ended, apply it with the same gusto.

God not only loves a cheerful giver, He honors a sincere singer.

This Sunday put yourself into the lyrics of each hymn,
considering them your own personal credo. See what a difference it makes.

A Mentor

❧ *1 Thessalonians 5:1–11* ❧

*T*here we sat, a cluster of six. A stubby orange candle burned at the center of our table flickering eerie shadows across our faces. One spoke; five listened. Every question was handled with such grace, such effortless ease. Each answer was drawn from deep wells of wisdom, shaped by tough decisions and nurtured by time. And pain. Mistakes and mistreatment. And honed by tests, risks, heartbreaks, and failures. Decades in the same crucible had made his counsel invaluable.

His age? Seventy-two. He had seen it all, weathered it all—all the flack and delights of a flock. Outlasted all the fads and gimmicks of gullible and greedy generations, known the ecstasy of seeing lives revolutionized, the agony of lives ruined, and the monotony of lives unchanged. He had paid his dues—and had the scars to prove it.

There we sat for well over three hours hearing his stories, pondering his principles, questioning his conclusions, and responding to his ideas. The evening was punctuated with periodic outbursts of laughter followed by protracted periods of quiet talk.

As I participated, I was suddenly twenty-six years old again. A young seminarian and pastoral intern existing in a no man's land between a heart full of desire and a head full of dreams. Long on theological theories but short on practical experience. I had answers to questions no one was asking but a lack of understanding on the things that really mattered. In momentary flashbacks, I saw myself in the same room with this man thirty years earlier, drinking at the same well, soaking up the same spirit. Thirty years ago he had been a model; now he had become a mentor. Thoroughly human and absolutely authentic, he had emerged a well-worn vessel of honor fit for the Master's use. And I found myself profoundly grateful that Ray Stedman's shadow had crossed my life.

As we said good-bye to Ray that evening, I walked a little slower. I thought about the things he had taught me without directly instructing me, about the courage he had given me without deliberately exhorting me. I wondered how it had happened. I wondered why I had been so privileged. I found myself wanting to run back to his car and tell him again how much I loved and admired him.

But it was late. And after all I was a fifty-five-year-old man. A husband. A father. A grandfather. A pastor. To some, a leader.

But as I stood there alone in the cold night air, I suddenly realized what I wanted to be when I grew up.

A mentor knows how to stretch without insulting,
affirm without flattering, release without abandoning us.

GIVING IS GODLIKE

❧ *John 3:16* ❧

*S*hortly after World War II, the saddest sight for American soldiers who were picking up the pieces in ravaged Europe, was that of little orphaned children starving in the streets of those war-torn cities.

One soldier driving along in his jeep spotted a little lad with his nose pressed to the window of a pastry shop. Inside the cook was kneading dough for a fresh batch of doughnuts. The hungry boy stared in silence, watching every move. The soldier pulled his jeep to the curb and got out to slip over to the boy's side. Through the steamed-up window he could see the mouth-watering morsels as they were being pulled from the oven, piping hot. The boy salivated and released a slight groan.

The soldier's heart went out to the orphan. "Son...would you like some of those?"

The boy was startled. "Oh, yes, would I!"

The American stepped into the shop, bought a dozen, put them in a bag and walked back to where the lad was standing in the foggy cold of the London morning. He smiled, held out the bag, and said simply: "Here you are."

As he turned to walk away, he felt a tug on his coat. The soldier looked back and heard the child ask quietly:

"Mister . . . are you God?"

We are never more like God than when we give.

HANDLING ADVERSITY

❧ *Job 1–2, 42* ❧

*S*tep into the time tunnel with me, and let's travel together back to Uz (not the wizard of, but the land of). Wherever it was, Uz had a citizen who was respected by everyone. Why? Because he was blameless, upright, God-fearing, and clean living. He had ten children, thousands of head of livestock, acres and acres of land, a great many servants, and a substantial stack of cash. No one would deny that he was "the greatest of all the men of the East." His name was Job, a synonym for integrity and godliness.

Yet, within a matter of hours, adversity fell upon this fine man like an avalanche of jagged rocks. He lost his livestock, his crops, his land, his servants, and all ten children. Soon thereafter he also lost his health.

The book that bears his name records an entry he made into his journal soon after the rocks stopped falling: "The LORD gave and the LORD has taken away. Blessed be the name of the LORD" (Job 1:21).

Following this incredible statement, God adds: "Through all this Job did not sin nor did he blame God" (1:22).

The logical questions are, Why didn't he? What kept him from bitterness or even thoughts of suicide?

At the risk of oversimplifying the situation, I suggest three basic answers that I have discovered from searching through this book.

First, Job claimed God's loving sovereignty. He believed that the Lord who gave had every right to take away (Job 1:21; 2:10). *Job looked up* claiming his Lord's right to rule over his life.

Second, he counted on God's promise of resurrection. "Even after my skin is destroyed, yet from my flesh I shall see God" (Job 19:25–26). *Job looked ahead,* counting on his Lord's promise to make all things bright and beautiful in the life beyond.

Third, he confessed his own lack of understanding. What a relief this brings! He didn't feel obligated to explain why (Job 42:2–4). *Job looked within,* confessing his inability to put it all together.

He rested his adversity with God, not feeling forced to answer why.

When we're looking in all the right directions, we won't take the wrong turn.

THINK IT OVER

❧❧❧

*T*ry to make time this weekend to read the entire book of Job, for only then do you really see the true extent of Job's honest dealings with God and his steadfast faith in the face of adversity.

Then, honestly look at your own life and your own dealings with the Lord. Think about your past . . . those times of adversity in your own life. Were you able to look up, look ahead, and look within?

Where are you now in your journey of faith?

If you are climbing over the ragged rocks of adversity, take His hand and let Him lead you through. In the midst of it all, it is His touch which comforts and guides.

If the road ahead is smooth right now, get ready. Watch out for falling rocks!

A MATTER OF OBEDIENCE

❧ *1 Timothy 2:1–7* ❧

*L*eading can be awfully lonely and terribly frustrating. I haven't always believed that. Fact is, when I was a starry-eyed seminary student back around '59 and '60, I had this crazy idea that a leader lived a charmed life. Especially a spiritual leader. My fantasy included contented people, smiling and grateful; plenty of time to think, study, and do relaxed research; no financial woes; short counseling sessions with folks who were eager and happy to adjust their lives according to Scripture; untold energy; sermons that virtually jumped from the text, then into my notes and out of my mouth. No conflicts. No confrontations . . . no kidding!

You're smiling. (I told you it was a fantasy.)

It's amazing what three decades can do to a wastebasket full of theories. Today I would tell anyone thinking about becoming a spiritual leader to think again. It's not that they're not needed; goodness knows, this ornery planet of depraved humanity can always use a few more leaders who are Christian to the core. The problem is, it's a lonelier task than it used to be. And the frustrations can be downright maddening.

In the midst of all this, it always helps me to return to my "call." Thousands of miles away from home, stationed on a tiny island in the South Pacific, I distinctly remember the inner surge of assurance that I would be neither fulfilled nor happy doing anything other than ministry. It meant changing careers and returning to graduate school. It meant retooling my mental machinery for a lifetime of study. It meant living my life under the always curious and sometimes demanding scrutiny of the public eye, and, if necessary, being willing to go to the wall for the sake of the gospel. None of this mattered. God had spoken to my heart, and there was no turning back. It was a matter of obedience.

We must recognize that the Lord, our God, is responsible for our appointment to any place of leadership. Over all other suggestions and advice, we must seek to hear the counsel of Almighty God as revealed in Scripture. We must take refuge in and rely on the Spirit of God rather than our own flesh and skill. With our whole heart we must fear Jesus Christ, our Lord, and acknowledge Him as the sovereign Head of the church, deserving of our unreserved faithfulness, submission, diligence, and commitment.

For me, there are no other options.

It's a matter of obedience.

How about you?

Take refuge in and rely on the Spirit of God rather than your own flesh and skill.

MUSING OVER MISTAKES

❧❧ *1 Samuel 15* ❧❧

*W*hen it comes to mistakes, we need a great deal of tolerance. And a sense of humor doesn't hurt, either.

I ran across an embarrassing mistake recently in the sports section of the newspaper. A volleyball coach was being featured, and the article went on and on about her background, superb ability, win-loss record, and style of coaching. The next day, tucked away in a much less obvious place, was a one-sentence apology, which said that the coach was, in fact, a man, not a woman. Ouch!

Who hasn't happened upon one every once in a while in a church bulletin? One of my all-time favorites was the announcement letting people know about a "sing-in" following an evening service. Unfortunately, this is the way it appeared: "There will be a sin-in at the Johnson home immediately following the pastor's evening message on 'Intimate Fellowship.'"

There are even a few human-error scenes in Scripture that strike me as nothing short of hilarious.

Among my favorites is the one tucked away in 1 Samuel 15 where King Saul was commanded by Samuel, very clearly, that he should not only destroy the Amalekites, but also every living creature in the region of the Amalekites. He went, he saw, he slew . . . but instead of total annihilation, he captured the king and also spared a lot of the animals.

When Samuel heard of the king's disobedience, the prophet showed up and asked why. Saul lied. "I have carried out the command of the Lord," he said.

Samuel's line is classic: "(You obeyed, huh?) What then is this bleating of the sheep in my ears, and the lowing of the oxen which I hear?"

Can't you just picture it? All the time old Saul's mouth was moving, there was this strange mixture of animal sounds in the distance. No, his sin wasn't funny . . . but the way he got caught red-handed was. The animals told on him!

So long as there is humanity on this old earth, there will be mistakes and failures. If you can't tolerate those who make them, I'd suggest you stop making them yourself!

General John Sedgwick did. In fact, his last words were spoken while looking over the parapet at the enemy line during the Battle of Spotsylvania in 1864. With great gusto he sneered, "They couldn't hit an elephant at this dist—"

*Remember, when it comes to mistakes, we need a great deal of tolerance.
And a sense of humor doesn't hurt either.*

ON BEING CONFIDENTIAL

🕸 *Romans 1:21–32* 🕸

*B*e honest now, can you keep a secret? When privileged information passes through one of the gates of your senses, does it remain within the walls of your mind, or is it only a matter of time before a leak occurs? Do you respect a person's trust or ignore it, either instantly or ultimately?

The longer I live, the more I realize the scarcity of people who can be fully trusted with confidential information. And the longer I live, the more I value those rare souls who fall into that category! As a matter of fact, if I were asked to list the essential characteristics that mark a person of integrity and trust, the ability to maintain confidences would rank very near the top.

A portion of the physician's Hippocratic Oath comes to mind: "And whatsoever I shall see or hear in the course of my profession . . . if it be what should not be published abroad, I will never divulge, holding such things to be holy secrets."

We would be justly offended by a doctor who treated our "holy secrets" lightly. The same applies to a minister or an attorney, a counselor or a parent, a teacher or a secretary, a colleague or a friend. Especially a close friend.

Solomon wrote some strong words concerning this subject in his Proverbs. Listen to his wise counsel and remember it the next time you are tempted to run off at the mouth:

> When there are many words, transgression is unavoidable, but he who restrains his lips is wise. (10:19)
> He who goes about as a talebearer reveals secrets, but he who is trustworthy conceals a matter. (11:13)
> The one who guards his mouth preserves his life; the one who opens wide his lips comes to ruin. (13:3)
> He who goes about as a slanderer reveals secrets, therefore do not associate with a gossip. (20:19)

In light of these scriptural admonitions, I suggest we establish four practical ground rules:

1. Whatever you're told in confidence, do not repeat.
2. Whenever you're tempted to tell a secret, do not yield.
3. Whomever you're talking about, do not gossip.
4. However you're prone to disagree, do not slander.

Be honest now, can you keep a secret? Prove it.

A confidence kept gives others confidence in you.

A PLACE TO UNLOAD

❧ *Galatians 5–6* ❧

*T*his thing called life is an awfully long journey. For some, it seems an end-less trip, filled with thankless responsibilities and relentless tasks, disappointments and deadlines, and daily demands.

Being imperfect doesn't help. Every so often we make stupid decisions. We say things we wish we could retrieve. Selfishly, we look out for number one and later regret it. We act impulsively and realize, after the fact, how foolish we were, how dumb we looked. On top of all that, we hurt the ones we love the most. All this stuff caves in on us at certain times, and we wonder how anybody could ever love us . . . especially God.

When we start thinking like this, we need to turn our mind to the "one anothers" in the New Testament. Here's just a sampling: Love one another, build up one another, live in peace with one another, confess your sins to one another, speak to one another, admonish one another, comfort one another, pray for one another.

I deliberately saved my favorite for last: "Bear one another's burdens" (Gal. 6:2).

Imagine two mountain hikers trudging along, each carrying a backpack. The one on the left has a tiny, light pack that a kid could carry, while the poor soul on the right is so loaded down we can't even see his head or his body.

Let's imagine what he might be lugging in that pack down that long road. It could be a long-standing grudge that's poisoning his insides. It might be a broken relationship with his wife or one of his kids. That pack could be loaded with unpaid bills, all of them overdue.

The question is, Where can that fella on the right go to unload so the fella on the left can help "bear the burden"? By sitting in church alongside a few hundred or a couple thousand other folks? Hardly. What he needs most is to be involved in an adult fellowship in a small-group setting, a place where there is person-to-person caring and the opportunity for authentic sharing. Where he will feel free, without embarrassment or shame, to tell his secret or state his struggle; where someone will listen, help him unload, and give him fresh strength.

Adult fellowships and small groups are not miniature church services. They are pockets of people who love Christ and believe in helping one another. They don't point fingers or preach or compare. They are your brothers and sisters in Christ.

Once you begin unloading that pack, you'll discover how much easier the journey seems.

Are you involved in a small fellowship group?
If not, consider joining or starting a group—especially if your load is too heavy.

RECONCILING UNFORGIVENESS

🍂 *Psalm 32:3–4* 🍂

*J*esus tells us to stop praying for forgiveness until we've made things right with people we need to forgive or ask forgiveness from. I believe most of us try to do that. But what if it is impossible for me to reconcile because the offended person has died? It's impossible to get a hearing, but your conscience remains seared. I suggest you share your burden of guilt with someone whom you can trust—your spouse, a counselor, your pastor. Be specific and completely candid. Pray with that person and confess openly the wrong and the guilt of your soul. In such cases prayer and the presence of an understanding, affirming individual will provide the relief you need so desperately.

After David had indirectly murdered Uriah, Bathsheba's husband, his guilt was enormous. Adultery and hypocrisy on top of murder just about did him in. Finally, when he was caving in, he broke his silence and sought God's forgiveness but Uriah was not there to hear his confession. He had been dead almost a year. The broken king called on the prophet Nathan and poured out his soul, "I have sinned . . .," Nathan followed quickly with these words: "The Lord also has taken away your sin; you shall not die."

When you have been the cause of an offense, that is, when you are the offender, have the heart of a servant. Stop, go, reconcile, and then return.

Confess your sins one to another. Only pride is stopping you.

GUMPTION

🎗 *Look up the scripture references mentioned below.* 🎗

*W*e don't hear much about *gumption* anymore. Too bad, since we need it more than ever these days. I was raised on gumption (my parents also called it "spizzerinctum")—as were my own children, especially when I was trying to motivate them.

Can't you just see it as a whole new academic field—"Gumptionology 101"—in some college catalog? That will never happen, however, since gumption is better caught than taught.

Most folks get a little gumption in their initial birth packet, but it's a tool that rusts rather quickly. Here are some pointers that will help you keep it well oiled:

Gumption begins with a firm commitment. Daniel "made up his mind" long before he was dumped in a Babylonian boot camp (Dan. 1:8). Joshua didn't hesitate to declare his commitment in his famous "as for me and my house" speech (Josh. 24:15). You want gumption to continue to the end? Start strong!

Gumption means being disciplined one day at a time. Rather than focusing on the whole enchilada, take it in bite-sized chunks. The whole of any objective can overwhelm even the most courageous.

Gumption requires being alert to subtle temptations. Gumption plans ahead, watching out for associations that weaken us (Prov. 13:20), procrastination that steals from us (24:30–34), and rationalizations that lie to us (23:4; 25:28). People who achieve their goals stay alert.

Gumption requires the encouragement of accountability. At David's low-water mark, his friend Jonathan stepped in. When Elijah was ready to cash in everything, along came Elisha. With Paul it was Timothy . . . or Silas or Barnabas or Dr. Luke. People need people, which is why Solomon came on so strong about iron sharpening iron (Prov. 17:17).

Gumption comes easier when we remember that finishing has its own unique rewards. Jesus told the Father He had "accomplished" His assignment (John 17:4). On more than one occasion, Paul referred to "finishing the course" (Acts 20:24; 2 Tim. 4:7). Desire accomplished is sweet to the soul.

If the journey seems extra long today, enjoy a gust of wind at your back from these words out of The Living Bible. It's one of those spizzerinctum scriptures: "Let us not get tired of doing what is right, for after a while we will reap a harvest of blessing if we don't get discouraged and quit" (Gal. 6:9).

Gumption may be hidden, but it always shows.

THINK IT OVER

❧❧ ❧❧

I ran across the word "gumption" again while reading Robert Pirsig's *Zen and the Art of Motorcycle Maintenance*. Singing the praises of all that gumption represents, he wrote:

I like the word gumption because it's so homely and so forlorn and so out of style it looks as if it needs a friend and isn't likely to reject anyone who comes along. It's an old Scottish word, once used a lot by pioneers, but . . seems to have all but dropped out of use.

A person filled with gumption doesn't sit around, dissipating and stewing about things. He's at the front of the train of his own awareness, watching to see what's up the track and meeting it when it comes.

A little later Pirsig applies gumption to life, hiding his comments behind the word picture of repairing a motorcycle:

> If you're going to repair a motorcycle, an adequate supply of gumption is the first and most important tool. If you haven't got that you might as well gather up all the other tools and put them away, because they won't do you any good.
>
> Gumption is the psychic gasoline that keeps the whole thing going. If you haven't got it, there is no way the motorcycle can possibly be fixed. But if you have got it and know how to keep it, there's absolutely no way in the whole world that motorcycle can keep from getting fixed. It's bound to happen. Therefore the thing that must be monitored at all times and preserved before anything else is gumption.

PREDICAMENTS

✣ *Romans 8* ✣

*A*h, those predicaments . . . life is full of them. Often they are of our own making. Other times they just seem to happen mysteriously to us. Occasionally, predicaments are comical or borderline crazy. Sometimes they can be irritating and troublesome. But one thing is for sure: Predicaments are unpredictable. And embarrassing. And confusing. And really weird.

Like the time I was leading a Bible study at a church I'd never attended before. Shortly after getting underway, I noticed two people (latecomers) standing at the door, reluctant to join us. The woman was much older than the man, so I paused, looked in their direction, and welcomed them to join our group, saying, "Why don't you and your mother pull up a chair and join us?" Well, you could've heard a pin drop. Too late I realized my mistake. She was his wife! Throughout the first part of the session (which seemed like an eternity), I felt like dead meat, and they glared at me like a couple of circling buzzards. When we took a coffee break, they were out of there.

At times like this, I find a measure of relief in knowing that Scripture records one predicament after another. Can you imagine how Peter felt immediately after he had deliberately denied the Lord for the third time . . . then heard that ominous cock crowing in the distance? Talk about embarrassing.

And what about Daniel, who refused to obey the injunction of King Darius. Though Daniel continued to obey God, he wound up spending the night in a den of lions. Talk about confusing!

And who can forget David's inexplicable actions when he fled from Saul and found himself in enemy territory and "disguised his sanity . . . and acted insanely in their hands, and scribbled on the doors of the gate, and let his saliva run down into his beard" (1 Sam. 21:13). Talk about weird!

I'm comforted when I realize that God is in sovereign control of all of life. He not only knows the times and the seasons; He is also Lord of the unexpected and the unpredictable. Our times and our trials are in His hands. Even when we feel embarrassed or confused or do something really weird.

Whether we're on cloud nine, enjoying His blessings, or caught in the thicket of some tangled predicament, He hasn't let us go. By His grace, He remains "for us" (Rom. 8:31).

Remember, He is the God of your soaring spirits
as well as your perplexing predicaments.

RESPONSIBILITY

❧ *Joel 3:14* ❧

One of George Bernard Shaw's statements frequently flashes through my mind: "Liberty means responsibility. That is why most men dread it." In a day when most people pass the buck with merely a shrug, those words bite and sting. It's one thing to sing and dance to liberty's tunes, but it's something else entirely to bear the responsibility for paying the band.

There are numerous examples of this. Leadership carries with it a few privileges and perks, but living with the responsibility of that task makes a reserved parking space and your own bathroom pale into insignificance. Conceiving children is a moment of sheer ecstasy, but rearing them as a loving and caring parent represents years of thankless responsibility. Running an organization that gets a job done, leaving those involved feeling fulfilled and appreciated, can be exciting, fun, and stretching, but it's a nightmare unless the details of responsibility are clearly set forth and maintained.

Big projects and meaningful achievements get done not by dreamers but by doers, not by armchair generals who watch and frown from a distance but by brave troops in the trenches, not by fans in the bleachers but by committed coaches and players on the field, not by those who stay neutral and play it safe but by those who get off the fence of indecision, even though their decisions are occasionally unpopular.

All this reminds me of a full-page advertisement I saw in the *Wall Street Journal*:

> DECISIONS, DECISIONS: Sometimes the decision to do nothing is wise. But you can't make a career of doing nothing. Freddie Fulcrum weighed everything too carefully. He would say, "On the one hand . . . but then, on the other," and his arguments weighed out so evenly he never did anything. When Freddie died, they carved a big zero on his tombstone. If you decide to fish—fine. Or, if you decide to cut bait—fine. But if you decide to do nothing, you're not going to have fish for dinner.

The secret of true liberty is responsibility. And that calls for decisions, decisions. Tough decisions. Lonely decisions. Unpleasant decisions. Misunderstood decisions. Courageous decisions.

As I recall, Jesus often had fish for dinner.

> *"Responsibility is the first step in responsibility"*
> *(William Edward Burghardt Du Bois).*

SHARING YOUR TESTIMONY

🍂 *Acts 22:1–21* 🍂

*A*time-honored, effective method of evangelism is your personal testimony. Just telling about your spiritual pilgrimage. The skeptic may deny your doctrine or attack your church, but he cannot honestly ignore the fact that your life has been cleaned up and revolutionized.

Now I'm not talking about some stale, dragged-out verbal marathon. That kind of testimony never attracted anyone! I'm speaking of an effective, powerful missile launched from your lips to the ears of the unsaved. Consider these five suggestions:

1. *You want to be listened to, so be interesting.* It's a contradiction to talk about how exciting Christ really is in an uninteresting way. Remember to guard against religious clichés, jargon, and hard-to-understand terminology. Theologians, beware!

2. *You want to be understood, so be logical.* Think of your salvation in three phases and construct your testimony accordingly: (a) before you were born again—the struggles within, the loneliness, lack of peace, absence of love, unrest, and fears; (b) the decision that revolutionized your life; and (c) the change—the difference it has made since you received Christ.

3. *You want the moment of your new birth to be clear, so be specific.* Don't be vague. Speak of Christ, not the church. Emphasize faith more than feeling. Be simple and direct as you describe what you did or what you prayed or what you said. This is crucial!

4. *You want your testimony to be used, so be practical.* Be human and honest as you talk. Don't promise, "All your problems will end if you will become a Christian," for that isn't true. Try to think as unbelievers think.

5. *You want your testimony to produce results, so be warm and genuine.* A smile breaks down more barriers than the hammer blows of cold, hard facts. Let your enthusiasm flow freely. It's hard to convince someone of the sheer joy and excitement of knowing Christ if you're wearing a face like a jail warden. Above all, be positive and courteous. Absolutely refuse to argue. Nobody I ever met was "arm wrestled" into the kingdom. Insults and put-downs turn people off.

Ask God to open your lips and honor your words . . . but be careful! Once your missile hits the target, you'll become totally dissatisfied with your former life as an earthbound, secret-service saint.

No persuasive technique will ever take the place of your personal testimony. If you have not discovered the value of telling others how God rearranged your life, you've missed a vital link in the chain of His plan for reaching the lost.

Short and Sweet

🐚 *James 4:13–17* 🐚

*A*verage life spans are shorter than most of us realize. For instance, a face-lift lasts only six to ten years; a dollar bill lasts for only eighteen months; a painted line on the road remains only three to four months; and a tornado seldom lasts more than ten minutes.

There are differences of opinion, but most agree that the human life span averages somewhere between seventy-five and eighty years. That may sound encouraging to the young and disturbing to those in their sixties, seventies, and eighties. The simple fact is, however, nobody knows for sure how long he or she may live.

When we read *and believe* the warnings in Scripture, there is little doubt that life is short. James pulls no punches when he writes, "You are just a vapor that appears for a little while and then vanishes away" (4:14).

The average life span may be seventy-five to eighty years, but who can say you or I have that long? We may have less than two years or, for that matter, less than two weeks. Vanishing vapors aren't known for longevity.

Since this is true, let's do our best to make the time we have count. Rather than live with reluctance, let's live with exuberance. Instead of fearing what's ahead, let's face it head-on with enthusiasm. And because life is so terribly short, let's do everything we can to make it sweet.

How? Three thoughts come to mind.

First, *act on your impulse.* Don't wait for the perfect moment. A woman in my former church took these words to heart and contacted a person she hadn't talked to for a long time. The person was surprised and thrilled. "You have no idea how much your call has meant to me," she said. Later the woman who had received the call admitted she had planned to take her life that very afternoon. The call had changed her mind.

Second, *focus on the positive.* Merchants of negativism may be strong and sound convincing, but their message is debilitating. Life's too short for that. Spread germs of cheer. Joy is contagious.

Third, *traffic in the truth.* Refuse to stake your claim on hearsay. Check out the facts. Be discerning. If you are a conduit of communication, speak only the truth. If you're not absolutely sure, keep quiet. Lies can outlive lives, unfortunately.

Short and sweet. That's the only way to go.

Have you been putting off something you really want or need to do?
You don't have forever. Get at it!

"Today"

*T*hose servants who refuse to get bogged down in and anchored to the past are those who pursue the objectives of the future. People who do this are seldom petty. They are too involved in getting a job done to be occupied with yesterday's hurts and concerns. Very near the end of his full and productive life, Paul wrote: "I have fought the good fight, I have finished the course, I have kept the faith" (2 Tim 4:7). What a grand epitaph! He seized every day by the throat. He relentlessly pursued life.

I know human nature well enough to realize that some people excuse their bitterness over past hurts by thinking: "It's too late to change. I've been injured and the wrong done against me is too great for me ever to forget it. Maybe Paul could press on, not me." A person with this mind-set is convinced that he or she is the exception to the command to forgive, and he is determined not to change.

But when God holds out hope, when God makes promises, there are no exceptions. With each new dawn there is delivered to your door a fresh, new package called "today." God has designed each of us in such a way that we can handle only one package at a time . . . and all the grace we need will be supplied by Him as we live out that day.

"I press on toward the goal."

PETTINESS

🐝 *Galatians 2:4–5* 🐝

*F*ew things turn our crank faster than being around big-minded, enthusiastic, broad-shouldered visionaries. They are positive, on the move, excited about exploring new vistas, inspired, and inspiring. While others are preoccupied with tiny tasks and nit-picking squabbles, these people see opportunity in every difficulty and helpful lessons in every setback.

Few things turn us off quicker than being around small-minded, pessimistic, narrow-world, tedious frowners. Engrossed in the minutiae of what won't work and remembering a half-dozen worst-case scenarios, they can throw more cold water on a creative idea than a team of fire fighters snuffing out a candle.

It's not caution we resent. Caution is necessary and wise. Caution keeps the visionary realistic. No, it's the tiny-focused, squint-eyed, tight-lipped, stingy soul that drives us batty. The best word is petty . . . as in petty cash, petty larceny, petty minded.

"Pettiness," writes George Will, "is the tendency of people without large purposes."

Petty people are worse than stubborn; they are negative and rigidly inflexible. While we work overtime to come up with some soaring idea, they've already thought up eight reasons it won't fly.

Whatever or wherever or whoever manifests pettiness isn't my concern, however. Stopping its effect on us is. Why? Because the church seems to be the breeding ground for this legalistic disease.

Pettiness takes a terrible toll. It kills our joy!

I have been studying the lives of several of the great visionaries of the church. They were extremely different, yet they all have one common denominator: Not one was petty. I mean *not one.*

Let me remind you of Paul's reaction to those who "sneaked in to spy out our liberty which we have in Christ Jesus." He declares, "We did not yield in subjection to them for even an hour" (Gal. 2:5). Nor should we.

Count on this: You will encounter petty types. So when you do, shrug it off and just keep on honoring God as you pursue those large purposes.

"Pettiness is the tendency of people without large purposes" (George Will).

THINK IT OVER

❧❧❧

*I*n one of his more serious moments, Mike Yaconelli, editor of *The Wittenburg Door,* addressed the issue of pettiness:

Petty people are ugly people They are people who have lost their vision. They are people who have turned their eyes away from what matters and focused, instead, on what doesn't matter. The result is that the rest of us are immobilized by their obsession with the insignificant.

It is time to rid the church of pettiness. It is time the church refused to be victimized by petty people. It is time the church stopped ignoring pettiness. It is time the church quit pretending that pettiness doesn't matter.

Pettiness has become a serious disease in the Church of Jesus Christ—a disease which continues to result in terminal cases of discord, disruption, and destruction. Petty people are dangerous people because they appear to be only a nuisance instead of what they really are—a health hazard.

—*The Wittenburg Door* December 1984/January 1985

SHOWING OFF

🕮 *Matthew 6* 🕮

*J*esus opened a five-gallon can of worms the day He preached His Sermon on the Mount. There wasn't a Pharisee within gunshot range who wouldn't have given his last denarius to have seen Him strung up by sundown. They hated Him because He refused to let them get away with their phony religious drool!

If there was one thing Jesus despised, it was the very thing every Pharisee majored in at seminary: showing off. Another word for it is "self-righteousness." The Messiah unsheathed His sharp sword of truth that day, exposing their pride. Like never before, the smug show-offs were put in their place!

Listen to Matthew 6:1: "Beware of practicing your righteousness before men to be noticed by them."

In other words, stop showing off! Stop calling attention to your righteousness! And then, to make the warning stick, our Lord gave three specific examples of how people show off their own righteousness so that others might ooh and aah over them.

In Matthew 6:2 Jesus says, "When therefore you give alms, do not sound a trumpet before you." In other words, when you perform acts of charity or assist someone in need, keep it quiet. Remain anonymous. Jesus promises that "your Father who sees in secret will repay you" (6:4).

In Matthew 6:5 Jesus talks about "when you pray." He warns us against being supplicational show-offs who stand in prominent places and mouth meaningless mush in order to be seen and heard. A show-off loves syrupy words. He's got the technique for sounding high and holy down pat. But Jesus says: Don't show off when you talk with the Father.

In Matthew 6:16 Jesus says, "Whenever you fast, do not put on a gloomy face as the hypocrites do." Fasting is when the show-off really hits his stride! He works overtime trying to appear humble and sad, hoping to look hungry and exhausted like some freak who just finished walking across the Sahara that afternoon. Instead, we ought to look and sound fresh, clean, and completely natural.

Our Lord reserved His strongest and longest sermon not for struggling sinners or discouraged disciples but for hypocrites . . . for glory hogs. Unfortunately, most of them never change because they don't hear what He says to them. Show-offs, you see, are terribly hard-of-hearing.

Is your righteousness showing off? Listen to His words!

SIMPLIFY!

❧ *John 17* ❧

*H*igh-tech times lead to high-stress tension. The never-ending drive for more, mixed with the popular tendency to increase production and intensify involvement, leaves most folks in the workplace not only exhausted but dissatisfied.

Instead of Saturday being a change-of-pace day, it has become an opportunity to squeeze in a second job. And Sundays? A time for renewal and refreshment? You're smiling. No, it's the day most type-A high achievers start another to-do list in preparation for the new week.

Every time I officiate at a funeral, I'm reminded of the things that really matter . . . things that last. Stuff that seemed so all-fired important yesterday loses its steam when you stand on a windswept hill surrounded by weather-beaten grave markers.

At that moment, something within you cries: Simplify!

Jesus mastered the art of maintaining a clear perspective while accomplishing every single one of His objectives. Though we never read of His hurrying anywhere, He managed to fulfill the complete agenda. Just before the agony of the Cross, He told the Father that He had "accomplished the work which Thou hast given Me to do" (John 17:4). And only seconds before He drew His last breath, He made that epochal statement, "It is finished" (19:30). Nothing essential was left undone.

I believe that a major reason for His being able to say those things was that He simplified His life. Jesus followed His own agenda instead of everyone else's. He set predetermined limits: He chose twelve (not twelve hundred) whom He trained to carry on in His absence. He maintained His priorities without apology. He balanced work and rest, accomplishment and refreshment, never feeling the need to ask permission for spending time in quietness and solitude. He refused to get sidetracked by tempting opportunities that would drain energy and time. He was a servant of His Father, not a slave of the people.

He was firm yet kind and gentle, quick to hear and slow to speak. The complexities that tie us into knots never complicated His life or cramped His style.

What's happened to us? When did we buy into all this hectic hassle that steals so much of the joy of just plain living? Who convinced us to feel guilty for taking time to balance work with play? Get off the treadmill and reorder your life. Go back three spaces and clean out the clutter that led to all this nonsense of busy-ness. Simplify!

How much longer will we keep adding nonessentials to our agenda? Simplify!

STORIES

❧ *Matthew 13* ❧

tories transport us into another world. They hold our attention. They become remarkable vehicles for the communication of truth and meaningful lessons that cannot be easily forgotten. If a picture is better than a thousand words, a story is better than a million!

Some of the best stories are those spun from everyday life or from our past. Family histories are held together and handed down from generation to generation in stories. And these strong cords of memory actually become the ties that bind.

Biographies drip with interesting accounts worth passing on. For example, *Human Options* by the late Norman Cousins is a treasure house of his recollections, impressions, and encounters distilled from his dozen or more trips around the world. He calls it an "autobiographical notebook."

Stories, real and imagined, told with care and color, can say much more than a planned speech. It is probably not surprising, then, that the use of story was Jesus' favorite method of preaching: "he did not say anything to them without using a parable" (Matt. 13:34, NIV).

In fact, I've never heard a great preacher who couldn't tell a good story. Woven into the tapestry of the strong message is the ability to communicate solid stuff through an attention-getting story.

Had I lived in Spurgeon's day, I would no doubt have subscribed to his material. He published one sermon per week for every year of his ministry, from 1855 until his death in 1892. So prolific was this prince of the pulpit, that at his death there were still so many unpublished Spurgeon sermons, they continued to be printed at the same rate for twenty-five more years. Many include wonderful, memorable stories.

Are you interested in getting truth to stick in your child's head? Use a story.

Can't seem to penetrate your teenager's skull? Try a story.

Need a tip for making your devotional or Sunday school lesson interesting? Include a story.

Want to add some zest to your letter-writing ministry? A brief story will do the trick.

Want to learn how to tell them so folks will stay interested? Listen to Paul Harvey.

Best of all, read your Bible. His Story is one you won't be able to put down.

Grandparents (and parents, too) need to be reminded that our little ones love to hear about how it was and what it was that brought us to this moment.
Tell your stories!
Consider recording them or writing them down for future generations.

Take It Easy

*M*aybe it's because I just had another birthday. Maybe it's because I'm a granddad several times over. Or maybe it's because of a struggling young seminarian I met recently who wishes he had been higher on his parents' priority list than, say, fifth or sixth. He was hurried and ignored through childhood, then tolerated and misunderstood through adolescence, and finally expected to "be a man" without having been taught how.

My words are dedicated to all of you who have the opportunity to make an investment in a growing child so that he or she might someday be whole and healthy, secure and mature. Granted, yours is a tough job. Relentless and thankless . . . at least for now. But nobody is better qualified to shape the thinking, to answer the questions, to assist during the struggles, to calm the fears, to administer the discipline, to know the innermost heart, or to love and affirm the life of your offspring than you.

When it comes to "training up the child in the way he should go," you've got the inside lane, Mom and Dad. So—take it easy! Remember (as Anne Ortlund puts it) "children are wet cement." They take the shape of your mold. They're learning even when you don't think they're watching. And those little guys and gals are plenty smart. They hear tone as well as terms. They read looks as well as books. They figure out motives, even those you think you can hide. They are not fooled, not in the long haul.

The two most important tools of parenting are time and touch. Believe me, both are essential. If you and I hope to release from our nest fairly capable and relatively stable people who can soar and make it on their own, we'll need to pay the price of saying no to many of our own wants and needs in order to interact with our young . . . and we'll have to keep breaking down the distance that only naturally forms as our little people grow up.

Time and touch. Listen to your boys and girls, look them in the eye, put your arms around them, hug them close, tell them how valuable they are. Don't hold back. Take the time to do it. Reach. Touch.

When you are tempted to get involved in some energy-draining, time-consuming opportunity that will only increase the distance between you and yours, ask yourself hard questions like, "Could my time be better spent at home?" and "Won't there be similar opportunities in the years to come?" Then turn your attention to your boy or girl. Hold nothing back as you renew acquaintances.

Take it easy!

The two most important tools of parenting are time and touch.

FORGETTING

❧ *Philippians 4:13–14* ❧

I honestly believe that "forgetting" is the hardest part of "forgiving." Forgetting is something shared with no other person. It's a solo flight. And all the rewards are postponed until eternity . . . but how great they will be on that day! Forgetting requires the servant to think correctly which means our full focus must be on the Lord and not on humanity. By God's grace, it can happen.

Ask yourself these two questions:

Is there someone or something I have refused to forget, which keeps me from being happy and productive?

Am I a victim of self-pity, living out my days emotionally paralyzed in anguish and despair?

If your answer is yes, stop and consider the consequences of living the rest of your life excusing your depression rather than turning it all over to the only One who can remove it.

And lest you are still convinced it's "too late" . . . you are "too old to change" . . . your situation is "too much to overcome," trust me. Listen, it is never too late to start doing what is right. Never!

Better late than never.

I Walked Where He Stood

❧ *Romans 5* ❧

*I*t doesn't take a Rhodes scholar to guess the country, though the towns may sound strange: Offenbach, Darmstadt, Mannheim, Coburg, Heidelberg, Worms. . . . The land of beer steins, sauerkraut, liverwurst, and black bread; cuckoo clocks and overflowing flower boxes; wide, winding rivers and deep green woods; stone castles on hillsides and quiet, efficient trains; and the greatest music ever written. The beloved homeland of Bach, Mendelssohn, Handel, Beethoven, and Wagner.

Germany is also where some of the severest yet most essential battles for the faith were fought. It was there that the chain that bound the Bible to ornate pulpits of spiritually dead religion was broken. It was there that the Word's truths were liberated from the secret language of a corrupt clergy and placed into the hands of the common people. And it was there those same people were first given a hymnal from which they could sing their faith. And it was all because a sixteenth-century German monk was willing to take his stand against all odds.

It was in his tiny, stark cell in the Augustinian convent at Erfurt, all alone with a Latin copy of the Word of God, that Martin Luther decided to believe God, to allow Scripture to mean what it says, and then to stand firmly on it, regardless of the consequences. It's that last part we tend to minimize.

Being officially branded a heretic did not hold him back. Being publicly defrocked, rebuked, and excommunicated merely fueled his fire. From the day he hammered those ninety-five theses onto the door of the Wittenberg church to the day he stood at Worms before the most impressive array of church prelates and political authorities ever gathered in his lifetime, the man remained the embodiment of authentic courage.

I have walked where he stood. Jeers no longer mark his pilgrimage; instead, one finds monuments and plaques and paintings. Time has a way of correcting faulty perspective.

I needed that visit to Luther's homeland. I needed to hear those guttural sounds he once spoke and to touch the stones he once touched.

I found myself seeing beyond the temporal stuff like steins and sauerkraut, castles and skyscrapers. I heard Luther's voice in the woodwork, and I felt his fire in the bronze and iron monuments now green with age. It was more powerful than my phrases can possibly describe, making me appreciate again the eloquent words from the sacred text, "He, being dead, yet speaketh."

When we stand on the shoulders of those saints who have gone before,
we gain a strategic vantage point.

THINK IT OVER

❦❦❦

*L*ike silent shadows, the heroes of the faith pass beside us, pointing us toward the upward way, whispering words of courage.

The memory of all those models of righteousness now gone from view puts needed steel in our spirit, prompting us to press forward, always forward.

The legacy of their powerful presence and penetrating pages adds depth to our otherwise superficial existence.

Because their convictions live on in words that challenge today's shallow thinking, we do not—we dare not—remain the same.

I would challenge you to do some further reading about these heroes of the faith. Their lives and their words are there for our edification.

"But as it is, they desire a better country, that is a heavenly one. Therefore God is not ashamed to be called their God; for He has prepared a city for them" (Heb. 11:16).

THOROUGHNESS

🐾 *Proverbs 13:4, 9; 20:4* 🐾

*J*ust looked up the definition of "thorough" in my dictionary. Mr. Webster says it means "carried through to completion, careful about detail, complete in all respects." Somehow, I find that a convicting definition. Few indeed are those who finish what they start—and even fewer do a complete job of it when they do finish a task.

Now I'm not referring to a neurotic fanaticism of extreme, some impractical and unbalanced preoccupation with mundane details. I'm talking about the rare but beautiful experience of carrying out a responsibility to its completion. A course at school. A project at home. An occupation. Everyday duties.

There is a verse in Proverbs that is commonly quoted around the Swindoll house when we really finish a job the way it should be done: "Desire accomplished is sweet to the soul" (Prov. 13:19). When you have accomplished or thoroughly fulfilled a task, you experience a feeling of satisfaction that cannot be expressed in words.

Listen to another proverb: "The soul of the sluggard craves and gets nothing, but the soul of the diligent is made fat" (13:4). The sluggard longingly craves, but because he is "allergic to work," he gets nothing in return! Proverbs 20:4 makes this clear.

So, what are you waiting for? Stop being satisfied with a half-hearted, incomplete job! Stun those around you with a thorough, finished product! AND STOP PUTTING IT OFF! As an oboe teacher of mine used to say when I would stare in disbelief at the difficulty of a piece of music, "Attack it, boy!"

The difference between something good and something great is attention to detail. That is true of a delicious meal, a musical presentation, a play, a clean automobile, a well-kept home, a church, our attire, a business, a lovely garden, a sermon, a teacher, a well-disciplined family.

Let's make a long-term commitment to quality control. Let's move out of the thick ranks of the mediocre and join the thin ranks of excellence.

I'm ready if you are.

Does something need doing? Dig right in and refuse to give up until that task is done. Tighten your belt a notch and wade into that unpleasant job with renewed determination to write "finished" over it.

TURTLES

❧ *Isaiah 51* ❧

*M*y younger daughter and I sat and stared in silence. It had been well over forty years since I'd seen the sight. For her, it was a first. It was a tiny, plain, unimpressive garage apartment, leaning and peeling with age. It was the place of my birth.

As the little South Texas town of El Campo faded in the rear-view mirror, the contrast between my life in the mid 1930s and my life today stood out in bold relief. I blurted out, "I feel like a turtle on a fence post." Startled, my daughter asked for an explanation.

I first heard this imagery used by Dr. Robert Lamont, a Presbyterian pastor who felt incredibly blessed by God. "When I was a schoolboy," he said, "we would occasionally see a turtle on a fence post, and when we did, we knew someone had put him there. He didn't get there by himself. That is how I see my own life. I'm a turtle on a fence post."

The Bible is chock-full of turtles: one person after another who knew that his or her position of power, authority, or promotion was given by Another.

Joseph was a turtle. How often, in his Egyptian chariot or his opulent surroundings, he must have sat back, closed his eyes, and reflected on his humble beginnings. His jealous brothers. The pit. Slavery. Prison. Now this! What an incredible fence post! How faithful of God . . . how gracious!

Moses was a turtle. As leader of the Israelites, he surely awoke many a morning in the wilderness shaking his head in disbelief, remembering his murderous and monotonous past. How good of God to have put him on the fence post!

Gideon was a turtle. Remember his response to the angel when he was informed that he was to be commander of the Israelite troops? "Sir, how can I save Israel? My family is the poorest in the whole tribe of Manasseh, and I am the least thought of in the entire family!" (Judg. 6:15, TLB).

The next time we are tempted to think we're self-appointed fence-post sitters, I recommend the prophet's counsel: "Listen to me, you who pursue righteousness, who seek the LORD: Look to the rock from which you were hewn, and to the quarry from which you were dug" (Isa. 51:1).

There's nothing better for a turtle temporarily elevated on a fence post than to return to those humble roots. Remember the quarry from which you were dug, the strong determination of a mother who bore you and the quiet commitment of a father who cradled you through poverty, hardship, and pain. It's enough to make you sit and stare in silence.

*Think about your own fence post and then call to mind the quarry
from which you were dug.*

CONTROL

🍃 *Galatians 3* 🍃

*I*t's easy to get confused these days. "Out of control" isn't what we want to be. People who drink too much are said to be "out of control." Those who worry too much become emotionally "out of control." The same goes for those who go too far with anything: prescription drugs, food, fitness, sex, work—you name it.

But wait. Does this mean we're supposed to be "in control"? Is that our goal? I know a boss (in fact I know several) who is definitely "in control." Folks who work for him either grin and bear it or jump ship as soon as another job surfaces. Some fathers are, without question, "in control." They intimidate, dominate, moderate, and manipulate.

But being "in control" doesn't necessarily mean "controlling." A healthy, happy life requires being in control of ourselves. To be punctual, we must control the use of our time. To be prepared and ready, we must be in control of our schedule. To be a good listener, our minds and tongue must be controlled. To get a project completed, our tendency to procrastinate must be under the firm control of our determination.

This means, then, that we need to be in firm control of ourselves . . . but not controlling of others. Our example? Christ, of course. He got the job done. Without wasted effort, personal panic, or extreme demands, He accomplished the objective. Right on schedule, He went to that cross. When He sighed, "It is finished," it was. Absolutely and completely.

Did most believe? Are you kidding? The vast majority back then, as now, didn't give Him the time of day. Could He have grabbed the controls and forced them to sit up and take notice? I hope to shout! Remember what He said? "Do you think that I cannot appeal to My Father, and He will at once put at My disposal more than twelve legions of angels?" (Matt. 26:53). I'd call 72,000 angels being in charge, wouldn't you? It was His own control that restrained Him from controlling others.

The Christian life boils down to a battle of the wills: Christ's vs. our own. Every day we live we must answer, "Who's in charge here?"

Recently I received a letter from a fine Christian couple, and I smiled understandingly at one line: "Although the Lord has taken good care of my wife and me for the past thirty-eight years, He has taken control of us for the past two and a half."

Tell me, how long has the Lord taken care of you? Be honest now . . . has He also taken control of you? It's easy to get confused these days. It's even easier to take control.

Don't get "out of control" because you're so determined to stay "in control."

THE FINAL WAR

❧ *Romans 11:33–36; 2 Peter 3* ❧

For the next few minutes, imagine this scene:

> But the day of the Lord will come like a thief, in which the heavens will pass away with a roar and the elements will be destroyed with intense heat, and the earth and its works will be burned up. Since all these things are to be destroyed in this way, what sort of people ought you to be in holy conduct and godliness, looking for . . . the coming of the day of God, on account of which the heavens will be destroyed by burning, and the elements will melt with intense heat! (2 Pet. 3:10–12)

Scary stuff, that business about the heavens passing away and the astronomical destruction and the twice-mentioned "intense heat" that will result in a total wipeout of Planet Earth. Makes me wonder *how.* Oh, I've heard the same things you have about superatomic warheads and World War III. But somehow that never explained how "the heavens will pass away" or how the surrounding atmosphere and stratosphere could be "destroyed by burning."

Since that would usher in "the day of God," I've always questioned whether He would use man-made, adult fireworks to announce His arrival. But in my reading recently I stumbled across a possible hint of how the Lord might be planning to pull off this final blast.

On March 9, 1979, nine satellites stationed at various points in the solar system simultaneously recorded a bizarre event deep in space. It was, in fact, the most powerful burst of energy ever recorded. Astronomers who studied the readings were in awe.

The burst of gamma radiation lasted for only one-tenth of a second . . . but in that instant it emitted as much energy as the sun does in 3000 years. If the gamma-ray burst had occurred in the Milky Way Galaxy, said one astrophysicist, it would have set our entire atmosphere aglow. If the sun had suddenly emitted the same amount of energy, our earth would have vaporized. Instantly.

As untrained and ignorant as we may be about the technical side of this, I suggest it might cast some light on the validity of Peter's remark. At least, in my estimation, it makes a lot more sense than atomic wars.

It's probably going to be more like star wars. The good news is this: I have no plans to be around at the premier showing.

How about you?

We may not understand all His ways, but we can know Him whose ways are "unfathomable."

A RENEWED MIND

❧ *2 Corinthians 10:11–12* ❧

*N*o hypocrisy, no competition. Wouldn't that be refreshing to live such a life? It all comes to those with a "renewed mind" . . . those who determine they are going to allow the Spirit of God to invade all those walls and towers, capturing the guards that have kept Him at arm's length all these years.

I can't recall the precise date when these truths began to fall into place, but I distinctly remember how I began to change deep within. My fierce tendency to compete with others started to diminish. My insecure need to win—always win—also started to fade. Less and less was I interested in comparing myself with other speakers and pastors. This growing, healthy independence freed me to be me, not a mixture of what I thought others expected me to be.

And now my heart really goes out to others when I see in them that misery-making "comparison syndrome" that held me in its grip for so many years. Not until you start thinking biblically will this independent identity begin to take shape.

It is when God is in control of the servant mind that we can realize as never before that life's greatest joy is to give His love away to those poor souls who are still stuck in the rut of comparative living.

The more you give, the more you'll get!

FINDING A REFUGE

🕯 *Joshua 20* 🕯

*T*he law of supply-and-demand is something we face every day. Because there are those who need, there must also be those who provide. There are employers and employees. There are counselors and counselees. There are teachers and teachees (I couldn't resist).

But it breaks down when it comes to refugees. There aren't enough "refugers" to meet the demand.

Back in the days when the Hebrews settled in Canaan, they set up cities of refuge. People who were in danger—even those guilty of wrongdoing—could escape to one of these six cities and find personal relief and refreshment.

Don't misunderstand. These weren't sleazy dumping grounds for hardened criminals. These were territories dedicated to the restoration of those who had made mistakes. People who had blown it could flee to one of these places of refuge and not have those inside throw rocks at them.

Today, we have lots of places to meet and sing. To pray. To hear talks from big wooden pulpits. To watch fine things happen. Yes, even to participate occasionally in the action. But where is the place of refuge for those whose lives have gotten soiled in the streets?

More often than we want to admit, we're bad Samaritans. We're notorious for not knowing what to do with our wounded. Getting in there and cleaning up those ugly wounds and changing bloody bandages and taking the time to listen and encourage, well . . . let's be practical, we're not running a hospital around here.

That makes good sense until you or I need emergency care. Like when you discover your husband is a practicing homosexual. Or your unmarried daughter is pregnant and isn't listening to you. Or your parent is an alcoholic. Or you get dumped in jail for shoplifting. Or you blew it financially. Or you lost your job and it's your own fault. Or your wife is having an affair. Or your dad or mom or mate or child is dying of cancer.

Thankfully, in the church today, there are a few lights to help the hurting find their way back. There are dozens and dozens of small groups in churches across our land comprised of caring, authentic, but very human Christians who are committed to growing friendships and deepening relationships. Good Samaritans who have compassion. May their tribe increase!

These are our modern-day cities of refuge.

Genuine, New Testament Christianity doesn't hang out at headquarters;
it gets into the trenches with the wounded and weary.

THINK IT OVER

❧❧

*A*certain man was going down from Jerusalem to Jericho; and he fell among robbers, and they stripped him and beat him, and went off leaving him half dead. . . . But a certain Samaritan, who was on a journey, came upon him; and when he saw him, he felt compassion, and came to him, and bandaged up his wounds, pouring oil and wine on them; and he put him on his own beast, and brought him to an inn, and took care of him. And on the next day he took out two denarii and gave them to the innkeeper and said, 'Take care of him; and whatever more you spend, when I return, I will repay you.' Which of these three do you think proved to be a neighbor to the man who fell into the robbers' hands?"

And he said, "The one who showed mercy toward him." And Jesus said to him, "Go and do the same" (Luke 10:30–37).

People don't want to listen to a cassette of some sermon when the bottom drops out. They want a place to cry—a person to care—someone to bind up their wounds—someone to listen—the security of a few close, intimate friends who won't blab their story all over the church—who will do more than say, "I'll pray for you." They want refuge.

Stop and think. Who and where is your refuge for bruised believers?

DETERIORATION

✺ *1 Kings 3,11* ✺

olomon's life reminds me of the swing of a pendulum. Smooth and graceful . . . silent and elegant . . . yet periodically given to extremes.

Wisdom, loyalty, diplomacy, and efficiency marked his attitude and acts during the early years of his reign. Best of all, "Solomon loved the LORD" (1 Kings 3:3). His achievements could not be listed on ten pages this size. When visited by surrounding magistrates, he was viewed with awe. And rich? Multiplied millions annually. And creative? He was an architect, songwriter, artist, author, and inventor of unparalleled ability.

Things slowly began to change, however, as the pendulum began its tragic swing. Farther and farther . . . and farther.

Solomon seized the reins of wrong and drove his glistening chariot of gold onto the misty flats of licentiousness, pride, lust, profanity, and paganism. Silently, gradually, like eroding soil near the banks of a deep, angry river, he began to believe the lie that has captured many a top executive . . . or super salesperson . . . or successful physician . . . or athletic prima donna . . . or film star . . . or TV celebrity.

Materialism, polygamy, brutality, and idolatry now crippled his steps. Revolts fractured his nation, and irrational decisions characterized his rule. All to him became "vanity and striving after wind" (Eccles. 2:26). Nothing satisfied him any longer. The normal, God-given drives lost their appeal as deterioration took its final toll. And when death finally came, Solomon left in his wake a confused following and a broken, rebellious family.

Deterioration is never loud. Never obvious. Seldom even noticed. Like tiny cracks in a stucco wall, it hardly seems worth our time and attention. Never sudden.

Character threads don't "suddenly" snap. As the British expositor of yesteryear, F. B. Meyer, once put it, "No man suddenly becomes base."

Slowly, silently, subtly, things are tolerated that once were rejected. At the outset everything appears harmless, maybe even a bit exciting. But with it comes an "insignificant" wedge, a gap that grows wider as moral erosion joins hands with spiritual decay.

Be on guard! Those of us who stand must take heed lest we fall.

The pitfalls are still present. Still real. As unobtrusive as the ticking of a clock. As attractive as the swinging of a pendulum . . . until . . .

"There is a way which seems right to a man, but its end is the way of death"
(Solomon, Prov. 14:12).

COST AND WORTH

❧ *Matthew 6* ❧

*H*ow much does it cost?" "What's it worth?" These two questions may sound alike, but they are different. Very different.

"Cost" is the amount of money it takes to complete a purchase . . . the bill, the tab, the monetary expense required to accomplish a financial transaction. "Worth" is the usefulness of the object . . . the benefit, value, and importance of the thing purchased. It is the long-lasting return we derive from the item. Justification for paying a certain cost is usually determined on the basis of the personal worth that accompanies the purchase.

One other distinction must be emphasized. "Cost" is cold, objective, and even painful. Nor is it necessarily easy to accept. That's where "worth" plays a vital role. In our minds we juggle the unemotional, hard facts of cost along with the subjective, magnetic appeals of worth. Worth, when it does its job, convinces the buyer that either the cost is acceptable, or it says, "Don't do it . . . it isn't worth that kind of money."

The difference between handling our money wisely or foolishly is largely determined by the interplay between these two forces. Obviously, we have spent wisely when the cost is eclipsed by the worth. Again, that must be determined individually. That is why, in the long run, we can usually determine a person's scale of values by the things he or she purchases. Or, to use the words of Jesus: "For where your treasure is, there will your heart be also" (Matt. 6:21).

So next time you ask, "How much does it cost?" think also about "What's it worth?" This is especially true when we are deciding how to spend the money God's people have given for the upkeep and ministry of the church. While our stewardship should guard against extravagance, we certainly do not want to clothe the riches of Christ in rags.

Think about Sundays—your church life and the motivation you receive. Think about your children and their future. And their children's future. Think about your neighborhood—unreached individuals by the hundreds. Think about the possibilities of radio or television outreach, perhaps a Christian school, enlarged missionary outreaches, room to grow, room to park! What's it worth?

Deciding whether something is worth the cost requires intense, effective, prevailing prayer, as well as the hard work of objective thinking. And then it requires courage to act on God's clear direction.

Ministries that stay alive are forever moving forward—walking along the ridge called "faith" overlooking that chasm called "impossibility."

GOING FISHING

🙈 *Acts 7, 17* 🙈

*B*illy Wilder, the great movie producer, openly admitted: "I have a vast and terrible desire never to bore an audience." With tacit agreement, Jack Parr once declared: "The greatest sin is to be dull."

Those two statements ought to haunt anyone who regularly practices the fine art of communication.

Communication is a competitive field. Like it or not, the teacher, writer, speaker, or preacher contends with ABC, NBC, CBS, CNN, Rush Limbaugh, magazines, paperbacks, CDs, the theater, the cinema, the thrilling excitement of sporting events, and a zillion other attractions. Pity the missionary whose mimeographed letter arrives in the same mail with *Sports Illustrated* or *Newsweek*. God help the Sunday evening services across America that do battle with *60 Minutes* and *Masterpiece Theater.*

Today's communicator faces a stiffer challenge than ever before. This means that we who communicate Christ must work especially hard at *winning* and then *maintaining* a hearing. This doesn't mean we need to put on a better show or shout louder or attack our competition. What it does mean is that we must meet at least three demands.

We must be prepared. Basically, it necessitates doing our homework. But it also means we must determine what ought to remain behind the counter, held in reserve, and what ought to be placed on display. It's the art of verbal economy.

We must be interesting. We must paint verbal pictures for the uninitiated, preoccupied mind to see. To do this we need energy, subtlety, relevance, and changes of pace.

We must be practical. Communicating the Scriptures is more than dumping out a truckload of biblical facts; it means using those facts to meet practical, everyday needs.

Communicating is like fishing. We need to provide the right lures and bait to attract our listeners.

Check out Paul's address on Mars Hill (Acts 17) or Stephen's defense before the Council (Acts 7) or Jesus' great sermon on the mountain (Matt. 5–7) or His conversation with Nicodemus (John 3). Not a rusty hook in the bunch!

Funny thing about fish: They keep their eyes open even when they're bored and sound asleep. Myopic communicators tend to forget that.

When we communicate Christ, we are like GE: We bring good things to light.

SURE CURE FOR P.E.B.

❧ *Psalm 75:6–7; Daniel 2:21; 4:26* ❧

*T*here's a new virus going around. It's called P.E.B.—Post Election Blues. The symptoms? Oh, stuff like moping around, whining, and feeling a mixture of self-pity, resentment, and smoldering anger, and even entertaining thoughts of moving to Tahiti or Australia because your candidate didn't win.

Well, I've got news for you. That won't help. The best antibiotic is to buck up, stand firmer than ever on the solid rock of God's sovereignty, and face the future with renewed confidence—no matter who's in office. Nothing that happens in this old world—even in the election booth—surprises or frustrates our Lord. These words are still in the Book: "For not from the east, nor from the west, nor from the desert comes exaltation; but God is the Judge; He puts down one, and exalts another" (Ps. 75:6–7).

Somehow those words are easier to read when my candidates get elected; they stick in my throat when the other folks get in! Ever noticed that?

And then I happen across Solomon's proverb: "The king's heart is like channels of water in the hand of the LORD; He turns it wherever He wishes" (Prov. 21:1).

Remember Daniel? He lived victoriously through strong and weak national leaders, yet he didn't hesitate to declare that "Heaven rules" and that it is the living God who "changes the times and seasons; he sets up kings and deposes them" (Dan. 2:21; 4:26, NIV).

So, then, I suggest we start thinking theologically and acting responsibly. Both are hard, hard work. That's right! Recovering from a bad case of P.E.B. requires being *hardy*.

The man or woman who is hardy can withstand adverse conditions, is firm in purpose, and has a vigorous outlook on life. We might say that many missionaries and most mountain climbers are hardy folks. The hardy person remains productive under difficult situations, all the while maintaining emotional, physical, and spiritual health.

It should be remembered, however, that hardiness is not an inherent attitude, temperament, or gift. It is a quality that must be consciously developed.

And it's the best treatment for the P.E.B. virus—and a number of others!

Measure your own "hardy" quotient. Do you measure up?

THINKING RIGHT

❧ *James 1:19–25* ☙

*W*ouldn't you love to live courageously in spite of the odds? Doesn't it sound exciting to be divinely powerful in day-to-day living? Aren't you anxious to become authentic in a day of copy-cat styles and horrendous peer pressure? Of course!

It all begins in the mind. Thinking right always preceds acting right. That is why I emphasize the importance of the renewed mind. It is really impossible to grasp the concept of serving others—or to carry it out with joy, without fear—until our minds are freed from the world's mold and transformed by the Lord's power.

Now some so-called religious leaders and gurus exploit others by calling them to "servanthood" in order to control them and use them for their own purposes. I feel the need to warn you against becoming a victim of some strong personality who wishes to "use" you. How easy it is to encourage servanthood so others might serve us. That is not the way our Master walked and neither should we.

Servanthood starts in the mind. With a simple prayer of three words:

"Change me, Lord."

"Lord, make me a servant who asks of you and of others, what can I do for you?"

COMMENCE PRAYER

❧ *Malachi 3* ❧

*I*t was in 1968 on an airplane headed for New York—a routine and normally very boring flight. But this time it proved to be otherwise. As the plane was on its descent pattern, the pilot realized that the landing gear was not engaging. Passengers were told to place their heads between their knees and grab their ankles just before impact.

Then, with the landing only minutes away, the pilot suddenly announced over the intercom: "We are beginning our final descent. At this moment, in accordance with International Aviation Codes established at Geneva, it is my obligation to inform you that if you believe in God you should commence prayer." Scout's honor . . . that's exactly what he said!

I'm happy to report that the belly landing occurred without a hitch. No one was injured and, aside from some rather extensive damage to the plane, the airline hardly remembered the incident.

Amazing. The only thing that brought out into the open a deep down "secret rule" was crisis. Pushed to the brink, back to the wall, right up to the wire, all escape routes closed . . . only then does our society crack open a hint of recognition that God may be there and—"if you believe . . . you should commence prayer."

There's nothing like crisis to expose the otherwise hidden truth of the soul. Any soul.

We may mask it, ignore it, pass it off with cool sophistication and intellectual denial . . . but take away the cushion of comfort, remove the shield of safety, interject the threat of death without the presence of people to take the panic out of the moment, and it's fairly certain most in the ranks of humanity "commence prayer."

Remember Alexander Solzhenitzyn's admission? "It was only when I lay there on rotting prison straw that I sensed within myself the first stirrings of good. . . . So bless you, prison, for having been in my life."

Those words provide a perfect illustration of the psalmist's instruction: "Before I was afflicted I went astray, but now I obey your word. . . . It was good for me to be afflicted so that I might learn your decrees" (Ps. 119:67, 71 niv).

After crisis comes, God steps in to comfort and teach.

There's nothing like crisis to expose the hidden truth of the soul.

THINK IT OVER

❧❧ ❧❧

*G*od's Word is filled with examples of those who believed God and "commenced prayer." David certainly did. "I waited patiently for the LORD; And He inclined to me, and heard my cry. He brought me up out of the pit of destruction, out of the miry clay; And He set my feet upon a rock making my footsteps firm" (Ps. 40:1–2).

Paul and Silas experienced the same thing in that ancient Philippian prison when all seemed hopeless (Acts 16:25–26). And it was from the deep that Jonah cried for help. Choking on salt water and engulfed by the Mediterranean currents, the prodigal prophet called out his distress:

"Then Jonah prayed to the LORD his God from the stomach of the fish, and he said, 'I called out of my distress to the LORD, and He answered me. I cried for help from the depth of Sheol; Thou didst hear my voice. . . . All Thy breakers and billows passed over me. . . . But Thou hast brought up my life from the pit, O LORD my God'" (Jonah 2:1–6).

Often it is the crucible of crisis that energizes our faith. Think it over.

CONTENTMENT

❧ *Philippians 4* ❧

*L*aurence J. Peter and I are close friends. Although I've never laid eyes on him, I've smiled at his comments and nodded at his conclusions . . . amazed at his remarkable insight into my own life and those around me.

The simple answer to the riddle is this: I own a copy of his book *The Peter Prescription*, and you should too! It's an insignificant looking paperback filled with significant, sound principles. He says it talks about "How to Be Creative, Confident, and Competent," but I think he's overlooked a better word: how to be *Content*.

Isn't it strange that we need a book to help us experience what ought to come naturally? No, not really . . . not when we've been programmed to compete, achieve, increase, fight, and worry our way up the so-called ladder of success (which few can even define).

Face it. You and I are afraid that if we open the door of contentment, two uninvited guests will rush in: loss of prestige and laziness. We really believe that "getting to the top" is worth any sacrifice. To proud Americans, contentment is something to be enjoyed between birth and kindergarten . . . retirement and the rest home . . . or (and this will hurt) among those who have no ambition.

Stop and think. A young man with keen mechanical skills is often counseled against being contented to "settle" for a trade right out of high school. A teacher who is competent, contented, and fulfilled in the classroom is frowned upon if she turns down an offer to become a principal. The owner of Super-Duper Hamburgers on the corner has a packed-out joint every day, but chances are selfish ambition won't let him rest until he opens ten other joints and gets rich—leaving contentment behind.

Now, listen to Jesus: "Be content with your wages" (Luke 3:14). Hear Paul: "I am well content with weaknesses," and, "If we have food and covering . . . be content!" (2 Cor. 12:10; 1 Tim. 6:8). And hear another apostle: "Let your character be free from the love of money, being content with what you have" (Heb. 13:5).

I warn you: This isn't easy to implement. You'll be outnumbered and outvoted. You'll have to fight the urge to conform. Even the greatest of all the apostles admitted, "I have learned to be content" (Phil. 4:11). It's a learning process . . . and it isn't very enjoyable marching out of step until you are convinced you're listening to the right drummer.

When you're fully convinced, however, you'll be free, indeed!

"Striving to better, oft we mar what's well" (William Shakespeare).

CORDIALITY

✿ *Proverbs 15* ✿

The heart of the term "cordial" is the word "heart." And the heart of "heart" is *kardia,* a Greek term that most often refers to the center of our inner life—the source or seat of all the forces and functions of our inner being. So when we are cordial, we are acting on something that comes from and affects the very center of life itself. Maybe that's why Webster defines "cordial" as "of or relating to the heart vital, tending to revive, cheer or invigorate, heartfelt, gracious."

Being cordial literally starts from the heart, as I see it. It begins with the deep-seated belief that the other person is important, genuinely significant, deserving of my undivided attention, my unrivaled interest, if only for a few seconds. Encouraged by such a belief, I am prompted to be sensitive to that person's feelings. If he is uneasy and self-conscious, cordiality alerts me to put him at ease. If she is shy, cordiality provides a relief. If he is bored, cordiality stimulates and invigorates him. If she is sad, cordiality brings cheer. What a needed and necessary virtue it is! How do we project cordiality? Try these four basic ingredients:

1. *A warm smile.* A smile needs to become a natural part of your whole person, reflecting genuine friendliness. Nothing is more magnetic or attractive than your smile, and it will communicate volumes to the other person.

2. *A solid handshake.* Never underestimate the value of this cordial expression, my friend. The handshake is a rare remaining species in the family of touch, and it is threatened with extinction.

3. *Direct eye contact.* Accompanying every handshake and conversation, no matter how brief, ought to be an eyeball-to-eyeball encounter. The eyes reflect deep feelings enclosed in the secret chamber of your soul . . . feelings that have no other means of release. Eye contact allows others to read these feelings. Cordiality cannot be expressed indirectly.

4. *A word of encouragement.* Keep this fresh, free from clichés, and to the point. Call the person by name and use it as you talk. Be specific and natural, and deliberately refuse to flatter the person. Let your heart be freely felt as your words flow.

"Oil and perfume make the heart glad, so a man's counsel is sweet to his friend" (Prov. 27:9). Spread some sweetness . . . have a heart . . . convey cordiality!

How are you doing in the cordiality department?
Try to be conscious of it this week, without being self-conscious.

COMING HOME

❧ *Ruth 1* ❧

*W*e must have resembled a family of Gypsies or a scene from *Grapes of Wrath* as we rambled along the highway. Several layers of redwood forest dust mixed with pine tree sap covered our car. The cartop carrier was loaded with miscellaneous stuff, including a bike wrapped in a blanket flapping in the air, piled on top of several boxes of "family fun stuff." We were homeward bound and glad of it.

As most of the family dozed, I hummed a tune from John Denver's best album, the main line of which says, "Hey, it's good to be back home again. . . ." Truer words were never sung!

Lake Tahoe had been crystal clear and beautifully therapeutic. Ten days out under the stars beside an open fire is good for what ails ya . . . but coming home is better!

Why? Why would anyone prefer the maddening pace, the freeways, the smog, the crowds, loads of laundry, stacks of mail (especially unpaid bills), a desk piled with a backlog of office details? What is so magnetic about coming home to all that? Why is the appeal of the familiar so powerful that we're always anxious to return?

I really have no profound answer. But consider this . . .

Home represents our point of identity, our base of operations, our primary realm of responsibility. Home gives life its roots, its sense of purpose and direction. Even with the hammer blows of pressure, stress, and struggles, home is the anvil used of God to forge out character in the furnace of schedule and demand. We count on it over the long haul and thereby develop security, stability, and consistency.

For me, coming home has an added benefit. It means returning to ministry. It means accepting the most exciting challenge life offers . . . one with eternal dimensions and incredible proportions. It means facing every new dawn with total dependence, living literally on the raw edge of reality.

To me, that's not an optional existence . . . that's the only way to live.

> *We are invariably drawn to come back home not because of where it is*
> *but because of what it represents.*

Act Medium

❧ *Matthew 20* ❧

*T*he children worked long and hard on their little cardboard shack. It was to be a special spot—a clubhouse, where they could meet together, play, and have fun. Since a clubhouse has to have rules, they came up with three:

Nobody act big.

Nobody act small.

Everybody act medium.

Not bad theology!

In different words, God says the very same thing: "Let each of you regard one another as more important than himself" (Phil. 2:3). "Through love serve one another" (Gal. 5:13).

Just "act medium." Believable. Honest, human, thoughtful, and down to earth. Regardless of your elevated position or high pile of honors or row of degrees or endless list of achievements, just stay real.

What is it Solomon said? "Let another praise you . . . a stranger, and not your own lips" (Prov. 27:2).

Meaning what? Meaning no self-reference to some enviable accomplishment. Meaning refusal to scratch a back when yours itches. Meaning no desire to manipulate and manufacture praise. Meaning authentic surprise when applauded.

Like the inimitable Principal Cairns, headmaster of an English school, who was walking onto the platform along with other dignitaries. As he stepped up, a burst of spontaneous applause arose from the audience. In characteristic modesty, Cairns stepped back to let the man behind pass by . . . as he began to applaud his colleague. He genuinely assumed the applause was for another.

But one final warning: Don't try to fake it. False humility stinks worse than raw conceit.

The answer is not in trying to appear worthless or "wormy." The answer lies in consistently taking notice of others' achievements, recognizing others' skills and contributions . . . and saying so. That's called serving others in love. And that's what Christ did.

"Nobody act big. Nobody act small. Everybody act medium."

Such good advice from a clubhouse full of kids who, by the way, are pretty good at practicing what they preach.

Make yourself a little plaque with this rule on it
and put it in a place where you will see it every day.

LIVING MERCY

❧ *Hebrews 4:14–15* ❧

*T*he apostle John asks: "If someone who is supposed to be a Christian . . . sees a brother in need, and won't help him—how can God's love be within him?" (1 John 3:17, TLB).

True servants are merciful. They care. They get involved. They get dirty, if necessary. They offer more than pious words.

And what do they get in return? What does Christ promise? "They shall receive mercy." Those who remain detached, distant, and disinterested in others will receive like treatment. But God promises that those who reach out and demonstrate mercy will, in turn, receive it. Both from other people as well as from God Himself.

That is exactly what Jesus, our Savior, did for us when He came to earth. By becoming human. He got right inside our skin, literally. That made it possible for Him to see life through our eyes, feel the sting of our pain, and identify with the anguish of human need. He understands.

Get inside someone's skin today to understand and give mercy.

PROPHET SHARING

❧ *Deuteronomy 18* ❧

N"ow a new king arose over Egypt, who did not know Joseph" (Exod. 1:8). Too bad. Tragic, in fact. Seems a shame Joseph had to die at the young age of 110(!), before he had a chance to impact the new king. What a difference that encounter might have made in the lives of the Hebrews, who were now reduced to the monotony of mixing mortar and making bricks.

Seems like some people die too soon. About the time you realize just how valuable their contribution is, it's too late. They're gone.

As a preacher, I think about this a lot. I think about how helpful it would be if some of the men who preached and wrote so well could have lived another twenty, maybe thirty years. Men like A. W. Tozer.

Aiden Wilson Tozer died the year I began studying for the ministry (1959). He had spent thirty-one years pastoring the unobtrusive Southside Alliance Church in Chicago. During his ministry, which included both the spoken and the written word, that intense, provocative little man functioned as the conscience of evangelicalism. Yet I never once heard him in person. Nor did most of my contemporary ministerial colleagues.

"To listen to Tozer preach was as safe as opening the door of a blast furnace!" says Warren Wiersbe, aptly describing the man's style.

I suppose I have ten or more of Tozer's tough-minded volumes that dare me to drift off course. I don't always agree with him, but he never fails to stimulate my thinking and challenge my way. Mystical and picky though he may have been, the man asked the right questions: Is God real to you? Is your Christianity a set of definitions? Or is it a vital relationship with Christ? Do you genuinely hunger after God?

With daring dogmatism, the man didn't stop with casual investigation. He assaulted with insightful and relentless determination. And it didn't take him a hundred pages to get to the point—something most of us would do well to remember.

Now a new generation of pastors has arisen over the church who did not know Tozer . . . or Moody . . . or Meyer . . . or. . . . Seems such a shame.

The truth of the matter is, God shares His prophets briefly. Often, only when it is too late, do we realize how much more time we wish we had spent at their feet.

There's nothing like the old to help us see all things new.

THINK IT OVER

❧❧❧

*T*here are two kinds of ground: fallow ground and ground that has been broken up by the plow.

"The fallow field is smug, contented, protected from the shock of the plow and the agitation of the harrow. Such a field, as it lies year after year, becomes a familiar landmark to the crow and the bluejay. . . . Safe and undisturbed, it sprawls lazily in the sunshine, the picture of sleepy contentment. . . . Fruit it can never know because it is afraid of the plow and the harrow.

"In direct opposite to this, the cultivated field has yielded itself to the adventure of living. The protecting fence has opened to admit the plow, and the plow has come as plows always come, practical, cruel, business-like, and in a hurry. Peace has been shattered by the shouting farmer and the rattle of machinery. The field . . . has been upset, turned over, bruised, and broken, but its rewards come hard upon its labors. The seed shoots up into the daylight, its miracle of life, curious, exploring the new world above it. Nature's wonders follow the plow.

"There are two kinds of lives also—the fallow and the plowed.

"The man of fallow life is contented with himself and the fruit he once bore. He does not want to be disturbed. He smiles in silent superiority at revivals, fastings, self-searchings, and all the travail of fruit bearing and the anguish of advance. The spirit of adventure is dead within him . . . he has fenced himself in, and by the same act he has fenced out God and the miracle.

"The plowed life is the life that has . . . thrown down the protecting fences and sent the plow of confession into the soul. . . . Such a life has put away defense and has forsaken the safety of death for the peril of life. Discontent, yearning, contrition, courageous obedience to the will of God these have bruised and broken the soil till it is ready again for the seed. And as always fruit follows the plow.

—A. W. TOZER, *Paths to Power*

HAVING FUN

❧ *Ecclesiastes 3:4; Proverbs 17:22* ❧

*A*l Michaels and his team turn the Swindoll family room into a stadium on Monday nights. That's one part of my week when all pressures shift into neutral. Even though I may shout and scream and jump and jeer, it's a relaxing and rewarding experience I thoroughly enjoy. What's more, it's the same for Michaels and those players and the refs and those nutty fans surrounding the gridiron. They're all having a ball!

In fact, I remember when Don Meredith was doing commentary and was interviewed, he stated that one of the reasons he retired from the Cowboys was he stopped "having fun." He caught himself getting so all-fired serious about the game that he was no longer able to hang loose, laugh off a mistake, and look forward to that next set of downs. When the fun stopped, so did the desire, the delight, and the determination. So what did he do? He got into another phase of his specialty that allowed him to bring back the fun that had departed. He exchanged the uniform for the microphone . . . and started smiling again. Good for him! May his tribe increase!

Now, some frowning, neurotic soul is reading this and saying, "Well, somebody's got to do the job. Life is more than fun 'n' games, Swindoll. Grow up and get down to business! Laughter is all right for kids, but adults, especially Christian adults, have a job to do that's serious."

Nobody's going to argue that life has its demands and that being mature involves discipline and responsibility. But who says we have to get an ulcer and drive ourselves (and others!) to distraction in the process of fulfilling our God-given role? No one is less efficient or more incompetent than the person on the brink of a breakdown. He really isn't much of an asset to society—or to the cause of Christ. And that's not a criticism; it's reality.

Old Solomon knew that. Remember his words of wisdom? "A joyful heart is good medicine, but a broken spirit dries up the bones" (Prov. 17:22). There is no more effective safety valve in all of life than balancing the serious, somber side with frequent flashes of fun, fun, fun!

If you're not enjoying most of your day, if you've stopped having fun, you're missing more than you are contributing.

Oops, gotta go. The stadium is almost full and it's kick-off time.

When was the last time you laughed till you cried?
Did you know that a good belly laugh is a proven stress reliever?

Start Seeking God

❧ *Lamentations 3:25* ❧

*L*ord, I'm back and I diligently seek you." How many times have we said this? This time stop stalking and sit silently. Wait patiently, seek diligently, sit silently. That means you need to pour out your heart and then deliberately be quiet. Spend a full day in quietness.

Meditation is a lost art in this modern, hurry-up world. I suggest you revive it. Not by endlessly repeating some mantra to get into some other frame of mind. Not that. Simply and silently wait before your faithful God. Read a passage of Scripture, perhaps a Psalm, and let it speak. Say nothing. Just sit silently. Let Him talk. Let Him reassure you that you are fully and completely forgiven and that your shame is gone. Feel His arms around you. Understand the cleansing that He's bringing. Feel again the freshness and relief of His presence.

God will give you a fresh start if you'll stop fighting. It works. I know. I've been there. Just submit to Him and accept His grace.

God will keep His promise to forgive and welcome you home.
His mercies are new every morning.

DON'T TAKE IT EASY

❧ *Psalm 90* ❧

*L*ast fall one day at the church, I spotted a visiting gentleman who was shaking hands with a half-dozen folks he'd never met before. Then he looked at me, and with a grin and a twinkle, he whipped out his hand. It was a hand you could strike a match on, toughened by decades of rugged toil.

"You look like a man who enjoys life. What do you do for a living?" I asked.

"Me? Well, I'm a farmer from back in the Midwest."

"Really? I guess I'm not surprised, since you've got hands like a tractor tire."

He laughed . . . asked me a couple of insightful questions, then told me about his plans for traveling on his own.

"What did you do last week?" I asked.

His answer stunned me. "Last week I finished harvesting 90,000 bushels of corn," he said with a smile.

I then blurted out, "Ninety thousand! How old are you, my friend?"

He didn't seem at all hesitant or embarrassed by my question. "I'm just a couple months shy o' ninety." He laughed again as I shook my head.

He had lived through four wars, the Great Depression, sixteen presidents, ninety Midwest winters, who knows how many personal hardships, and he was still taking life by the throat. I had to ask him the secret of his long and productive life. "Hard work and integrity" was his quick reply.

As we parted company, he looked back over his shoulder and added, "Don't take it easy, young feller. Stay at it!"

The Bible is filled with folks who refused to take it easy. Remember our friend Caleb, who, at age 85, attacked the Anakim in the hill country and successfully drove them out (Josh. 14)? Or Abraham, who had a baby (well, actually Sarah did) when he was "in his old age" . . . he was 100, she was 90 (Gen. 21)? Or Noah or Moses or Samuel or Anna, the 84-year-old prophetess . . . significant people, all.

Age means zilch. Wrinkles, gray hair, and spots on your hands, less than zilch. If God chooses to leave you on this old earth, great. If He makes it possible for you to step aside from your work and move on to new vistas with fresh challenges, that's also great.

And whatever else you do, don't take it easy!

"No disease is more lethal than the boredom that follows retirement"
(Norman Cousins).

REFLECTIONS

❧ *Psalm 104* ❧

*T*ime to reflect." That would be my answer to the question: "What do you like most about end of the year?" Time to stand in front of the full-length mirror of memory and study the scene. Thoughtfully. Silently. Alone. At length. To trace the outline of the past without the rude interruption of routine tasks. Taking time to stop and listen. And think.

Invariably, those occasions leave me feeling grateful to God. Often I end up thanking Him for something or someone specifically that He provided in the yesterday of my life that makes my today much more meaningful.

It happened again last week. As one by one the rest of the family drifted off to bed, I put a couple more logs on the fire, slid into my favorite chair, and read for well over an hour. I came across a few thoughts put together by Ed Dayton, a longtime leader in the World Vision ministry. He mentioned watching a short film called *The Giving Tree,* written by Phil Silverstein—a simple, fanciful piece about a tree that loved a boy.

> When the boy was young, he swung from the tree's branches, climbed all over her, ate her apples, slept in her shade. Such happy, carefree days. The tree loved those years.
>
> But as the boy grew, he spent less and less time with the tree. "Come on, let's play," invited the tree on one occasion, but the young man was interested only in money. "Take my apples and sell them," said the tree. He did, and the tree was happy.
>
> He didn't return for a long time, but the tree smiled when he passed by one day. "Come on, let's play!" But the man was older and tired of his world. He wanted to get away from it all. "Cut me down. Take my large trunk and make yourself a boat. Then you can sail away," said the tree. The man did, and the tree was happy.
>
> Many seasons passed—and the tree waited. Finally, the old man returned, too old and tired to play, to pursue riches, or to sail the seas. "I have a pretty good stump left, my friend. Why don't you just sit down here and rest?" said the tree. He did, and the tree was happy.

How many Giving Trees have there been in my life? How many have released part of themselves so I might grow, accomplish my goals, find wholeness and satisfaction? So, so many. Thank you, Lord, for each one. Their names could fill this page.

It was late as I crawled into bed. I had wept, but now I was smiling. "Good night, Lord," I said. I was a thankful man. Thankful I had taken time to reflect.

Reflect upon the Giving Trees in your own life. Thank God for them.
Is it your turn to do the same for another?

How to Be Salt and Light

❧ *John 8:12, Matthew 5:13* ❧

*G*od calls us to be salt-and-light Christians in a bland, dark society. We need to remember salt must not lose its taste and light must not be hidden. Let me suggest three statements that declare and describe how to fulfill this role:

- "I am different." We should not become like the world. We must guard against being sucked into the prevailing culture and conforming to society's expectations.
- "I am responsible." Every once in awhile we need to ask some hard questions: Are we making contact with others? Are we seeking isolation? It's up to us to spread the salt and light.
- "I am influential." Let's not kid ourselves. The very fact that we belong to Christ—that we don't adopt to the system, that we march to a different drumbeat—gives us an influence in this society of ours. We are influencing others in our every behavior, be it good or bad. Even when we aren't trying, out comes the salt and on comes the light.

Remember to keep your light "on" and your saltshaker tipped!

COUNT YOUR BLESSINGS

❧ *Psalm 95* ❧

*S*ometimes when you don't feel like praying, or you're consumed with needing to speak to the Lord but can't gather the words, try that old standby—count your many blessings, count them one by one.

It's amazing how you can get carried away from worries and woes and self concern when you start naming out loud what you're thankful for. Right away your focus shifts from your needs to the Father's graciousness and love. Try this:

LOOK UP . . . thank You, Lord . . .

      for Your sovereign control over our circumstances

      for Your holy character in spite of our sinfulness

      for Your Word that gives us direction

      for Your grace that removes our guild

LOOK AROUND . . . thank You, Lord . . .

      for our wonderful country

      for close family ties

      for an opportunity to help others

      for a place to live, clothes to wear, food to eat

LOOK WITHIN . . . thank You, Lord . . .

      for eyes that see the beauty of Your creation

      for minds that are curious, creative, and competent

      for memories of pleasures and recent accomplishments

      for broken dreams and lingering afflictions that humble us

      for a sense of humor that brings healing and hope

He is worthy of our highest praise and gratitude. To Him goes all the glory.

If you can't pray, make a personalized list of blessings.

THINK IT OVER

❧❧❧

*W*hy not try counting your blessings now?

LOOKING UP . . . thank You, Lord, for _____

LOOKING AROUND . . . thank You Lord, for_____

LOOKING WITHIN . . . thank You, Lord, for_____

SELF-PITY

❧ *1 Kings 19* ❧

A severe case of ingrown eyeballs strikes all of us every once in a while. In both dramatic and subtle ways, the stubborn enemy of our souls whispers sweet little nothings in our ears. He reminds us of how unappreciated and ill-treated we are . . . how important yet overlooked . . . how gifted yet ignored . . . how capable yet unrecognized . . . how bright yet eclipsed . . . how valuable yet unrewarded.

But the most damaging impact of self-pity is its ultimate end. A frown will replace your smile. A pungent criticism will replace a pleasant, "I understand." Suspicion and resentment will submerge you like a tidal wave, and you will soon discover that this sea of self-pity has brought with it urchins of doubt, despair . . . and even the desire to die.

An exaggeration? If you think so, sit with me awhile beneath the shade of a juniper tree located at 19 First Kings, the address of a prophet named Elijah.

Elijah had just won a great victory over Ahab and his Baal-worshiping pawns. In fact, God stamped His approval upon Elijah in such a way that all Israel knew he was God's mouthpiece. As a result, Jezebel, Ahab's spouse (he was her mouse), declared and predicted Elijah's death within twenty-four hours.

Now, the seasoned prophet had surely been criticized before. But this threat somehow found the chink in his armor.

So Elijah ran for his life. Then, beneath the tree, overwhelmed with self-pity, he said, "I've had enough . . . take away my life. . . . I've worked very hard for the Lord God of the heavens; but the people of Israel have broken their covenant with you and torn down your altars and killed your prophets, and only I am left; and now they are trying to kill me, too" (1 Kings 19:4, 10, TLB).

Yet God didn't rebuke His man, nor strike him dead. He encouraged him to take a rest, enjoy a catered meal or two . . . and get his eyes off himself and his situation so that they might get back on the Lord. God even gave him a close friend, a fella named Elisha, with whom he might share his life and his load.

Feeling sorry for yourself today? Why not try God's remedy: Take a break, stop trying to work things out yourself. And take a long, loving look at your Savior in His Word . . . and then spend some time with a friend. You'll be amazed at the outcome.

Self-pity is the smog that pollutes and obscures the light of the Son.

SURPRISE ATTACKS

🍃 *1 Peter 5* 🍃

*A*s an ex-marine I am often the brunt of jokes told by ex-dogfaces and ex-swabbies. Since my outfit is viewed as the guys with more muscles than brains, the jokes usually portray leathernecks as disciplined yet dull, brawny oxen with IQs about six points above a plant. I heard another hilarious one last weekend at a men's conference I attended.

In America they say, "It's 10:00. Do you know where your children are?"

In France they say, "It's 10:00. Do you know where your wife is?"

In Italy they say, "It's 10:00. Do you know where your car is?"

In the marines they say, "It's 10:00. Do you know what time it is?"

Marines aren't the only ones notorious for being thick and tired of life. Evangelical Christians run a close second!

We get our theological ducks in a row, we make sure our eternal destination is sealed in a fireproof safe, we surround ourselves with a predictable schedule that protects us from contamination with the lost world, and then, like a 600-pound grizzly, we settle down for a long winter's snooze.

Only one problem. The battle continues to rage, no matter what the season. Whether we choose to believe it or not.

It is so easy to forget that our adversary, like our Advocate, neither slumbers nor sleeps. With relentless, unslacking energy . . . as sure as this morning's dawn, he's on the prowl, "seeking someone to devour" (1 Pet. 5:8).

He's been at it for centuries. By means of a brilliant strategy, an insidious scheme, he takes advantage of our mental dullness. Surprise attacks are his specialty.

Small wonder Jesus kept urging His followers to "be on the alert," to "watch," to "resist," to keep a clean crop, free of stuff that "chokes the word, making it unfruitful."

Why? Because you never know when you are in the cross hairs of the enemy's high-powered rifle. It could be today that you will be the target. When you least expect it . . . in the lazy days of summer, in the cool days of autumn, in the fog of false security, under the frost of a laid-back lifestyle.

He's looking for you. He's primed and ready to fire. And he doesn't wait for hunting season. In fact, as far as Satan is concerned, it's always open season on Christians.

Are you alert to the danger?

If you're going to stand firm in the faith, you can't be lying down.

RALLYING POINTS

❧ *Exodus 40* ❧

*T*o rally: "to muster for a common purpose . . . to arouse for action . . . to come together again to renew an effort." That's the way Webster defines the verb. He says the noun means: "a mustering of scattered forces to renew an effort; a summoning up of strength or courage."

Throughout Scripture, we encounter God's rallying points: places where His people assembled for a common purpose, for recovery and refreshment, for mustering forces and getting recharged for battle.

For Abraham it was Bethel, the place of the altar. For Moses it was the bush in the desert. For the Hebrews en route to Canaan? Well, they had several. During the day, a massive cloud overhead. At night, an enormous column of fire. Along the way, the tabernacle, that portable sanctuary where the Lord met with His chosen ones. Later, it was the temple. Then, following the terrible years of Babylonian captivity, Nehemiah envisioned a plan for "mustering scattered forces to renew an effort" as he led a ragtag group of dejected Hebrews back to Jerusalem to rebuild the city walls.

Jesus Himself became a rallying point for a handful of men whose lives were otherwise destined for mediocrity. And after His departure, His Spirit came at Pentecost and ignited a spark as the church universal came into existence, offering perpetual hope for fractured, lost humanity.

Finally, today, you and I can look back and recall a specific place—our own Bethel or desert bush—where God became real to us again.

Where would we be without rallying points? Places that catapult us into new dimensions we would otherwise never inhabit.

Today, rallying points are often provided by evangelistic crusades. Critics, of course, want us to believe these are nothing more than some old-fashioned revivals where church folks gather, sing a few songs, listen to Bible preaching, then promptly go back to business as usual. You and I know, however, that these meetings can be some of the most significant events ever held in America, for they may provide a fresh spiritual awakening that will be nothing short of revolutionary.

So, thank God for your own Bethel. And pray that He will provide the same for others.

Pray that He will arouse us for action and muster us for a common purpose in these days when our forces often seem scattered and when we need a summoning up of strength and courage.

Rallying points replace flabby faith with the grit and gristle of godliness.

THE DIFFERENCE

❧ *Matthew 5:13–16* ❧

*O*urs is a hell-bound, degenerate world, and you know it. Political corruption abounds. International peace, a splendid ideal, continues to blow up in our faces. The crime rate escalates as domestic violence and gang wars and drug traffic and overcrowded jails continue to plague society. Pending legal cases choke the courts of our land with an endless litany of litigation. And even when cases are finally brought to trial, no courtroom or prison cell can remove madness from minds or hatred from hearts.

Satan, our relentless enemy, has a game plan, and it's on the board. Knowing that his days are numbered, knowing that he has an appointed amount of time before the scoreboard counts him out, he holds the world in his lap and gives it directions, implementing his strategy day after day.

If our Christian message is a mirror image of the message of the world, the world yawns and goes on its way, saying, "What else is new? I've heard all that since I was born." But if the Christian lifestyle and motivation and answers are different, the world cannot help but sit up and take notice, thinking: *How come they live in the same place I live, but they are able to live a different kind of life? Why is their love so deep and lasting and ours so shallow and fickle? How is it that she can forgive and never hold a grudge? Why do these people have so much more compassion, kindness, integrity, and patience than anyone else I know?*

Do you get the message? It's the difference that makes the difference!

Think about it: Do people feel more alive when they're around you? Do you create within them a thirst for God? Does anyone ever wonder why you are so unselfish, so thoughtful, so caring? Do the neighborhood children want to be in your home because of the way you treat your children?

What do people see when they look at you? Do they see your good works? Do they hear your courtesy? Do they detect your smile? Do they notice that you stop to thank them? Do they hear you apologize when you are wrong? Do they see every visible manifestation of Christ's life being normally lived out through you? When they see all that, Jesus said, they "will glorify your Father who is in heaven" (Matt. 5:16).

Isn't it a pleasure when someone says to you, "Why are you like that?" And isn't it a natural thing to respond, "I'm glad you asked. Let me tell you what's happened"?

"When the Church is absolutely different from the world, she invariably attracts it. It is then that the world is made to listen to her message, though it may hate it at first" (D. Martyn Lloyd-Jones).

A SELF-DESCRIPTION OF JESUS

❧ *Matthew 11:28–29* ❧

*I*n all my studies I've found only one place where Jesus Christ—in His own words—describes his own "inner man." In doing so, He uses only two words. He doesn't say: "I am wise and powerful," or "I am holy and eternal," or "I am all-knowing and absolute deity." Do you know what He said? Hold on, it may surprise you.

"Come to Me, all who are weary and heavy-laden, and I will give you rest. Take My yoke upon you, and learn from Me, for I am gentle and humble in heart; and you shall find rest for your souls" (Matt. 11:28–29).

I am gentle. I am humble. These are servant terms. Gentle means strength under control. Humble in heart means lowly—the word picture of a helper.

Frankly, I find it extremely significant that when Jesus lifts the veil of silence and once for all gives us a glimpse of Himself, the real stuff of His inner person, He uses gentle and humble.

When we remember that God wants us to conform to His son's image, we realize he wants us to have qualities like Jesus had. We must let gentleness and humbleness emerge.

We are never more like Christ than when we fit into His description of Himself.

FAITH OR FAMILY

Hebrews 11:8–10

*O*ver forty-five years ago, my parents were not convinced that Cynthia was the best mate for me. They were sincere, but on that matter, they were wrong. Had I listened to them, I would not have married the woman I should have married. We recently celebrated our forty-fourth wedding anniversary.

Now, if they are believers and if they're walking with the Lord, parents are usually good counselors on most things. But they don't walk on water. Sometimes parents can be short-sighted and selfish. This is also true of other family members, and sometimes your immediate family represents the most difficult part of your obeying the will of God. They may even become resentful or angry when they disagree with your life decisions. But when a crisis of belief occurs, faith and obedience must prevail. Releasing and risking will be required. First and foremost we are to do God's will. That's Obedience 101!

Faith, not sight is what works here. Just turn your decisions over to the Lord, and rest in the confidence that He is working out His plan for your life, and He will fix things up with your family.

The One to Whom we should be faithful invented the family!

THINK IT OVER

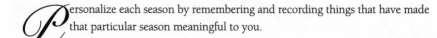

*P*ersonalize each season by remembering and recording things that have made that particular season meaningful to you.

Spring

Summer

Fall

Winter

DOING THE UNEXPECTED

❧ *John 1* ❧

*T*here are various ways to describe it: turning the other cheek . . . going the extra mile . . . doing good to those who hate us . . . loving our enemies. We may say it in different ways, but the action amounts to the same thing. By doing the unexpected, we accomplish a twofold objective: (1) we put an end to bitterness, and (2) we prove the truth of the age-old axiom, love conquers all. I've seen it happen over and over again.

Why are we so hesitant? What keeps us from doing the unexpected for the undeserving so that we might watch God accomplish the unbelievable? Because it goes against our human nature. Furthermore, it's a major risk. Of course, that is where faith comes in: to believe the Lord against all odds and to obey Him even if the action backfires. But some of you are frowning, thinking, *Yeah, that sounds good, but nobody could pull it off.*

Rabbi Michael Weisser did. It happened in Lincoln, Nebraska, where for more than three years, Larry Trapp, a self-proclaimed Nazi and Ku Klux Klansman, spread hatred through mailings and ugly phone calls. Weisser became one of Trapp's targets, receiving numerous pieces of hate mail and offensive phone calls. At first, the Weissers were so afraid they locked their doors and worried themselves sick over the safety of their family.

Then one day Rabbi Weisser decided to do the unexpected. He left a message on Trapp's answering machine, telling the man of another side of life . . . a life free of hatred and racism.

Trapp was stunned. He later admitted, through tears, that he heard in the rabbi's voice "something I hadn't experienced. It was love."

Slowly the bitter man began to soften. One night he called the Weissers and said he wanted out but didn't know how. They grabbed a bucket of fried chicken and took him dinner. Before long they made a trade: In return for their love he gave them his swastika rings, hate tracts, and Klan robes. That same day Trapp gave up his recruiting job and dumped the rest of his propaganda in the trash. "They showed me so much love that I couldn't help but love them back," he finally confessed.

Christmas is right around the corner. How about giving the gift of forgiveness, a cup full of kindness, a sincere phone call of grace to someone who would never expect it and might not deserve it . . . with no strings attached? It's risky . . . but you wouldn't be the first to try it.

God's gift to us came wrapped in swaddling clothes, lying in a manger.
Talk about doing the unexpected for the undeserving!

DIVINE PREPARATION

🎝 *2 Corinthians 4:10–11, 16–18* 🎝

*A*mericans like things to be logical and fair. We operate our lives on that basis. Meaning this: If I do what is right, good will come to me; and if I do what is wrong, bad things will happen to me. Right brings rewards and wrong brings consequences.

That's a logical and fair axiom of life, but there's one problem. *It isn't always true.* All of us have had the unhappy and unfortunate experience of doing what is right yet suffering for it. And we have also done what is wrong on a few occasions without being punished. The latter we can handle, but the former is a tough pill to swallow.

This can even happen in a life of servanthood. You will give, forgive, forget, release your own will, obey God to the maximum, and even wash dirty feet with an attitude of gentleness and humility. And after all those beautiful things, you will get ripped off occasionally.

The Bible doesn't hide this painful reality from us. In 1 Peter 2:20–21 (addressed to servants, by the way—see v. 18), we read:

> For what credit is there if, when you sin and are harshly treated, you endure it with patience? But if when you do what is right and suffer for it you patiently endure it, this finds favor with God.
> For you have been called for this purpose, since Christ also suffered for you, leaving you an example for you to follow in His steps.

If a person does wrong and then suffers the consequences, even though he or she patiently endures the punishment, nobody applauds. *But*—now get this clearly fixed in your mind—when you do what is *right* and suffer for it with grace and patience, God applauds!

When you feel as if God is taking things away, maybe He's just trying to make room in your life for better things that He wants to give you.

RELAXING

❧ *Psalm 27* ❧

I love memories. Today I've been remembering a perfect Monday evening from years back. . . .

The smell of homemade clam chowder greeted me as I walked through the front door. After kissing the kids and hugging the cook, I settled into my favorite chair, loosened my tie, and kicked off my shoes—just in time to watch the beginning of the game.

Our two youngest were upstairs fiddling around with a rabbit, two hamsters, and a guinea pig. Our older daughter was on the phone with her best friend, whom she hadn't seen for at least two hours. Curt was sitting on the floor in his room strumming his guitar and singing "Raindrops Keep Fallin' on My Head." In between chopped onions and diced potatoes, Cynthia was doubled over with laughter in the kitchen as she tried to finish a chapter of Erma Bombeck's latest book.

No amount of money can buy that feeling of incredible contentment, that inner sense of fulfillment, that surge of release and relief as the noise and pace of the world are muffled by the sounds and smells and sights of a happy, relaxed evening at home.

What therapy! How essential! And yet how seldom we really relax. It's almost as though we are afraid to slow down, shift into neutral, and let the motor idle.

We place such a high priority on achievement that we actually feel guilty when we accomplish nothing over a period of several hours. This is underscored by the number of churches who literally brag about "something for everybody every night of the week"!

Relaxing isn't automatic, is it? It's a skill that must be learned. Here are a couple of suggestions to help you cultivate that skill:

Block out several evenings each month on your calendar. Make special plans to do nothing except something you (or your family) would enjoy.

Each day, look for times when something humorous or unusual makes laughter appropriate . . . then laugh out loud! That helps flush out the nervous system.

And when you relax, really relax.

A relaxed, easy-going Christian is far more attractive and effective than the rigid, uptight brother who squeaks when he walks and whines when he talks.

ETERNAL DIMENSIONS

✣ *1 Timothy 6:6–20* ✣

*C*ontentment is something we must learn. It isn't a trait we're born with. But the question is *how?* In 1 Timothy 6 we find a couple of very practical answers to that question:

A current perspective on eternity: "For we have brought nothing into the world, so we cannot take anything out of it either" (v. 7).

A simple acceptance of essentials: "And if we have food and covering, with these we shall be content" (v. 8).

Both attitudes work beautifully.

First, it really helps us to quit striving for more if we read the eternal dimension into today's situation. We entered life empty-handed; we leave it the same way.

The truth of all this was brought home forcefully to me when a minister friend of mine told of an experience he had several years ago. He was in need of a dark suit to wear at a funeral he had been asked to conduct. He had very little money, so he went to a local pawn shop in search of a good buy. To his surprise, they had just the right size, solid black, and very inexpensive. As he forked over the money, he asked how they could afford to sell the suit so cheaply. With a wry grin the pawnbroker admitted that all their suits had once been owned by a local mortuary, which they used on the deceased, then removed before burial.

My friend felt a little strange wearing a suit that had once been on a dead man, but everything was fine until in the middle of his sermon he casually started to stick his hand into the pocket of the pants . . . only to find there were no pockets!

Talk about an unforgettable object lesson! There he stood, preaching to all those people about the importance of living in light of eternity today, as he himself wore a pair of trousers without pockets that had been on a corpse.

Second, it helps us model contentment if we'll boil life down to its essentials and try to simplify our lifestyle. Verse 8 spells out those essentials: something to eat, something to wear, and a roof over our heads. Everything beyond that we'd do well to consider as extra.

God's Word offers this advice: Contentment is possible when we stop striving for more. Contentment never comes from externals. Never!

As a Greek sage once put it: "To whom little is not enough, nothing is enough."

Great wealth is not related to money.
We are being enriched by our investment in eternity.

COPING WITH CONSEQUENCES

❧ *2 Corinthians 4:10–11, 16–18* ❧

I have found great help from two truths God gave me at a time in my life when I was bombarded with a series of unexpected and unfair blows (from my perspective). In my darkest hours these principles still become my anchor of stability, my only means of survival.

Because they work for me, I pass them on to you. Memorize them. Write them on a card and carry it at all times.

- Nothing touches me that has not passed through the hands of my heavenly Father. Nothing. Whatever occurs, God has sovereignly surveyed and approved. We may not know why, but we do know our pain is no accident to Him who guides our lives.

- Everything I endure is designed to prepare me for serving others more effectively. Everything. Since my Heavenly Father is committed to shaping me into the image of His Son, He knows the ultimate value of this painful experience. It is being used to empty our hands of our own resources, our own sufficiency, and turn us back to Him—the faithful Provider. And God knows what will get through to us.

Things may not be logical or fair, but when God is directing the events of our lives, they are right.

SIMPLE FAITH

❧ *Matthew 7* ❧

*W*hen it came to clear communication, Jesus was a master. Children and adults alike had no difficulty understanding His words or following His reasoning.

This was never truer than when He sat down on a hillside with a group of His followers and talked about what really mattered. His hillside chat was an informal, reasonable, thoughtful, and unpretentious presentation.

People were fed up with the manipulation, the pride, and especially the hypocrisy of their religious leaders. Man-made systems of complicated requirements and backbreaking demands shut the people behind invisible bars, shackled in chains of guilt. They could not measure up. Many were losing heart. But who dared say so?

Then out of the blue came Jesus with His message of liberating grace, encouragement to the weary, hope for the sinful. Best of all, everything He said was based on pristine truth— God's truth—instead of rigid religious regulations. He talked of faith in terms anyone could understand. No wonder the people found Him amazing! No wonder the scribes and Pharisees found Him unbearable! Hypocrisy despises authenticity. When truth unmasks wrong, those who are exposed get very nervous.

So what does Jesus want? What was He getting at?

He was simply saying that He wanted His followers to be people of simple faith, modeled in grace, based on truth. Nothing more. Nothing less. Nothing else.

Jesus put it straight: "Beware of practicing your righteousness before men to be noticed by them" (Matt. 6:1). In other words, stop acting one way before others when you are really not that way at all.

Following His passionate reproach against hypocrisy, Jesus also warned the people against judging each other. "How can you say to your brother, 'Let me take the speck out of your eye,' and behold, the log is in your own eye?" (Matt. 7:4).

Jesus was encouraging tolerance. Be tolerant of those who live different lifestyles. Be tolerant of those who don't look like you, who don't care about the things you care about, whose fine points of theology differ from yours, whose worship style is different. Be tolerant of the young if you are older . . . and be tolerant of the aging if you are young.

Jesus' words that day on the hillside were powerful. When He finished speaking, nobody moved. Small wonder. His words were like spikes nailing them in place.

People of faith mean what they say and do what they hear. They do not substitute words for action or pious discussion for personal involvement.

THINK IT OVER

❧❧❧❧

*S*ome years ago I was given a book of Puritan prayers called *The Valley of Vision*. I have worn out one copy and had to purchase another. I recommend this volume to you. Read the following prayer from the Puritan's pen slowly (preferably aloud).

> O LORD,
> I am a shell full of dust,
> but animated with an invisible rational soul
> and made anew by an unseen power of grace;
> Yet I am no rare object of valuable price,
> but one that has nothing and is nothing,
> although chosen of thee from eternity,
> given to Christ, and born again;
> I am deeply convinced of the evil and misery of a sinful state,
> of the vanity of creatures,
> but also of the sufficiency of Christ.
> When thou wouldst guide me I control myself,
> When thou wouldst be sovereign I rule myself.
> When thou wouldst take care of me I suffice myself.
> When I should depend on thy providings I supply myself,
> When I should submit to thy providence I follow my will,
> When I should study, love, honour, trust thee, I serve myself;
> I fault and correct thy laws to suit myself,
> Instead of thee I look to man's approbation,
> and am by nature an idolater.
> Lord, it is my chief design to bring my heart back to thee.
> Convince me that I cannot be my own god, or make myself happy,
> nor my own Christ to restore my joy,
> nor my own Spirit to teach, guide, and rule me. . . .
> Then take me to the cross and leave me there.

GOODS VS. GOD

🕭 *Colossians 3:2* 🕭

*W*hile we think we may be immune to the endless litany of television commercials, newspaper ads, our friends' gadgets and gizmos, the constant admonition to spend, spend, spend, we Christians need to be alert to how Satan tempts us with the temporal. I'll mention a few ways to avoid the magnetism of the cash register or the credit card.

Doctinal danger . . . substituting the temporal for the eternal. Don't let physical and earthly "things" get between you and the things that are above.

Personal danger . . . trying to impress instead of imparting the Word. We are doing God's business, not ours.

Economical danger . . . spending more than you have. Before every purchase, think: *Is this within my budget? Is it appropriate?*

Psychological danger . . . believing your purchase will make things "all right." Money won't buy happiness.

Make Hebrews 12:3 your aim: "Consider Him . . . so that you may not grow weary and lose heart."

Rule of thumb: If you don't have the cash, don't buy it.

GOD'S GUIDANCE

🖤 *Psalm 119:66* 🖤

*M*any Christians complain that God doesn't speak to them when they're in need of guidance. For some reason they have forgotten the first and most basic way God leads His children—through His written Word!

As the psalmist said, "They word is a lamp to my feet, and a light to my path" (Psalm 119:105). Whenever you see the scriptural phrase "This is the will of God," you know for sure that's His will. You also know that to disobey is to break His Word. Other clear indications of His leading are the precepts and principles in the Scripture.

Precepts are clearly marked statements like "Abstain from sexual immorality." That's like saying, "Speed Limit 35." What is speeding? Anything over thirty-five miles an hour. That's a precept.

Then there are principles in the Scriptures that are general guidelines that require discernment and maturity if we are to grasp them.

So often in the emotion of the moment or the pressure of the day, we make a decision that we would never make in the clear, discerning light of God's Word. Make a habit of reading the Word when you're facing tough decisions or moves, and study it prayerfully. God will talk to you!

You will never, ever go wrong in consulting the Scriptures.

CHRISTMAS ALL YEAR

❧ *Matthew 1–2* ❧

*H*ave you ever thought about giving something away every day of the year leading up to Christmas? These daily gifts could be called our "Christmas projects," one per day, every day till Christmas. Just think of the fun of being able to say "Merry Christmas" in July!

Here are a few suggestions:

Mend a quarrel.
Seek out a forgotten friend.
Write a long overdue love note.
Hug someone tightly and whisper, "I love you so."
Forgive an enemy.
Be gentle and patient with an angry person.
Gladden the heart of a child.
Find the time to keep a promise.
Make or bake something for someone else. Anonymously.
Release a grudge.
Listen.
Speak kindly to a stranger.
Enter into another's sorrow.
Smile.
Laugh a little.
Laugh a little more.
Take a walk with a friend.
Lessen your demands on others.
Play some beautiful music during the evening meal.
Apologize if you were wrong.
Turn off the television and talk.
Treat someone to an ice-cream cone (yogurt would be fine).
Do the dishes for the family.
Pray for someone who helped you when you hurt.
Fix breakfast on Saturday morning.
Give a soft answer even though you feel strongly.
Encourage an older person.
Point out one thing you appreciate most about someone you work with or live near.
Offer to baby-sit for a weary mother.

Let's make Christmas one long, extended gift of ourselves to others. Unselfishly. Without announcement. Or obligation. Or reservation. Or hypocrisy.

This is Christianity, isn't it?

When you give yourself, the gift never has to be returned.

TRUST GOD TO REMEMBER YOU

❧ *Lamentation 3:25–29* ❧

*I*f you want to trust God to remember you, stop running and start waiting! "The Lord is good to those who wait for Him" (Lamentations 3:25a). Stop running! Wait patiently.

Next, start seeking Him. "The Lord is good to those who seek Him" (v. 25b). So, instead of ignoring Him, return to His open arms and start seeking Him again.

"Lord, I'm back. I know You've heart it before, and I know You remember me. I'm ashamed to tell You what I've been doing (as if You didn't know), but it's good for me to rehearse it. Here's where I've been, here's what I've done; here are the things that brought shame to Your name and hurt me as well as others. I'm back and I still diligently seek you. I'm not going to ignore You any longer."

Just dump the full load of guilt on Him. He can handle it. Then stop talking and wait silently. Wait patiently, seek diligently, sit silently. Feel His arms around you, feel His reassurance, feel the freshness and relief of His presence.

His mercies are new every morning.

THE SAFEST PLACE ON EARTH

❧ Genesis 6 ❧

*T*he longer we walk with the Lord, the more we realize that we really don't know what each new day may bring. A phone call can come in the middle of the night shattering our joy. Suddenly everything changes. It's amazing what a knock at the door can bring or what the opening of a letter can do.

I don't say these things to conjure up fear in our hearts, but simply to remind us that God alone knows our future. And there's no safer, no better, no more rewarding place to be than in the nucleus of His will, regardless of where that may be.

We are only finite human beings. We can only see the present and the past. The future is a little frightening to us. So we need to hold onto His hand and trust Him to calm our fears. And at those times when we're stubborn and resisting and God shakes us by the shoulders to get our attention, we're reminded that we don't call the shots, God has a plan for us, mysterious though it may seem, and we want to be in the center of it.

All the risks notwithstanding,
the center of His will is still the safest place on earth to be.

A TREE FELL IN FULLERTON

❧ *1 Corinthians 10:11–13* ❧

*O*ne year a large section of a tree fell not far from where we had lived for over twenty-two years. Within minutes several of us had gathered to grieve the loss. As I stood there staring in disbelief, the thought struck me, *This happened only minutes ago . . . but it's been in the process of happening for a long, long time.* No tree just suddenly breaks apart. Once we were able to see beneath the thick bark at the break, it was obvious that some kind of killer disease had been at work for years.

The city was notified, and within an hour or two they came in their orange trucks with heavy equipment, chain saws, rakes and brooms, and had everything whisked away in no time.

Not so with a fallen life. Unlike trees, people don't grow up all alone or exist in a world of stoic and hard independence. We mingle and we merge into one another's lives. All the while there is appropriate respect for each other—and for one another's privacy. So we back off, trusting one another in realms too personal and intimate to share.

But herein lies "the rub." A core disease in the thought-life goes unnoticed and untreated. No one knows that the pulp behind our healthy looking bark is neither wholesome nor healthy. And so the erosion continues its slow, silent, secret process. And then one day there is a sudden collapse, a terrible break, that allows everyone to see what no one expected. But because fallen people are not like fallen trees, many around the fallen one are always injured. A family, a circle of friends, a body of fellow believers, a group of distant admirers. And the cleanup is never efficient. In fact, there is no crew to remove the evidence and sweep away the debris, so the damage lingers . . . sometimes for years.

What can we learn from this analogy?

First: A good start doesn't necessarily assure us of a strong finish.

Second: Erosion could be at work, even though the bark looks healthy and the fruit tastes good.

Third: Strength comes from deep within. Invite a few to keep watch over your pulp.

Fourth: Never try to convince yourself that your fall won't hurt anyone all that much.

Hear and heed this warning: "Let him who thinks he stands take heed lest he fall!"

Truly, "man looks at the outward appearance, but the LORD looks at the heart"
(1 Sam. 16:7).

THINK IT OVER

❧❧❧

*W*hen I think of fallen people, my mind returns to an ancient example, King Saul, the tall, dark, handsome monarch of the Hebrews. What an impressive specimen of humanity! He was the one of whom the Lord had said to Samuel, "Behold the man of whom I spoke to you! This one shall rule over My people" (1 Sam. 9:17).

With humility and genuine reluctance Saul accepted the appointment, acknowledged God's anointing, and graciously stood before the cheering masses as Samuel announced:

"Do you see him whom the LORD has chosen? Surely there is no one like him among all the people." So all the people shouted and said, "Long live the king!" (1 Sam. 10:24).

To save you pages of reading and a long, depressing list of facts, let me hurry to the dismal end of Saul's story where the man takes his own life. Observing the scene, David wrote a song of grievous lyrics as he lamented

"How have the mighty fallen in the midst of the battle! . . . How have the mighty fallen!" (2 Sam. 1:25–27)

Like the sickening sound of an enormous tree plunging to the ground, Saul fell, and anyone caring enough to look inside his life can analyze why He became diseased to the core. An erosion of character went on, unchecked, a destruction of substance, which took a dreadful toll on the man who once stood tall.

Someday, when you die, someone will speak for you and sing of you. Think about what you'd like them to say and sing on that day in the future. Then live like it today.

THE SECRET PLACE

❧ *Psalm 27:8; Psalm 91:1* ❧

The psalmist said, "He who dwells in the shelter of the Most High will abide in the shadow of the Almighty" (Ps. 91:1).

Do you have a place of shelter where you seek only His face? Do you spend time in that secret place?

Have you given prayer the priority it deserves? And when you pray, do you remember that it is the Lord's face you seek?

It is possible to be engaged in the work of ministry, in the work of the church, yet be in secret very seldom. There is this great tendency to think our best work is done at our desk or on our feet . . . but it's really done on our knees.

It is easy to become so caught up in people's needs (which are endless and usually urgent) and to be so preoccupied with meeting those needs that we miss "the shelter of the Most High."

It is so easy to emphasize all the involvements of being with people, rather than being alone in a secret place with Him. And I do mean alone with God, as though there is not another care, another need, another person . . . only "the Almighty."

In the last year and a half, maybe two, I have begun to realize the value of this. As a result of time invested in the secret place, we gain an invincible sense of God's direction and the reassurance of His hand on our lives, along with an increased sensitivity regarding iniquity in our lives.

Being alone with God is not complicated, but it is tough to maintain. Nevertheless, we need secrecy, especially in this hyperactive, noisy, busy world of ours.

Consider the beauty, the wonder, the magnificence, the awe-inspiring times of praise in the secret place! There is nothing to be compared to it. As great as corporate worship may be, with a magnificent pipe organ and full orchestra and a congregation singing at full volume, it cannot compare to the secret place where our best work is done and where God's best work is accomplished in us.

When Jesus was instructing His disciples regarding prayer, He said, "Pray to your Father who is in secret, and your Father who sees in secret will repay you" (Matt. 6:6).

Our best work is done on our knees.

THE REAL THING

❧ Galatians 2:20 ❧

*B*ack in 1958 when I was a young marine stationed on the island of Okinawa, I became closely associated with a man I deeply admired. His name was Bob Newkirk.

I didn't know what it was exactly that first drew me to Bob. More than anything else, I guess, there was something refreshingly unpretentious about him. He was devoted to the things of the Lord, no question, but it was never on parade, never for the purpose of public display. And I loved that.

I never got the idea that Bob was interested in making big impressions on me or other people. He was what he was, plain and simple—far from perfect, but authentic. Real.

I remember dropping by his home late one rainy afternoon to pay an unexpected visit. His wife met me at the door and informed me that he was not home. She added, "You've probably noticed lately that he has been under some stress. I think he may be down at his office. I'm not really sure. But he told me he just wanted to get alone."

I decided to try Bob's office, a little spot down in Naha. I caught the three-wheel jitney that took me from the village where the Newkirks lived down to the capital city of the island. It was still raining lightly, so I stepped around and over the puddles as I made my way down a street, across an alley, then another alley until I came upon his unassuming, modest office.

Before I arrived, however, I could hear singing in the distance . . . "Come, Thou Fount of every blessing, tune my heart to sing Thy grace."

It was Bob's voice! I'd know it anywhere.

I stood outside in the rain for a few moments, listening, as my friend continued singing the simple hymn. Then, I confess, I peeked in the window and saw a candle on a table, my friend on his knees, and not another soul around. He was spending time with the Lord . . . all alone.

As I stood outside, the soft-falling rain dripping off my nose and ears, my eyes filled with tears of gratitude. Bob never knew I came by that evening, but without his knowing it, I got a glimpse of authentic Christianity that night. Not piety on parade . . . not spiritual show-time, but a man "in the shelter of the Most High."

In the back streets of Naha I learned more about simple faith than I would later learn in four years of seminary.

When it comes to faith, there is no substitute for the real thing.

HELPING EACH OTHER UP

❧ *Hebrews 10:19–25* ❧

*S*everal years ago my family and I were invited to spend Thanksgiving weekend at a picturesque ski resort in Colorado with about five hundred single young adults, most of whom were staff personnel with Campus Crusade. I spoke all week on the subject of servanthood, emphasizing the importance of believers being those who help, encourage, affirm, and care for others.

By Friday of that week I decided to take a break and hit the slopes (emphasis on hit, since it was the first time I had ever attempted to ski). It had snowed all day Thanksgiving, so the ski areas were absolutely beautiful and in perfect condition. I struck out on my virgin voyage with a positive mental attitude, thinking, "I'm going to be the first person who learns to ski without falling down. *Guinness Book of World Records* will hear of this and write me up!"

Don't bother to check. I'm not in the book.

Working with me that humiliating day was the world's most encouraging ski instructor (yes, I had an instructor!) who set the new world record in patience. She is the one Guinness needs to interview. Never once did she lose her cool. Never once did she laugh at me. Never once did she yell, scream, threaten, or swear. Never once did she call me "dummy." Never once did she say, "You are absolutely impossible. I quit!"

That dear, gracious lady helped me up more times than I can number. She repeated the same basics time and again—as though she had never said them before. Even though I was colder than an explorer in the Antarctic, irritable, impatient, and under the snow more than I was on it, she kept offering words of reassurance.

That day God gave me a living, never-to-be-forgotten illustration of the value of encouragement. Had it not been for her spirit and her words, believe me, I would have been back in the condo, warming my feet by the fire, in less than an hour.

What is true for a novice on the snow once a year is all the more true for the people we meet every day. Harassed by demands and deadlines; bruised by worry, adversity, and failure; broken by disillusionment; and defeated by sin, they live somewhere between dull discouragement and sheer panic.

All of us, even Christians, need encouragement. All of us need somebody to believe in us. To reassure and reinforce us. To help us pick up the pieces and go on. To provide us with increased determination in spite of the odds.

We all need encouragement . . . and we all need to be encouragers.

The beautiful thing about encouragement is that anybody can do it.

SALT AND LIGHT

🕏 *Matthew 6:1—16* 🕏

*O*urs is a tough, rugged, wicked world. Aggression, rebellion, violence, cutthroat competition, and retaliation abound. Not just internationally, but personally. What is true in the secret council chambers of nations is also true behind closed doors of homes. We are stubborn, warring people. Outside of riots and war, studies have concluded, the most dangerous place to be is in the American home! With domestic violence and child abuse on the rise in our hard, hostile society, one might wonder what possible influence the servants of Christ can have.

What impact—how much clout—do the poor in spirit, the gentle, the merciful, the pure in heart, or the peacemakers actually have? Such feeble-sounding virtues seem about as effective as pillow fighting in a nuclear war.

Can our presence do much good? Isn't it pretty much a wasted effort?

Jesus, the One who first painted the servant's portrait, both in words and with His own life, did not share this skepticism. But neither did He deny the battle. Remember these words!

> Blessed are those who have been persecuted for the sake of righteousness, for theirs is the kingdom of heaven. Blessed are you when men revile you, and persecute you, and say all kinds of evil against you falsely, on account of Me. Rejoice, and be glad, for your reward in heaven is great, for so they persecuted the prophets who were before you. (Matt. 5:10–12)

Our Lord admitted that the arena of this world is not a friend of grace. Nevertheless, strange as it may seem, He went on to tell that handful of Palestinian peasants (and all godly servants in every generation) that their influence would be nothing short of remarkable. They would be "the salt of the earth" and "the light of the world." And so shall we!

So far-reaching would be the influence of His servants in society that their presence would be as significant as salt on food and as light on darkness. Neither is loud or externally impressive, but both are essential.

Without our influence this old world would soon begin to realize our absence. Even though it may not admit it, society needs both salt and light.

God has called us to be light-and-salt servants in a dark-and-bland society.

GENUINE JOY

❧ *Philippians 4* ❧

*I*n my words, the apostle Paul would tell us that joy isn't fickle; it doesn't need a lot of things to keep it smiling. Joy is deep and consistent—the oil that reduces the friction of life.

Well, we know what joy is, but how do we get it and keep it? Once again, it's the attitude of our mind. Our minds can be kept free of anxiety as we dump the load of our cares on the Lord in prayer. By getting rid of the stuff that drags us down, we create space for joy to take its place.

Think of it like this: Circumstances occur that could easily crush us. They may originate on the job or at home or even during the weekend when we are relaxing. Unexpectedly they come. Immediately we have a choice to make . . . an attitude choice. We can hand the circumstance to God and ask Him to take control, or we can roll up our mental sleeves and slug it out. Joy awaits our decision. Peace replaces panic and joy moves into action.

Deliberately choose to give your "stuff" to God the moment it happens.

GOD DOESN'T HAVE TO EXPLAIN HIMSELF

Psalms 139:1–6

*E*ven in the midst of disappointment, surprise, and mystery, you will discover an amazing thing. You will discover how very reliable and trustworthy God is—and how secure you are in His hands. And oh, how we need that in this day of relativism and vacillation, filled with empty talk and hidden behind a lot of semantic footwork. In the midst of "Spin City," it is the Lord who talks straight. It is the Lord who has preserved Truth in black and white in His Word. And it is the Lord who has the right to do as He wishes around us, to us, and in us.

Puzzling as the process may be to us, He stays with His plan. There is no need for us to know all the reasons, and He certainly doesn't need to explain Himself. If we're going to let God be God, then we're forced to say He has the right to take us through whatever process He chooses.

Let Him have His way with your life, for nothing is worse than resisting and resenting the One who is at work in you.

WORDS

🎵 *Ecclesiastes 12:9–14* 🎵

A word fitly spoken," wrote the wise Solomon, "is like apples of gold in settings of silver" (Prov. 25:11, KJV).

Like Jell-O, concepts assume the mold of the words into which they are poured. Who has not been stabbed awake by the use of a particular word . . . or combination of words? Who has not found relief from a well-timed word spoken at the precise moment of need? Who has not been crushed beneath the weight of an ill-chosen word? And who has not gathered fresh courage because a word of hope penetrated the fog of self-doubt? The word "word" remains the most powerful of all four-letter words.

Fitly spoken words are right words . . . the precise words needed for the occasion. Mark Twain, a unique wordsmith himself, once wrote: "The difference between the right word and almost the right word is the difference between lightning and a lightning bug."

One set of words purifies our thoughts, transplanting us, at least for an instant, to the throne room of God; another set of words ignites lust, tempting us to visit the house of a harlot. Some words bring tears to our eyes in a matter of seconds; others bring fear that makes the hair on the back of our necks stand on end.

Now, let's return again to more choice words from the pen of Solomon: "The words of wise men are like goads, and masters of these collections are like well-driven nails; they are given by one Shepherd" (Eccl. 12:11).

J. B. Phillips correctly assessed the impact of such words when he wrote: "If words are to enter men's hearts and bear fruit, they must be the right words shaped cunningly to pass men's defenses and explode silently and effectually within their minds."

The finest examples of that are the words and phrases of Jesus Christ. His choice of words. His placement of words. His economy of words. Even His eloquent turn of a phrase. The life-changing message of Jesus.

Being the ultimate wordsmith, Jesus wrapped up some of His most significant words in a brief statement we commonly call the Golden Rule: "Therefore, however you want people to treat you, so treat them, for this is the Law and the Prophets" (Matt. 7:12).

What a classic example of "apples of gold in settings of silver."

Are your words fitly spoken?

GOD'S SOVEREIGNTY

❧ *Romans 11:33–36* ❧

*S*ome people mistakenly use God's sovereignty as an excuse for complacency, passivity, and uninvolvement. All is of God they say; God does everything. God's sovereignty does not mean that I am released from responsibility. It does not mean I have no interest in today's affairs, or that I cannot be bothered about decisions, or that I need not concern myself with the eternal destiny of the lost. It doesn't mean that at all. Somehow there has to be a balance using the privilege of choice that He has given us.

We can choose for, or we can choose against. But we cannot choose the consequences. If we choose against the person of Jesus Christ, we thereby step into God's decree of eternal punishment. If we choose in favor of the Lord Jesus Christ, then we inherit all the rewards of heaven—the blessing of forgiven sins and eternity with God. God rules. God reigns. And His way is right.

Don't fight with God over who is in control.

OTHERS AND US

❧ *Matthew 5* ❧

"herefore, however you want people to treat you, so treat them, for this is the Law and the Prophets" (Matt. 7:2). That single sentence is perhaps the most famous statement Jesus ever made. It is the "Everest of Ethics," as one man put it. In some ways it is the cornerstone of true Christianity, certainly the capstone of Jesus' Sermon on the Mount.

I appreciate the positive emphasis. Instead of saying, "Don't do this," He says, "Do this." If you have wondered about how to get started in a lifetime of simple faith, here it is.

• The principle? *Modeling must accompany our message.*

• You want to be forgiven? Forgive.

• You need affirmation? Affirm.

• You feel hurt, wounded, broken, and could stand a gentle touch? Be gentle with others.

• You have discovered the value of tact when something sensitive needed to be addressed? Be tactful.

The examples are endless. Unfortunately, models of such greathearted behavior are rare. Is it any wonder the non-Christian world looks with suspicion in our direction?

The best part of the whole principle? It is so simple. Living by the Golden Rule prevents the need for laying down an endless list of little rules and regulations to govern conduct. Just put yourself in the other person's place and think, *What is it I would need if I were him or her?* And then? Do it. When you do, you will fulfill the essence of "the Law and the Prophets."

Do you know the greatest message we can deliver? It is the message of Christlike character. No message on earth is more needed or more powerful.

You want to impact your family, your church, your community, your place of employment? You want to make a difference in the life of your mate, a family member, a friend (Christian or not), some person in the workplace? Demonstrate the characteristics of Christ.

It has been said that the only Bible most folks ever read is the daily life of the Christian. If that is true, I believe the world needs a *revised version*. Our problem is not that too many of us are being ignored; it's that we are all being observed!

Words fitly spoken are powerful,
but they are nothing compared to the power of a life fitly lived.

A BETTER WAY

❧ *Romans 12:10–13* ❧

*Y*ourself. Yourself. Yourself. We're up to here with self! How very different from Jesus' model and message! Instead of a "philosophy" to turn our eyes inward, He offers a fresh and much-needed invitation to our "me first" generation. There is a better way, Jesus says. "Be a servant. Give to others!" Just listen: "Do nothing from selfishness or empty conceit, but with humility of mind let each of you regard one another as more important than himself; do not merely look out for your own personal interests, but also for the interests of others" (Phil. 2:3–4).

Know what all that means? Well, for starters, "nothing" means just that. Stop permitting two strong tendencies—selfishness and conceit—to control you! Let nothing either of them suggests win a hearing. Replace them with "humility of mind."

But how? By regarding others as more important than yourself.

Look for ways to support, encourage, build up, and stimulate the other person. And that requires an attitude that would rather give than receive.

"Humility of mind" is really an attitude, isn't it? It's a preset mentality that determines ahead of time thoughts like this: I care about those around me. Why do I always have to be first? I'm going to help someone else win for a change. Today, it's my sincere desire to curb my own fierce competitive tendencies and turn that energy into encouraging at least one other person. I willingly release my way this day. Lord, show me how You would respond to others, then help me do the same.

To get started in this unselfish lifestyle, let me suggest three basic ingredients: giving, forgiving, and forgetting.

Once we make up our minds to implement the truth of Philippians 2:3–4 (taking a special interest in others) or Galatians 5:13 (serving others in love), those three basics will begin to emerge. Instead of always thinking about receiving, we'll start looking for ways to give. Instead of holding grudges against those who have offended us, we'll be anxious to forgive. And instead of keeping a record of what we've done or who we've helped, we'll take delight in forgetting the deed(s) and being virtually unnoticed.

It is impossible to give yourself away at arm's length.

THAT SUBTLE SIN

🍃 *Matthew 6:25, 33—34; Luke 10:38—41* 🍃

*D*o you know which sin is the subtle enemy of simple faith? Materialism and greed? Anger? Lust? Hypocrisy? No. All of these sins are certainly our enemies, but none of them qualify as *subtle* enemies.

The most notorious faith killer in all of life: *worry.* "For this reason I say to you, do not be anxious for your life, as to what you shall eat, or what you shall drink; nor for your body, as to what you shall put on. Is not life more than food, and the body than clothing?" (Matt. 6:25).

Being something of a wordsmith, I find the term "worry" fascinating. To begin with, the word used by Matthew (translated here as "anxious") is the Greek term *merimnao.* It is a combination of two smaller words, *merizo,* meaning "to divide," and *nous,* meaning "the mind." In other words, a person who is anxious suffers from a divided mind, leaving him or her disquieted and distracted.

Of all the biblical stories illustrating worry, none is more practical or clear than the one recorded in the last five verses of Luke 10. Let's briefly relive it.

Jesus dropped by His friends' home in Bethany. Martha, one of those friends, turned the occasion into a mild frenzy. To make matters worse, Martha's sister, Mary, was so pleased to have the Lord visit their home that she sat with Him and evidenced little concern over her sister's anxiety attack.

As Luke tells us, "Martha was distracted with all her preparations" (Luke 10:40). But Martha didn't have help, and that was the final straw. Irritated, exasperated, and angry, she reached her boiling point, and her boiling point led to blame. "Lord, do You not care that my sister has left me to do all the serving alone? Then tell her to help me" (10:40).

But Jesus was neither impressed by her busyness nor intimidated by her command. Graciously, yet firmly, He said, "Martha, Martha, you are worried and bothered about so many things; but only a few things are necessary, really only one, for Mary has chosen the good part, which shall not be taken away from her" (10:41—42).

Worry occurs when we assume responsibility for things that are outside our control. And I love the Lord's solution: "only a few things are necessary, really only one." What a classic example of simple faith!

All Mary wanted was time with Jesus . . . and He commended her for that. Mary's simple faith, in contrast to her sister's panic, won the Savior's affirmation.

Worry and faith just don't mix.

MARKS OF MATURITY

❧ *Ephesians 4:14–15* ☙

To be mature is to be fully developed, complete, and "grown up." Becoming mature is a process of consistently moving toward emotional and spiritual adulthood. In that process we leave childish and adolescent habits and adopt a lifestyle where we are fully responsible for our own decisions, motives, actions, and consequences.

I heard someone say recently that maturity is developing and discerning competence as to how to live appropriately and to change rightly. In a word, it is stability.

We never "arrive." We are always in the process of moving toward that objective. I have also observed that when maturity is taking place, balance replaces extremes and a seasoned confidence replaces uneasy feelings of insecurity. Good choices replace wrong ones.

Do you have these marks of maturity:

- Concern for others that outweighs personal concerns.
- Detection of the presence of evil before it's obvious.
- Self discipline.
- Compassion and involvement.
- Tempered emotions.
- Consistently growing in God's Word.

How do your "marks" stand up?
Will you work on improving them before the next scoring period?

FINISHING WELL

❦ *1 Corinthians 3:10–14* ❦

One of the great doctrines of Christianity is our belief in a heavenly home. Ultimately, we shall spend eternity with God in the place He has prepared for us. And part of that exciting anticipation is His promise to reward His servants for a job well done.

Most rewards are received in heaven, not on earth. God reserves special honor for that day when "each man's work will become evident" and "he shall receive a reward" (1 Cor. 3:13–14).

All rewards are based on quality, not quantity. God's eye is always on motive.

No reward that is postponed will be forgotten. When that day in eternity dawns, no act of serving others—be it well-known or unknown to others—will be forgotten.

Someone once counted all the promises in the Bible and came up with an amazing figure of almost 7500. Among that large number are some specific promises servants can claim today.

When we did what was right, with the right motive, but received no credit, no acknowledgment, not even a "thank you" . . . we have God's promise that "we shall reap."

When any servant has served and given and sacrificed and then willingly stepped aside for God to receive the glory, our heavenly Father promises he will receive back.

And then there are the eternal rewards. Some of them are referred to as "crowns" that are being set aside for God's servants. The Bible speaks of at least five crowns:

The imperishable crown (1 Cor. 9:24–27), awarded to those believers who consistently bring the flesh under the Holy Spirit's control.

The crown of exultation (Phil. 4:1; 1 Thess. 2:19–20), distributed to those servants who are faithful to declare the gospel.

The crown of righteousness (2 Tim. 4:7–8), awarded to those who live each day with eternity's values in view.

The crown of life (James 1:12), promised to those who endure trials, loving the Savior all the way.

The crown of glory (1 Pet. 5:1–4), promised to those who faithfully "shepherd the flock."

What a scene! All God's servants before His throne. They are bowing in worship, having cast all crowns before their Lord in adoration and praise, ascribing worth and honor to the only One deserving of praise—the Lord God!

God alone is perfectly and consistently just. We forget; God remembers.
We see an action; God sees a motive. This qualifies Him as the best recordkeeper
and judge.

THINK IT OVER

❧❧❧

*W*e have reached the end of another year and now face a new one. When we stood in this same spot 364 days ago, we looked ahead to what the Lord was going to teach us in the coming year and we anticipated the many ways we were going to see Him at work in our lives.

We said, "By the end of this year we will discover that God had wondrous things for us which we would never have known or experienced had we not accepted the challenge changes inevitably bring."

Today, as you look back over the past weeks and months, what do you see? How have His grace, joy, and love touched your life?

When we began the year, we also talked about finishing well. The reality is, of course, we are not finished. The race is not over. Our lives are still being perfected. We still need much more of the Master's touch.

"Wherefore seeing we also are compassed about with so great a cloud of witnesses, let us lay aside every weight, and the sin which doth so easily beset us, and let us run with patience the race that is set before us, looking unto Jesus the author and finisher of our faith" (Heb. 12:1–2, KJV).

CHARLES SWINDOLL

DROPPING YOUR GUARD

Charles Swindoll unveils a biblical blueprint for rich relationships in this life-changing classic. In this updated version of his best-selling book, Swindoll poignantly and honestly portrays the need for authentic love and transparency.

FINISHING TOUCH, THE

When the going gets tough, most people just quit. This daily devotional challenges us to persevere and to finish well the race set before us as God finishes in us the good work He began. This popular volume is Swindoll's first collection of daily readings.

FLYING CLOSER TO THE FLAME

Best-selling author Charles Swindoll explores the void that exists in many Christian's lives due to a lack of understanding about the Holy Spirit. In *Flying Closer to the Flame,* he challenges readers toward a deeper, more intimate relationship with the Holy Spirit.

GRACE AWAKENING, THE

In this best-selling classic, Charles Swindoll awakens readers to the life-impacting realities of God's grace, the freedom and joy it brings, the fear it cures, the strength it lends to relationships, and the ever-increasing desire to know God. A modern-day classic from Charles Swindoll.

GREAT LIVES SERIES

Throughout history, people have faced the same challenges and temptations. In his Great Lives Series, Charles Swindoll shows us how the great heroes of the faith offer a model of courage, hope, and triumph in the face of adversity.

GROWING UP IN GOD'S FAMILY

Growing older doesn't necessarily mean growing up or maturing in Christ. Using the stages of physical growth—birth and infancy, childhood, adolescence, and adulthood—to describe the phases of spiritual maturity, Swindoll encourages Christians to pursue spiritual growth.

HAND ME ANOTHER BRICK

Most of us could benefit from wise advice on how to be a more effective leader at work and at home. Charles Swindoll delves deep into the life of Nehemiah to show how to handle the issues of motivation, discouragement, and adversity with integrity.

HOPE AGAIN

Combining the New Testament teachings of Peter and the insights of one of the most popular authors of our day, *Hope Again* is an encouraging, enlivening, and refreshing look at why we can dare to hope no matter who we are, no matter what we face.

IMPROVING YOUR SERVE

In this classic volume, Charles Swindoll uniquely shows the important aspects of authentic servanthood, such as: What it takes to serve unselfishly, why a servant has such a powerful influence, and what challenges and rewards a servant can expect.

LAUGH AGAIN

Discover outrageous joy in this modern classic. Charles Swindoll shows how we can live in the present, say "no" to negativism, and realize that while no one's life is perfect, joy is always available. Applying scriptural truths in a practical way, Swindoll shows readers how to laugh again.

LIVING ABOVE THE LEVEL OF MEDIOCRITY

Charles Swindoll tackles the problem of mediocrity in one of his most popular books. With his trademark stories and practical insight, he boldly confronts the issues of self-discipline, laziness, and our tendency to accept less than what we deserve, drawing clear lines between the pursuit of excellence and the pursuit of success in the eyes of the world.

LIVING ON THE RAGGED EDGE

Here is an intimate glimpse into Solomon's ancient journal, Ecclesiastes, in which the young king's desperate quest for satisfaction—in work, in sexual conquest, in all the trappings afforded by his fabulous wealth—was as futile as trying to "catch the wind." For those struggling with the anxieties and frustrations of our modern era, the good news is that you can find perspective and joy amid the struggle.

ROAD TO ARMAGEDDON, THE
Various Authors

The end of a century. A new millennium. For Christians everywhere, there is little doubt that these are the last days, as we move down the road to Armageddon. This book features six of the most respected scholars and teachers on Bible prophecy and coming world events. An important tool for understanding the future.

SIMPLE FAITH

Must we run at a pace between maddening and insane to prove we're among the faithful? Is this really how the Prince of Peace would have us live? In this book, Swindoll answers with a resounding, "No!," showing how Christians can break free from exhausting, performance-based faith, back to the simplicity of the Sermon on the Mount.

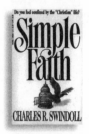

START WHERE YOU ARE

"To start fresh, to start over, to start anything, you have to know where you are," says Charles Swindoll. "Seldom does anybody just happen to end up on a right road." In *Start Where You Are*, Swindoll offers upbeat and practical advice on creating a life worth living, no matter what the circumstances are now or where they may lead in the future.

STRENGTHENING YOUR GRIP

As only he can, Charles Swindoll combines biblical insights with unforgettable stories that inspire readers to strengthen their spiritual grip on issues such as family, prayer, integrity, and purity.

SUDDENLY ONE MORNING

Through the eyes of a shopkeeper on the main street of Jerusalem, readers experience the life-changing events of a week that begins with a parade and ends with an empty grave. This Easter gift book combines an original Swindoll story with beautiful full-color art.

TALE OF THE TARDY OX CART, THE

In *The Tale of The Tardy Ox Cart*, Charles Swindoll shares from his life-long collection of his and others' personal stories, sermons, and anecdotes. 1501 various illustrations are arranged by subjects alphabetically for quick and easy access. A perfect resource for all pastors and preachers.

THREE STEPS FORWARD,
TWO STEPS BACK

Charles Swindoll reminds readers that our problems are not solved by simple answers or all-too-easy clichés. Instead, he offers practical ways to walk with God through the realities of life—including times of fear, stress, anger, and temptation.

You and Your Child

Best-selling author and veteran parent and grandparent Charles Swindoll believes that the key to successful parenting lies in becoming a "student" of your children—learning the distinct bent and blueprint of each child. Here's practical advice for parents wishing to launch confident, capable young adults in today's ever-changing world.